James Connolly
and the
United States

James Connolly
and the
United States

The Road to the
1916 Irish Rebellion

by
Carl Reeve
and
Ann Barton Reeve

HUMANITIES PRESS, INC.
Atlantic Highlands, New Jersey

Distributed by
The Academy Press
124 Ranelagh,
Dublin 6.

AIMS HISTORICAL SERIES NO. 10

Library of Congress Cataloging in Publication Data

Reeve, Carl.
 James Connolly and the United States.

 1. Connolly, James, 1868-1916. 2. Irish question. 3. Ireland -- History
-- Sinn Fein Rebellion, 1916. 4. Labor and laboring classes -- United
States. 5. Socialists -- United States -- Biography. 6. Revolutionists --
Ireland -- Biography. 7. Socialists -- Ireland -- Biography. I. Reeve, Ann
Barton. II. Title.
DA965.C7R44   941.5082′1   78-17273
ISBN 0-391-00879-X

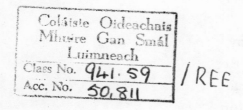
Printed in the United States of America

TABLE OF CONTENTS

Dedicated --

To the memory
of the unconquerable
Mother Ella Reeve Bloor
and to the brave young
who devotedly are following
in her path and that of
James Connolly
for "singing tomorrows."

AUTHORS' PREFACE

On May 12, 1916, in Dublin, Ireland, James Connolly, gravely wounded, was taken from prison on a stretcher, strapped into a chair and shot to death, by troops of the British imperialist government. He was not quite forty-eight years of age.

The "Easter Rising," in which, he held the key military post of Commander of the Dublin Garrison, began on the morning of Easter Monday, April 24, 1916. Its purpose was to free Ireland from domination by Great Britain. The Irish Citizen Army, of labor, and the Irish Volunteers, of the nationalists, held control of Dublin for nearly a week. The first Irish Republic was proclaimed and it took British forces six days to overcome the Irish Republicans.

The seven signers of the Proclamation of the Provisional Government of the Irish Republic were executed, Connolly being the last to die. Though defeated, the Rising changed the course of Irish and world history. In the United States, it was one of the main factors which halted for a year President Woodrow Wilson's plans for taking the country into World War I, as England's ally. The Rising and the struggles which followed marked the beginning of the decline of British imperialism, presaging the rise of the United States as the dominating world imperialist power.

In a few years, the British government was forced to grant a form of "Home Rule" to Ireland and the Irish Free State was established. Many Republicans felt that the independent republic had still to be won and continued fighting.

Connolly spent the years 1902 to 1910 in the United States. It is recognized by Irish historians that these years forged and tempered him for the serious tasks he faced upon his return to Ireland.

Returned there, he was the leading Marxist socialist of that country. He became the outstanding labor leader, heading the Irish Transport and General Workers Union, after James Larkin, ill, left for America, in the Fall of 1914.

With Larkin, in 1913, he led the greatest labor struggle in Ireland's history. He demonstrated his mastery of strike strategy and, in the face of the employers' all-out offensive against the workers in a massive lockout, he saved the union and achieved some victories for the workers. He was one of the founders and the leader of labor's Irish Citizen Army. He initiated the formation of a Labor Party in Ireland. Under his leadership, the Socialist Party of Ireland was formed on a national scale, as a worker-based party of struggle. From the outbreak of the World War, in August, 1914, Connolly was the center of the fight against the imperialist war. Recruiting for the war and conscription were defeated in Ireland as a result.

Padraic Colum, the Irish poet, author and playwright, who lived most of his life in the United States, said, after Connolly's execution by the British Government: "Now that heavy, earnest man, that brave and clear-minded fighter has been shot to death, it is hard to think that the loss to Ireland is not irreparable. I find it difficult to believe that we will see in our time a man who will give the Irish workers such brave and disintereseted service-- who will give, as Connolly gave them, his mind, his heart, his life."*

When Connolly was executed, a wave of protest arose in the labor movements of the large citites of the United States. Central Labor bodies of the American Federation of Labor, in New York, Chicago, Detroit, and other large cities, had demanded his release from prison and then passed resolutions denouncing his murder.

This book focuses chiefly on Connolly's important American years. We feel it has been a serious omission that Connolly's substantial theoretical and organizational contributions to the American working class movement are largely unknown in this country and have been almost completely ignored by American labor historians.

Connolly's theoretical battles for involvement of American socialists in labor's mass struggles for workers' needs, particularly for higher wages, influenced the course of labor and socialism in this country. Connolly fought against sectarianism and in 1904 crossed swords with Daniel De Leon, a leader of the Socialist Labor Party and editor of the *Daily* and *Weekly People.* De Leon and his followers waged a battle against Connolly which lasted, on and off, for years, with Connolly leaving the SLP and joining the Socialist Party.

One of the IWW's first national organizers, Connolly was an able exponent of industrial unionism. Professor Walter Kendall, a labor historian of Oxford University, credits Connolly and De Leon, by their propaganda for industrial unionism, with providing the inspiration and the blueprint for the large shop steward movement in Great Britain.

Connolly's most important works, *Labor in Irish History, Socialism Made Easy* and *Labor, Nationality and Religion,* were all written in the United States, and distributed in all English-speaking countries. He worked among the foreign-born workers, advocating Socialism; he taught

---

*Mother Earth, Vol. 2, No. 4, pp. 505-507, June 1916.

himself German and Italian so as to reach workers of these nationalities effectively.

The attention which he paid to the political development of Elizabeth Gurley Flynn and to his oldest daughter, Nora, while in the United States, was evidence of Connolly's interest in the development of women leaders. He was in the forefront of the fight for women's economic and political rights, in the United States, England, and in Ireland.

This book takes up De Leon's career only as it affected Connolly.* It is a fact that De Leon, more than anyone else, exposed the corrupt, class-collaborationist policies of the Gompers machine in the AFL. He also made available to the American workers the classics of Marx and Engels and was for many years, the editor of the only socialist daily paper printed in the English language in the United States. He was one of the founders of the IWW in 1905. However, De Leon became increasingly hide-bound and inflexible in his sectarianism, his dogmatism and bureaucracy, during the time of Connolly's stay in the United States.

Against the wishes of the anti-religious sectarians in the socialist movement, Connolly established a socialist dialogue with Irish-American Catholic workers and intellectuals. From 1908 to 1910, he was editor of the *Harp*, the monthly publication of the Irish Socialist Federation, which he founded to appeal to Irish-American workers. In the *Harp*, appeared some of his finest writing.

He was dogged by poverty most of his life in the United States, often barely managing to feed his family. Their extreme need did not harm his family relationships. On the contrary, Connolly's family was close-knit, loving and understanding and proud of Connolly's work.

In 1909, when he went to work as a national organizer of the Socialist Party of America, at three dollars a day, plus expenses, it was the best paying job he had ever had. In the Spring of 1910 a few months before returning to Ireland Connolly was asked by the SPA to go into the Pittsburgh steel area, where workers at a number of large mills, led by the IWW and members of the Socialist Party, had gone on strike against unbearable conditions, confronting the Steel Trust. U.S. Steel, owners of the struck mills, had ordered the arrest of the editor of the *New Castle Free Press,* a Pennsylvania-based Socialist Party weekly newspaper, on charges of sedition as well as technical violation of laws governing issuance of newspapers. Connolly went to New Castle and became Managing Editor.

---

*For a detailed study of De Leon, see Carl Reeve's *The Life and Times of Daniel De Leon,* AIMS and Humanities Press, New York, 1972.

His daughter, Nora Connolly O'Brien, wrote us about this period: "I remember that my father went to Pennsylvania... to replace a number of men who were assisting in a strike and were arrested and accused of almost treasonable activity in speeches and articles..."

The Steel Trust was unable to destroy the Socialist movement and was forced to release the editors. Connolly was able to leave for New York and prepare to return to Ireland.

We have had the good fortune to have been able to examine and use hundreds of unpublished personal letters, reports, documents and articles by Connolly, from a tremendous body of material which was turned over to the National Library in Dublin, after the death of William O'Brien several years ago. He had stubbornly refused to make this vast library available to writers or to the general public. He had saved everything Connolly wrote, for many years, including socialist and labor union documents. Many letters used here were addressed from the United States to his friend, John Matheson, in Scotland, others to William O'Brien. These documents form an unprecedented picture of socialism and unionism in the United States during the period. Numerous reports, statements and letters, regarding Connolly's controversies with De Leon within the SLP, which were suppressed by the *People's* editor, see the light of day here, for the first time in this country. Included are portions of a particularly able essay on Marxian economics, written by Connolly.

In his personal letters, Connolly spoke against the sectarianism of the SLP and the chauvinism of some American leaders. He gave his opinions of the Second International, the IWW, Eugene V. Debs, Elizabeth Gurley Flynn, Morris Hillquit and other socialists. He analyzed the hierarchy of the Catholic Church and denounced Gompers' leadership of the AFL. He commented on the inability of the craft unions to unite the workers as compared to industrial unionism.

Dr. P. Henchy, Director of the National Library, in Dublin, made available to us copies of hundreds of pages of these documents. We have Dr. Henchy to thank, too, for making known to us two capable research workers, to whom we gave the task of going through the voluminous papers.

In 1907, a brochure, "Songs of Freedom by Irish Authors," was published. Connolly wrote an introduction and many of the poems appearing in it. We have secured from a number of sources what we believe is the most complete collection of Connolly's poems in existence. We regret that space prohibits us from including them here. The same problem applies to Connolly's play, "Under Which Flag?" which was performed in

Liberty Hall, union headquarters, a few weeks before the Rising. This play, which many years later was performed by the Abbey Theater, has also never been published in the United States. We also regret that the limitation of space prevents us from including a transcript of a recording by Peadar O'Donnell and members of the Irish Citizen Army who survived the Easter Rising. O'Donnell sent this recording to the Transport Union of Greater New York in 1949, when he was denied a visa to come to the United States and speak for the union at a Connolly Memorial meeting. All of this material, we hope to publish at another time.

Time and distance notwithstanding, Connolly's principles, in many ways, paralleled those of Lenin. Connolly was a proponent of the policy which Lenin expounded, combining the nationalist struggle for freedom from oppression by a foreign government, with the class struggle for socialism. Like Lenin, when the great international crisis of capitalism emerged in World War I, Connolly called on the workers and farmers and their allies to turn the imperialist war into a civil war, to establish a socialist road to peace.

Connolly had a special ability for uniting socialists and non-socialists in mass movements of the Irish people. Maud Gonne, the Irish heroine, fought side by side with him in dramatic actions and he was supported even by Arthur Griffith, who founded Sinn Fein, in his fight for Irish independence and against the imperialist war.

In his early career, Connolly was a semi-syndicalist who saw the industrial unions as the instrument of revolution. As the class struggle matured, his approach changed. He accepted as one solution, winning Socialism through the ballot, at a time when the Socialist Party Ireland needed broadening and unifying. Even then, he admonished that such a solution might be impossible. British repressions that accompanied World War I brought him to the conclusion that armed uprising was necessary to free the Irish people from oppression.

Today in Ireland, streets are named for Connolly. The railway station on Amiens Street, Dublin, is "Connolly Station." Two city avenues bear his name. Commemorative stamps, bearing Connolly's likeness, were issued in 1966. Souvenir china pieces, decorated with Connolly's picture among other leaders of the Rebellion, are offered in Irish shops.

Nora Connolly O'Brien, his eldest daughter, wrote us, when we described the book we were writing: "My book *(Portrait of a Rebel Father)* was more concerned with portraying the human person. I have always felt that in most biographies of historical characters the human person is lost in the tale of his activities and philosophy and loses warmth and life as a result. The brief outline you have given me of your intended work promises a combination of the two."

We feel we have learned to know Connolly, the person. We hope through these pages he does emerge -- his family life, his struggles, triumphs, disappointments, as well as his politics.

We have received help from many sources. For all of it, we are most grateful. We could not have gone forward without the conscientious work of the two research workers who labored at the National Library in Dublin. Rupert J. Coughlan, who sent us material from July to November, 1972, was a founding member and past president of the County Donegal Historical Society. The second research worker, Don O'Broin, began his research on the O'Brien papers in February, 1973 and concluded his work in April of that year.

We are greatly indebted to Gerald O'Reilly, for the programs and correspondence of the Connolly Commemoration Committee of the Transport Workers Union of Greater New York, which, for a number of years, with him as its moving spirit, commemorated James Connolly's life and death. He made available to us letters to him from Maud Gonne and Sean O'Casey. We made use of the *Official Minutes of the Royal Commission of Inquiry* (into the Rising) printed by the *Dublin Times,* in 1916, as well as a number of other rare, out-of-print books and pamphlets from his library.

Herbert Aptheker, Director of the American Institute for Marxist Studies, permitted us to examine the papers of Elizabeth Gurley Flynn, then in the AIMS' library. His editorial help on the entire manuscript is deeply appreciated.

We are grateful to Ina Connolly Heron, Connolly's daughter, for sending us a copy of a manuscript of several lectures about her father, delivered by her. The late John Williamson, who was deported from the United States during Cold War days, and became, in London, Librarian of the Marx Memorial Library, sent us photo copies of articles by Arthur MacManus, devoted friend of Connolly, who later became Chairman of the Communist Party of England. We also received from him material in connection with Connolly's son, Roderick, and others.

Interested friends, from time to time, forwarded material they thought might be useful. Among theses were Morris Pasternak and the late Solon De Leon, son of Daniel. We are grateful.

We have particularly benefited from the advice of Herbert Aptheker, Dirk Struik and the late Oakley Johnson.

We have had very fine cooperation from many libraries and librarians. We must single out several of them: The Free Library of Bucks County, at Doylestown, Pennsylvania, secured a quantity of books and microfilm for us through inter-library loan. Through this library, we used material from the Labadie Collection of the University of Michigan, St. Joseph's College, Penn State University, the College of Lower Bucks County, Villanova, and others.

Dionne Miles, Archivist of the rich IWW collection in the Wayne State University Walter P. Reuther Library, Detroit, responded in a particularly helpful manner and went beyond the call of duty in finding important material for our use. We want to thank Dorothy Swanson, Librarian for the Tamiment Collection, Elmer Holmes Bobst Library of New York University, for providing us with valuable material in connection with the Socialist Party of America and the Socialist Labor Party, including microfilm of the *People*, the *New York Socialist Call*, and the *International Socialist Review*.

We wish to acknowledge, from the National Library in Dublin, the rich material, photo-copied, of a biography of Connolly by Ina Connolly Heron, which was printed serially in *Liberty Magazine,* publication of the Irish Transport and General Workers Union.

Villanova University Library made available to us the McGarrity papers, a treasure trove of Irish American history, the history of the Fenians, the Irish Republican Brotherhood, the Clan na Gael and material on the relationship of Irish Americans to the Republican movement in Ireland. In this collection, John Devoy's privately printed *Recollections of an Irish Rebel* has been very important.

From the International Institute for Social Science (Internationaal Instituut voor Sociale Geschiedenis) in Amsterdam, Holland came *Songs of Freedom by Irish Authors*. The Wisconsin Historical Society sent us microfilm of the *Harp*, the *New Castle Free Press,* and additional material from the De Leon papers.

From the library of the University of the Pacific, Stockton, California, we obtained a copy of the fine thesis of Kara P. Brewer, "The American Career of James Connolly" (October, 1972). The University of New Hampshire provided Manus O'Riordan's interesting thesis: "James Connolly in the United States" (January, 1971).

We would like to mark our special indebtedness to C. Desmond Greaves, London, author of *The Life and Times of James Connolly*. In letters to us, he gave us encouragement and valuable advice, leading to fruitful research. Without the Rabinowitz Foundation and a special person, the late Rose Malkind Portal, whose friendship and faith in us, helped us to finish this book,it might not have seen the light of day. From her early teens into her eighty-third year, Rose fought for the freedom, dignity and fraternal unity of the working class. Her contribution was constant, selfless and unsung. Picketing, collecting strike funds, workers' education, mobilizations, circulating petitions for working people's causes were her day to day concern. It is understandable that her friends love and respect her memory and see her life as following a path of working class devotion, illuminated so brightly by the life of James Connolly.

Finally, a bibliography which we have included at the end of this book fully details every publication mentioned in the text and the Reference Notes.

Carl Reeve
Ann Barton Reeve

CHAPTER I

SEVEN CENTURIES UNDER ENGLAND'S YOKE

The Easter Rising of 1916 differed singularly from the more than seven hundred years of Irish revolt against England which preceded it. This time a man of the poor, a labor leader and Marxist Socialist led the forces of revolt. James Connolly's intensive study of the history of Irish rebellion was one of two principal forces which shaped his life. The second was the philosophy of Karl Marx, which illuminated for him the position of classes and the directions of forces arrayed against one another as Irish history unfolded.[1]

His masterful work, *Labor in Irish History*, written in the United States, examines from a Marxist viewpoint the position of the peasants and workers in the various epochs. It indicates the framework of Connolly's thinking for most of his life and throws additional light on his pathway to Easter Monday, 1916. Connolly analyzed the hundreds of years of suppression and revolt and urged the Irish people to use their past history to provide lessons for the time in which they lived.

Ireland's history, to him, proclaimed the failure of middle-class leadership to attain freedom for Ireland. Such leaders throttled rebellion at the point at which their own class interests had been satisfied.

"Only the Irish working class remain as the incorruptible inheritors of the fight for freedom in Ireland," said Connolly, in this scholarly treatise.[2]

He wrote his work in the midst of organizing and while he edited the *Harp,* in which it first appeared, serially. He wrote at home, with his lively children about him; while riding on stagecoaches and trains; between speaking dates; in libraries; and in the homes of his comrades while away from home. He contended: "...the capitalist system is the most foreign thing in Ireland...".[3] A form of communal society existed in ancient Ireland and continued as late as 1600. Feudalism was imposed from foreign shores. Connolly envisioned a reconversion of Ireland to the Gaelic principle of

---

[1]James Connolly, Fragmentary Notes, in *The Communist Review.*
[2]James Connolly, *Labor in Irish History,* pp. xxxiii, 9, 10.
[3]*Ibid..* p. xxx. See T.A. Jackson, p.25.

common ownership by a people of their sources of food and maintenance.

The Irish defended themselves from waves of invaders--Dane, Norseman and Anglo-Norman. England repeatedly invaded Ireland. The pattern was repeated for three centuries. The English conquerors and their supporters took the fertile land, killed and maimed the Irish peasants, driving them off the land to starve on the rocky slopes or in the woods and bog-land. From these positions, the victims bitterly attacked their enemy and their enemy's cattle and barns.[4]

The Lords were forced to come to terms with the peasants, who returned from the hills; but their homes and fields, however, now belonged to the Lord and they paid him tribute.[5]

Queen Elizabeth, in the sixteenth century, instructed Lord Essex to rid Ireland of the Irish. A document of the time had the ring of contemporary imperialist policies: "Let us... connive at their disorders, for a weak and disordered people can never attempt to detach themselves from the Crown of England." Thus early was the agent provacateur and the spy projected as a force in the domination of peoples.[6]

James I, at the beginning of the 17th century, confiscated one-half million acres in Ulster and colonized thousands of Scottish and English Presbyterians. The British Government, according to Connolly, had placed "in the heart of Ulster a body of people who, whatever their disaffection to that Government, were still bound by fears of their own safety, to defend it against the natives." The Presbyterian planter, however, could claim neither civil nor religious liberty. "The Episcopalians were in power, and all the forces of government were used by them against their fellow Protestants...".[7]

At the end of the century, though the Irish Catholics fought stubbornly for James II of England, the war in which victory was won by the Protestant William III, Prince of Orange, had little to do with religion. Connolly saw this war as setting the stage for modern Irish history. In his book, he pointed out that William and the Pope were joined in the League of Augsburg, which aimed at containing Catholic Louis XIV of France, James' ally. The Pope poured his treasury into William's effort and, at his victory, Te Deums were sung in Rome.

---

[4]Jackson, pp. 38, 39. Karl Marx, Frederick Engels, *Ireland and the Irish Question*, p. 217. George Creel, p. 61.

[5]Jackson, p.40.

[6]Marx, Engels, *Ireland*, etc., pp. 259, 260; "Outline of a Report on the Irish Question," p. 127. Creel, p. 65.

[7]James Connolly, *ReConquest of Ireland*, pp. 9, 10.

Connolly mourned the "splendid opportunity" which had been lost for the Irish people to bid for freedom while their two oppressors fought. Instead, the "people took sides on behalf... of their enemies."[8]

The Penal Code of 1697 deprived Irish Catholics of all rights but also attacked non-Episcopalian Protestants. Irish industry was virtually wiped out by prohibitive taxes. All export of live-stock and dairy products to England was forbidden.[9] Later, when disease attacked cattle in England, export of cattle became a source of huge profits to Irish landlords. Tenants were evicted by the thousands and every available acre put to pasture.

The peasants organized in secret societies, tore down fences enclosing cattle and burned the houses of the shepherds. They dug up and harassed the land until it became useless for pasture. Thousands suspected of affiliation with the secret societies were hanged. Many of the rebels fled to America.[10]

Two huge people's movements marked the last several decades of the eighteenth century. One of them resulted in a full-fledged revolt against England. The Irish Volunteers sprang out of the military and financial weakness of England, as a result of its war with America. The British government called for troops of volunteers, to be financed by Irish contributions, to act for the defense of Ireland. By the end of 1779, 100,000 citizen soldiers were marching with 130 cannon.[11]

Henry Grattan, lawyer and small proprietor, who led the Patriot Opposition in the Irish Parliament became the leader of the vast organization. Karl Marx described him as "a parliamentary rogue."[12] An enormous contingent of volunteers followed him in "review" outside Parliament. Emblazoned on a large cannon was the sign: "Free Trade or Else." The message of this immense presence was not lost upon the meeting inside. The movement halted, for a time, the dominance of the English Parliament over the Irish Parliament in Dublin and established free trade for Irish merchants. The Volunteers now numbered a half million men.[13]

Captain James Napper Tandy recruited Catholic artisans into the Volunteers, although they were officially excluded, since they were forbidden to carry arms. He contended that the Catholics neither owned nor carried arms, individually, since these belonged to him as Treasurer.[14]

---

[8]Connolly, *Labor in Irish History,* p.6.
[9]*Ibid.,* p. 33. Jackson, pp. 84, 85. John Devoy, p. 454.
[10]*Labor in Irish History,* pp. 13, 16. Jackson, pp. 103, 104. Elinor Burns, p. 14.
[11]Jackson, p. 106. *Labor in Irish History,* p. 25.
[12]Marx, Engels, Letter Marx to Engels, December 10, 1869, p. 285.
[13]*Labor in Irish History,* p. 35.
[14]Jackson, p. 107.

He was one signer of a Manifesto which declared, in part: "We cannot but lament that distinctions injurious to both [Catholics and Protestants] have too long disgraced the name of Irishmen, and we most fervently wish that our animosities were entombed with the bones of our ancestors; and that we and our Roman Catholic brethern would unite like citizens and claim the *Rights of Man*."[15]

A movement developed within the Volunteers for popular representation in Parliament, which was strongly opposed by Grattan and his aristocratic friends. The Volunteer's Commander-in-Chief, Lord Charlemont, repudiated a convention called for this purpose and, echoing him, Grattan called the convention "an armed rabble."

Connolly, in *Labor in Irish History,* deplored once more the lost opportunity. "...An Irish Republic could have been won as surely as Free Trade," he wrote, "but when the rank and file of the Volunteers proceeded to outline their demands for the removal of their remaining political grievances... all their leaders deserted. The people had elected aristocrats, glib-tongued lawyers and professional partriots to be their officers..."[16] The poor in the towns and the peasants knew no improvements and continued to go hungry.

Theobald Wolfe Tone was the leader of the rebellion of 1798. He was a founder of the United Irishmen and defender of the Catholics. He declared: "Our freedom must be had at all hazards. If the men of property will not help us, they must fall; we will free ourselves by the aid of that large and respectable class of the community--the men of no property."[17]

Tone, a Protestant from Dublin, was trained as a lawyer. Yet "a foolish wig and gown" did not sustain his interest.[18] The French Revolution had encouraged the aspirations of the Irish; the principal demand of the United Irishmen was a democratic Parliament, with representation for all. The program included agrarian reform and opposed rack-renting by the landlords.

The Protestant poor, through development of industry, were being drawn from agriculture into the factories. They were learning they had more common interest with the Catholic poor than with the Protestant master. The two diverging streams in Ireland were being unified, wrote Connolly, by "waters of a common suffering."[19]

---

[15]*Labor in Irish History,* p. 59.
[16]*Ibid.,* pp. 35, 37.
[17]*Ibid.,* p. 43.
[18]From Padraic Pearse's speech at commemoration ceremony at Wolfe Tone's grave, June 22, 1913, Joseph Deasy, p. 13.
[19]*Labor in Irish History,* p. 53.

The United Irishmen was declared illegal. The pro-England Orange Society emerged as a counter-revolutionary force and provided spies and provocateurs. Tone was one of those charged with treason. Grattan demanded that the Catholic Committee, which employed Tone to help redress Catholic grievances, disavow him. Their refusal saved his life. He and his family embarked for the United States but he soon left for France, to enlist aid for the Irish cause.[20]

Several attempted invasions of Ireland by the French failed. On September 20, 1798, Tone again sailed to Ireland, on the flagship of a fleet which carried 3,000 men. When they arrived on October 10th, the British Navy was waiting for them. After a six hour battle, the French fleet was destroyed. Tone was put in irons and taken to prison, where he died, his family charging he had been murdered by his jailers.[21]

The nineteenth century opened (January 1, 1801) with the British Parliament passing an Act of Union. The century was to see greater numbers than ever before involved in bitter struggles to rid Ireland of British shackles.

Robert Emmet led a conspiracy to seize Dublin Castle, as the first call for revolt. The intended rebellion, however, had been kept too secret and no mass support had been sought. Consequently, it failed.[22]

Daniel O'Connell, "The Liberator," appeared on the scene before the century reached the half-way mark. Thousands of workers and peasants were drawn into a vast movement for "Catholic Emancipation," under his leadership.[23] They were convinced that his objective was rebellion against England. Actually, O'Connell, a banker, a brewer, and a large landowner, hated democratic "French ideas." He organized giant meetings for "Repeal of the Union" and attacked the tithes levied upon the people for support of the established church.

As Frederick Engels described the meetings, in a letter published in *Der Schweizerische Republikaner,* June 27, 1843: "...What huge numbers are moved by him! The day before yesterday, 150,000 men at Cork; yesterday 200,000 men in Nenagh; today 400,000 men in Kilkenny... If O'Connell... were really concerned with the elimination of misery--and not with his miserable, petty middle-class objectives... I should like to know what demand advanced by O'Connell... could be refused."[24]

---

[20]Jackson, pp. 138, 142, 144, 145, 146. *Labor in Irish History,* pp. 52, 53, 56, 57. Creel, p. 91. Devoy, p.3.
[21]Sean Cronin, p. 21. Jackson pp. 170, 185. *Labor,* etc., p. 44.
[22]Jackson, pp. 193, 194. *Labor,* etc. p. 63. Cronin, p. 27.
[23]Devoy, p. 6.
[24]Cronin, pp. 33, 34. Marx, Engels, *Ireland,* etc., p. 35.

O'Connell's failure to lead Irish revolt was demonstrated at Clontarf. Though the authorities had announced that the meeting to be held there was prohibited, a million persons marched toward the town. At last, now, the marchers believed, O'Connell would give "the word" for the rebellion.[25] O'Connell did not give "the word" but sent messengers along all roads ordering the marchers to turn back. Later, when he was arrested, his attorney claimed the consideration of the court for O'Connell, for standing between the people of Ireland and British authority.[26]

A group of men who called themselves the "Young Irelanders" were moved by the tides of democratic thought engaging Europe and felt themselves part of the revolutionary currents which were agitating the minds of men, though, as Connolly commented: "...without ever being able to comprehend the depth and force of the stream upon whose surface they were embarked."[27]

Three hundred thousand persons had died of starvation in the famine of 1845. Connolly wrote: "There was food enough in the country to feed double the population, were the laws of capitalist society set aside and human rights elevated to their proper position." In the fifty years before 1888, 3,668,000 persons had been evicted under the Poor Relief Bill. The Corn Laws, repealed in 1846, had robbed Ireland of the protective tariffs which supported her economy.[28]

James Fintan Lalor, whose writings importantly influenced Connolly, understood the economic relationships that lay at the root of the disease. The famine fanned his determination to fight English domination of Ireland and save the peasantry from extinction. He reasoned with the Young Irelanders: "A mightier question moves Ireland today than that of merely repealing the Act of Union... On a wider fighting field... must we close for our final struggle with England... Ireland her own... and all therein, from the sod to the sky. The soil of Ireland for the people of Ireland, to have and hold... forever, without suit or service, faith or fealty, rent or render, to any power under heaven...".[29]

Connolly later resurrected and published Lalor's *Faith of a Felon,* which called for the Irish people to pay no more rents, but to arm themselves and protect their harvest with "a peaceful, passive resistance." He added: "...and should need be, and favorable occasions offer, surely we may

---

[25]Jackson, p. 234. Devoy, p. 6. *Labor,* p. 60.
[26]*Labor,* p. 102. Cronin, p. 36.
[27]*Ibid.,* p. 105.
[28]*Ibid.,* pp. 105, 111.
[29]Brian O'Neill, pp. 53, 54.

venture to try the steel."[30]

The insurrection, which began July 26, 1848, lasted three days. The Young Islanders did not follow Lalor's advice. According to Connolly, with few exceptions, they "failed to rise to the grandeur of the opportunity offered them." They chose property rights instead of human rights, "as a basis of nationality, and the measure of their failure was the measure of their country's disaster."[31]

In 1867, James Stephens, who, with John O'Mahony organized the Fenian Brotherhood, also refused to give "the word" for revolt, although his fellow patriots felt the time was ripe. In Dublin, on March 5, 1867, when the revolt actually began, it was a night of "hail, rain, storm and snow." Hundreds stood ready, though arms were few. The snow piled up in the largest drifts anyone could remember. The British Government had been informed in advance, once again, and its large forces readily put down the rebellion.[32]

Writing in the *Workers Republic* on March 11, 1916, a month before the Easter Rising, Connolly viewed the past history of Ireland: "The United Irishmen waited too long, the Young Irelanders waited too long, the Fenians waited too long... But...in these days of March, let us remember that generations, like individuals, will find their ultimate justification or condemnation not in what they accomplished, but rather in what they aspired and dared to attempt to accomplish."[33]

When Connolly was a lad, living with his family in Edinburgh, Scotland, the Land League, led by Michael Davitt, was defending peasants against dispossession by the landlords. Charles Stewart Parnell was addressing huge meetings, advising: "Pay no rents and hold a firm grip on your homesteads."[34] An old Fenian uncle of the boy was telling him about past battles for Irish freedom and James was beginning to absorb the story of Irish rebellion, as he experienced the hard life of a working class family.

[30]*Ibid.,* pp. 56, 57.
[31]*Labor,* etc.; p. 112. Referring to America, Lalor wrote: *"Somewhere,* and *somehow,* and by *somebody,* a beginning must be made... Lexington was premature, Bunker Hill was imprudent and even Trenton was dangerous." (From *Labor,* p. xiv.)
[32]Devoy, pp. 235, 236. O'Neill, p. 63. *Labor,* p. 134. Jackson, pp. 275, 276. Henri Le Caron.
[33]James Connolly, *Labor and Easter Week,* p. 154.
[34]O'Neill, pp. 66, 67, 68, 69.
For additional material on Irish history, see *The Unbroken Tradition,* by Nora Connolly; *Ireland's Case Stated,* by Very Rev. T. N. Burke, O.P; *A History of the Irish Working Class,* by P. Berresford Ellis. Important letters and articles in *Ireland and the Irish Question,* not previously cited, can be found on pp. 129, 143, 279, 280, 281, 290, 327, 328, and Note 39 on p. 425. (The article by Jenny Marx, written February 27, 1870, p. 380, exposed the brutal treatment accorded the Fenians, particularly O'Donovan Rossa, and resulted in his release from prison.)

CHAPTER II

SOCIALIST BEGINNINGS

James Connolly was born in the Irish ghetto in Edinburgh, Scotland, June 5, 1868.[1] His father, John Connolly, worked as a "carter" for the Edinburgh Corporation, the city administration. His job was to empty and cart away the waste buckets of Edinburgh families. His wages were low, the work hard and disagreeable. But poverty dictated that he hold the job.[2]

He and Mary McGinn Connolly had three children, the first-born, John; the middle child, Thomas; James the third son. Bronchitis often left the mother suffering and incapacitated. Before James' birth, John Connolly's work was upgraded to lamplighter and the family moved into more comfortable quarters. The promotion proved temporary, however, and the family was forced to return to the old slum neighborhood, the symbol of their destitution.

Murtagh Lyng, friend and associate of Connolly as a young man, said "Connolly was 'dragged up' like most proletarian boys," though he was, nevertheless, "well educated" as the result of the difficult circumstances under which he lived. He developed "a deep hatred of those institutions which have weighed so heavily on the working class."[3]

His father was able to contribute to the education of his sons to the extent of seeing to their attendance at the local Catholic School for a short time, to learn the rudiments of reading, writing and arithmetic.[4] In later years, when Connolly was publishing *The Harp* in the United States, he described himself as a boy: "...(my father) would set me to do ten minutes work," he wrote, "and find me an hour after sitting, dreaming with the job not yet commenced."[5]

Very early he began to read omnivorously, an enjoyment and a discipline which he never relinquished and used as a weapon in all his

---

[1]C. Desmond Greaves, p. 17.
[2]Joseph Deasy, p. 4.
[3]Desmond Ryan, p. 12.
[4]Kara P. Brewer, p. 4.
[5]*The Harp,* June, 1908.

work. Reminiscent of Abe Lincoln's youth, in Connolly's boyhood, the light of the fire had to serve as illumination. He later told his daughter, Nora: "When the fire was going out, I couldn't read...".[6] It is probable that the rigors at this stage of his life resulted in the squint and poor eyesight which marked him.

His lesson in the limited options of working-class Irish boys came early. At ten years of age, family conditions forced James to go to work. He became a printer's devil for the *Edinburgh Evening News,* where Thomas had worked before him. James "fetched" for the printers. He also washed the inky rollers. As well as being under-age, he was small. When the regular visit of the Factory Inspector was due, James was taken from his regular duties and placed on a high stool. The Factory Inspector discovered the truth and James' services at the newspaper were terminated.[7]

At age twelve, he found employment in a bakery. The boy hated the hard work, which lasted from six in the morning until late at night. His health was undermined and at night he suffered nightmares. He later told Nora: "...the few shillings I could get were needed at home... Often I would pray fervently all the way that I would find the place burnt down when I got there."[8] His next job, in a mosaic tile factory, was less difficult, physically, and lasted only until someone even younger than he could be found for even lower wages.

By age fourteen, he had "devoured" the literature of the Irish Land League. Charles Stewart Parnell led a vast alliance of revolutionary Fenianism, which called for national revolt, and constitutional nationalism. He declared a "true revolutionary movement in Ireland should partake both of a constitutional and illegal character." The movement was widely supported in the United States.[9]

In 1881, the British Government decimated the agrarian struggle by arrests. Davitt and Parnell and many agrarian leaders were jailed. Parnell offered to divert the peasant movement into political channels, in exchange for release of the prisoners. Many of Parnell's followers believed his agreement with British authorities was a sell-out. Davitt joined the damning chorus. Parnell's dominance in the Irish anti-British struggle diminished. The period was still marked by sporadic outbursts of peasant action against eviction. The spirit of the Land League was alive in spite of

---

[6]Nora Connolly O'Brien, pp. 91, 92.
[7]Greaves, p. 18.
[8]Nora Connolly O'Brien, p. 86.
[9]Cathal Shannon, p. 75. John Devoy, pp. 286, 313, 314. Sean Cronin, p. 118. Elinor Burns, p. 28.

continued repression. This was the climate in which young Connolly was growing up and learning.[10]

Following in the footsteps of his brother, John, James discovered a place where an unemployed Irish lad might find a niche which would release his family from the burden of supporting another growing boy. Undoubtedly falsifying his age, he enlisted in the British Army under the name, Reid, also used by his brother.[11]

John J. Lyng wrote to William O'Brien on April 29, 1951: "...Here in the U.S.A. Irish Socialist Clubroom, Jim said of his military service: "I was carried away by the John Boyle O'Reilly [a Fenian] propaganda to infiltrate the British Army and found myself in India like most of the other Irishmen who enlisted for the same reason. They scattered the Irish recruits all over the Colonies...".[12] Later Connolly was to write burning words against Irish youth enlisting in the British Army, in order to learn weaponry.

James' son, Roderick, records that the only time he saw his father in a "towering rage" was when he was discovered, at age twelve, talking to a British recruiting sergeant. Connolly ordered his son into the house and proceeded, stormily, to give the sergeant his thoughts on the British Army. To his son, he made clear, that he would expect him never to accept the King's shilling.[13]

John Leslie, leader of the Social Democratic Federation in Scotland, who importantly influenced Connolly's early Socialist years, wrote to William O'Brien from Edinburgh, November 1, 1916: "He was away from Edinburgh for a considerable time and about this period of his life he was reticent... Understand me, I know the reason and to my mind, there was no occasion for reticence, but such was his wish."

In Dublin, with his battalion, returning from an evening's excursion, James met Lillie Reynolds, his future wife. He was waiting on a street corner for a tram as Lillie, too, waited. She was small, quiet and fair. The tram rushed past them. They laughed and talked and decided they would enjoy seeing more of each other. The romance quickly developed.

Four months before the termination of his term of military service, Connolly walked away from the army. Two reasons were responsible for

---

[10]Brian O'Neill, pp. 84, 85.
[11]Connolly Archives, William O'Brien Collction, Manuscript note dated February 2, 1957, written by O'Brien. He wrote: "It is believed he enlisted under a false name. A man in Edinburgh thought it was Reid but was not sure."
[12]Connolly Archives, Letter, John J. Lyng to William O'Brien, April 29, 1951.
[13]Samuel Levenson, p. 29.

this action. He had heard that his father had been discharged by Edinburgh Corporation after a disabling accident and was in desperate circumstances; secondly, he and Lillie wanted to marry. To his permanent surprise, the British Army overlooked his absence, possibly through the confusion in records, due to the move of the battalion out of Dublin.

He married Lillie, in Perth, after an interval in Dundee, Scotland, where he found a temporary job. He wrote Lillie from there: "I could get plenty of work in England but you know how England might be unhealthy for me...".[14]

His arrival in Dundee coincided with a militant free speech fight conducted by the Socialists, whose several organizations united in this purpose. There were meetings and protest marches against local bans on their meetings. The following October, the Social Democratic Federation and the Socialist League united into the Scottish Socialist Federation.

At the time Connolly left the Army, there was an unprecedented growth in trade unionism in Great Britain. The year 1889 was marked by huge strikes and working class solidarity. Socialist societies and clubs burgeoned.[15]

James and his brother, John, attended the meetings and demonstrations in Dundee. John Leslie was one of the principal speakers. The demand for the eight-hour day was the dominant slogan. Connolly and his co-workers tackled the problem of struggle for the shortened work week on their own job. He wrote Lillie, asking for a week's postponement of their wedding: "If we get married next week, I shall be unable to go to Dundee as I promised, as my fellow-workmen on the job are preparing for a strike at the end of this month, for a reductin of the hours of labour. As my brother and I are ringleaders in the matter, it is necessary we should be on the ground." He added: "If we were not, we should be looked upon as blacklegs, which the Lord forbid."

Sympathetic Lillie could understand, then as ever, James' loyalty to his fellows. She has been described by her children and others who knew her as gentle, loving and compassionate, "thoroughly in accord with her husband's ideals."[16]

James and Lillie established their first home in Edinburgh. He was soon attending meetings with his brother, who was secretary of the Scottish Socialist Federation. John Leslie described Connolly's early talent for combatting opposition: "I noticed the silent young man as a very interested

---

[14]Greaves, p. 29.
[15]Deasy, p. 4.
[16]Desmond Ryan, pp. 14, 15.

and constant attendant at the open air meetings... Once when a sustained and virulent personal attack was being made upon myself and when I was almost succumbing to it, Connolly sprang upon the stool, and to say the least of it, retrieved the situation. I never forgot it. The following week, he joined our organization, and it is needless to say what an acquisition he was...".[17]

The undefeatable will-power that characterized Connolly was displayed at this time. Leslie said: "When he started... he had a decided impediment in his speech, which greatly detracted from the effect of his utterances, but by sheer force of will, he conquered it and became what you know...".[18]

James now had also gone to work for the Edinburgh Corporation, a job as carter the only one available. His employment was sporadic, since he was hired on a provisional basis.

In May, 1893, brother John was one of the speakers at a demonstration for the eight-hour day which was jointly organized by the Scottish Socialist Federation, the Independent Labour Party and the Trades Council. John was dismissed by the Edinburgh Corporation, despite efforts in his behalf by the Trades Council. He had to leave Edinburgh to find work and James succeeded to his position as secretary of the Scottish Socialist Federation.

The Connolly flat now housed that organization, Keir Hardie's Independent Labour Party, and a women's branch of the SSF which Connolly had organized.

Lillie was called on for advice and help with his first letters and articles for the socialist movement. She carefully reviewed the material he wrote, correcting spelling, punctuation and grammar.[19] Connolly, by this time, had attained a solid knowledge of literature, poetry, economics, ancient and modern history (particularly concerning revolutionary traditions in Irish history). He seriously studied Marx and Engels and attended lectures given by prominent socialists on economics and socialism.[20]

He became Edinburgh correspondent to *Justice* published by the Social-Democratic Federation and wrote a regular column for the *Edinburgh and Leith Labour Chronicle*, which he signed "R. Ascal."

In the beginning of his socialist apprenticeship, he performed the chore of the novice speaker -- carrying the platform to street corner meetings for the principal speaker. Leslie was his teacher. Connolly developed his talent and learned to hold the attention of his listeners with wit and authority.

[17]Connolly Archives, Letter, John Leslie to William O'Brien, November 1, 1916.
[18]*Ibid.*
[19]Nora Connolly O'Brien, p. 26.
[20]Desmond Ryan, p. 15.

He ran for a seat on the Town Council on the Socialist ticket. His vote totalled third, out of four candidates. He was opposed by the Irish National League, which supported the Conservatives, and two candidates of the Liberal Party. The local clergy kept a watchful eye on those who attended Connolly's meetings and attempted to warn them away. The next Spring, Connolly again was a candidate for a seat on the Poor Law Council; this time he was defeated by a priest.

His election activity had done nothing to increase his popularity with his employers. Calls to work were becoming infrequent. It was the worst winter of the century. An economic slump hit Edinburgh and many unemployed were searching for work. The Corporation "solved" the problem by cutting out extra men and putting the regulars on more intensive work and longer hours.

Connolly was trying to provide for two daughters, Mona and Nora in addition to Lillie and himself. The Corporation now closed to him, he set up a cobbler's shop. He had no aptitude for cobbling and was more preoccupied with the problems of the socialist and labor movements of Edinburgh. A customer could be sure of getting a political discussion with the shoes, which, often, might be unwearable. It is told that Connolly addressed a friend at the end of this unsuccessful enterprise. Taking off his apron, he announced: "I am going out to buy me a mirror so I can watch myself starve to death!"

In 1894, at twenty-six years of age, he had become, also, secretary of the Scottish Labour Party (the Edinburgh name for their Independent Labor Party branch). He was friendly with Keir Hardie, secretary and moving spirit of the parent organization.[21] That the association was one of mutual respect can be seen by the tone of the letters that were written to the veteran by the young Connolly, who was not reluctant to contribute advice and criticism.

The middle class parties, Connolly wrote Hardie, used the land question only in the interests of political maneuvering. This could be exposed by the ILP through a great meeting in Dublin, which Hardie should address "strong and straight, without reference to either the two Irish parties, but rebellious, anti-monarchical and outspoken on the fleecings of both landlord and capitalist, and the hypocrisy of both political parties for a finale...".[22]

[21]Kara Brewer, p. 11.
[22]Connolly Archives, Letters, James Connoly to Keir Hardie, Reprinted in the *Socialist Review*, pp. 117, 118, 119.

Hardie did not take Connolly's advice lightly and organized a demonstration in Dublin, in which more than 10,000 persons participated.

The Scottish Socialist Federation affiliated with the Social-Democrat Federation and maintained a Scottish District Council. In order to issue propaganda, Connolly often dipped into his own scant funds.

A series of lectures arranged by Connolly brought to Edinburgh such prominent socialists as Eleanor Marx Aveling; Edward Aveling; Tom Mann; H.M. Hyndman, founder of the SDF; Harry Quelch, editor of *Justice;* Ben Tillet, labor leader, and others.[23]

The family's poor economic situation was deteriorating further. Connolly's attempts to meet his difficulties by lecturing were met by disappointment. It became virtually impossible for the family to exist in Edinburgh. James Connolly made arrangements to emigrate to Chile.[24]

Lillie was frantic and appealed to Leslie.

"As the result of my conversation [with Connolly] the project was given up...," he recorded.

Leslie pressed Connolly's cause in a special appeal in *Justice.*

He wrote: "I am not much given to flattery... yet I may say that very few men have I met deserving of greater love and respect than James Connolly... no man has done more for the movement than Connolly... Certainly nobody has dared one-half what he has dared in the assertion of his principles... he is the most able propagandist in every sense of the word that Scotland has turned out." He pleaded: "...is there no comrade in Glasgow, Dundee or anywhere else who could secure a situation for one of the best and most self-sacrificing men in the movement? Connolly is, I have said, an unskilled labourer, a life-long total abstainer, sound in wind and limb. (Christ in Heaven! how often have I nearly burst a blood vessel as these questions were asked of myself!) Married, with a young family, and as his necessities are therefore very great, so he may be had cheap."[25]

The Dublin Socialist Club responded with an offer of a job as paid organizer. Leslie and other friends raised the money for the family's move. Lillie and James' third daughter was born two months before the family's departure. She received the Irish name, Aideen.

The Socialist Club of Dublin became the Irish Socialist Republican Party in May, 1896, the month of Connolly's arrival. In several years, under his leadership, it was to become the inspirer and leader of a number of significant mass protests against British imperialism, which drew into its

[23]Kara P. Brewer, p. 13. Greaves, p. 68.
[24]Connolly Archives, Letter, John Leslie to William O'Brien, November 1, 1916.
[25]Greaves, pp. 69, 70.

orbit nationalists, poets and intellectuals, together with Irish workers. Its program, drafted by Connolly, united precepts of socialism and nationalism. It called for "The establishment of an Irish Socialist Republic, based upon the public ownership by the people of Ireland of the land and instruments of production, distribution, and exchange." Agriculture and industry were to be administered "as a public function" by elected boards of management. It called for organizing "the forces of democracy in preparation of any struggle which may precede its realization." Interim demands were placed to "palliate" the effects of the existing social system, to be achieved by political (voting) means. Included were demands for the 48-hour week; universal suffrage; free education "up to the highest University degree"; graduated income taxes; free maintenance of all children; abolition of private banks and nationalization of railways and canals. For the farmers, the program proposed that the best machinery should be made available.[26]

Edward Aveling was the first man outside Ireland to become an associate member of the ISRP. Eleanor Marx Aveling wrote to Connolly, offering whatever help she might give.[27]

In the uneasy period following the inception of the organization, Connolly found that his financial position was far from secure. Strikes and unemployment dominated the lives of Dublin workers. The building trades were on strike and since it was the young workers in this trade who formed the basis for the financial agreement which brought Connolly to Dublin, his one pound a week wages could not be raised. He found work as a laborer with Dublin Corporation.

He was unequal, physically, to the heavy work. His daughter, Nora, described his return after the first day's work, following a period of unemployment. Exhausted, he could barely speak.

"I cannot do the work," he moaned. Nora recalled their dismay, when, seeing him set out for the new job, Lillie discovered that his boots had rotted from dampness. Lillie, unhappily, suggested that he wear bedroom slippers tied to his feet with rope.

Lillie could not endure seeing her husband in this rare, dispirited mood. She left quietly, and pawned her gold watch, her last treasure.

"You'll have good meals tomorrow and you'll be strong again," she told James, who many times had gone searching for work without taking food

---

[26]James Connolly, *Socialism and Nationalism,* Irish Socialist Republican Party program, pp. 184, 185, 186. Desmond Ryan, pp. 19, 20.

[27]*Socialism and Nationalism,* p. 21.

for himself from the family's small larder.

"I'll make it up to you, Lillie... I'll make it up to you," Nora quoted her father.[28]

During periods of unemployment, Connolly spent some of his time studying in the National Library. He published a phamphlet on the writings of James Fintan Lalor, rescuing his essays from virtual oblivion. In *'98 Readings,* prepared for the 1898 Centenary Commemoration of Wolfe Tone and other martyred Irish heroes, he further popularized Lalor's writings. He taught himself German and French. Among the Irish intellectuals who frequented the library with him, the extent of his knowledge and ability became legendary.[29]

In the Celtic Literary Society, he talked with the poet, W.B. Yeats, and with Arthur Griffith and other men who espoused varied types of nationalism.[30] Anti-labor and opposed to Connolly's politics, Griffith, nevertheless published in his newspaper, *United Irishmen,* Connolly's letters and articles, a "single honorable exception," at a time "when the ISRP had to suffer under the boycott of the entire Irish press,", Connolly later declared.[31]

Connolly became friends with the remarkable Maud Gonne, whose militant nationalism was oriented toward improving the life of the Irish people. She was never a Socialist but found Connolly a man she could admire.

She was called "the most beautiful woman in Europe." Yeats, who courted her, wrote his play, "Cathleen ni Houlihan," symbolizing Ireland, for her and refused to have it performed unless she played the leading role. It was the only time she acted upon a stage. When the Land League had been ordered to disband, she organized the Ladies Land League, which carried on the fight courageously. She was refused membership in the all male Celtic Literary Society and found that other nationalist organizations also excluded women. In response, she founded "Inghinidhe na H'Eireann" ("Daughters of Ireland"). The organization, which grew rapidly, was pledged to "...work for the complete independence of Ireland."[32] Influencing her nationalist friends and the Dublin literati to follow her example, she supported Connolly and the Irish Socialist Republican Party in the burgeoning movements of the late 1890s.

---

[28]Nora Connolly O'Brien, pp. 19-25.
[29]Kara P. Brewer, p. 15.
[30]Padraic Colum, *Ourselves Alone,* p. 52.
[31]*The Harp,* March, 1908.
[32]Maud Gonne MacBride, *Servant of the Queen,* pp. 227, 233, 291, 300, 317.

The activities of the '98 Centenary Committee developed and its
popularity attracted Home Rule and other middle-class politicians and
businessmen. Connolly argued that the philosophy of Tone was
revolutionary and should be revived to throw light on present problems.
Yeats argued with him and Maud Gonne that a union of classes was
desirable and, indeed, even those loyal to England should be invited to join
the activities.[33] The Centenary Committee finally became completely
dominated by non-working class delegates. At this point, Connolly
withdrew and formed the Rank and File '98 Club, over which he presided.
As always, he combined theoretical writing with agitation and organizing.

In 1897, the ISRP countered plans for the celebration of Queen
Victoria's Diamond Jubilee with a projected anti-Jubilee Celebration. The
response was hearty. Maud Gonne came from Paris to be one of the
speakers and to help with the organization of the protest. The main slogan
was to be: "Down with Monarchy! Long Live the Republic!"

Dublin had the largest anti-Jubilee action of any city and the most
spectacular. The Manifesto of the ISRP, written by Connolly, described
the destitution caused by Britain's armed invasion of Ireland through the
centuries.

"Ireland has seen 1,225,000 of her children die of famine," it stated.
"Starved to death whilst the produce of her soil and of their labor was eaten
up by a vulture aristocracy--enforcing their rents by the bayonets of a hired
assassin army in the pay of the 'best of the English Queens'; the eviction of
3,668,000, a multitude greater than that of the entire population of
Switzerland; and the reluctant emigration of 4,186,000 of our kindred, a
greater host than the entire people of Greece."

And the present! "Seventy-eight percent of our wage earners receive less
than one pound per week, our streets are thronged by starving crowds of
the unemployed, cattle graze on our tenantless farms and around the ruins
of our battered homesteads, our ports are crowded with departing
emigrants, and our workhouses are full of paupers..."

The Irish working class was asked to "Join your voice with ours in
protesting against the base assumption that we owe to this Empire any
other debt than that of hatred of all its plundering institutions."[34]

Jubilee Day arrived. Maud Gonne had arranged to have a large window
available at the National Club on Parnell Square. Hundreds of black flags
were prepared, white lettering displaying the names of those who had died

---

[33]*The Harp*, June, 1908.
[34]*Socialism and Natinalism*, pp. 192, 193, 194.

in the famine, under Victoria's reign. Preparations were carried on under great secrecy.

Maud Gonne described the events which followed: "James Connolly had arranged for the making of a big coffin, symbolic of the fate of the British Empire, and had obtained the services of a workers' band whose instruments were so old and battered that if they were broken by the police, it would be no great loss." [35]

The Centenary Commemoration Committee was meeting at City Hall on Jubilee Day, with delegates from all over Ireland. Maud Gonne, for whom the Committee had lost most of its attraction, was waiting, impatiently, "listening anxiously for the harmonious sounds of Connolly's band." At 8 o'clock, the first sounds of the band were heard. Maud asked the chairman, John Leary, to call the meeting to a halt and "invite all the delegates present to come out on the steps... to see our Jubilee procession." James Connolly leading, members of the ISRP pushed "a rickety hand-cart," draped to resemble a coffin. Maud Gonne, Yeats, and a number of members of the Centenary Committee fell in with the marchers, paced by the "cracked instruments of the band," playing a "Dead March."

Police, mounted on horses, moved on the marchers and brutally swung their clubs. Ambulances began taking people away. The procession stubbornly continued to O'Connell Bridge where the viciousness of the fighting brought Connolly to a quick decision. The coffin was in danger of being captured. Connolly ordered that it be thrown into the Liffey River. "Here goes the coffin of the British Empire. To hell with the British empire!" he shouted. At this point, he was arrested.

The police attacked those watching in Parnell Square. Their indiscriminate blows resulted in the killing of an old woman. The infuriated crowd smashed windows in every shop which displayed Jubilee decorations. The next morning, Maud Gonne went to the jail to see Connolly. "Let my wife know," he said to her. It was the first time he had been arrested.

She drove to the one room where the Connollys were living. Lillie was bathing the baby. Nora listened silently. "I was sure something like that had happened when he didn't come home," said Lillie.[37] The prisoners were released the next day. The battered musical instruments appropriated by the police were carefully returned to Connolly. The Diamond Jubilee had brought no honor to the Queen in Dublin nor the several other Irish

---

[35]Maud Gonne MacBride, p. 272.
[36]*Ibid.,* p. 276.
[37]*Ibid.,* p. 277.

cities where the ISRP had a following.

Ireland's potato crop was devastated by the blight and drought which struck the countryside. Landlords once again evicted thousands of starving tenants for non-payment of rents. Floods followed drought. The bogs, upon which the peasants depended for fuel, became impossible to reach. A fuel famine added its harassment to the potato famine and disease.

The old methods of redress arose again out of the dreadful suffering. At night, landlords who had deprived their tenants of home and land were themselves punished. Peasants' meetings demanding relief became a frequent occurrence. Maud Gonne visited County Mayo to see what was being done. The Government had done nothing. A question, raised in the House, in regard to famine deaths in County Mayo and plans for saving the lives of the peasants, brought the arrogant reply from J.A. Balfour: "You can't expect us to supply your farmers with champagne."[38]

She returned to Dublin to confer with Connolly, "chiefly because he was. the bravest man I knew."[39] If the famine was to be conquered, she reasoned, the people must be taught to be without fear. Connolly seconded Maud Gonne's plea: "The people must be roused to save themselves and not die as in 1847." A day's work at the National Library supplied him with material for a Declaration, "The Rights of Man and the Rights of Property," which he wrote with Maud Gonne. The words of Pope Clement I, Pope Gregory the Great, St. Thomas Acquinas and Cardinal Manning were used to support the contention: "In case of extreme need of food, all goods become common property... The very highest authorities on the doctrine of the church agree that no *human* law can stand between starving people and the right to Food, including the right to take that food whenever they find it, openly or secretly, with or without the owners' permission...".[40]

Maud Gonne provided the money for printing the leaflet and arranged to have it sent to her. Meanwhile she returned to the countryside to work with the beset farmers and their families who were fighting police and soldiers against eviction. After a series of demonstrations, the authorities capitulated. Relief work on a large scale was initiated. The Declaration had freed the farmers for action.

Connolly, at the request of Daniel De Leon, toured the famine area to supply articles on the famine for the *Weekly People*. To his disgust, the

[38]*Ibid.*, p. 226.
[39]*Ibid.*, p. 233.
[40]*Ibid.*, pp. 227 ff.

Home Rulers appeared oblivious to the famine. They had completely captured the Commemoration movement and theirs was the only voice being heard. These facts drew Connolly to the conclusion that the ISRP must have its own publication.

The Workers' Republic was issued in August, 1898, after a tour in Scotland by Connolly, to secure finances for its publication. The paper, which advocated "an Irish Replublic, the abolition of landlordism, wage slavery, etc.," appeared in time for the commemoration meeting held by Connolly's Rank and File '98 Committee. It attacked the actions of Irish Americans, who were "distinguishing themselves in the war against Spain." As Connolly put it, the objective of the publication was: "To *unite* the workers and to bury in one common grave the religious hatreds, the provincial jealousies and the mutual distrusts upon which oppression has so long depended for security."

The paper had an uneasy, though influential life, with recurrent demises, followed by rebirths. Police smashed its presses in 1899 in a raid of ISRP headquarters. It emerged again, in 1900 and in 1902. In order to conserve money, Connolly was "printer's devil," printer, editor, contributor and composing-room staff. Its issues appeared most regularly when Connolly was unemployed.

Great Britain had gone to war against the Boers. In August, in the *Workers' Republic,* Connolly called the war "one of the most iniquitous wars of the century..." The war had "valuable lessons," especially for those who hoped for the "peaceful" resolution of the aims of socialism. He did not, said Connolly, like to theorize "upon the functions of force as a mid-wife to progress -- a matter to be settled by the enemies of progress. If, then, we see a small section of the possessing class prepared to launch two nations into war, to shed oceans of blood and spend millions of treasure, in order to maintain intact a *small portion of their privileges,* how can we expect the entire propertied class to abstain from using the same weapons, and to submit peacefully when called upon *to yield up forever all their privileges?*"[41]

The ISRP was expanding, with branches in Cork and with supporters in Belfast, Limerick, Dundalk, Waterford and Portadown. In Dublin, the organization held the first public meeting in sympathy with the Boers to be held in Ireland. A series of anti-recruiting meetings followed with James Connolly the spearhead in a vast movement. "Dangerous rough and tumbles," Maud Gonne described them.

---

[41]James Connolly, *Labour and Easter Week,* pp. 27-31.

One such meeting announced as speakers: Michael Davitt, William Redmond, Arthur Griffith, James Connolly and Maud Gonne. The old Fenian, John O'Leary, presided. The platform was a horse-drawn wagon, or "brake." Davitt and Redmond did not appear. Connolly commented to Maud Gonne: "Our M.P.s are conspicuous by their absence." He climbed on the box seat, alongside the driver.

Maud Gonne described what followed: "As we turned out of Abbey Street, a group of police came forward and stopped the cart. 'Go back, you can't pass, the meeting is banned'... (Connolly) seized the reigns... drove right through the police cordon, the brake swaying dangerously over the rough ground, the crowd cheering wildly and rushing in through the broken cordon." Beresford Place was "a seething mass of people, all shouting 'Up the Boers! Up the Republic.' "

"Quick, put the resolution. We are not likely to have much time," Connolly told her. The police, mounted and on foot, finally had succeeded in surrounding the brake. By this time there had been a rousing acclamation of the resolution, which moved that the meeting "denounces the interference of the British capitalist government in the internal affairs of the Transvaal Republic, as an act of criminal aggression..."[42]

The brake was driven into the police station yard. "We were all prisoners," recounted Maud Gonne. "...I heard the station sergeant say 'We can't keep them here.' Two inspectors went inside the station house and the station sergeant said abruptly: "You can't stay here."

"We don't want to," said Connolly. The gates were opened, and Connolly, asking no questions, drove the horses away.[43]

Widespread support for the pro-Boer position even included some of the clergy. As a result of the general agitation, enlistments had fallen off drastically. It was announced by the authorities that Victoria herself was coming to Ireland to promote recruiting.

Connolly later praised Maud Gonne ("a female Bayard") and the "fearless women of Ireland" for the role they played in the massive protest which the arrival of the Queen exploded.

The Royal Procession advanced, with the people of Dublin confined by police to a safe distance. The crowds on the quays surged forward, broke the glass of the Lord Mayor's carriage, battered the coach, and, according to Maud Gonne, would have given him "a dip in the Liffey," had it not been for police intervention.

[42]*Ibid.*, p. 30.
[43]*The Harp*, March, 1909. Maud Gonne MacBride, pp. 291ff.

The Queen was to give a treat to the children of Dublin. Maud's Inghinidhe na h'Eireann announced, instead, a "Patriotic Children's Treat," to all children who had not participated in Queen Victoria's treat. Twenty-thousand children responded. Assisting Maud Gonne were the men of the Celtic Literary Society and the Gaelic Athletic Association. They marshalled the children and led them in a tremendous parade to Clonturk Park, "An unforgettable sight," wrote Connolly in retrospect. Queen Victoria's treat had been eclipsed. The parents and children of Dublin had refused the royal bon-bon.[44]

---

[44]*Ibid.*

CHAPTER III

TOURING THE "LAND OF THE FREE" -- 1902.

Connolly's emphasis that the fight for socialism in Ireland must be tied to independence from England had its first reward in 1900, when the Congress of the Second International, meeting in Paris, recognized the Irish Socialist Republican Party as an entity, entitled to recognition apart from the Socialist Party of Great Britain. Though poverty made it impossible for Connolly to attend, the Irish delegates carried on the fight and won their point. It was a source of jubilation among Irish socialists and even the anti-socialist, Arthur Griffith, was highly pleased.

One of the supporters of the action had been Daniel De Leon, the leader of the American Socialist Labor Party and the editor of its paper, the *People*. The delegates of the ISRP backed De Leon's stormy struggle against opportunism and reformism, in the debate around approval of Alexander Millerand's acceptance of a post in the French Cabinet. Millerand's colleague there was the notorious Gallifet, who had butchered thousands of Paris Communards.[1]

The final compromise resolution of the Congress, offered by Karl Kautsky, was called "Kaoutchouc" (India Rubber) by Lenin. It was evasive and while ostensibly criticizing class collaboration, offered an escape clause which made it acceptable to the right wing: "Whether in a particular case, the political situation necessitates this dangerous experiment [of entering bourgeois cabinets] is a question of tactics and not of principle...".[2]

Connolly left no doubt as to his position. In a letter, published May 25, 1901 in *Justice*, official publication of the Social Democratic Federation, he characterized the Kautsky resolution: "Millerand could still logically claim to be considered a good socialist, differing only in tactics from the socialists of the world, who agreed with him in principle. I would like to know how you are going to get out of the difficulty... except by repudiating

---

[1]Carl Reeve, p. 125.
[2]*Ibid.*, p. 131.

23

the Kautsky resolution and accepting the definite and uncompromising resolution proposed against it, viz.: that the revolutionary proletariat should, through its delegates, accept no government position which it cannot conquer through its own strength at the ballot box."[3]

During this period, Connolly issued *The New Evangel,* a pamphlet consisting of a series of articles from the *Workers' Republic.* It attacked Home Rule as "...a cloak for the designs of the middle-class, desirous of making terms with the Imperial Government it pretends to dislike. It is but capitalist Liberalism speaking with an Irish accent...". He polemicized against the theory of "state monopoly" or "state capitalism," which had been proposed in opposition to socialism and refuted the position that socialism and atheism were synonymous.[4]

The generally desperate economic situation prompted Connolly to promote a lecture tour for himself in England and Scotland. His Scotch comrades welcomed him but in England, the tour was unsuccessful, his stand on Millerandism being unpopular with H.M. Hyndman and other leaders of the Social Democratic Federation.

The uncompromising political approach of De Leon against opportunism and reformism held much appeal for Connolly at this time. The principles of De Leon and the SLP were also becoming attractive to Socialists in Scotland, where John Carstairs Matheson was fighting opportunism, exemplified by Hyndman and his associates in the SDF. John Matheson, later to become Connolly's close friend and political confidante, was a school teacher from the small town of Falkirk, centre of the iron industry. His group of dissidents saw the SDF leadership as weak in theory and lax in practice.[5] He and his associates were named "the unholy Scotch current," by the SDF leaders. Harry Quelch, editor of *Justice,* called them "impossibilists" after those who had followed Jules Guesde's revolutionary fight against Millerand's reformism.[6] The SLP's *Weekly People* increased its circulation among SDF members, both in Edinburgh and Glasgow.[7]

The desire for a Marxist revolutionary theory and revolutionary party was an important bond between Connolly and the Scottish Socialists, most of them shop workers and trade unionists. Another area of mutuality between them was antipathy to alcohol and its effects on the workingman.

---

[3]C. Desmond Greaves, *The LIfe and Times of James Connolly,* p. 132.
[4]James Connolly, *The New Evangel,* pp. 27 ff.
[5]Walter Kendall, p. 13.
[6]Thomas Bell, p. 371.
[7]*Ibid.,* p. 14.

Connolly, throughout his life a teetotaler, in his early Edinburgh years, abhorred the Corporation's practice of paying wages to the workers in the local pub. Matheson and his group severely criticized the heavy drinking of Hyndman, Quelch and other SDF leaders, which became a political issue.[8] The Scotch SDF branches expelled heavy drinkers.

Matheson and his political friends found their disagreements with the SDF leadership mounting. Their contributions to *Justice* suppressed by Quelch, they found their outlet in the newspaper of the American SLP. It was inevitable that the idea of a newspaper of their own should develop. In 1902, with the help of Connolly, the *Socialist* was born, at first printed on the small press of the ISRP in Dublin.

Thomas Bell, a protege of Connolly, who was later to become the first national organizer of the Communist Party of Great Britain, hawked the papers in the foundry where he worked, and at public meetings. "Under the influence of the *Socialist*," he said, "I, too, became an "Impossibilist.""[9]

Connolly's tour of Scotland and England did not solve his financial problems nor improve his family's well-being. A projected tour of the United States had his complete approval.

As early as 1900, overtures had been made by the ISRP to the SLP to arrange such a tour. At that time, Henry Kuhn, SLP National Secretary, had replied that the desperately insecure financial position of the *People* made practical arrangements impossible.[10] On April 10, 1902, a letter arrived from Kuhn to: "M. Deering, Secretary of the Irish Socialist Republican Party." It declared: "We have just emerged from a series of internal troubles that did at one time threaten the future existence of the Daily People. We are over it now, practically so, and will soon get in shape again... But in the meantime, we would be pleased to hear from you as to the details of arrangment that is to be made in case our sections decide in favor of the proposition, which we have every reason to believe they will do."

He requested the name of the person to come to the United States. "Our impression is that comrade Connolly will be selected, but we want to know for certain..." The ISRP would "stand the cost of the inward sea voyage, we to pay for the passage back to Ireland."[11]

By July 30, 1902, Kuhn had outlined a preliminary itinerary. Connolly

[8]*Ibid.*, p. 42.
[9]*Ibid.*, p. 38.
[10]Connolly Archives, Letter, Henry Kuhn to Martha J. Lyng, July 14, 1900. Also letter, Kuhn to Murtagh J. Lyng, Sptember 1, 1900.
[11]Connolly Archives, Letter,Kuhn to M. Deering, April 10, 1902.

had written on July 15th requesting that the tour be extended to San Francisco, where Connolly wanted to visit a cousin. If necessary, he wrote, the additional cost could be taken from his salary. Kuhn replied that he would attempt to arrange dates through the San Francisco SLP and would try to "see it through without making use of Connolly's offer..."[12].

Connolly had been elected to the Dublin Trades Council of the United Labouring Union, during his tour of England and Scotland. This organization promised financial support to the proposed American tour. The ISRP also had been preparing. In Dublin, Daniel O'Brien wrote a letter to its members, in connection with finances for the tour: "I am instructed to remind you that the funds towards defraying the expenses of sending out Comrade Connolly as agitator to the States will be closed on Tuesday next the 26th inst. I need scarcely inform you what an important event in the history of the Party the tour will be..."[13].

The ISRP was enthusiastic at the prospective tour. It was hoped that Connolly would build the subscription list of the *Workers' Republic* in the United States and collect funds for the paper. The United States, of course, was a prime source of financial contributions to many Irish causes. In addition, the membership avidly awaited first-hand information on the American SLP and Daniel De Leon.

Connolly was the man to make the connection. He was already well known by the American SLP. The New York Labor News Co. had reprinted several thousand copies of the ISRP Manifesto. Connolly's articles on the famine of 1897 were published in the *Weekly People*. In addition, excerpts from the *Workers' Republic* had appeared from time to time in the People and Connolly's *Erin's Hope* had been published in full by the SLP.[14]

Connolly left Dublin at the end of August, 1902. He was given a rousing send-off by his comrades. He told his disconsolate daughter, Nora: "I am not going away forever, only long enough to get enough money to print the paper."[15] Lillie packed his box and on August 30, 1902, James Connolly was on his way. He eagerly awaited meeting Daniel De Leon and his revolutionary Socialist Labor Party.

Advertising of the tour had already begun in the *People*. "Mr. Connolly, the foremost representative of Socialism in the Emerald Isle," would tour the United States under SLP auspices. Murtagh Lyng had prepared a

---

[12]*Ibid.*, Letter, Kuhn to Mark Deering, July 30, 1902.
[13]*Ibid.*, Undated Letter marked "Handwriting of Daniel O'Brien, Ms. 13924."
[14]Kara P. Brewer.
[15]Nora Connolly O'Brien, p. 63.

biography for the paper, which he signed, "His Old Friend."[16] Prior to leaving, regarding his "old friend's" article about him, Connolly quipped: "The friend who wrote that preposterous biography and created a new birthplace and a new year of birth for me, will, I hope, suffer in this life all the tortures of the damned..."[17].

The itinerary planned by Kuhn took Connolly to New Jersey, Connecticut, Rhode Island, Massachusetts, New York, Ohio, Michigan, Kentucky, Indiana and Missouri. It was later extended to include California, Arizona, Illinois and Colorado. The three and a half months tour also included stops in Canada, at the invitation of the Canadian SLP. As many dates as possible were scheduled before October 16th, in order to use the meetings on behalf of upcoming state elections. The majority of branches were eager to cooperate in scheduling Connolly meetings. Kuhn, several times, was forced to warn the sections that arrangements must include some time off for Connolly.[18]

At home, in Dublin, the postman was eagerly awaited by Connolly's family. He wrote regularly and enclosed newspaper clippings. According to Nora, every Monday morning, she arose early and ran outside to meet the postman who "brought the letter from daddy."[19]

His first meeting, in Jersey City on September 13th, preceded by several days the large New York reception which had been scheduled to open his tour. It was a "rainy, disagreeable evening," but Union Hall was crowded. "His speech fairly bristled with telling points in the indictment against the Irish skinners of Irish labor," wrote the *Daily People* correspondent. The Irish Socialist Republican Party had experienced a steady growth, Connolly said, in spite of the use of religion to divide the people.

The official greeting to Connolly took place at Cooper Union in New York City on September 15th.[20] Reporters from the major newspapers asked Connolly the stock question: "Where did your ancestors come from? Did they have estates or castles in Ireland?" Visiting Irishmen in the past had provided many a bright tale of ancient kings and chiefs.

Connolly answered briefly: "I have no 'ancestors.' My people were poor and obscure like the workers I am speaking to now!"[21]

The *People* reported: "At 7:30 o'clock all the approaches to the hall were

[16]*Weekly People,* September 16, 1902.
[17]Samuel Levenson, p. 87.
[18]Connolly Archives, Letter, Kuhn to Connolly, September 30, 1902.
[19]Nora Connolly O'Brien, p. 63.
[20]*Daily People,* September 15, 1902.
[21]Desmond Ryan, p. 11. R.M. Fox, pp. 57, 58.

jammed with the waiting crowd. There was little standing room left..."
Frank D. Lyon chaired the meeting. Connolly's speech was preceded by
that of Daniel De Leon who gave a send-off to the SLP campaign in the
state elections, in which he was running for Governor.

De Leon then introduced Connolly, who had come from Ireland, not
only to give greetings from the "Socialist Labor party of Ireland," but also
to "urge his fellow wage slaves in America to hasten the day when the
'American Invasion' of Europe will be, not the invasion of ultra
capitalism... but the invasion of that Freedom dreamed of by the Franklins
of old, carried now as a live possibility in the folds of the Socialist Labor
Party of America..." This position of the dominance of the American
socialist movement was repeated more explicitly by De Leon in the
farewell meeting to Connolly at the end of the tour in December.[22]

A resolution welcoming Connolly gave endorsement to his mission:
"Enlisting the interest of Irish-Americans in the Socialist movement of
Ireland... and... in his mission, aims to destroy the influence of the Irish
home rulers and bourgeois in Ireland, and their allies, who trade on the
Irish vote in this country, to the economic detriment of the Irish
workingmen of this country...".

Connolly, arising to speak, according to the report, was "received with
cheers and applause that increased in volume for several minutes." He was
"visibly affected" by the responsiveness of the New York audience.

"I never stood before such a crowd before," he commented. "Judging
from your hearty and vigorous conduct, for a Party that is supposed to be
dead, you appear to be as lively as an Irish wake in full blast."

He declared: "I represent only the class to which I belong... I could not
represent the entire Irish people on account of the antagonistic interests of
these classes, no more than the wolf could represent the lamb or the
fisherman the fish."

He reiterated his basic position: "The Irish situation is two-fold, political
and economic. Politically the people of Ireland are under the rule of
another country, and even if the Irish were to resolve to effect important
economic changes, they could not, because of the political domination of
this other country..." The Irish Socialist Republican Party had as its task,
first, the emancipation of Ireland. "No person can be economically free

---

[22]Later, in 1906, De Leon wrote, in *Flashlights of the Amsterdam Congress:* "America is
the theater where the crest of capitalism would first be shorn by the falchion of Socialism...
Europe on the whole is decidedly behind. While, so far, decidedly in advance of America in
the tangible and visible part of the Socialist movement, the facilities, capabilities and ripeness
of continental Europe for ringing the tocsin of the Social Revolution and successfully
carrying out the revolution, are, to all appearances, infinitely behind America." (p. 133)

who is not politically free and no person can be politically free who is not economically free... While... political dependence destroys the racial and other characteristics of the Irish, economic dependence destroys the people themselves."

In Dublin, Connolly continued, the majority of workers lived seven or eight families to one house. Such houses, for the most part, were owned by "the shining lights of the Home Rule executive committee." Children could not be raised decently under the circumstances. Connolly's eloquence came from personal experience. As to wages, the Irish worker earned less than one pound ($5.00) a week, when working, "so that it is not possible for Irishmen to live as becomes intelligent human beings." Under international competition, the small farms of Ireland could not survive, without the vastly improved machinery used abroad, which economically was unobtainable. The Socialist demand was for the social ownership of agricultural land, "and the means whereby to exploit it."

On Home Rule: "Fighting foreign tyrants to put a native one in their place is no remedy." It was necessary to own the factories and the machinery.

The Irish workingmen were uniting, slowly, on the class-conscious lines of Socialism and were making headway against religious prejudice. In ˙concluding, Connolly urged the Irishmen present to vote for the Socialist Labor Party and work for it. Whatever promoted Socialism in America and destroyed capitalism, would help advance Socialism and destroy capitalism in Ireland.

According to the *People,* Connolly's "fervent appeal" ended "amid tumultuous applause. The audience cheering at the top of their voices, rising in their seats and throwing their hats in the air."[23]

This was an auspicious launching of Connolly's tour. The report gave the necessary impetus to the sections and branches throughout the country to schedule the Irish socialist for their home areas.

In Yonkers, New York, the next evening, Connolly spoke, in Getty Square, to an estimated four hundred people. His lecture, as in every city, was along the lines of his New York City speech.[24]

From every city of the tour, subscriptions to the *Workers Republic* continued to trickle into SLP headquarters after the meetings. Typical of the letters accompanying the subscriptions was that of Joseph H. Sweeney. He wrote Henry Kuhn from Yonkers on December 17th: "Enclosed you

---

[23]*Daily People,* September 16, 1902; *Weekly People,* September 20, 1902.
[24]*Daily People,* September 19, 1902.

will find check for one dollar and five subscription cards returned." [Subs were advertised at 50 cents for one year. Probably the branches received a small percentage.] "...we will try and get subscribers in the future among our Irish friends for the Paper."[25]

In Paterson, New Jersey, Connolly spoke on a Friday night, September 19th. Despite stormy weather, 300 people came to hear him.[26] SLP members from Elizabeth, New Jersey, however, reported the audience on Saturday night, September 20th, was "not large but very intelligent." They listened closely and interrupted only for "hearty applause," the one and a quarter hours "masterly address."[27]

In Germania Hall, in Hartford, Connecticut, the evening of September 24th, during the question period, a man arose and announced he was a capitalist. He had saved $300 in 25 years. His question was how should he vote? Predictably, Connolly's reply was that he should vote the SLP ticket. Socialists, if they came into power, would treat him better than the capitalists, who had forced him to spend so many miserable years in the effort to save $300. "Connolly put this advice in such bewitching language that the whole audience roared with laughter," it was reported, and the "capitalist" left the hall.

The scheduling of Connolly's meetings by the SLP sections left much to be desired. In a letter to Kuhn, written September twenty-third from Providence, Rhode Island, Thomas F. Herrick projected a tight schedule. Connolly was expected to arrive in Providence at noon on Saturday, the twenty-seventh. A street meeting would be held in Woonsocket that evening. A hall in Pawtucket would be hired for 2 o'clock Sunday afternoon, to be followed by a meeting in the evening in a hall in Providence. Probably aware of the exhausting demands on Connolly's physical endurance, Herrick added: "If he is not able to speak at all meetings, the meeting will be held with local speakers." A reception committee would meet Connolly at the Providence train station. They would be identified by red SLP buttons in their lapels.[28]

Kuhn responded to the obviously protesting Connolly: "Providence told me that they would let you out for one day and I don't see why they did not... Troy has been notified and as to St. Louis, I have simply left one day open. After that there is another day open on October 30."[29]

---

[25]Connolly Archives, Letter, Joseph H. Sweeney to Kuhn, December 17, 1902.

[26]*Daily People,* September 24, 1902.

[27]*Daily People,* September 23, 1902.

[28]Connolly Archives, Letter, Thomas Herrick to Kuhn, September 23, 1902.

[29]*Ibid.,* Letter, Kuhn to Connolly, September 30, 1902.

The Troy arrangers, too, ignored Kuhn's exhortation that Connolly be given some rest. Three meetings, one after the other, had been organized for him. Connolly refused to speak at all three meetings and exchanged angry language with several Troy members. The argument reached its peak with Frank Passano, Troy organizer, hurling insults at him.

Connolly protested to the National Executive Committee. On October 31st, Kuhn wrote Connolly at St. Paul: "Enclosed please find letter just received from Section Troy. Boland [member of Troy SLP] writes me that Passano, the member who made the offensive remark you quoted in your last, himself realized that he had allowed himself to be carried away by momentary anger and that he will retract the statement made... The National Executive Committee, at the first meeting held after the receipt of your letter reporting the Troy affair, without hesitation took the stand that the members of Troy... acted utterly without warrant and that the remarks made by Passano were an insult that cannot be countenanced by anyone..."[30].

Later, in 1903, when Connolly returned to Troy to live, and, subsequently, to fight his important theoretical battle with De Leon on the relation of wages to prices, Passano was his bitter enemy and did his best to force Connolly out of the SLP.

Trouble flared, also, in the wake of the Rhode Island meetings. This incident illuminated the straight-laced refusal of the NEC leadership to work among non-socialist workers. James O'Gara, a Scotsman, who had travelled with Connolly away from the Woonsocket meeting, in order to talk with him about the movement in Glasgow, wrote a letter to the NEC. As Kuhn described the letter to Connolly, O'Gara "accuses you of having trained with the ILP, spoken at meetings arranged by them, etc. De Leon has the letter and is keeping it for you." The question asked by O'Gara was: if Connolly could speak for the Independent Labor Party across the water, why were members of the SLP in the United States prohibited from speaking on behalf of organizations other than the SLP?[31]

Before he left the country, Connolly sent a letter and a gift to an SLP member in Providence who had befriended him. In the letter, he complained of the unexpected attack by O'Gara. The Providence comrade, obviously agitated, wrote that O'Gara had been misunderstood: "...For some time... the NEC and the Rhode Island SLP had been growling at each other. The NEC says you must not speak a word, only under the

---

[30]*Ibid.,* Letter, Kuhn to Connolly, October 31, 1902.
[31]*Ibid.,* Kuhn to Connolly, December 18, 1902.

auspices of the SLP, while we in R.I. insist on speaking when, wherever you can get a hearing. You do it on the other side of the water and you are right... I will tell Mr. O'Gara... to write you. I can assure you he meant well in trying to get De Leon to see we must all speak when anybody else will let us in." The letter ended: "Don't let this... keep you from spending a very Merry Christmas. I only wish you were here in Providence with us...".[32]

It could hardly have escaped Connolly's attention that all was not calm in the internal affairs of the SLP during his 1902 visit. On October 23d, a major front-page article appeared in the *Daily People,* addressed to the members of the Socialist Labor Party of Pennsylvania. It charged the "defunct" Pennsylvania State Committee with trying to "smash" the Party. The State Committee had levelled a series of charges against the NEC and, in turn, was called "anarchists and corrupt ward heelers."

A little less than a month and a half later, while Connolly was on tour, the convention of the Socialist Trades and Labor Alliance endorsed the action of its General Executive Board in suspending all Pittsburgh locals, since the members had been expelled from the SLP. This was in accordance with an amendment to the Constitution which provided that: "no expelled member of the Socialist Labor Party shall be a member of the Socialist Trade and Labor Alliance."[33]

In Boston, Faneuil Hall was filled before Connolly's meeting opened, according to the fluent correspondent of the *People,* "despite the wretched condition of the streets," and the game "which Jupiter Pluvius was playing with the clouds overhead." The meeting resulted in 25 subscriptions for the *Workers Republic.* Connolly presented "...a fine speech, interspersed with telling points and witty allusions." The Irish Socialist Republican Party, said Connolly, recognized the Socialist Labor Party as the only real Socialist party in the United States. As in every speech until election day, Connolly urged his audience to support the SLP at the polls. Present at the meeting, Socialist Party "Kangaroos" (the SLP saw them as jumping from one reform to another) created a short interruption by heckling.[34]

An open-air meeting in Haverhill, Massachusetts, on October second, was followed by a hall meeting, Saturday night, October fourth, in Lowell. Connolly had written a note to the *People* that he preferred indoor meetings, since these were "not subject to all the chances of bad weather, brass bands, dog fights and other such circumstances against which

---

[32]*Ibid.,* D.S. Roughen to Connolly, Undated.
[33]*Daily People,* December 3, 1902.
[34]*Daily People,* October 6, 1902.

Demosthenes himself would contend in vain."[35]

Connolly's schedule took him to Cleveland, Ohio, on October 17th, following meetings in Buffalo, New York and Woburn, Massachusetts.[36] James Matthews, organizer for the area, arranged to meet him at the train. "You will be able to distinguish me... with the red button in the lapel of my coat, also being minus the left arm...".[37]

The SLP members had worked hard to secure a large audience for the meeting, which was held in Germania Hall. In addition to advertisements in the newspapers,they had requested permission to raise a banner in the public square on the afternoon of the meeting, Mayor Tom Johnson, called a progressive, had advertised his own public election meeting in this way. The Director of Public Works refused the request.

The audience numbered between "400 to 500," according to the report. "The capitalist parties were holding meetings in different parts of the city, one of them being in the same building where Connolly spoke." A planned disruption made only a small impact. At a signal, about 18 supporters of the Mayor arose from their seats and marched out of the hall, "expecting to stampede the crowd." But, according to the *Daily People,* "It didn't work."

In the public square, where a huge tent had been pitched, the Mayor appeared. The entertainment consisted of booming cannons, fireworks lighting the sky, and loud brass bands. Connolly's meeting, however, had its own "beautiful band," whose rendition of the "Marseillaise" brought down the house.[38]

Connolly commented on current unemployment and the misery it brought to the workers. Basic was the fact,he continued, that the interests of wage workers of all countries were the same, despite religious prejudices.

In Chicago, in the SLP, shortly before Connolly's visit, 17 members quit, leaving a party of only five members. Those who had separated themselves had taken the money and property at hand. This state of affairs was described in a letter written October 14th by John Keegan to J. Matthews. It was doubtful that a Connolly meeting could be organized. By October 25th, however, another letter informed Connolly that a meeting had been arranged at Horan's Hall. Once more someone would meet him at the railroad station; this time Connolly was to wear the red SLP button

[35]Kara P. Brewer, p. 27.
[36]*Daily People,* October 10, 1902.
[37]Connolly Archives, Letter, James Matthews to Connolly, October 11, 1902.
[38]*Daily People,* October 20, 1902; *Weekly People,* October 25, 1902.

for identification.[39] At the meeting, he was called upon to handle "freaks, frauds, fakers, and Kangs," according to the report. This he did, to the satisfaction of the local SLP.[40]

The Minneapolis audience at Century Hall (capacity 800) on Sunday, November second, was "large and enthusiastic." Every seat on the lower floor was occupied and the gallery was well filled. The reporter wrote that Connolly, "...must be heard to be appreciated. In print, his wit suffers; but spoken in his genuinely Irish proletarian style, it creates both mirth and thought."[41]

The next day, at Federation Hall, in St. Paul, the day before election, Connolly gave the "last shots in the campaign" of the section.[42] He left for Salt Lake City, for a November eighth meeting, after a "racial supper" and reception given him by members from St. Paul and Minneapolis.[43]

The rosy reports from Minneapolis and St. Paul that appeared in the *People* did not reflect the unpleasant situation which arose between Connolly and the local SLP Section. The *Workers Republic* had arrived late and to Connolly's chagrin, an ineptly worded story in connection with a letter from Father Haggarty was featured. Kuhn referred to Father Haggarty as "a Kangaroo speaker who has been floating around the country a good deal."[44] The Minneapolis Section, according to Connolly, "claimed it was an endorsement of the Social Democrats, and wanted me to repudiate it."

Though he angrily rebuked his Dublin comrades for "getting me into a devil of a row over that foolish note about Father Haggarty's letter -- (Why you did not print it as a letter and let it go at that, or put your comment in a fashion that the average man could discriminate between your letter and his... I do not know and can not imagine...".) nevertheless, Connolly was furious at the ultimatum of the Minneapolis SLP. He denied the story was an endorsement of the Social Democrats and said: "The *Workers' Republic* was published for Ireland and not for America, and if the comrades in Minneapolis thought we were going to publish the paper to suit American politics, they were vastly mistaken...". The local SLPers refused to push Connolly's paper as the result of the hassle.

---

[39]Connolly Archives, Letter John Keegan to J. Matthews, October 14, 1902 and letter, Henry Ide to Connolly, October 25, 1902.

[40]Connolly Archives, Unsigned letter to *Workers' Republic,* Ms. 13923.

[41]*Daily People,* November 10, 1902.

[42]*Ibid.*

[43]Connolly Archives, Letter, Charles Davidson to Kuhn, October 10, 1902.

[44]*Ibid.,* Letter, Kuhn to Connolly, December 20, 1902.

He revealed in his letter of November third to Daniel O'Brien, written with several additions during the course of several days, that this was not the first time he had rebuked members of the American SLP.

"You people think, no doubt, that I have quite a picnic on, but I have not," he wrote. "In quite a few cases, I have had to turn sections down very sharply for their manner of talking about this trip of mine. They... appear to imagine that their share of the business is quite a piece of philanthropy but I have set them right on it in a way that sobered them very rudely. I have always insisted that the ISRP stood on an equal footing with the SLP, or any other body...".

Connolly was unreservedly sharp, in this letter, with those he had left behind in the ISRP. The delays in getting out the *Workers' Republic* infuriated him. "Here am I," he wrote, "knocking life out of myself, travelling from 200 to 600 miles every day, at least, and talking every night, canvassing hard for subscriptions and in order to get them telling everybody that the paper will appear more regularly in the future than in the past, and you people at home have not the common manliness to try and stand by my word by getting out the paper as promised... you all ought to be damned well ashamed of yourselves... If some of you do not think the cause of the Socialist Repbulic worth working for, why in Heaven's name do you not get out of the Party?"

Connolly attempted to lighten the sombre tone of his letter with a P.S.: "Last night I received a letter from Troy, New York, apologizing for their conduct, and this morning, I received a deputation from Minneapolis, apologizing for theirs. So all is friendship again."[45]

Among the letters preserved in the Connolly archives, O'Brien Collection, are several written requests of that period, in which the visitor was asked to state his views on America. These few existing letters, doubtlessly, reflect similar requests by additional SLP members. It was from Salt Lake City, November 10th, that Connolly finally responded. There might well have been mixed reactions to the letter which appeared in the *People*.[46] By this time many SLPers were acquainted with Connolly's biting wit. They could not be familiar with the forceful interchange between the Irish and Scotch Socialists, who took and gave forthright ideological blows in their dealings with one another. Furthermore, the biting wit had been directed to events in Ireland. This time it hit a very sensitive area -- themselves -- Americans.

---

[45]Connolly Archives, Connolly to Daniel O'Brien, November 3, 4, 1902.
[46]*Weekly People*, November 22, 1902.

Connolly wrote: "Doubtless my comrades of the SLP would be interested in learning what are the impressions of America I have acquired so far, as the result of my trip in this country. At least when I consider that every Socialist Labor Party member whom I have yet met, as soon as he had got through the necessary preliminary process of shaking my hand, inquired: 'What do you think of America?' I am venturing to set down here some of my opinions." The letter was a brew of humor, obviously high spirits, and thoughtful, but no-punches-barred analysis.

"When it was arranged between the ISRP and the SLP of America that I should honor this country by my presence, an acquaintance suggested to me that I had better hurry or there would be no SLP left in the United States when I got there." Such information came from the Socialist publications of Great Britain, whose correspondents used every possible slander against the SLP. Though he did not believe these newspapers, Connolly wrote, they had their effect. He had expected to find the SLP in the United States weakened by secessions and resignations.

"To me, it was sufficient that the SLP was following in America the same line of action which we, in Ireland, had mapped out for ourselves before we came in touch with SLP literature." The SLP, with the Socialists of France, Poland and Italy, had supported the delegations of Ireland and Bulgaria at the International Congress, against the reformist Kautsky resolution. The SLP had but one vote at the Congress, but "as long as their cause was just, it did not matter whether the SLP vote [within the United States] was 34,000 or 1,000,000... I believe firmly that the revolutionary Socialist movement will always be numerically weak, until the hour of revolution arrives, and then it will be as easy to get adherents by the thousands as it is now to get single individuals."

After he reached the United States, "...the real state of affairs in the sections exceeded my fondest expectations." The members of the SLP were not disheartened nor disorganized. They were hopeful, energetic and active. Defections did not deter them. They were, in fact, "a real revolutionary movement."

And De Leon? A Salt Lake City "Kangaroo" said that "hundreds of thousands of men" had been driven out of the party by him. When he met "the tyrant," Connolly said, he was surprised to find "a somewhat chirpy old gentleman with an inordinately developed bump of family affection... a new sort of 'Socialist of the Chair' who stated a politico-sociological proposition which scalps a traitor or reveals a corruption, with as little personal feeling as a surgeon in the dissection room."

He proceeded to other evaluations, referring to a trait which he was to confront often in later years. "Permit me also to say that in one respect, the SLP is thoroughly American. It has its full share of the American national disease--Swellhead. When the average SLP man now asks me what I think of America, I have got into the habit of replying that I don't think much of it." The man, who in the past had often signed his articles, "R. Ascal," continued: "and it does me good to watch the dazed, mystified expression that creeps across his face. Then after a while, his face clears up and I know then that he has said to himself, 'Well, Connolly is only an Irishman after all, and, of course, he knows no better.' "

His vacation in San Francisco lasted less than five days. His meeting took place there on November 18th, after having been publicized by handbills and advertising wagons drawn through the streets by horses. According to Kuhn, the section was "under the sway of a hostile element."[47] The San Jose SLP had scheduled him for November 19th; on November 20th, he was to be in Bakersfield; November 21st, Los Angeles; November 24th, Phoenix, Arizona. Then on to Colorado, November 27th.

Kuhn, from New York, continued to negotiate with the section organizers for meetings and the sections continued to gather subscriptions to the *Workers' Republic* and contributions to the "Irish Agitator's Fund," to underwrite Connolly's expenses. The *People* on November 15th, reported receipt of $99 from branches and sections, having previously acknowleged $376.72.

In San Jose, his meeting took place during "a cold rain." His competition was a meeting of the Republican Party, dedicated to the Grand Army of the Republic and also "a free literary entertainment on behalf of the Catholic Church." Connolly made the point that most of the members of the Irish Socialist Republican Party were Catholics who had the good sense to lay aside religious beliefs when considering politics. To a question on the differences between Irish and American labor unions, Connolly replied that although Irish unions were "pure and simple," they endorsed men of their class, not men of the capitalist class, as in the United States. At the root of the corruption in the American "pure and simple" unions was the large number of political jobs bestowed as political favors. "Labor fakirs" held "all kinds of jobs from that of cleaning spittoons in city halls to that of Commissioner General of Immigration,"[48] he declared.

"Some foolish Kangs who asked some silly questions" in the Los Angeles meeting "were crushed," according to the *People*,[49] by Connolly.

---

[47]Connolly Archives, Letter, Kuhn to Connolly, September 30, 1902.
[48]*Weekly People,* December 13, 1902.
[49]*Daily People,* December 8, 1902.

From Pueblo, Colorado, under date of November 29th, came William Knight's report to the *People*. "...Two hundred workingmen listened to Comrade Connolly." His theme was: "The greatest power the master class uses against the workers was political power, in other words, the government... It makes no difference whether the robber is Irish, American, Jew or German... a robber he will remain so long as the workingmen give to him the political power by their votes."

In Denver, an estimated 500 persons filled Columbia Hall; a number had to be turned away. In the question period, it became apparent that members of the Socialist Party had given up their own meeting to attend, according to the correspondent, to create trouble for the SLP. The SPA members were routed when they "arose in different parts of the hall and made all kinds of statements." Connolly answered all questions.

A single taxer declared: "...in your Irish impudence, you call us 'American slaves and oppressed wage earners.' This gall is unpardonable." Connolly's "delicately sarcastic and witty" reply brought applause and the single taxer subsided.[50]

Connolly's last scheduled meetings met with difficulties, aggravated, perhaps, by lack of enthusiasm of members, due to Connolly's now well-known criticism of American chauvinism. His schedule called for routing through Cripple Creek and Grand Junction, Colorado on December second and fourth; then to St. Louis on December seventh, followed by stops in Jacksonville and Springfield, Illinois on the eighth and ninth. He was to speak in Marion, Indiana on December 10th and Detroit on December 11th.

At Grand Junction, according to the Daily Sentinel, a successful meeting at the Court House attracted a large crowd, in spite of the enticing presence of "Captain Jinks of the Horse Marines" at the Opera House.[51] The *Weekly People,* providing the itinerary through December 11th, carried the note: "December 12 and following days in Canada. This will conclude the tour of comrade Connolly in America."[52]

The Detroit meeting had not been held because train connections could not be made. St. Louis party members did not accept their date since: "the venture would not warrant undertaking at this time... especially as the intervening period to advertise is so very short." Jacksonville SLP members were unable to hire a hall for the scheduled date. The Marion people could only schedule a meeting on week-ends. That date was

50*Ibid.*
51Greaves, p. 151.
52*Weekly People,* December 13, 1902.

accepted by the Indianapolis members, who requested that Connolly speak on American conditions, specifically, "The Socialist Movement in America."[53] His visit to Indianapolis was referred to by Connolly in a letter to the *People,* in 1904, which ignited the theoretical controversies between himself and Daniel De Leon, and served to underline his own position against sectarianism.

The negotiations for a short tour of Canadian branches in Toronto had begun several months before. The National Secretary of the Canadian SLP wrote him: "From Detroit, kindly come to London (Ontario)... you will be met by comrades wearing the red button."[54]

Connolly offered to speak at a meeting in Troy before he left for Ireland, since he wanted to visit his cousins again. On December 19th, he was the principal speaker at a meeting there, his subject the history of the "Political and Economic Situation." He spent Christmas 1902 with the Humes, his relatives.[55]

On one of his last days in the United States, Connolly wrote an article for *Detroit Today* on the vast migration of the Irish people. Had the emigrants benefited by the change? Could they not have achieved "as great a change for the better... by making a more determined stand at home?... The intensification of labour is greater here than at home... and, in my opinion, the worker is an old man in this country when he is still regarded as being in the prime of life at home. In other words, the emigrant sacrifices his future... for the sake of a few extra dollars."[56]

The demanding tour was now behind him. Passage had been booked for him by Kuhn, second cabin, *Etruria,* for December 27th.[57] Connolly was anxious to arrive in Ireland in time for the upcoming election campaign in Dublin which was to culminate on January 15th. Kuhn informed Daniel O'Brien that Connolly would arrive in Queenstown about January second, 1903 and that "he has been doing quite well in the matter of getting subscriptions."[58]

Evidence of some annoyance and exasperation by the SLP leadership toward Connolly is seen in a difference of opinion on money due Connolly. Kuhn sent $40 to Troy "which will see you through, until you come down

[53]Connolly Archives, Letter, Kuhn to Connolly, December 18, 1902. Also letters Hugh Richards to Connolly, December 6, 7, 1902.
[54]*Ibid.,* Letter, W.S. Corbin to Connolly, December 18, 1902.
[55]*Ibid.,* Letter, Kuhn to Connolly, undated, Ms. 13926.
[56]Greaves, pp. 151, 152.
[57]Connolly Archives, Letter, Kuhn to Connolly, December 8, 1902.
[58]*Ibid.,* Letter, Kuhn to Daniel O'Brien, December 8, 1902.

to the city when final settlement can be made." He reported an inaccuracy of $2.10 in Connolly's figures, "but we can straighten that out when you are here."[59] To Connolly's letter of the 19th, Kuhn responded: "You have made the point in several of your letters that you wanted a week to yourself at the end of the tour and the idea that salary would be asked for that period never entered my mind." Kuhn stated he could not decide any dispute on the point. "I am not the National Executive Committee. Neither can I make payments which, so it appears to me, I am not justified to make and the NEC itself will have to pass upon the matter."[60]

The matter was, no doubt, resolved, and all that remained for Connolly in the United States was the New York farewell meeting on December 26th, at the Manhattan Lyceum, the night before he was to set sail.[61]

The reporter for the *People* referred to an "interchange of ideas... between the representative countries of both the Old and New World." In fact, the meeting again exposed differences between De Leon and Connolly on the SLP's role in America and Europe, as the revolutionary situation developed.

"James Connolly proved that he was not only a witty and eloquent expounder of Socialism, but also an observer of great philosophical depth... His speech was replete with impressions of the capitalist and Socialist development of this country, which were modestly and unostentatiously delivered."

Introducing Connolly, the chairman declared that the meeting was called not only to bid farewell to Connolly but "also to give him an opportunity to state his impressions of this country and our movement." Connolly, rising to his feet, was received with "tremendous cheers ending with a rousing tiger."

Any deficiencies in his remarks, Connolly began, rose from the fact that he was more used to addressing the enemy than talking to Party members. He was not completely prepared, he said, to express his thoughts on America, which was "far too big a proposition to take in all at once." His reservations, however, did not keep him from expressing his unresolved impressions. A first impression of the "greenhorn" coming here is the attitude of the people that the United States is like "nothing under the sun."

"This is true in a great many respects," Connolly continued, "but there are a great many things here that will require improvement." He had been surprised by a general disregard for law, true particularly among the

---

[59]*Ibid.*, Letter, Kuhn to Connolly, December 18, 1902.
[60]*Ibid.*, December 20, 1902.
[61]*Daily People*, December 26, 1902.

capitalist class of the United States. In the United States, more than any other country, individualism is systematically practiced, "both as a theory and as a policy." Even the trade unions are affected by this general lawlessness. They, too, looked on labor fakirs, generally, as displaying smartness, "rather than a matter calling for disapproval." Then came a remark which, undoubtedly, must have irritated De Leon -- an evaluation of the American movement. As a matter of fact, said Connolly, the country as a whole, was behind, in its conception of the class struggle.

"Connolly reaffirmed his belief in the policy of the Socialist Labor Party," the report continued, "stating that it was the only one that is likely to carry the working class to emancipation."

Capitalism had run its course, Connolly concluded. It was a class which no longer performed a useful function. He ended with a poem, written by an English Chartist: "Come, I preach a new crusade... Labor is lord of the earth and we should be lords of our labor." There was prolonged applause as Connolly sat down.

Now Daniel De Leon spoke. The Connolly tour was over and it was time to present his clear, theoretical approach. He rejected Connolly's evaluation of American Socialist backwardness. Through Connolly, he said, some messages should be sent to the Socialists of Europe. Connolly should "knock into their heads" that they had better begin to study the importance of American conditions, of which they were crassly ignorant. He repeated a prophecy made eight or nine years before, at a meeting welcoming Keir Hardie, that in America, where there is no deterrent to the growth of capitalism, would be the strategic battleground in the conflict between capitalism and Socialism. America was the country upon which the emancipation of the workers of Europe depended, and which, therefore, they must learn to know. De Leon's address, according to the report, was "eloquent, and at times, impassioned." It received "round upon round of applause."[62]

In the early afternoon, the next day, Connolly sailed. He had made an impact on the American SLP. He had augmented the subscription list of the *Workers' Republic,* had stabilized its financial condition, and he was bringing back money for his family.

In Dublin, Nora was awakened by knocking at the door. It was still dark. "Who is it?" Nora asked.

"Open and see."

---

[62]*Weekly People,* December 27, 1902; *Weekly People,* January 3, 1903. Reeve, pp. 125-137, for further discussion on this point.

"Daddy! Daddy!" screamed Nora.

"Where's mama?" Connolly asked his daughter.

"She's in bed. Oh, daddy, she's got a great surprise for you."

Connolly ran to Lillie's bed, to see her after the long separation, and to see, for the first time, the new baby, Roderick (Ruaidhre).

Afterward there were presents -- a book on China for Mona, an American history for Nora, Indian moccasins for Edie, a ball for Agna (Ina) and a doll for Moira.

"There's no place like Dublin," said James Connolly.

He said to Lillie: "At practically every meeting I received subscriptions for the paper, enough to help keep it going for a while. If we can only keep it going, it should pay."

"Thank God," said Lillie, "you won't have to go away again."[63]

---

[63]The Connolly archives in the O'Brien Collection has supplied many letters on this period, some of which are used here and a number not quoted. These have added enormously to the picture of Connolly's introduction to the United States.

CHAPTER IV

GOODBYE TO IRISH COMRADES

On his return, Connolly found that all was far from well with the ISRP. The greeting by some of his fellow Socialists was surprisingly cool. The reason soon became clear. His efforts had not stabilized the finances of the *Workers' Republic*. A large part of the money sent home for subscriptions had been used to pay the deficits of a licensed bar, which had been set up in ISRP headquarters against Connolly's advice, his strong concern having been expressed during his tour. In addition, he had seen no reason to temper his criticism of the membership on their laxity in publishing the *Workers' Republic* regularly. Connolly discovered, also, that inadequate financial records had been kept during his absence. He furiously declared that the committee who was accountable should be suspended. The club did not support him.

It was in this atmosphere that Connolly became a candidate in the municipal elections in Wood Quay Ward, again supported by his union, the United Labourers. Arthur Griffith wrote in the *United Irishman,* on January 10, 1903: "The able and honest men who are going forward as candidates can be counted on the fingers of one hand. Foremost amongst them is Mr. James Connolly, the Irish Socialist Labour Party's candidate in the Wood Quay Ward. He is opposed by the shoneens, the tenement house rack-renters of the poor, the publicans, and we regret to say, the priests. We are not Socialists, but we would be intensely gratified to see a man of Mr. Connolly's character returned to the Dublin Corporation..."[1].

The inner confusion in the ISRP a contributing factor, Connolly's vote, in comparison to the previous election, was almost halved -- 243 to 431.

With no funds and chaotic conditions within the ISRP, regular issuance of the paper was virtually impossible. To add to the financial difficulties, in March, the Scotch Socialists who had used the ISRP press in Dublin, decided to print the *Socialist* in Edinburgh. Foreclosure of the printing plant was imminent. Connolly demanded that payment of this outstanding

---

[1]R.M. Fox. p.47.

bill must be made by the Dublin local. The ISRP could not lose its publication and still function as a party. Furthermore, the Americans who had subscribed had a right to receive the paper, after paying for subscriptions The membership voted a resounding "No!"

The look on his face when he arrived home led Lillie to ask: "What's wrong?"

"Everything," Connolly told her and recounted the evening's events.

"What will you do now?", asked Lillie.

"I've done it. I resigned as a protest..." Lillie refused to believe the club would accept his resignation. "They did;" said Connolly, "it hurts, Lillie."[2]

In the two weeks which followed, he made application for membership in the SDF, obviously feeling he had to function within a socialist organization. But a reconciliation of sorts took place with the ISRP and his membership application was put aside.[3] Stewart, leader of the fight against Connolly, resigned. William O'Brien, Tom Lyng (brother of Jack Lyng, who supported Connolly) and others, dropped out of activity.

On March 21st, Connolly wrote a letter of humility and self-abnegation to William O'Brien: "...I feel your loss to the movement so keenly that after due deliberation upon it, I have resolved to make you an offer. It appears that... you and your friends, (of course I except Stewart) were activated by the belief that I am an obstacle to the progress of the party, that I am a danger to Socialism in Dublin. I do not know upon what facts such reasoning is based, but that is beside the point.

"I believe that you, being a much younger man, and having fewer ties to embarrass you than I have, are a help and a hope of the Socialist movement here, and also that you could be depended upon to run the movement upon the same lines as in the past--the only line that can be permanently successful.

"I am willing, if you agree, to retire from all participation in the party, to resign my membership and go out in order that you may come in... If you consider my presence in the party an irreparable obstacle to your resuming your membership, say so, and I am willing to go out. It shall never be said of me that I kept back the movement."[4]

The inner-party situation continued to deteriorate and for all purposes, the ISRP ceased to be. Connolly accepted the invitation of the District Council of the SDF to lecture in Scotland for five months. He wrote

[2]Nora Connolly O'Brien, p. 66.
[3]Connolly Archives, Letter, J.B. Armstrong to ISRP, March 10, 1903.
[4]*Ibid.,* Letter, Connolly to William O'Brien, March 21, 1903.

Matheson on April 8th: "I am wearying for my Scotch tour to commence. It is the centrepiece of my plans for the whole year as I intend (D.V.) to go to America in the Autumn and bring my family out after me... in any case I consider that the party here has no longer that exclusive demand on my life which led me in the past to sacrifice my children's welfare for years in order to build it up. I only wish I had known it in America before I came home, as when there I received tempting offers to stay, and it is not likely that having rejected them once I will receive them again... You are the only Socialist to whom I have mentioned my intention on America. Do not send it over here yet." The balance of the letter was an effort to forewarn and arm Matheson against attacks against him and his group by the SDF leadership.[5]

Although Connolly's tour was to begin May first, he arrived in Edinburgh in April. He used the time to study linotype operation at a technical school. Though he qualified, Connolly was refused admission into the trade union.

In Glasgow, Connolly worked with the lively dissidents within the SDF. He spent several days each week with them and applied himself to teaching them to become speakers and leaders. Tom Bell described Connolly as he appeared at the time: "A short, stocky man, with heavy auburn moustache, a rougish twinkle in his eye, a pleasant Irish brogue in his speech, Connolly made friends everywhere. His quiet, reticent disposition concealed the store of knowledge he had acquired from extensive reading and wide travel. But, provoked into discussion or debate, he would route opponents with incisive and merciless logic... A proletarian of proletarians, he had none of that snobbery and pretentiousness that mar so many of our leaders. He was... devoted and self-sacrificing for the cause of the workers' emancipation from capitalist slavery."[6]

The situation between the "impossibilists" and the SDF officials came to the point of crisis. The SDF leadership warned that unless the *Socialist* changed its tone, publication would have to stop. Expulsion of Matheson, its editor, and others followed. The May issue of the *Socialist* carried the important announcement that a conference to form a new party would be held June sixth and seventh, 1903, at Edinburgh.[7]

At Glasgow headquarters, with a bucket of paint in readiness, members awaited news of the outcome of the SDF conference at Shoreditch. Learning there had been a split, they used their paint to erase the letters

[5]*Ibid.*, Letter, Connolly to John Carstairs Matheson, April 8, 1903.
[6]Thomas Bell, pp. 46, 47.
[7]Walter Kendall, p. 20. C. Desmond Greaves, *The Life and Times of James Connolly*, p. 160.

"SDF" from the headquarters. They named themselves the Glasgow Socialist Society and took over Connolly's contract.

Connolly chaired the June conference to form the new party. In general, the principles of the American SLP were supported. Some sentiment was expressed that they should not be considered "tools of the SLP." Connolly told Tom Bell: "It does not matter what you call yourselves; you'll be dubbed the Socialist Labor Party anyway." The new organization became the SLP.[8] Echoing the American SLP, it was decided that no official of a trade union could join. The manifesto opposed "pure and simple" (non-revolutionary) trade unions.[9]

Connolly travelled throughout Scotland organizing and lecturing for the Scottish SLP. As national organizer, his salary was thirty shillings a week. Most of the Scottish branches of the SDF came into the De Leonist fold.[10]

Tom Bell wrote: "Connolly's speeches were a model of simplicity, conciseness and burning class invective; always backed up by quotations and statistics of fact... he went to no end of pains to clear up doubts in the minds of workers honestly seeking the truth. A brilliant writer, he not only wrote his articles, but hand-set them, ran the printing machine, and did everything in connection with the production of a newspaper, including its sales at meetings..."[11].

The enthusiastic young Scotch militants "shamelessly exploited" Connolly. Once more Connolly spoke everywhere, holding as many as 12 meetings in one week. His 30 shillings were not always forthcoming. "But never a murmur or complaint did we hear," commented Bell.[12]

After three months in Scotland, in July, Connolly announced that he would return to the United States to live. He had been unable to find in Ireland or Scotland the means with which to support his family.

There was sadness among his young comrades. "We were all filled with emotion when he sailed from the Broomielaw one September night, in the Irish boat, to go to Dublin, in preparation for emigration to New York."[13]

In Dublin, the state of the organization was depressing. Connolly spoke at several open-air meetings. Michael Rafferty, ISRP Secretary, described it in a letter to the *Weekly People,* dated September 15th:

"As you are perhaps aware, there has lately been very stormy times in

[8]Kendall, pp. 20, 21. Bell, pp. 40, 41.
[9]Kendall, p. 68.
[10]*Ibid.,* p. 66.
[11]Bell, p. 48.
[12]*Ibid.*
[13]*Ibid.,* p. 49.

Ireland in connection with the ISRP. We have an attempt to disrupt the party by the wholesale resignation of an element which made the pretext of its resignation the charges of "bossing" against Comrade Connolly, said bossing consisting in his insistence on our duty to our American subscribers... The ISRP, however still lives and will breast the storm..." In a P.S., Rafferty added: "Comrade Connolly sails this week for the States. He has the well wishes of the party here, who are all sorry for losing such a good comrade."[14]

Margaret Hume, in Troy, New York, had forwarded passage money to Connolly. She wrote: "I was so glad to hear you paid a visit to my mother and father... Now dear James... so long as you are determined to come here and bring your family and make this your home, I will do all in my power to assist you... the time is short and it would be a bad time to wait until October; the sooner you get here the better. I will send you a draft for your fare so you will have it by the first of August, so you can make your arrangements."

In view of the accidental death of Connolly's eldest daughter, Mona, after her father's departure, many unhappy hours must have been spent by Connolly and his cousin in retrospect, on the situation which made the next paragraph necessary: "I am sorry you said anything to Mona about coming with you for I think we cannot manage that at present and she will be disappointed. But with the help of God, it may not be so long until the family can come..."[15].

On September 18, 1903, Connolly once more left his family in Dublin and embarked for the United States. Matheson had written him on the fifteenth: "Just a short note to bid you goodbye and good luck... I had looked forward to many years work alongside of you for the cause and many years of your comradeship but destiny and capitalism have been against it... I feel pretty damned blue about it now that the time has come... Take good care of yourself, old chap, and get rich if you can, without being altogether a beast... Yours in the Cause."[16]

Another letter had come to Connolly before he left Dublin. William O'Brien wrote him. "I cannot express with what surprise and sorrow I read in the *Socialist* of your intention of emigrating to America. I have always regarded you as too much bound up with the movement in Great Britain in general, and Ireland, in particular, to ever think you would leave it for

[14]*Weekly People,* October 13, 1903.
[15]Connolly Archives, Letter, Margaret Hume to Connolly, June 29, 1903.
[16]*Ibid.,* Letter, Matheson to Connolly, September 15, 1903.

good... I regret your decision all the more because of the recent dispute, and the part I felt it my duty to take in it. But although you may not take an active part in the Socialist agitation in this country again, no one can question what you have already done -- invaluable work which can never be undone. To you, in a great measure, is due the honour of planting in Ireland a thoroughly straight and scientific movement, and very few men in these islands can, with any truth, say as much. The best tribute, I suppose, we can pay to your memory is to continue that work which you started and so ably carried on for the past seven years, and I can promise you that, personally, I will not lag in the task. I am sure that in our uphill fight, we will often miss your ability, and particularly your enthusiasm under the most adverse circumstances. That you may succeed and prosper, both in your advocacy of the cause of Socialism and in your own material condition, is the earnest wish of Yours fraternally, William O'Brien."[17]

On his arrival in the United States, the *Weekly People* printed a first-page interview with Connolly, on the inner strife in the SDF and the formation of the SLP of Great Britain.[18]

It has been somewhat of a mystery why Connolly's return to the United States was greeted so coolly by De Leon. It is true that the ISRP, whose hero he was when he made his first trip, now was fragmented and nearly non-existent. Connolly had expressed his disagreement that American Socialism could lead the world movement. On the other hand, Connolly had been largely responsible for the existence of the Scottish SLP, with a membership which was completely devoted to Daniel De Leon and his principles. Nevertheless the SLP gave Connolly no help in finding work.

In a letter to Matheson, Connolly described this period:

"When I came here," he wrote, "I meant to work at the printing trade, and might have succeeded... if I (had) not unfortunately placed myself in the hands of a comrade (?) Mr. Frank Lyons, who was then the manager of the Labor News Co. and he succeeded in squelching my hopes of admission into the union... It was not until I found that this gent had squeezed all the STLA men out of the Labor News Co. and manned it exclusively with pure and simple men out of Big Six [AFL] that I had any suspicion of his advice, but as he was enjoying the bosom confidence of De Leon, Kuhn, et al., I dared not breathe my suspicions... He has been found out after he had swindled the party out of about $200 and the leading members, Kuhn amongst the number, out of $500 more..."

[17]*Ibid.,* Letter William O'Brien to Connolly, Undated, Ms. 13908 (3).
[18]*Weekly People.* October 17, 1903.

In the same letter, written in 1905, Connolly mentioned a letter he had seen which was addressed to a comrade then living in New York, but "who had voted against me in Ireland who was told to tell Connolly 'they all would welcome me if I returned.' "[19]

A letter written by Connolly to Matheson, December 20, 1908, after he had become disenchanted with the SLP, offers a possible explanation of De Leon's unfriendliness. Connolly forcefully polemicized against De Leon's *Socialism vs. Anarchism,* which the *Socialist* was reprinting. Connolly called it "De Leon's absurd and unscientific pamphlet" and recalled: *"You will remember that it was a criticism of this work that first set De Leon up in arms against me, and you will remember that I submitted the manuscript to yourself and Neil MacLean at your home in Falkirk before mailing it to New York.* You both agreed as to the justice of this criticism. *Since that time I have publicly before a general party meeting of the SLP pointed out the absurdity of his position to the satisfaction of most of the members and his own intense discomfiture.* [Our italics.]

"Now you will remember that in the speech as originally printed in the *People* and as printed and published in the American pamphlet, he quotes from an article by Rae, author of a 'History of Contemporary Socialism' this phrase: "The assassination of individuals can never produce a social revolution" and goes on to say that the man who said so was ignorant of history and of Socialism. He then goes on for the greater part of the pamphlet giving instances to prove his contention. My point was that Rae's statement was correct, and would be endorsed by every scientific Socialist in the world, and that the 'instances' given were all political revolutions and not social ones. That in short, De Leon's position was utterly opposed to all our teaching. His only defense was that I was 'too technical' in my definition of a 'social revolution,' as if Socialists could afford to be anything else but technical in dealing with such a subject...".

He accused the *Socialist* of incorrectly quoting Rae in order to safeguard De Leon's reputation, in a "so-called 'reprint'... Where Rae has used the words 'the assassination of individuals,' you have substituted 'the act... of small groups... You have altered de Leon's speech to suit the purpose of *hiding* this *forgery*..."[20] It seems obvious that Connolly wrote to De Leon about the pamphlet before he returned to the United States in 1903 and

---

[19]Connolly Archives, Letter, Connolly to Matheson, November 19, 1905.
[20]*Ibid.,* Letter, Connolly to Matheson, December 20, 1908. See Daniel De Leon, *Socialism vs. Anarchism* (1962 edition) p. 12: "A small group may concoct an isolated crime but it can do little toward bringing about a social revolution."

persisted in continuing the discussion in SLP meetings in which De Leon
participated. In a political atmosphere where those who disagreed with De
Leon were regarded as his enemies, no favors would be given Connolly.
Events to come made this clearer.

CHAPTER V

ARE STRIKES USELESS? CLASH WITH DE LEON

Of the disagreements and debates which occurred between Connolly and De Leon, the most important to the future of the labor movement in the United States was based on whether or not workers should struggle for higher wages in the advance toward Socialism. De Leon said this was useless, expressing his customary opposition to raising immediate demands. In view of capitalist domination, he claimed, prices always rose with wages. The controversy centered largely around Marx's position in *Value, Price and Profit,* and the practical application of that treatise in the day to day workers' struggles.

When the discussion began, Connolly was living with his cousins in Troy and working for an insurance company. He hoped to save enough money to bring his family to the United States. His entry into the theoretical fray was low-keyed and, in a sense, off-hand. He did not realize that this was to become a major theoretical battle between himself and De Leon, to be fought fiercely and doggedly during the time he remained in the SLP and, afterward, as an organizer for the IWW. It was to result, eventually, in his final separation from De Leon and the SLP.

Connolly first expressed his differences on "Wages, Marriage and the Church," in a brief letter to the *Weekly People* dated March 23, 1904. It was printed in the April ninth edition.[1] Connolly visualized a friendly discussion and did not imagine the bitterness which the controversy would engender.

His letter explained: "I run up against things in our movement contrary to my own views of Socialism and the essentials of Socialist propaganda." He was, he said, "in complete accord with the SLP, (of which I am proud to be a member) on questions of policy and discipline and revolutionary procedure..." He had, he stated, always defended the SLP against all attacks and criticism. "Yet I have found in the party, speakers and writers and comrades... [who] "gave expression to views... with which I would not

---

[1] *Weekly People,* April 9, 1904.

51

for a moment agree."

His disagreement was three-fold: (1) On the position of SLP speakers that a struggle for higher wages was useless. Strikes were pointless, since prices inevitably rose with wages; (2) There was too much talk on free love and agitation against monogamy in the party; and (3) The constant anti-religious agitation in the party unnecessarily antagonized religious workers. Controversy around the latter two points will be discussed in later chapters.

On wages: "Lately," he wrote, "when reading the report of one of our organizers in the West, I discovered that in the course of a discussion with a spokesman of the Kangaroos, this comrade held that the workers could not even temporarily benefit by a rise in wages, as every rise in wages was offset by a rise in prices--. When the Kangaroo quoted from Marx's *Value, Price and Profit* to prove the contrary, our SLP man airily disposed of Marx by saying that Marx wrote in advance of and without anticipation of the present day combinations of capital. I am afraid that the SLP speaker knew little of Marx except his name... The theory that a rise in prices always destroys the value of a rise in wages, sounds very revolutionary, of course, but it is not true, and, furthermore, it is not part of our doctrine. If it were, it knocks the feet from under the Socialist Trades and Labor Alliance [the small union for revolutionary education established by De Leon in 1895] and renders that body little else than a mere ward-heeling club for the SLP."

He concluded: "Until our party is a unit upon such points, our propaganda in one place will nullify propaganda in another." He requested an "earnest" discussion and intimated he would have more to say later.

De Leon responded to Connolly's letter in the same issue of the *People*. Regarding wages and prices, he declared: "The SLP organizer was right... the conclusion drawn against him and as to the effect of his position on the STLA are wrong." De Leon's polemic was circuitous. He admitted that even the "pure and simple" unions of the AFL, let alone the STLA, could prevent "the coolie stage by acting as a brake on the decline" of wages. He then negated this appraisal of the economic function of unions. The main function of the STLA, he reasserted, was to eliminate private ownership of the means of production. "...That is the reason for its existence--and that is why even though prices rise in tempo with the alleged rise of wages and even though pure and simple unionism checks the decline in Labor's earnings, the STLA form of unionism is a necessity."[2] De Leon added a

---

[2]*Ibid.*

venomous attack against Connolly.

Discussion followed in the SLP press for several months, until the national SLP convention in July, 1904. Connolly, however, was not given an opportunity in the *People* to expand his original letter to further clarify his views, nor refute ciriticism against him. Troy Section summoned him to a meeting on May 29th for "considering and investigating Comrade James Connolly in the matter of Wages, Marriage and the Church and also to' decide whether his attitude and actions are an attack on the party."[3] Several fervent apostles of De Leon demanded Connolly's expulsion or other disciplinary action. Notice of the "trial" was only announced in the *Daily People* on the day it took place. Several days earlier, on May 23d, a note signed by "F.E. Passono, Secretary," was addressed to De Leon. Passono asked if he had "any matter that would be of any service to the Branch in its investigation of the Connolly matter. The Branch is determined to arrive at some definite conclusion in the matter... We feel here that if Connolly is guilty of attacking the Party, he should be punished."[4]

Connolly presented a statement to the Branch dated April, 1904, headed: "Reply by James Connolly to Editor of the Daily People." The document, an able Marxian exposition of the relationship of prices to wages, never saw the light of day in the SLP press and for more than sixty-five years has remained unpublished. It was buried among the papers of William O'Brien, which were released after his death in 1968 to the National Library in Dublin.[5]

"I believe the question of wages and prices to be the only one of the three which would even, by the most straining of language, be considered vital," he wrote. "I wrote my first article in a spirit of good-natured criticism, quietly and calmly stating the points I wished to discuss. But De Leon replied, to my astonishment, with a torrent of florid English, passionate rhetoric." Connolly said that in his preliminary statement, he "gave no argument at all," but only told his reasons for thinking the matter "worthy of discussion."

"The opinion of the SLP," he said to his comrades, "is the only Public Opinion I care about." If the charges against him were found to be true, he should be expelled. But "if they... cannot be substantiated, then they ought to be withdrawn as publicly as they were made." Connolly wanted to

---

[3]*Daily People,* May 29, 1904.
[4]*Daily People,* June 4, 1904.
[5]Connolly Archives, Ms. 13, 929.

remain in the SLP "...where I belong."

De Leon had acted as prosecutor and judge at the same time, Connolly charged. He "wishes to act as referee while he is boxing in the ring."

The "most astonishing mistake" of Connolly's critics, he declared, was the assumption, underlying their agreement, that the worker is exploited as a consumer. Marx had "effectually demonstrated that exploitation takes place in the workshop, and affects the workingman as a producer, not as a consumer...

"Observe the tangle," wrote Connolly, "into which such a position leads our usually logical Editor. He declares that a rise in wages leads to a rise in prices, in other words that wages determine prices. Then he quotes Marx, who said that the value of labor is governed by the cost of maintenance, and he agrees with that too. He does not seem to realize that they are two antagonistic propositions, each excluding the other. The first is that wages determine prices; the second is that prices determine wages. De Leon agrees with both."

Connolly discussed capitalism's contradictions, in which overproduction brings unemployment and crises. "We know that the greater productivity of labor itself will glut the market with commodities, produce an industrial crisis, throw hundreds of thousands out of work and bring wages down again with a slump. We know, in short, that all the tendencies of capitalist society are against the worker maintaining a high rate of wages." High wages, then, is not the basic cause of economic crisis.

In his "Reply," Connolly accused De Leon of falsifying Marx. Though C. Desmond Greaves did not see Connolly's "Reply," in examining De Leon's response to Connolly's first letter, he used even sharper language against De Leon: "If De Leon had Marx's *Value, Price and Profit* in front of him when he wrote, he was guilty of questionable subterfuge."[6] De Leon omitted a very significant phrase in Marx's classic, which reversed the meaning of the quotation.

Marx wrote: *"I might answer by a generalization, and say that* [our emphasis, showing De Leon's omission] as with all other commodities, so with labour, its market price will in the long run adapt itself to its value; that therefore despite all the ups and downs, and do what we may, the workingman will, on an average, only receive the value of his labour, which resolves into the value of his labouring power, which is determined by the value of the necessaries required for its maintenance and reproduction, which value of necessaries finally is regulated by the quantity of labor

---

[6]C. Desmond Greaves, p. 176.

wanted to produce them."[7]

In the very next sentence, Marx gave the reason for the qualifying: "I might answer by a generalization," etc. *"But"* he wrote, "there are some peculiar features which distinguish the *value of labouring power* or the *value of labour* from the value of all other commodities. The value of the labouring power is formed by two elements -- the one merely physical, the other historic or social. Its *ultimate limit* is determined by the physical element, that is to say to maintain and reproduce itself... On the other hand, the length of the working day is also limited by ultimate but by very elastic boundaries." The standard of life of the workers, Marx explains, varies from country to country. This historical or social element may be "expanded or contracted."

Clearly, eliminating the "I might say," and the "But," De Leon was turning Marx around.

Connolly paid his respect to this muddling of Marx's theory of value: "I challenge De Leon, or any of his supporters, to show anything in the context, anything in Marx from A to Z to justify the attributing of such reason to Marx. Our comrade has so cleverly intertwined his own reasoning with Marx's conclusion that it is difficult to tell where one begins and the other ends. In fact, it cannot be done unless you have the book in hand while doing it."

Connolly concludes his evaluation of De Leon's position on *Value, Price and Profit:* "Stripped of all the verbiage and sophistry with which our comrade strives to cloak this economic heresy, here are the two conclusions he attempts to foist upon Marx: (I) A rise in wages does not mean a rise in prices. (II) The worker can not get more than the full value of his labor because a rise in wages DOES mean a rise in prices."[8]

Connolly's "Reply" confesses: "I say to you in all candor that although I have been fifteen years in the socialist movement, I have seldom, if ever, met a more slip-shod examination of a grave economic problem than that which our Editor has treated us to in this case."

He explained that his original letter had not been an attack on the STLA but "...was an attempt to free that body from the incubus of a false doctrine, and to enable it to take a real live part in the struggles of the workers.

"Comrade De Leon spins some fine theories upon the mission of the ST&LA to resist the lowering of the standard of the workers' living, but the

---

[7]Karl Marx, *Selected Works,* Vol. I., "Value, Price and Profit," pp. 332-334.
[8]Connolly Archives, Ms. 13,929.

most effectual temporary way to resist a lowering of the standard of comfort is to encourage the worker to strike for higher wages, but you cannot do that and at the same time preach that a rise in wages is no good. De Leon's theory would keep the ST&LA, as far as its economic work is concerned, perpetually on the defensive...".

The practical consequences of De Leon's position on wages -- surrender of the fight for immediate economic demands--is described: "Imagine a union which would fight against a reduction of wages, but prevented from fighting for a raise because taught by its organizers that a raise was no good. What a picnic the Employer would have; every reduction they could enforce would be a permanent one, as our principles would forbid us demanding a rise, it being no benefit."

Connolly concluded his section on the wages question: "The statement that high prices follow high wages is to my mind the very reverse of the truth. The truth is that high prices PRECEDE high wages. Prices go up with lightning-like rapidity and wages slowly and painfully climb after them...".

It is clear that De Leon did not understand Marx's position on wages but based himself on Lassallean conceptions. Ferdinand Lassalle presented an anti-Marxian theory, the "Iron Law of Wages," which was popular in the United States, even after his death in 1864, and lingered on into the 20th century.

The "law" was summarized by Lassalle, as follows: "The iron economic law which, under present day conditions under the domination of supply and demand, determines the wages of labour, is this: that the average wage always remains reduced to the necessary subsistence which is required by the people according to its habits, for the maintenance of existence and reproduction."[9]

Lassalle concluded that the struggle for immediate demands should be abandoned. Wages could not be increased. Thus trade-unions had no function and their efforts were useless. De Leon's position was almost identical. His amendment to this theory was his sanctioning of the formation of small, revolutionary unions, whose objective was to propagandize for socialism, and after socialism was achieved, would take

---

[9]Ferdinand Lassalle, *Gessammelte Reden u. Lehriften,* p. 342. Reeve, pp. 148-155. One labor historian comments on the Lassallean influence: "The Lassallean's... point was that under capitalism wages were determined by the cost of bare subsistence; this law ruled out or at least minimized the value of trade unions. For if wages could not be raised above the level of subsistence, workers had little, if any, urgency to unite along economic lines." Samuel Bernstein, pp. 245-248.

over the country's administration. The Socialist Trades and Labor Alliance, organized by De Leon and later, in 1905, merged with the IWW, remained small, with only a few hundred members, most of them also members of the SLP.

It is ironical that De Leon was the first to translate into English Marx's *Value, Price and Profit,* which was written, specifically, to refute the wages theories of Lassalle and others like him. The treatise consists of two addresses by Marx to the General Council of the First International, in response to a speech of Citizen Weston, also a member of the International, against trade union efforts for wage increases.[10] In declaring the value of labor to be variable, Marx repeatedly called for struggle to achieve the needs of the workers.

"...The value of labor itself is not a fixed but variable magnitude even supposing the values of all other commodities to remain constant... The fixation of its actual degree is only settled by the continuous struggle between capital and labor."[11]

Connolly understood Marx's concept. De Leon fastened upon only those passages which spoke of the ultimate working-class aim. "The working-class ought not to exaggerate to themselves the ultimate working of these every day struggles," Marx wrote. "They ought not to forget that they... are applying palliatives, not curing the malady." He advocated, therefore, that the workers should not be *exclusively* absorbed in "guerrilla fights" or the immediate struggles. The socialist goal should remain. "Instead of the conservative motto, 'A fair day's wage for a fair day's work, they ought to inscribe on their banners 'Abolition of the Wage System.' "

In *Capital,* Vol. I, Marx countered the purely economic outlook of the anarcho-syndicalists. The class struggle had to be fought both on the political and economic front. He wrote: "The limitation of the working day in England... has never been settled except by legislative interference. Without the workingmen's continuous pressure from without, that interference never would have taken place..."[12]. Marx used the example of the history of the Factory Laws in England.

Engels attacked the Lassallean "fixed law" theory and reiterated Marx's insistence on the need for trade union struggle, in a letter to August Bebel in 1875 criticizing the German socialists.[13]

---

[10]Karl Marx, *Ten Classics of Marxism,* "Value, Price and Profit," p. 5.
[11]Karl Marx, *Selected Works,* Vol I, "Value, Price and Profit," pp. 291, 332, 333.
[12]*Ibid.,* p. 334.
[13]Engels wrote Bebel: "Our people have allowed the Lassallean 'iron law of wages' to be

These Marxian concepts did not find their way into the "discussion," which De Leon opened in the columns of the *Daily People.*

On May 15, 1904, E.C. Dieckmann, of St. Louis, wrote: "There is entirely too much 'rag chewing' about what Marx said or meant," he wrote. "Most every workingman... knows from experience that prices always rise in advance of a general rise in wages." Furthermore, "the rise in wages is never equal to the rise in prices." If he had thought out his position, he would have realized that on this point he was in agreement with Marx and Connolly.[14]

In many letters, Connolly was severely taken to task for his "errors" in economic theory. Patrick Twomey, of New York City, agreed "with the national editor that to get for the commodity, labor power, any more than its market value, is in the end an economic absurdity."[15] Charles Zolot, of Peekskill, New York, reprimanded Connolly for using the term "ward-heeling club" regarding the STLA.[16]

Although few letters offering clear-cut support to Connolly on the wages question were published, a number protested De Leon's refusal to permit Connolly to reply to questions raised in the discussion. Frank P. Janke, of Indianapolis wrote sharply: "...I wish to criticize as entirely unfair... the denial of comrade De Leon to grant comrade Connolly further space in the *People* to answer the questions and opinions put forth by the editor... Comrade Connolly should have at least one chance to answer his opponents." Janke continued that De Leon, in one article, had asked Connolly the same question "no less than seven times."[17]

In the midst of the discussion, early in May, Connolly wrote an agitated letter to his old friend and comrade, John Matheson. His side of the controversy was not being heard and he feared expulsion from the SLP.

---

foisted upon them and this is based on a quite antiquated point of view, namely that the worker receives on the average the *minimum* of the labour wage, because according to Malthus' theory of population, there are always too many workers... Now Marx has proved in detail in *Capital* that the laws regulating wages are very complicated, that sometimes one predominates and sometimes another, according to circumstances, that therefore they are in no sense iron but on the contrary, very elastic." Engels criticized the German socialists for immersing themselves in Lassallean utopianism to the extent of dropping from their programs all mention of trade union struggles. "There is not a word about the unions. And that is a very essential point, for this is the real class organization of the proletariat in which it carries on its daily struggles with capital, in which it trains itself." Marx and Engels, *Correspondence,* p. 335.

[14]*Daily People,* May 26, 1904.
[15]*Ibid.,* May 14, 1904.
[16]*Ibid.,* May 18, 1904.
[17]*Ibid.,* April 26, 1904.

Accompanying the letter was a satirical article Connolly had prepared for the *Socialist.* "As a favor, I ask you to print the accompanying article as it stands. I have veiled it so that none but the readers of the *People* will see that it is really an answer to De Leon's charges upon me. I simply answer him out of his own mouth. All the quotations are verbatim and complete."

The language reflected his desperation. "I would not ask you to do this, only I fear that unless I can get my side heard by some such means, he will intrigue me out of the party.

"God knows why; I don't... It is well to remember also that you will probably have to combat the wages heresy also, if it is allowed to go without his imprimatur."[18]

Matheson printed Connolly's article in the Edinburgh *Socialist* of June, 1904. It quoted, with praise, the De Leon of 1901 and 1902 on Wages, Marriage and the Church, which agreed with Connolly's position. It quoted, in opposition, the De Leon of 1904. In conclusion, it extracted from the *Weekly People* of January 18, 1902, a footnote by De Leon to a letter from W. McCormick, of Fairhaven, Washington. De Leon had commented: "The theory that increased wages means increased prices... is one frequently advanced by half-baked Marxists. The theory was never wholly correct; it is now substantially false..."[19]

Connolly wrote Matheson after the appearance of the article: "I notice that since the *Socialist* arrived in this country, there has been a sudden stop to all the correspondence... Possibly Dan sees the point, even if his devotees don't."[20]

On June 4th, De Leon responded to the letters demanding that Connolly be given an opportunity to reply in the *People.* He would not grant space to Connolly but would submit "all the documents" to the national convention in six weeks. The editor of the *People,* said De Leon, did not have the function "of a pneumatic tube that must allow anything through that is blown into it... He must stand as a rock against disorder."

Several days before his "trial" by Troy Branch, Connolly had written Matheson: "By the time this letter reaches you, I will have been tried by the Troy section, and if they decide against me, I will be expelled. If they refuse to decide, then I will escape until the convention when, Dan says, the whole matter will be laid before the National Delegation... I am convinced that the game is not worth the candle. The candle being Dan's friendship... I am

---

18Connolly Archives, Letter Connolly to Matheson, May 6, 1904.
19Edinburgh *Socialist,* June, 1904.
20Connolly Archives, Connolly to Matheson, June 22, 1904.

going to put up a stiff fight, and I promise you all the wounds won't be on one side. I think Dan is up against a tougher proposition than he is aware of..."[21].

Connolly was apparently struggling for objectivity and self-control. Matheson had asked him whether many of those who left the party had not been run out by De Leon's "dogmatism." Connolly answered: "I am inclined to think that some few men *may* have been irritated at Dan's dogmatism and rather unscrupulous handling of their case, that they struck out too wildly, and without justification committed something like treason.

"But they ought not to have allowed themselves to be irritated into such action, and their self love must have been rather pronounced to make them so act. Personally, I am resolved to fight the best I know how, but to fight so that when passion against me cools down, no reasoning man can point to any act of mine to help the enemy."[22] Connolly was anxious that the branches in Scotland see his defense before the Troy section. "The opinions of my comrades in Scotland are very dear to me... Of course it must not be published. It could do no good...".

Troy Section, however, did not expel Connolly. Instead it requested that the National Executive Committee ask De Leon to print Connolly's statement. The N.E.C. refused to act.[23]

Connolly wrote Matheson, June 22, 1904: "Troy has been converted and sent my defense on to the N.E.C. ... The prevailing opinion in Troy is that the defense will *not* be published."[24] The prophecy proved to be correct.

The proceedings of the 1904 national convention of the SLP, printed July fourth and July ninth in the *Daily People,* contained a one paragraph report by De Leon on "the so-called Connolly matter." De Leon declared that the reason for not publishing the various documents involved had been "...their incorrect and misleading contents..." The convention upheld De Leon but no action was taken against Connolly.[25]

In writing to Matheson, Connolly did not hide his dismay at the results of the convention. "Of course I could not be present, was not a delegate, and had my nose too close to the grindstone of exploitation to attend anyway,"[26] he wrote. "Dan played a very smart trick..." He "read my

[21]*Ibid.,* Letter, Connolly to Matheson, May 26, 1904.
[22]*Ibid.*
[23]*Daily People,* June 26, 1904, N.E.C. Minutes.
[24]Connolly Archives, Letter, Connolly to Matheson, June 22, 1904.
[25]*Daily People,* July 4, July 9, 1904.
[26]Connolly Archives, Letter, Connolly to Matheson, July 22, 1904.

correspondence, paragraph by paragraph, *adding his own criticism in between* so that the delegates could not discern where I ended and *my quotations* began... As a result, he had no difficulty in tearing me to pieces--and thus succeeded by this trick... in preventing publication of the letters, and in preventing the delegates and the party at large from having an opportunity of studying and calmly reviewing the evidence in cold print... The result is that throughout the SLP, I am looked upon as an incipient traitor... I must patiently await the ax."

He did not contain his bitterness: "How revolutionary we all are. Of course there is no hero-worship amongst *us*. We believe that the emancipation of the working-class must be the achievement of the working-class, but neither in Great Britain nor American can a working-class Socialist expect common fairness from his comrades if he enters into a controversy with a trusted leader from a class above them. The howl that greets every such attempt, whether directed against a Hyndman in England or a De Leon in America sounds... wonderfully alike, and everywhere is but the accents of an army, not of revolutionary fighters but of half-emancipated slaves."

He chided Matheson for equivocating on the wage controversy: "I see by the NEC report in this week's *People,*" he wrote, "the Executive Committee of the SLP of Great Britain have apologized for the insertion in the *Socialist* of a letter bearing upon the controversy in the *People,* and has also (as it was expressed to me) *promised to be good and behave* better in the future." He rebuked his friend for not speaking out "on the wages and prices issue, on which I know you *hold very decided opinions.* But... you are not the only person who differs from Dan and is afraid to say so."

In closing this letter, Connolly acknowleded Matheson's friendship. "I can assure you your sympathy has been very welcome to me in this very unfortunate controversy. Amid a sea of doubts... it was very sweet, to have even so far away, some whose faith in me never faltered."[27]

Matheson replied to Connolly's reprimand on August 3, 1904. He wrote that De Leon's conduct at the convention, "...has all been a great surprise, not to say disappointment to me."[28] The letter was written while De Leon was en route to the Amsterdam Congress of the Second International.[29] Before returning home, he toured Scotland. Matheson undoubtedly wanted to support Connolly but De Leon's tour placed the contradictions in his own position in sharp focus. De Leon was strengthening the SLP

---

[27]*Ibid.*
[28]Connolly Archives, Letter, Matheson to Connolly, August 3, 1904.
[29]Daniel De Leon, *Flashlights of the Amsterdam Congress.* Reeve, pp. 125 ff.

branches and after all, it had been only a year since the split from the Social Democratic Federation had occurred.

Matheson continued his letter: "I think you are a little less than just to me... Dan never asked me for my opinions on those points [wages and prices] at all. He asked me about you. I didn't think any the more of him for doing so, but concluded that not to answer would have the effect of confirming suspicions. I told him about your splendid work in this country... I did not, and no one in this country did, realize the hellish gravity of your situation. Neither did the Executive Committee promise to be good boys. They did not believe and I could not persuade them, that you had been refused the right of reply... I am going to write on the wages question in the September issue, taking up your standpoint. Furthermore, if you are expelled, I shall rip up the whole matter and discuss the case in all its bearings... if they object, I shall resign the editorship. Your stand is a question of international importance."

Matheson reported, "Your statement to the Troy section made a great impression here and it is everywhere stated that it is the most brilliant piece of work you ever did. Leith branch, the only branch that ever SNORTED to any great extent, about the publication of your article in the *Socialist* were simply carried off their feet and converted *en masse*. If you are flung [expelled] I shall publish your defense in the paper."[30]

Connolly did not break with De Leon for three years, basically because of common ideology. He, as De Leon, believed in the principles of industrial unionism and semi-syndicalism. As De Leon, he was a "dual unionist," believing that working within AFL craft unions was useless. Both men were opposed to the opportunism of the right-wing leadership of the Socialist Party of America. In this period, De Leon was still playing an important role in the American radical movement. He was one of the principal founders of the IWW in 1905--for which Connolly held very high hopes.[31]

Until 1907, an uneasy truce existed between the two men. In that period, Connolly refrained from public attacks on De Leon. But he held tenaciously to the position he had expressed in his "Reply".

"As a humble member of the SLP, as one who has absolute confidence in the revolutionary principles and sterling honesty of its rank and file, as one who believes implicitly in the political integrity and incorruptibility of its Officers... as one who believes that the SLP is where I belong, I am yet

---

[30]Connolly Archives, Letter, Matheson to Connolly, August 3, 1904.
[31]Fred Thompson, *The IWW, Its First Fifty Years.*

willing to stake my membership in the party on the absolute soundness and correctness of my position on Wages and Prices and the equally absolute unsoundness and incorrectness of Comrade De Leon's present position."

CHAPTER VI

A LOVING FAMILY SHARES HARD TIMES

In his Introduction to Nora Connolly O'Brien's book, *Portrait of a Rebel Father,* Robert Lynd described James Connolly's relationship to his family: "There have been few revolutionary leaders, I imagine, in whose life the affection of the home played a greater part. Poverty was there -- poverty sometimes so overwhelming that it became a question whether there was anything else in the house left to pawn -- but it is difficult not to think of that devoted family as being happy beyond the common lot. There was laughter as well as anxiety in the air. The family in *Little Women,* indeed, did not live in an atmosphere richer in human kindness than did the family of this dangerous agitator."[1]

And, the childrens' response to Connolly: "Connolly... found in his family a happy mirror of his own enthusiasm. We get the impression, at times, from his daughter's book, of the young people's throwing themselves into the work of agitation and assisting in strikes as gaily as if they were taking part in a birthday party. This gaiety, this high-spiritness, is, of course, common enough among those who have committed themselves to great causes."

The late Padraic Colum, Irish poet, too, described this family: "In James Connolly's household, between husband and wife, and father and children, there was a wonderful comradeship..."[2]

A few critics of Connolly are incapable of understanding his aspirations and drives, "merged in a purpose greater than self," as he was. To them, he failed his family, not being solely devoted to its welfare. His responsibility for his fellow workers, which he felt, fervently, the depth of his commitment to establish a new society in which the poor might live in economic security, happiness and human dignity is foreign to them. He would have understood Annie Clemence, who, in 1913, cried bitterly when she saw the bodies of children of striking miners carried out of a union hall,

---

[1]Nora Connolly O'Brien, pp. 9, 10.
[2]Padraic Colum, *Solidarity,* June 17, 1916.

where they had been enjoying a Christmas party. A Calumet-Hecla Copper Company thug shouted up the staircase leading to the hall, "Fire, Fire!" In the resulting panic, many children suffocated. Taunted by deputies as to why she grieved for children who did not belong to her, Annie screamed: "They are all my children!"[3] Connolly deeply loved his own family but also greatly loved all the children of the working class. In all his activities this was evident.

He carefully nurtured his family's understanding of his work. He gave his attention to each of his children, from the smallest to the eldest. When he was lying weakened and emaciated in prison in Ireland, as the result of a hunger strike, after being jailed during the 1913 strike and lockout, he wrote to Lillie: "Aideen and Moira must now begin to read so that they will understand what their father is working for and not think of him as an ordinary criminal..."[4].

The seeds of knowledge of class which Connolly so carefully planted in his family garden could not have thrived without the nutrient of the warmth and richness of his love for his family, which none of them ever doubted. He also taught them lessons of self-discipline, self-reliance, self-control, which he deemed necessary to enable them to face the problems of living and growing. The quality of his fatherhood left its mark on the members of his family all their lives.

When Nora, at that time his second eldest daughter, was a tiny child in Dublin -- before Connolly first went to the United States -- she overheard him use the word "Socialist."

"A Socialist, Daddy," said Nora. "What's that?"

"A Socialist, Nono," he replied, "is a person who wants to change things so that everyone - every man, woman, boy and girl, will have enough to eat, and that no little boy or girl will have to go barefoot, or without clothes. That's what a Socialist is."

"But everyone should want that," said the little girl. "Have you told everyone?"

Her father said to her: "You are like a young man who told me last week that when he first became a Socialist, he was afraid to go to sleep, for fear the revolution would begin before he awoke."

"What's a revolution?" Nora asked him.

"We'll require a revolution, Nono, before we change things and have enough for everyone."

---

[3]Ella Reeve Bloor, p. 123.
[4]Nora Connolly O'Brien, p. 146.

"Let's get a revolution," Nora said.

"Good girl! We will," said her father.[5]

In the first issue of the *Harp,* the publication of the Irish Socialist Federation, he wrote: "Let us laugh while we may, though there be bitterness in our laughter. Let us laugh while we may, for capitalism has tears enough in store for all of us."[6] The Connollys' life together was an experience of pitiful hardship, often hunger and tears. But the laughter was ever present.

There is no doubt that the strength of character of their remarkable mother, Lillie, was an important ingredient of the close-knit family unit. When she died, the *Irish Press,* January 24, 1938, commented: "She was not known to the public, never seen on a platform, we only know about her that wherever the fortunes of a tempestuous life led James Connolly, she went also and there made her home... she was comrade as well as dependent, encouraged him when times were bad, rejoiced with every improvement. Lillie Connolly lived a hard life but she was satisfied that it should be so because she knew, even when her children were hungry and her husband unemployed, when the fire was small and everything that could be sold was gone, that this was all to be suffered in the cause of changing the miserable lives of the workers and the poor and making the world a better place for all.

"She loved all children and among the wreaths on the coffin yesterday was one from the children of the neighborhood of Belgrave Square, who all knew her and reciprocated her affection for them..."

Ina, Connolly's fourth daughter, also described her mother as loving all children. "She said there was never a child born that was not beautiful..."[7] Lillie was the safe haven whose arms around her children were enough to keep troubles at a distance. She was adviser and playmate and disciplinarian.

Occasionally, as the family was again preparing to move on, a word or two would tell of Lillie's yearning to put roots down in a particular place and stay there. But her deepest wish was to be with her husband.

Nora's devotion to both parents was expressed in her dedication to *Portrait of a Rebel Father.* She wrote: "To My Mother Is Dedicated This Attempt To Portray A Brave, Loving and Lovable Father."

It was not for almost a year after September, 1903, when Connolly

---

[5]*Ibid.,* p. 57.
[6]*Harp,* January, 1908.
[7]Ina Connolly Heron, "James Connolly," *Liberty,* March, 1966, p. 19.

arrived in the United States for the second time, that he was in a position to send for his family. Competition on the part of the steamship companies, and the ensuing price-cutting war, finally made it possible for him to buy steamship tickets for his family. He impatiently awaited their coming.

In June, Matheson received a letter from him, Connolly apologizing for its brevity. "I have just received word from Dublin that my wife is dangerously ill and may not recover, my children have all had to be taken away in the homes of neighbors and friends. I am too upset to think of anything else now," he wrote. He signed the letter: "Your unfortunate comrade."[8] A month later, he was able to write that his wife was out of bed for the first time in nearly two months, "and expects to join me in the middle of August. Her boat leaves Liverpool on the fifth of that month."[9]

Disillusionment with the SLP and its leadership weighed heavily on Connolly. But a deeply personal tragedy lay at hand. The day before his family was to arrive, Connolly left Troy to meet them in New York. Walking around the city, he confronted Jack Mulray, a former ISRP comrade who had fought against him after his return from the 1902 tour. In spite of past quarrels, they were both happy for the encounter. Connolly was invited to Mulray's home to spend the night before the expected arrival. The ship which came into port the next day arrived without his family, however. An entire week passed, with Connolly meeting every incoming steamship.

In Dublin, the family had been preparing for departure. No one was more ecstatic than Connolly's eldest daughter, Mona. She had often accompanied him to meetings. At a very early age, she had attempted to read his pamphlets and understand his ideas.[10] When he was preparing to leave for America for the second time, Mona pleaded to go along. He told Mona that she must stay with her mother and help with the smaller children until they could all be reunited. He appealed to her to be "mathairin" (little mother).[11]

The family was to leave Dublin in the evening. During the day, the excited children were "falling over one another." A friend of Lillie, "Aunt Alice" had come to help the last minute preparations. She asked Mona to take Ina with her and go to her house to tidy up. Mona cheerfully agreed. At the house she went from room to room, looking for work to be done, all

[8]Connolly Archives, Letter, Connolly to Matheson, June 22, 1904.
[9]*Ibid.,* July 22, 1904.
[10]Ina Connolly Heron, *Liberty,* March, 1966, p. 23.
[11]*Ibid.*

the time talking about the coming reunion with her father.

She discovered a pile of wash waiting to be finished. There was fire in the kitchen range and Mona decided to boil the clothes. She lifted the hot kettle with her pinafore. Before the children were aware of what was happening, the apron was afire. Ina screamed. The "little mother," still aware of her responsibilities, ordered Ina away, as she ran to the water tap in the garden. A passing neighbor saw what was happening, jumped over the garden wall and put the fire out. It was too late; Mona died in the hospital.

A week later, the family sailed from Dublin. A cablegram was sent to Connolly to explain the delay but, waiting for them in New York, he did not receive it. On arrival in the United States, Lillie and her children sat all day on one of the long benches that filled the hall at Ellis Island. By this time, they were the only unclaimed family. James Connolly, meeting the boat, had asked for a wife and six children. A man's voice called out: "Is there a family called Connolly, from Dublin?"

"Yes," said Lillie, rising. They followed the man into a hall filled with huge wire cages. They were placed inside one of them and the man left. When he returned, he said: "There's some mistake. He said a wife and six children. There's only five children." Tears came to Lillie's eyes. "One died before we sailed," she told the guard. He, in turn, told Connolly and brought him to them. Connolly learned of the death of his daughter, thus, through a stranger. The children fought to hug him. Connolly went to Lillie. There were tears and Connolly took his family away.[12]

A short item appeared in the *Daily People* from Troy, New York. Headed "Mona Connolly," it recorded: "Died, August 5, Mona, eldest daughter of James and Lillie Connolly, late of Dublin, Ireland. The death at the early age of thirteen years and four months was the result of burns sustained in the house of a friend in Dublin... She only survived the lamentable accident twenty-four hours, and died on the day she was to have sailed to join her father in America. Her grief-stricken parents thank their many friends for condolences received..." It was signed by James and Lillie Connolly and carried the address of their new home, 96 Ingalls Avenue, Troy, New York.[13]

De Leon, on tour in Scotland, was informed of the tragedy. For a time the attacks on Connolly were called off. Subsequently, Connolly was invited several times to lecture in New York.

---

[12]Nora Connolly O'Brien, p. 73.
[13]*Daily People,* August 27, 1904.

In Troy, where the textile industry developed around the manufacture of shirts, cuffs and collars, a large number of Irish immigrants had settled. A number of them were interested in Socialism. The SLP had its own meeting room and headquarters.

There were many women, unable to go out to work in the factories, who worked at home, stitching collars. "Even my job depends on collars," Connolly told Nora. "The people are dependent on the collars for their money and I am dependent on the workers for mine. So we all live on the collars."[14]

Lillie and the children became attached to their home in Troy where they were all together again. Lillie enjoyed working in the garden and grew large, beautiful tomatoes. The children went nutting and sold the excess to the stores. The family had ample for their own enjoyment. There were apricots, quinces, apples and pears and jars in the pantry filled with jam.[15]

In the winter, the snow offered new delights. Even Lillie was coaxed to take a ride on a sled. When there was no sled, Nora, Ina and the others used a large tin tray and went sliding wildly down the hills. That year they had a "wonderful Christmas," according to Ina. "...A big Christmas tree of our own in the parlor, lit up with lights and hung with presents for every member of the family..."[16].

The boys and girls of Troy pulled little wagons through the streets, collecting the collars from the home workers and delivering unfinished work from the factories. When a neighbor asked Nora if she would be willing to bring collars from the factory to her and deliver the finished work for fifty cents a week, Nora became one of the Troy children who did this work. Ina, too, joined her.[17]

Connolly's approach to his children was richly sensitive and understanding. No reproach for a child's misdeed was given without a lesson defined for the future, as well as a warmly expressed belief in the good intentions of the child, whatever the gravity of the fall from grace.

When Nora started school in Troy, she found herself ahead of her Troy class in scholarship. Her insistence that she be put forward earned the hostility of the school principal, Mother Joseph, who told her she was too young and too little for a higher class.[18]

"I can't help it if I am small," said the outspoken Nora. Mother Joseph

---

[14]Nora Connolly O'Brien, pp. 82, 83.
[15]Ina Connolly Heron, *Liberty,* April 1966, p. 14.
[16]*Ibid.,* p. 13.
[17]Nora Connolly O'Brien, pp. 82, 83; Ina Connolly Heron, *Liberty,* April 1966, p. 13.
[18]Nora Connolly O'Brien, pp. 78-82.

walked away, saying: "Don't be impertinent."

Nora approached her father that evening and asked for help. "here's one lesson you can't learn too early," answered her father, "and that's self-reliance. The earlier you begin to fight your own battles... the better.. If you can make your principal put you in a higher class, you can say, 'I proved that I was fit for a higher class,' but if I write and she promotes you, you'll say, 'Daddy made her.' And the next time you have a battle to fight, you'll want your daddy to do it, you won't have faith enough in yourself to do it on your own. Do you understand?"

Nora once more began waiting in places where the principal might pass. At last Mother Joseph impatiently agreed that Nora could take the examinations for the higher class and, if she passed, she could be promoted.

Nora passed the examination. Before she revealed the good news to her father, her mother advised her, she must permit him to finish his supper. Nora could hardly contain herself until the time came. Finally she cried, "I've passed. I've passed. Mother Joseph told me today and put me in the high class...".

"You won your battle all alone, Nono," said her father. "Daddy can't tell you how proud he is of you." He turned to Lillie. "Aren't we proud of her, Lillie?"[19]

"Hard times" set in throughout the Troy area. The workers of Troy could no longer afford the insurance premiums that were regularly due. Connolly lost his job with Metropolitan. There were no jobs to be had in Troy and at the end of the month, Connolly had to look elsewhere.

It was an especially hard winter, Ina records: "The weather did not show us any favors, but sent out long cold winds, accompanied by snow and sleet... Slates were tossed off roofs; homes were wrecked, and railways were blocked, leaving us without any letter to tell us of father's whereabouts..."[20].

In New York, Connolly was given a place to sleep by John Mulray. At no one time were both men employed.[21] Connolly got a job for the Hancock Insurance Company in New York but found his expenses were greater than his income. In May, 1905, he was hired by the Pacific Mutual Life Insurance Company as its Troy representative. In the same month, the young girl starchers of Troy, who formed the bulk of the shirt and collar

[19]*Ibid.,* pp. 84, 85.
[20]Ina Connolly Heron, *Liberty,* April 1966, p. 13.
[21]Greaves, p. 183.

workers, rebelled against factory conditions. They had been organizing into the AFL Starchers' Union. With the introduction of new machinery, they were subjected to intense speed-up. A system of fines, imposed on them, applied not only to spoiled work, but to small personal infringements of the employers' rules. One girl was dismissed for sneezing. On May 14th, the workers walked out in a city-wide strike and closed nine factories. They demanded restoration of the eight hour day, "modification of the fines system and an end to petty tyranny."[22]

The strike lasted fourteen weeks. Connolly's earnings from the insurance business diminished to the point of extinction. He could not bring himself to dun the strikers for their insurance premiums. He used much time collecting strike relief.

Connolly was again unemployed. The Pennsylvania SLP discussed the possibility of hiring him as organizer. The plan fell through for lack of financial support. In the meantime, the section had forwarded fifteen dollars to him for expenses. The money was all too soon absorbed by the needs of Connolly and his family. On September 1, 1905, to add to the harassment of his again desperate economic situation, he received a letter from Pennsylvania section demanding: "a statement as to whether you expect to be in a position to return to the Section Executive Committee the 15 dollars advanced to you about 5 weeks ago, within a reasonably short time... The refusal to answer this letter could not possibly be understood in any other light than that you have made up your mind not to return the money..."[23].

There is no record of further correspondence and it is likely that somehow Connolly was able to raise the money to repay his debt.

In November, Connolly wrote his friend, Matheson, from Newark, New Jersey: "...As the Americans phrase it, I have been 'up against it good and hard' and had no heart to write and bore you with a recital of my personal woes." Connolly continued: "I have now left Troy and settled in Newark. I was working for six weeks as a machinist in a shop here. What we call an engineer at home... I had a Socialist foreman and he employed me at lay-out work, as it is called, and between us we buncoed the capitalist into the belief that I was an expert mechanic... At present I am running a lathe in Singer's Sewing Machine factory at Elizabeth... Employs...9,000 men and a special train runs every morning from Newark..." He already missed

---

[22]*Ibid.*, p. 186.
[23]Connolly Archives, Letter, L. Katz to Connolly, September 1, 1905.

Ireland. "If ever I am fortunate enough to escape from this cursed country and get back to Europe..." he wrote, inquiring about a mutual friend: "I am thirsty for news... let me have it good and strong..."[24].

The concept of socialist unity was beginning to appear among American radicals and in Newark, Connolly was becoming increasingly involved in this movement. He wrote Matheson: "In this state, the Social Democratic Party have voted to come to an agreement with the SLP...and the SLP here voted to appoint a committee to confer...as to the basis of reconciliation..." He felt that the Socialist Party, having state autonomy, would not be compromised, nationally, by the New Jersey action. The centralized SLP was a different story and the move "must be taken as having the endorsement of the party as a whole...Nothing keeps them apart but their leaders." He added: "With the development of the IWW, the tendency for both parties to get together will grow stronger.."[25]

In early summer, 1905, the Founding Convention of the IWW was held in Chicago. Very soon Connolly was speaking at Newark street corners, calling on workers to join the new industrial union. At the State Convention of the SLP, where he represented Essex County, he proposed that the IWW should establish its own political party. Socialists of all kinds would undoubtedly merge with it.

Connolly participated in Unity Conferences between the two parties and helped organize the New Jersey State Unity Conference in 1906. The Manifesto, unanimously adopted by members of both parties present, was largely De Leonite in character. During this time, Socialist Party and Socialist Labor Party workers formed a United Labor Council in Newark.[26]

The Socialist Party, however, finally squelched the unity movement. Connolly informed Matheson June 10, 1906: "The New Jersey State Convention of the Socialist Party turned down the unity proposal by an overwhelming majority, and from many other states, the same story is coming in. New York... at its State Convention, had the face to pass a resolution condemning unity conventions...".

In the autumn of 1905, Connolly had brought his family to Newark. Ina recalled: "We left Troy with sad hearts." The family arrived at their new home to find that their furniture had not arrived. They slept on the floor

[24]*Ibid.,* Letter, Connolly to Matheson, November 19, 1905.
[25]*Ibid.*
[26]Kara P. Brewer, pp. 49, 50.

but a neighbor, learning of the situation, took them in until their furniture came the next day.[27]

The unity movement was strongly affected in 1906 by the defense built around the frame-up of Bill Haywood, Secretary-Treasurer of the Western Federation of Miners, Charles Moyer, President, and George Pettibone, a friend of the union. Governor Frank Stennenberg, of Idaho, who had originated the "bull pen" to terrorize unionists, was killed by a bomb, in the yard of his house. The three influential trade unionists were kidnapped, separately, in Colorado and secretly taken to Boise, Idaho. They were charged with Stennenerg's murder and held without trial for a year and a half, with no evidence placed against them.

The powerful united front which was formed to defend them included IWW members, socialists from both parties, rank and file workers, trade unionists, professionals, etc.[28] Connolly, now named by the SLP to the New Jersey press and literature committee, organized a protest meeting, with Patrick Quinlan, his co-worker in outdoor IWW meetings. On April third, the Kurz Coliseum in Newark was packed. The Brewery Workers marched to the meeting behind their fife and drum corps. Connolly was chairman and De Leon was the main speaker. There were also speakers in Italian and German. The Newark Workingmen's Defense Committee, formed that night, continued to hold meetings for the balance of the year.

Later, in 1907, Elizabeth Gurley Flynn was invited to Newark to speak at a defense meeting. Since it had been arranged by the SLP, the New Jersey Socialist Party protested. She wrote in her autobiography, *I Speak My Own Piece:* "I felt I should go anywhere to speak for this purpose."[29]

During this period, Connolly suffered poor health. He performed heavy physical work fourteen hours a day and, despite Lillie's protests, whether or not he felt ill, he never missed a meeting. After his long work-day, coming off the train that ran from the Singer factory, his first sight would be his children, running as fast as they could to meet him. They took short cuts and crossed lots, competing to be the first to kiss him and tell the tales of the day. On Saturdays, Nora, sometimes, with her mother, would be on hand, and as a special treat they would occasionally stop at a restaurant before going home.

Nora had decided to leave school and find work. Thirteen years old, going on fourteen, the bright child was mindful of the precarious position of the

---

[27]Ina Connolly Heron, *Liberty,* April 1966, p. 14.
[28]Reeve, pp. 119-124. Greaves, p. 194.
[29]Elizabeth Gurley Flynn, p. 63. Greaves, pp. 194-197.

family. Her father could not dissuade her. He advised that she must consistently read books and newspapers. He passed books on to her which he had completed. "Read that, Nono; you will find it interesting," he would tell her. She worked hard at her father's assignments.[30]

There were other, less earth-shaking events, but nevertheless important to a growing young woman. Nora had her first long skirt. Her mother pinned her hair up around her head. "Do you like me, Daddy?" she asked. He answered: "Will the young lady like to go out with me as much as the girl?... Miss Connolly, will you come with me this afternoon to a meeting in New York?"[31]

The girl was proud to hear her father's speeches. If he was to speak in nearby Newark at a street meeting, she would go without supper, in order to be on time to hear him. When anyone said, "Hear, hear!", she wanted to thank the one who cheered. When she went to meetings in New York with him, she listened carefully to his arguments and explanations. He spoke simply, she felt. He was easy to understand.[32]

Many evenings, when her father was at home, he would read to his children. First they had to finish their lessons. When, one by one, the lesson books had been closed, he would begin. Once he read them a story about the French Revolution, "The Reds of the Midi," which was the tale of a little boy who listened to an old man tell of his revolutionary experiences.

The children would beg: "Don't stop, daddy; don't stop." Connolly would answer: "As the grandfather said to the little boy, 'It's bedtime now. The rest must come another night!' "[33]

In Newark, Ina had her troubles. One summer morning, Lillie awakened her very early and presented her with a list of errands. First she must stop at the doctor's house and tell him to come by as quickly as possible, before his rounds. Then Ina was to join Nora with Aideen, Moira and Roderick at a picnic in the park. Ina was warned not to go near the swimming pool. When she returned home, "If I am having a lie-down, you mustn't disturb me."

Warm from the exertion of completing her chores, the swimming pool looked very inviting to Ina. "Surely, mother won't mind my going into the water for just a few minutes, only long enough to cool off," she told herself. And she did, before joining Nora.

[30]Nora Connolly O'Brien, pp. 86, 87, 90, 91.
[31]*Ibid.,* pp. 94, 95.
[32]*Ibid.,* pp. 89, 90.
[33]*Ibid.,* pp. 98, 99.

When they arrived home, a new baby sister had been born. Her mother seemed very well and was making a great fuss over Fiona, as she called the baby.

"Did you do everything I asked of you?" she asked Ina. Ina admitted her dip in the swimming pool. Lillie refused to accept Ina's excuses and apologies and told her she would have to be punished. Her father, looking on, did not interfere. The baby was tenderly placed in the arms of each member of the family. When it was Ina's turn, Lillie quietly remarked that Ina was not to touch the baby that day.

"No other punishment could have hurt me so much," said Ina. She burst into tears and ran out of the bedroom. After the evening meal, with the chores of clearing the table, washing the dishes and tidying completed, Ina still dallied in the kitchen.

"Father was sitting at the table, writing. It struck me strange that he did not tell me to go off to bed..." When Ina, at last, decided it was time to kiss her father goodnight, he took her in his arms and explained why she was being punished. Going into the water, unsupervised, possibly drowning, was very serious. "...but that mother could not rely on my doing as I was told...was the worst possible thing I could do to her..."

Her father said: "I'm sure if you go to your mother now and tell her how sorry you are to have distressed her, and you hope never to let this incident recur, you will both feel much better. Remember your mother... does not like to see her children sad, but she knows they must be taught to be honest and reliable... To be able to do the right thing at a given moment--so that your friends and associates will know what way you will turn under trying circumstances--is more valuable than all the gold in the British Exchequer."

Her father took her to her mother. It was after midnight. The apologies were offered and accepted. James Connolly said now that the day was over and Ina had taken her punishment, he did not see why she could not be the first to hold the baby that day. "Mother laid the baby in my arms. I was so thrilled I thought my heart would jump out of my body. I gave the baby back to mother and made my way to bed..."[34].

Early in November, 1906, a visiting SLP organizer, Bernine, held several meetings at the Singer factory gates. By the second meeting, word had spread and the workers hurried through lunch, in order to attend. A literature stall was set up and an appeal made for 50 men to picket at the

[34]Ina Connolly Heron, Liberty, April 1966, pp. 15, 16.

gates, in behalf of organizing into a union and the SLP.[35] Connolly organized a series of noon hour meetings, to which many Singer workers came.

The New Jersey SLP responded to his work by electing him delegate to the National Executive Committee of the SLP. Singer management became aware of attempts to unionize the workers and put pressure on his foreman to fire him.[36]

As Ina described it: "He had become well known as a Socialist agitator and union organizer. This didn't phase him, but his friend, Magnette (who was foreman on the job and had given father employment in the first place) was on the spot and likely to get the sack himself. Father knew Magnette was too decent a fellow to let him go, so he quit..."[34].

Another freezing winter swept down on the Connollys. Often their mother played games after school, to keep the children moving around so they could be warm. The scanty fuel had to be hoarded. One blustery day, their mother, after giving them a slice of bread, said they would play a game of "three men in a boat -- the bed will be the boat." All were put in one bed and huddled to warm themselves while Lillie told a story. The children stayed in bed, until, towards evening, the fire was lit and the room warmed, ready for the arrival of "the breadwinners," Nora and their father.

It was impossible for the children not to recognize the conditions in which they lived. They attempted to pick up whatever money they could earn for odd jobs for the neighbors.

Lillie was grateful when an Italian neighbor presented them with vegetables from the garden. She remarked that it was "like the old country, where neighbors shared their surplus." She had misunderstood. One weekend, the neighbor announced that the Connllys had been taking his vegetables for a month, without paying for them. Connolly, astonished, replied that they believed the vegetables had been a gift. It was a misunderstanding by all parties, apparently. The family had heard Connolly speak Italian and believed his family, too, was familiar with the language and understood the arrangements to pay the account at the end of the month. Connolly explained the truth of the matter. All laughed and the debt was cleared up in a couple of weeks.[38]

Interrupting the pattern of their everyday lives were visitors from

[35]Greaves, p. 197.
[36]Brewer, pp. 53, 54, 55.
[37]Ina Connolly Heron, *Liberty,* April 1966, p. 17. Also May 1966, p. 21.
[38]Ina Connolly Heron, *Liberty,* April 1966, p. 17.

Ireland. Mr. and Mrs. Dudley Digges, of the Abbey Theatre, came to visit. Ina remembers there were great preparations to welcome their prominent visitors.

Connolly, at the time when the need to make the decision to leave the Singer factory was troubling him, was offered the kind of work to which he could be totally committed. The IWW asked him to take an organizing job as head of the District Council of New York City. No work could have pleased him more. At first he attempted to travel between Newark and New York. Knowing how much his wife and children enjoyed their suburban life, he delayed moving his family to New York. As his work developed and meetings multiplied, however, the move could not be avoided.[39]

"I couldn't stay much longer at Singer's, Lillie," Connolly told his wife. "Mother smiled," reminisced Ina. "Oh, well, let's get on with it. So long as we're together, I shan't complain," said Lillie.[40]

"You won't be lonely in New York, Lillie," he told his wife, "I've got a flat on the same landing as some Scotch friends. Another friend lives around the corner and there are several Irish names on the bells."[41]

The family moved to a six-story tenement building on Elton Avenue in the Bronx. Nearby lived the family of Elizabeth Gurley Flynn. Typical of this husband and wife, both responded to the needs of their neighbors. One night Lillie accompanied a mother and her child, desperately ill with diphtheria, to the hospital. Ina recalled: "We suffered no ill effects from her kindness to our distressed neighbors."[42]

At home with his family, another night, Connolly was told a tragic story about a former neighbor, an old Scotswoman. Her son had gone to work the morning of the day before and had not returned. The old lady, not knowing what to do, was almost mindless with worry. Connolly, though exhausted and ill, with a heavy schedule to fulfill the next day, went to the woman's home with Lillie, to see what could be done. James and Lillie contacted various city agencies, while Ina stayed with the old woman. In the morning, police came and took the woman to a mortuary, where among half a dozen corpses was that of her son.

Connnolly went to the carpenters' union to which he had belonged and made sure funeral arrangements would be taken care of and

---

[39]Greaves, p. 205.
[40]Ina Connolly Heron, *Liberty,* April 1966.
[41]Nora Connolly O'Brien, pp. 96, 97.
[42]Ina Connolly Heron, *Liberty,* April 1966, p. 18.

responsibility taken for the mother.[43]

Connolly's children kept the newspaper clippings telling about his tours. "A man of pleasing personality. His manner is that of an orator and his language that of a scholar," wrote the *Boston Herald.* "A forceful speaker, well-versed in the history and literature of his country, and in speaking draws from an abundant store of knowledge gained both from great study and wide experience," from the *Cleveland Plain Dealer.* "An eloquent Irishman," announced the *Salt Lake City Tribune.*[44]

For all his brilliance, Ina, with some reason, considered that her father "was not always practical." He objected to his family submitting to excesses of capitalist exploitation, though their economic position was often disastrous. When they returned to Ireland and Nora and Ina found work in Belfast, the two sewed aprons. "We were proud that our earnings helped support the family and kept the three younger members at school," said Ina. The articles were paid for on a piece basis. In order to earn any appreciable money, they took the work home at night, to turn up the hems and have them ready for sewing the next morning. Connolly objected strenuously and called it "slavery." So they practiced "minor deceptions." Callers on the girls were also put to work creasing the hems. When their father's footsteps drew near, they all quickly hid the piece work.[45]

In New York, Lillie, often short of money, did washing for neighbors, to make up the deficiency. This, too, was kept from James Connolly.[46]

A happy occasion, in New York, was the arrival of a check for one hundred dollars from Connolly, on tour, the financial product of *Socialism Made Easy*, his pamphlet.

To Ina, the changing state of family fortunes was reflected in the daily shopping list. "If all was going well, I was told to fetch a bag of rolls for breakfast--and if not so good, a rye loaf. A bottle of milk was also a good sign--a step higher than a tin of condensed milk."[47]

Toward the end of April, 1910, after being away lecturing for almost a year for the Socialist Party, Connolly returned home. His daughter, Nora, thought he looked shabby and tired. But, she records, there was the old twinkle in his eye and he was in good spirits. As after every trip, there were presents for all, followed by exclamations of appreciation and thanks.[48]

[43]*Ibid.,* p. 19.
[44]*Ibid.,* p. 20.
[45]Ina Connolly Heron, *Liberty,* June 1966, p. 14.
[46]*Ibid.,* April 1966, p. 23.
[47]*Ibid.,* p. 24.
[48]Nora Connolly O'Brien, p. 108.

Connolly carefully took a very small package from his vest pocket and handed it to Lillie. "Open it, mama; open it." The children crowded around her.

"It's a gold watch, a lovely gold watch," Ina crowed.

Lillie's eyes filled with tears. "James, oh, James," she murmured. She recalled the watch she had pawned so long ago so she could see whole boots on his feet.

"You see, Lillie, I didn't forget." Lillie put her head on his shoulder and wept.

Connolly was back in Ireland, the book he had worked on for so many years, *Labor in Irish History,* written in the United States, was published and acclaimed. He sent a copy to Lillie, in New York. Nora came home from work one evening to find her mother fondling James Connolly's book.

"Do you remember, Nono," asked Lillie, "when daddy sent me a check for one hundred dollars which he got for his pamphlet? Do you remember how pleased and proud we were?" Nora, of course, did.

"Look inside, Nono," said Lillie. "See what daddy has written inside. I'd rather have that than all the checks for a hundred dollars there are in the world."

The book was dedicated: "To my dear wife, the partner of all my struggles and the inspirer of my achievements." It was dated: "Dublin, November 8th, 1910."

"Oh, mama," said her daughter, "it must be wonderful to have someone able to write that about you."[49]

---

[49]*Ibid.,* pp. 109, 110.

NOTE: Ina Connolly Heron's story ran in eight issues of *Liberty* -- from March, 1966 through October, 1966. It provides a moving story of the Connolly family, largely upon their return to Ireland.

CHAPTER VII

WORKING AMONG HIS FELLOW IMMIGRANTS

There were good reasons for the Connolly family and the Flynns to gravitate toward each other. Not only did both families feel deeply their exploitation as workers and as foreign-born in the United States but both were socialists.

Elizabeth Gurley Flynn, the "Rebel Girl," was born in the United States, as was her father. Her mother, however, was an Irish immigrant. Elizabeth described her mother's background: "My mother, Annie Gurley, was born in Galway 83 years ago. [The article was written in 1942.] Both her grandfathers fought in the Irish Revolution of 1798, which was inspired by the victory of George Washington." Elizabeth's great-grandfather, on the Flynn side, came from Mayo. He also fought in this "gallant but unsuccessful uprising." She spoke many times of the tradition for independence which was brought to America by the immigrants from Ireland.[1]

In her childhood, Annie Gurley spoke only Gaelic. She came to America at the age of seventeen. Three years later, in 1869, she went to work as a "tailoress." She worked at this trade for more than thirteen years. Elizabeth commented: "The growing industries of this country were hungry for cheap labor." Annie was a staunch suffragist and a Socialist at an early age.[2]

The problems of the foreign-born were to Connolly, himself an immigrant, strongly personal. From 1860 to 1900, the population of the United States grew from thirty-one million to seventy-six million. There were fourteen million immigrants who arrived in this forty-year period, with Ireland supplying the largest number. In the year 1905, alone, 1,250,000 more immigrants added their numbers. When Connolly lived in the United States, immigrants and their children formed the majority of the population in many northern industrial cities.[3]

---

[1]Elizabeth Gurley Flynn Papers, *The Worker,* March 17, 1942.
[2]*Ibid.,* March 17, 1963.
[3]*American History, A. Survey,* pp. 305-507; 600-603; 700.

In 1908, he wrote in the *Harp,* "Soon, very soon, there will be none left in Ireland, except old men and women, lunatics, paupers, policemen and British government officials." He condemned the politicians of the United Irish League in the United States, who raised funds for Ireland without lifting a finger to change the terrible exploitation of the immigrant. "Go down to the harbor," he advised, "and see the great Atlantic liners emptying through the portals of Ellis Island. See the healthy faces of the. young Irish *cailini* and *bucailine,* girls and boys, watch the life and vigor in their every action, note the latent strength of limb and reflect on what they will be after years of fierce struggle...". What confronts the Irish immigrant in America? "Immigration does not bring the Irish worker from slavery to freedom. It only lands him into a slavery swifter and more deadly in its effects...". Not upon the flag that flies overhead, declared Connolly, but on "our control of the necessities of life," does freedom depend.[4]

The Irish had the advantage of speaking the English language. Some later became foremen and superintendents in industry or became skilled in the building trades, or, as in New York particularly, entered politics. The majority worked at low wages in heavy industry, in unskilled jobs, and they lived in unsanitary tenements. The very young were child laborers. More than 5,000 Irish boys, seven to sixteen years of age, were breaker boys in the coal mines.[5]

The Italians, Germans, Slavs and Hungarians, newer immigrants, who came in great numbers after 1880, could not speak English and existed under even more difficult circumstances.

Connolly had worked among Italian workers, both as an IWW organizer, among the harbor workers of the port of New York and, earlier, in Newark, where two-thirds of the population were foreign-born, including fifty thousand Italians. He learned the language.

In 1907, Elizabeth Gurley Flynn and Connolly were speakers at a meeting in Newark, held under the auspices of the Italian Socialist Federation. During a short intermission, Elizabeth asked Connolly who the Italian speaker would be. He smiled and replied: "We'll see; someone surely." Returning to the platform, he arose and "spoke beautifully in Italian," amazing young Elizabeth and highly pleasing his audience, who "viva'd loudly," according to her later account.[6]

Connolly was delighted with the very evident talent as a working-class

[4]*The Harp,* February 1908. Flynn Papers, *The Worker,* March 3, 1940, March 16, 1947.
[5]*The Worker,* December 11, 1938.
[6]Elizabeth Gurley Flynn, *I Speak My Own Piece,* p. 64.

agitator, of seventeen year old Elizabeth and taught her to understand "the causative factors of the Irish struggle and the relationship of the Irish economic problems to those of other peoples throughout the world...". He was strong for encouraging "the young people", she said of him.[7]

In a letter to John Matheson, he gave his estimate of the young woman, who, later in life, became an outstanding leader, first in the IWW and then in the Communist Party. Matheson had asked him whether Elizabeth was the usual run-of-the-mill prodigy. Connolly replied: "La Bell Flynn... is allright. Like you, I have a distrust of prodigies. But Lizzie is entirely free from the stereotyping characteristic. In fact, the really wonderful thing about her is the readiness [with] which she evinces a desire to learn, and to abandon her former opinions when they are proven untenable. She started out as a pure Utopian, but now she laughs at her former theories. Had she stuck by her first set of opinions, she would have continued *a persona grata* with the Socialist Party crowd, which, of course, commands the biggest purse and the biggest audience, but her advocacy of straight revolutionary socialism and industrial unionism alienated them..."[8].

Connolly's response to the situation of the foreign-born is revealed in a singularly emotional and colorful description of an Italian family, that appeared in the *Harp,* January, 1909. Changing trains in Youngstown, Ohio, on a tour, Connolly saw an Italian woman attempting to shepherd a flock of children onto a train. The sight, he related, "called up in my old heart some very deep emotions."

The woman was poorly dressed, spoke no English and was 3,000 miles from home. Several native-born Americans were laughing. "The old mother ran from one to the other [child] gathering them under her care 'as a hen gathereth its chicks.' To me, the solicitude and anxiety of the old woman was deeply touching. To my mind's eye, there came the vision of that great army of proletarian women, of whom that poor peasant woman was no unworthy example. I could not see... the rude garb, the clumsy shoes and all the other marks of poverty and unrequited toil... I could only see the love and unselfishness and abiding faith exemplified in that poor member of my class, in her venture upon the cold world of capitalist America."

He reflected on the "poor, despised, unskilled Italian laborer in some of our construction gangs -- toiling under the eyes of a harsh, unfeeling boss, sleeping at night in a rude, uncomfortable, unhealthy slum or shack, living

---

[7]*Ibid.,* pp. 64, 65. Also Flynn papers, *Daily Worker,* March 17, 1942.
[8]Connolly Archives, Letter, Connolly to Matheson, October 28, 1907.

on the cheapest food, and all the time scraping every cent together with his thoughts fixed upon the wife and children he had left thousands of miles away." The wife and children waited, "in penury and suffering, anguish and hunger... until the husband and father would send the American dollars--sanctified with his sweat and blood... And then I could see that... woman...tear herself from home and set sail for America." The sacrifice, in thousands of cases, brought no relief from poverty.[9]

Connolly made the decision that he would attempt to direct the attention of the SLP to work among the foreign-born. There were independent Swedish, Hungarian and Italian Socialist Federations. Most of their members spoke little English, read their own language newspapers and were influenced, largely, only by events in their native lands.

He began to work with the Italian Socialist Federation. The IWW had helped to draw the Italians away from their isolation and their focus on the anti-religious activities which absorbed radicals among them. The Federation drew closer to the SLP, especially after Connolly, Pat Quinlan, and other speakers defended their meetings from police harassment. One meeting of the Federation had been broken up by police, who were infuriated by the display of a red flag. Connolly led a protest to the Mayor. Following this, an open-air demonstration was held, with speakers addressing the crowds in both English and Italian. In the face of the mass protest, the police, who had been mobilized, refrained from attack.[10]

On September 15, 1906, there appeared in the *Weekly People* a statement by Connolly, introducing an article by Guiseppe Bertelli, editor of *Il Proletario*, publication of the Italian Socialist Federation. The article, translated by Connolly, related to a possible alliance with the SLP. Connolly, apparently, had been working with the Italian socialists toward this for months. The statement began: "Some few months ago, in a preface to my translation of the article of the editor of *Il Proletario*... I expressed the belief that some closer understanding than at present exists, was possible between that body and the SLP. I am glad to be able to say that that belief has been justified... Our comrade... declared in favor of an alliance with the SLP, affirmed his belief that the isolated position of the Italian Federation was untenable, and proposed that that body revise its constitution to meet the need of alliance with the American comrades...". It was proposed that the constitution of the Italian Socialist Federation be revised to provide: "On the political field, to ally with the SLP. On the

[9] *The Harp,* January, 1909.
[10] Greaves, pp.. 164-166.

economic field, to make it obligatory on all members to join the IWW."
The two proposals were to be discussed at the Congress of the Italian
Federation in November. The indication was that the proposals would be
accepted.

The lengthy article of Bertelli which accompanied Connolly's statement
bore this out. He polemicized against those in the Federation who wanted
an alliance with the Socialist Party, pointing to its opportunistic leadership
as the reason for his opposition. "Our Congress," he concluded, "ought to
proclaim which of the two American Socialist parties are nearest to the
ideas and tactics of the majority of the Federation, and with that enter into
official relations. I believe that the SLP is that party, because the majority
of our Federation is composed of revolutionists."[11]

Connolly's statement and the proposals of Bertelli were given no
encouragement by De Leon. As a result, when the Congress of the Italian
Socialist Federation was held, it endorsed the IWW but deferred affiliation
with the SLP.

Connolly and his Irish co-workers of the SLP proposed to organize an
Irish Socialist Federation, with the purpose of attracting Irish-Americans
to Socialism. It was not to be affiliated to either Socialist party, thus
avoiding factional activities among its members. Rather, Connolly
proposed a fraternal relationship with the Socialist Party of Ireland. Irish-
Americans, he stated, were attuned to literature, speakers and news from
their native land. The Socialists should supply this, rather than corrupt
Irish politicians of the Tammany Hall type.[12]

Irish SLP members responded enthusiastically. Mayor George B.
McClellan, of New York City, had declared: "There are Russian Socialists
and Jewish Socialists and German Socialists. But thank God there are no
Irish Socialists!" They would show, for all to see, the inaccuracy of that
statement.

The Call for the Conference to form the new organization appeared in
the *Daily People* on February 1, 1907. The purpose of the ISF would be: to
educate the Irish-Americans in the principles of Socialism; give support to
the Irish working-class movement, and carry on education in Irish labor
history.[13]

Several Irish-American socialist organizations had preceded the Irish
Socialist Federation. Actually an Irish Socialist club, called the "Unity

---

[11]*Weekly People,* September 15, 1906.
[12]*Daily People,* February 1, 1907.
[13]*Ibid.*

Club," had been in existence among a group of Irish socialists "for several months," according to Thomas Flynn, writing to the *Daily People* six weeks later. Its function had been mainly social, until a dinner, where Connolly met with them. He proposed the organization of the Irish Socialist Federation.

Flynn wrote: "The Irish Socialist Club is not to be a separate political organization but simply an educational organization... with the object of presenting the truths of Socialism to the Irish race... The Irish Club will not draw strength away from the SLP; rather it... will be the means of bringing a large number of men and women within the sphere of influence of the SLP..."[14].

He was defending the ISF from an attack in the *People* of February twenty-third by J.A. Stromquist, of Globe, Arizona, a loyal De Leonite, whose letter was prominently crowned with a large headline. Stromquist said he opposed "Race Federations," particularly the proposal of the Irish SLP members to form a Federation, affiliated directly with the Socialist movement in Ireland... The project is not only absurd, but disruptive and harmful. Better fewer members with higher quality."

A discussion was precipitated in the *People*. Many SLP rank and filers, by now, however, had begun to realize that Connolly's efforts were based on his attempt to widen the influence of the Socialist Labor Party and supported this aim.

Connolly answered Stromquist in the *Weekly People* of March 2, 1907. He opposed race and language branches within the SLP and "would vote to abolish them all." English should be the language of the SLP branches. But, "I am in favor of Race or Language Federations, to organize all the sections of our heterogenous population." The Irish, he wrote, even though they spoke the English language, as Stromquist had said in his letter, were more in need of a Federation than other nationalities, since the Irish-American capitalist politicians had tricked Irish workers into associations which took their money and their time, but not for the sake of Ireland, as they were told. Instead these were used by American capitalist political parties.

"...To the capitalist organizations of Irish-America, we will oppose a Socialist organization of Irish-America," he declared. The ISF would

---

[14]*Weekly People,* March 16, 1907; *Daily People,* March 8, 1907. Thomas Flynn, Elizabeth's father, earlier, had opposed Connolly in the SLP. Many years later, she recalled, after Connolly's execution by the British Government, "My father, to the day of his death, never said 'British government,' without adding 'Damn them for what they did to Connolly.'" (*Sunday Worker,* April 13, 1952, Flynn Papers.)

"broaden and develop the mental horizon of our countrymen" with literature from Ireland,. "and prepare them to take their place in the revolutionary army of the American proletariat...".

He concluded with a plea for an international approach. "Is socialism an international movement or is it not? If it is, why do you object to us trying to help the movement in Ireland?" He reported that 30 applications for membership had already come from the New York area and "many inquiries and promises from all over the country."[15]

The *People* of March second carried a notice for a *Ceilidh* (social gathering) at Fraternity Hall, 100 West 116th Street, New York, on Sunday, March 3, 1907, at 8 P.M.: "to commemorate the Irish revolutionary movements of 1803 and 1867 and to launch a permanent organization of Irish Socialists in this district." There were to be songs, recitations, toasts, short speeches. Speakers listed were Elizabeth Gurley Flynn, M.D. Fitzgerald (an old Fenian); Coady; Donahue; O'Shaughnessy, Connolly "and others."

The January, 1907 meeting of the National Executive Committee, Patrick Quinlan reminded SLP members, had recognized Language Federations. He wanted, he said, to "join hands with the boys in Ireland."[16]

The January meeting had unanimously approved resolutions for a constitutional change, setting up a dues apparatus for language federations. The De Leonites got their wires badly crossed in the discussions in the *People.* There was thorough confusion on the NEC resolutions. Frank Bohn, National Secretary, in the March twenty-third *Daily People,* declared that the Irish Federation was not the subject of the resolution. It was the Hungarian Federation which had asked for membership in the SLP and had been endorsed and ·accepted. The difficulty was the double dues, to the Federatin and to the SLP, which increased the burdens of the Hungarian members. In addition there was the problem of too many meetings.

"It was and is unpleasant, if not impossible, for them to take part in meetings where English is used," he said. The NEC had found an "easy" solution, which applied, as well, to the Swedish Federation.

"The Federations could be connected with the NEC if they wished and still conduct their propaganda, their papers and other matters which concerned them alone as federations." Members of the Federations, if affiliated, would belong to the SLP, subject to its discipline and activities.

---

[15]*Weekly People,* March 2, 1907.
[16]*Daily People,* February 25, 1907.

Federations would be represented at conventions and each Federation would have one member on the National Executive Committee of the SLP. A per capita tax of seven cents per month per Federation member would go to the NEC.[17]

The July convention postponed action on the language federations.[18] The N.E.C., in August, reopened discussions.[19] Continuous postponement of action eventually turned the Federations towards the Socialist Party. Later they formed a large bloc in the SPA left wing. In 1919 and early 1920, many of them joined in the formation of the Communist Party.

Elizabeth Gurley Flynn and her father were among the first members of the Irish Socialist Federation. She commented: "The Unity Club required us to be too placating, too peaceful." The new organization was much more attractive. The Federation organized regular street meetings in Irish neighborhoods, which were "stormy, but finally accepted."[20]

In June, 1906, Connolly had written to Matheson: "I have no word from Ireland for over a year." This relationship was soon to change. In the interim, the Irish Socialist Party had been formed. A number of newcomers added freshness of approach and had little interest in the squabbles of the past. Connolly's work was beginning to become familiar among the Irish socialists. His letter announcing that the Irish Socialist Federation wanted to become affiliated with the Irish Socialist Party was welcomed.

On February 13, 1907, a letter, drafted on the official stationery of the Irish Socialist Party, agreed that the party "accept your offer to affiliate with our party and also to assist us in publishing literature." It covered arrangements for joint publishing and distribution of Connolly's *New Evangel,* which he had written in 1901. The American Socialists would take 1,000 copies. The letter, which was probably written by William O'Brien (the signature is obliterated) proposed to reprint in the *New Evangel* an article by Connolly from the *Workers' Republic* of August 15, 1898, on Wolfe Tone, "The Man We Know." The letter ended: "If you decide to have these pamphlets printed [also mentioned was *Socialism and Nationalism*] let us know whether your name is to appear on them, and also if any advertisement of the proposed club, or of our pamphlets, *The Historical Basis of Socialism in Ireland* and *The Rights of Ireland* and *The*

---

[17]*Daily People,* March 23, 1907.
[18]*Weekly People,* July 20, 1907.
[19]*Weekly People,* August 3, 1907.
[20]Elizabeth Gurley Flynn, pp. 65, 66.

Faith of a Felon should appear on them. The latter pamphlet, with your introduction to it, has been reprinted by us last year."[21]

This important letter marked the beginning of closer relations between the Irish socialists and Connolly, which culminated in his return to Ireland in 1910.

At the end of September, 1907, Connolly announced the forthcoming appearance of the *Harp*, the publication of the Irish Socialist Federation.He wrote to Matheson: "By the way, the Irish Socialist Federation intends publishing a monthly journal here shortly. Could I rely on you for an article and for an exchange of advertisements?"[22]

The Declaration of Principles of the ISF, printed in the second issue of the *Harp*, February, 1908, summarized its intent:

"The ISF is composed of members of the Irish race[23] in America, and is organized to assist the revolutionary working-class movement in Ireland by a dissemination of its literature; to educate the working-class Irish of this country into a knowledge of Socialist principles and to prepare them to cooperate with the workers of all other races; colors and nationalities in the emancipation of labor."

In the Declaration, Connolly again combined agitation for socialism with the fight of Ireland against English imperialist domination. Along with the fight to liberate the workers economically, must be the movement "to free nations from domination of nation over nation as of man over man." The Federation "on the field of Irish politics is organized against every party recognizing British rule in Ireland, in any form or manner, in all its moods and modifications and as the final solution of the Irish, as of every other struggle for freedom, it seeks the Workers' Republic -- the administration of all the land and instruments of labor as social property in which all shall be co-heirs and owners."[24]

In the first issue of the *Harp*, in January, 1908, Connolly attempted to clarify the position of the ISF on affiliation with the Socialist Party of Ireland, in relation to the confusion resulting from the existence of two rival parties of Socialism in the United States. The Federation was not making membership in either of the parties a test of Federation membership. It would not participate in "the campaigns of slander which

---

[21]Connolly Archives, Letter, William O'Brien to Connolly, February 13, 1907. (Signature obliterated.)

[22]*Ibid*, Letter, Connolly to Matheson, September 27, 1907.

[23]The words "Irish *Race*" were generally used at the time, both in Ireland and the United States.

[24]*The Harp*, February, 1908.

form the stock in trade of the American Socialists, when they condescend to refer to each other." He frankly deplored their "mutual recriminations." Had they found grounds on which to agree, he said, they might have had "a great party... in unity, in essentials, great in numbers..." Until such unity, the ISF would "confine its work to the making of Socialists."

His dilemma was apparent. Ready to leave the SLP, he could not, then, bring himself to embrace the SPA. He hoped, still, that the IWW would launch its own political party.

De Leon did not express opposition to Connolly's plan for the formation of the Irish Socialist Federation in the *People*. Toward the end of 1907, however, he launched an attack on the *Harp*. But Connolly had been caught in troubled inner-party currents as early as April, and he could not dismiss the idea that De Leon's opposition to his work among the Irish Americans was the actual cause for his other attacks.

On April 15, 1907, Connolly wrote O'Brien: "I have been getting such a hard hammering from so many different quarters that I could not afford to have my attention distracted from the immediate task of defending myself. It commenced on the week of our inaugural banquet (*ceilidh*) and was doubtless intended to put a damper on our project. To some extent it succeeded, for when De Leon's attack on me was published, a number who had promised to come got cold feet and stayed away. But we pulled it through, nevertheless, and although the *People* has been publishing lots of letter against us... we have formed our organization and are getting down to work. One curious result of our move is that it has created such a feeling against all race federations that the proposal to admit [them] into the SLP, although approved by the NEC, will, without doubt, be voted down."

There follows an understandable outpouring of bitterness at the attempts to frustrate his work: "The Americans love us so much. They fancy we have no rights except to be their valiant soldiers, they to be the officers, we the rank and file. My friend, Dan, has made a particularly dastardly attack on me directly, and on the ISRP, on which matter I am appealing to your party as an organization."[25]

The bitter resumption of the attacks by De Leon on Connolly, which were both theoretical and personal, will be discussed in further chapters. In their course, Connolly was subject to a number of varied charges by De Leon and his followers. Among them, the charge that Connolly had "wrecked" the Irish Socialist Republican Party was particularly painful to

---

[25]Connolly Archives, Letter, Connolly to O'Brien, April 15, 1907.

him. He often referred to the significant movements of that period and the influence which the ISRP exerted on the political movements of the day. A number of articles in the *Harp* were refutations of De Leon's charges.

O'Brien, in a letter written to Connolly on April thirtieth, indicated his sympathy for Connolly. The SLP Labor News Company had ordered 5,000 copies of the pamphlet, *The Rights of Ireland,* from the Irish party. O'Brien had turned them down. "For various reasons," he wrote, "we declined to supply the pamphlets but offered them a thousand of Fintan Lalor's instead."[26] The latter carried Connolly's introduction.

In reply, Connolly gave O'Brien a lesson in objectivity, and non-sectarianism. He wrote: "Re. the Labor News order, I think you should supply any order from any source. *The main thing is to get your party and your literature known."* (Connolly's emphasis.)[27]

The members of the Irish Socialist Federation proudly displayed their banner at every meeting they attended. It was a "large green and white banner..." Prominent was the Gaelic slogan: *"Faugh-a-Balach"* (Clear the Way) which was surrounded by harps and shamrocks.

In 1914, Jim Larkin arrived in the United States from Ireland. The year before, with James Connolly, he led the vast general transport strike which was opposed by city-wide lockouts of the workers by the employers, particularly in Dublin. Elizabeth Flynn's mother presented the ISF banner to Jim. He displayed it at all his meetings, "where he thundered against British Imperialism's attempts to drag us into [World War I]", according to Elizabeth Gurley Flynn.[28]

---

[26]*Ibid.,*Letter, O'Brien to Connolly, April 30, 1907.
[27]*Ibid.,* Letter, Connolly to O'Brien, May 20, 1907.
[28]Elizabeth Gurley Flynn, p. 173.

CHAPTER VIII

A LETTER FROM THE TRANSVAAL

In the early part of 1907, the *People* carried on another prolonged anti-Connolly campaign, characterized by name-calling and petty spite. On the surface, this controversy occurred over a technicality -- whether two words were used in defining the responsibilities of the subcommittee of the National Executive Committee of theSLP. The real causes went deeper -- disagreements on the functioning of an effective socialist party and the rights and duties of membership.

In this period, Connolly rebelled against the one-man, undemocratic leadership of the party. He believed in party discipline, combined, however, with free discussion within party committees and clubs. During the course of the polemics, he emphatically defended the necessity for developing initiative of the rank and file and promoting working-class activists to leadership in the party. De Leon envisioned the SLP as a small, elite corps of well-trained revolutionists, who would lead the workers. Connolly placed great value upon mass involvement. The differences became sharply apparent and once more Connolly was regarded as a dangerous political enemy by De Leon.

De Leon had passed the zenith of his leadership. SLP membership was dwindling; the Socialist Party of America was growing rapidly. Although the SPA apparatus was controlled by the right-wing, an active, revolutionary left-wing was developing. The days when De Leon led the only socialist party (1890 to 1900) and edited the only socialist daily paper in the United States were past.

Looking back, Connolly saw the chief error of the SLP as its ingrown, sectarian character. "Chief among those mistakes," he wrote in a letter to Matheson, "if we accept the personality of Dan, was its refusal to recognize *growth* in the Labor movement, and its consequent absurd insistence that all workingclass movements which fell short of clearness were capitalist conspiracies against the SLP... Recognize that the developing class consciousness of the labor movement in Great Britain is healthier and more potent for good than the 'clearness' of a sect which insists on cutting the umbilical string uniting it to the general movement of the working class. And such a spirit does not call for nor imply any lack of strenuous or bitter criticism, nor for a condonation of treachery or incapacity on the part of the leaders."[1]

---

[1]Connolly Archives, Letter, Connolly to Matheson, May 7, 1908.

Connolly's acceptance of dual unionism contradicted his struggles against sectarianism. This he did not realize. But he was in the process of reevaluating past attitudes and developing as a theoretician.

The extent of Connolly's activities in 1907 was amazing. He was a very active IWW organizer and lecturer, writing "Notes from New York," for the Industrial Union Bulletin of the IWW; he was intent on organizing the foreign-born workers, particularly the Irish-Americans; he was writing his masterpiece, *Labor in Irish History;* he was arranging for the publication in Ireland of a new edition of his pamphlet, *The New Evangel.* In addition, he was writing articles for the socialist press of Scotland and Ireland.

It was in the midst of such intensive activity that he and De Leon tangled. While De Leon was away on a speaking tour, a letter had arrived from the Independent Labor Party of the Transvaal (South Africa). Dated September 30, 1906, it contained a request for funds for their upcoming election campaign. The main election plank called for stricter laws barring Chinese immigration, which "had for one of its objects, the crushing of the labor movement... by supplanting the white workers by a cheap, servile, non-voting class of labor."[2] The subcommittee of the NEC unanimously rejected the racist appeal. Frank Bohn, SLP National Secretary, wrote the Transvaal organization that it was "not a revolutionary party...". He confined criticism of the appeal's racism to the following: "If you would give to the revolutionary societies of the world a guarantee that in case you are successful in the coming elections, you would banish all capitalists from the Transvaal instead of the doubly enslaved Chinese workingmen, I am sure the response would be as enthusiastic as so glorious a purpose could justify."[3]

A copy of the letter was given to the *People* for publication but De Leon, home from his tour, refused to print the subcommittee's reply. He declared it had serious shortcomings but did not elaborate. The subcommittee overruled De Leon's decision and appealed to the January, 1907 meeting of the National Executive Committee.

By January, Connolly had been elected by the New Jersey party to the NEC and was part of its subcommittee. The NEC, with membership from all over the United States, met twice a year. The subcommittee, composed of NEC members from New York and nearby, functioned between meetings. In the argument which took place in the meeting, De Leon defended the Editor's right to exclude material. Connolly offered a

---

[2]Weekly People, January 26, 1907.
[3]*Ibid.*

motion: "Resolved, that the NEC and its subcommittee have the power to insert official matter and correspondence in the official organ." The motion was defeated, in a four to three vote. Nevertheless the September letter of the subcommittee did appear in the *Weekly People* of January 26th.

Connolly reported on his motion's defeat to the February New Jersey State Convention. From then on, he stated, the NEC and its subcommittee could claim no right of access to the party press. A group of New Jersey De Leonites asked De Leon to respond. De Leon's reply in the *People* was a blast against Connolly's report to the New Jersey convention. He charged that Connolly and the subcommittee were attempting to usurp the powers of the NEC by ruling on foreign affairs. He stated the subcommittee had no power to make any important decisions. Everything should be referred to the NEC except "emergencies."[4] De Leon said he had no disagreement with the rejection of the financial appeal of the Transvaal ILP. "I pointed out," he said, "serious defects of omission in the answer, although that answer, so far as it went, was excellent..."[5].

Connolly, however, was fair game and De Leon moved to defend what he saw as an attack on his hold on the SLP. He launched a series of maneuvers to assure control of committees. For months he opened the columns of the *People* to attacks on Connolly. The basic issues--the answer to racism in the Transvaal, the functions of party committees, party democracy, the right of members to friendly disagreements--did not emerge. Discussion was shifted to technicalities and De Leon's disciples attacked Connolly's integrity. Connolly fared better than in 1904, with more rank and file members supporting him and even some of the SLP leadership. He was becoming aware of the fact, however, that he and the SLP might soon part.

The New Jersey De Leonites mailed letters to each NEC member, charging that Connolly, in reporting to their convention, changed his motion in the National Convention, by adding the words "and its" to his original motion. They accused him of attacking the NEC by attempting to assign equal powers to the subcommittee. Connolly proved that he had reported his motion correctly. On March 30th, the *Weekly People* printed a letter from Connolly to Frank Bohn, asking: "Was my resolution as I have stated it or not? Please answer in the *People*."

Frank Bohn replied that the NEC minutes were "properly transcribed.

---

[4]*Daily People,* February 28, 1907; *Weekly People,* March 9, 1907.
[5]*Ibid.*

The Resolution... is before me in the handwriting of Comrade Olpp [secretary of the meeting] and is as stated in the copies mailed by me to the NEC members, and as stated by you in your communication to the *People.*"[6]

Both sides were guilty of heated arguments, not strictly confined to the issues. N.M. Hemberg, of Jersey City, answering an attack on Connolly by Julius Eck, denied that Connolly had called De Leon a Pope, and concluded that Eck "does not know enough to cool himself with a fan when it gets warm."[7]

A delegate to the New Jersey State meeting, W.H. Woodhouse, from Jersey City, defended Connolly's report to the State convention: "Connolly made himself so plain that there was no room for misunderstanding."

Pat Quinlan, secretary of the New Jersey convention, observed that a number of those who criticized Connolly had attended the convention but had not criticized him there. De Leon's assertion that Connolly had not presented opposing points of view in the discussion on Connolly's motion was incorrect, he said. Connolly had given the New Jersey convention the complete story.

As the discussion continued throughout the summer, the De Leon followers mustered their forces. Factional letters appeared in the *People,* many personally abusive. Peter Jacobson, of Yonkers, said he had supported Connolly, but after talking it over with a number of people, he now supported De Leon.[8]

Boris Reinstein, later an internationally known member of the Communist Party, demanded that a party bulletin should be issued to cover such discussions. The controversy should have been kept out of the *People.*[9]

A testament to the sympathy and support for Connolly is a surprising letter addressed to him on May 28, 1907, by Bohn, in the midst of the turmoil. On the letterhead of the SLP, he wrote: "You have been nominated delegate to the International Socialist Congress at Stuttgart, Germany. The Congress will be held August 12-18, 1907. Expenses will be met by the Party. Please inform me, *at once,* whether or not you will accept the nomination. Ballots for election must be issued at the earliest possible date."[10] There is no record of a reply but Connolly did not attend the

[6] *Weekly People,* March 30, 1907.
[7] *Ibid.*
[8] *Weekly People,* March 9, 1907. *Daily People,* March 14, 1907.
[9] *Weekly People,* July 20, 1907.
[10] Connolly Archives, Letter, Frank Bohn to Connolly, May 28, 1907.

Congress.

Olive Johnson, DeLeoniteNEC member from California, writing about this period years later, revealed her fears that De Leon would lose control of the SLP leading bodies. She rushed from Idaho, where she was attending the Boise trial, to New York, to the June 1907 NEC meeting, to add her tie-breaking vote to De Leon's support. She saw the "combination" of "Bohn - Connolly - [Justus] Ebert... each aspiring to replace De Leon..." as a grave threat. Seven members attended the NEC meeting, she wrote, "Three stood solidly with Bohn, three with De Leon, while one wobbled...". De Leon "would have been forced to resign... the damage would have been irreparable."[11]

At its sessions, the NEC elected a new subcommittee and prohibited dual membership in the two committees in the future. The *Daily People* reported on the meeting, after noting Connolly's absence: "The matter of Connolly's report to the New Jersey State Convention was taken up. After some discussion, the motion, made by Johnson, seconded by Kirsher, that Connolly be removed from the Subcommittee was carried, Gilchrist voting in the negative."[12] In fact, Connolly had already resigned.

The next motion reported was a "correction" of the minutes of the January NEC meeting, to support the anti-Connolly version, in spite of the testimony of Olpp, who had taken the minutes, and Bohn, who had mailed them. The NEC now ruled: "The Connolly motion, as corrected in the minutes of the January session should have read: 'Moved that the NEC ["and its" now excerpted] subcommittee have the power to insert its official correspondence in the party organ.' "

Gilchrist, during a session of the NEC, announced he had received a note from Connolly, asking for the floor, "to appeal from the decision of the New Jersey membership recalling him from the NEC." The request was granted and Connolly took the floor. The result, reported in the *People:* "After a lengthy discussion, it was moved by Kirsher and seconded by Johnson to dismiss the appeal. It was carried with two dissenting opinions."[13] The details of Connolly's defense were not made public.

In the *People,* John Duffy, in a vitriolic defense of Connolly, charged that the NEC had not "corrected" the minutes, but "falsified" them. He termed the action "roguery."[14]

---

[11]Olive Johnson, *Socialist Labor Party,* pp. 76, 77.
[12]*Daily People,* July 3, 1907.
[13]*Weekly People,* July 20, 1907.
[14]*Ibid.*

Until recently, the only material available on this period consisted of stories in the *People* or accounts written by pro-De Leon writers. Now Connolly's viewpoint is available through the letters and papers in the O'Brien Collection in the National Library in Dublin.

Even before the 1907 discussions in the *People,* Connolly realized that his concept of the manner in which the SLP should function was different from De Leon's. In June, 1906, he discussed this in a letter to Matheson: "I agree with his attitude towards the AF of L, towards the Labor Fakirs, towards the other Socialist (?) [Connolly's question mark] parties, but I disagree utterly with his attitude towards the membership of the SLP." As an example of bureaucracy, Connolly cited the narrow circle of writers given access to the *People.* "Did it never occur to you," he asked, "that it was a strange thing that the *Edinburgh Socialist* has more contributors who contribute regularly than the *Daily* and *Weekly People?* The SLP is supposed to be the flower of the working class in the U.S. ...and yet we have not one regular contributor whose name would immediately rise to your lips if you were asked to name another writer of the SLP than Dan." Were there other writers who could be used? "There are many, but they are discouraged... Scarcely any production of the pen of a comrade can get into the *People* unless it is in the correspondence column, as a letter, or comes as a report of progress in propaganda work. Every kind of literary initiative is frowned upon, as is every other kind of initiative."

Connolly referred to the New Jersey Unity Conference in 1906. Before each meeting, SLP delegates were invited to meet with De Leon. "The resolutions we passed were brought to us, typewritten, from the same quarter... there was a hell of a row because I succeeded in getting one clause of one of the resolutions stricken out by the committee on literature, of which I was a member."

Connolly rebelled against this ignoring of the abilities of the rank and file: "We are not treated as revolutionists capable of handling a revolutionary situation but as automatons whose duty it is to repeat in varying accents the words of our director general. Everything must filter through Dan."[15]

All his socialist life, Connolly had attached prime importance to training younger, less experienced men and women. He explained to Matheson: "I believe that the duty of a true Socialist editor or trusted leader is to train as many comrades as possible to fill *his* position, to make editors and writers, and propagandists, and to encourage every member to develop the cool-

---

[15]Connolly Archives, Letter, Connolly to Matheson, June 10, 1906.

headedness and readiness needed in a revolutionary movement; in short, that it is the duty of a man in Dan's place to train the comrades and equip the movement that there should be scores ready to fill his place in the case of death or removal in any form." In a classical description of bureaucratic control, Connolly added: "But Dan's settled policy is the direct antithesis of this. His policy is to make himself indispensable, so much the pivot on which the movement turns that in every dispute with a member on any point, Dan will be sure to secure the victory because of the honor attaching to his name as the only author, writer or tactician the party has been allowed to know about."

Connolly added a wry postscript, a jibe at himself, the irony of which he had no doubt his friend could understand: "I can write the foregoing without any personal feeling in the matter, because he has always published any articles or notes that I sent in on the question in general."[16]

Justus Ebert, Assistant Editor of the *People,* during one of De Leon's tours, had attempted to bring new writers to the paper. He had proposed to hold a discussion on methods of bringing this about. Connolly, in a letter to Matheson, in January, 1908, noted that he believed these activities were the main reason for De Leon getting rid of Ebert.[17]

Connolly's longest manuscript of this period -- it comes to ten pages -- is the text of an emotional, forceful speech, an appeal against the actions of the NEC.[18] It was delivered, possibly, before the New York SLP, which, in the course of events, compelled De Leon to appear and defend himself against Connolly, "and others on matters in dispute," Olive Johnson said. She mourned: "Never had it been thought possible that De Leon and the Party should be submitted to such a grueling ordeal."[19] It is clear that Connolly here confronted De Leon face to face. He elaborated his theories on inner-party democracy. De Leon had called the debate, the "Connolly controversy."

Connolly was sharp: "The exceedingly astute manner in which the discussion over the relative rights and duties of the NEC and its subcommittee has been twisted to make it appear... as being a personal affair of mine is thoroughly characteristic of our innocent and unsophisticated editor..." He had nothing to gain, personally, by his position, said Connolly, "...but for the sane and proper administration of

---

[16]*Ibid.*
[17]*Ibid.,* Letter, Connolly to Matheson, January 30, 1908.
[18]*Ibid.,* Undated Statement, Mr. Chairman, Ms. 13930.
[19]Olive Johnson, p. 77.

the party affairs..." there was very much at stake.

Connolly's defense exhibited a decided change from his 1904 discussions. His long statement was peppered with sharp, personal attacks on De Leon. He did not state a basic agreement on principle and no longer spoke of the SLP as the only working-class party. He believed that only working-class leadership could save the SLP from ruin.

"The discussion has really become one to decide whether the working-class organized in the SLP are capable of the initiative and self-reliance required of them or whether they require a superior intelligence from above to shape their speech and decide their actions...".

He described the discussion on the Transvaal letter at the January, 1907 meeting of the National Executive Committee, the first such meeting Connolly had attended. "I came to the conclusion," he asserted, "that De Leon was... simply maneuvering to... club Bohn into a properly submissive frame of mind...". Connolly charged that De Leon wanted to write everything himself. But, in addition, he had said that another reason for not publishing the letter in the *People* was because he wanted to tone it down, to conciliate some of the leaders of the Second International, in order that the letter "might not be used against him at Stuttgart." Connolly called this "the strange theory that we were to denounce the fakirs in America, but to the fakirs in S. Africa, we were to speak in terms of loving gentleness, in case somebody might get offended...".

On the essence of the discussion -- the powers of the subcommittee -- Connolly declared: "If De Leon's interpretation of the constitution was adopted, we would have an NEC with powers to act but unable to meet, and a subcommittee able to meet with no powers to act -- an impossible position and one whose practical results would be to leave all effective power of initiation in the hands of the editor...practically the situation today." In effect, Connolly advocated what was later called by Lenin, "democratic centralism."

Connolly pled for worker's advancement into SLP leadership, citing the "absurdity of preaching to the working class that the redemption of the working class must be the act of the working class themselves, and at the same time acting as if we believed that [it] must be the act of De Leon...". Connolly challenged the De Leon leadership: "I told the NEC...there was a higher power than they were--the membership of the SLP, and now, speaking to you without heat or excitement...I accuse these members of conspiring to commit a fraud upon the membership and I accuse Comrade De Leon of being the inspirer and the originator...There is but one supreme test of a man's soundness in the SLP...the man must be prepared to burn incense at the Shrine of De Leon...".

In the document, Justus Ebert was described as: "the clean-living, honest and faithful worker, who, for years... had borne the drudgery and thankless toil which had given De Leon the opportunity to do any literary work he chose." But because of Ebert's disagreements on policy, Connolly had heard De Leon say: "Oh, if you only knew how I have longed for years to get rid of that man, and how relieved I was when I heard of his resignation." Connolly, therefore, "could not wonder at his attitude toward me. I also had crossed swords with him and... opposed his garbled history and his slip-shod economics."

Justus Ebert was soon lost to the SLP completely. Bohn did not finish the year in the organization.

In his speech, Connolly criticized the administration of the *People*. In private letters to his Scottish friend, he went deeper into the matter and included deficiencies in the running of the New York Labor News Company, the SLP publishing organization.[20] He proposed reorganization of the publishing work, printing additional pamphlets to those written by De Leon and reflecting current labor struggles in SLP literature. He suggested immediate publication of a pamphlet on the Moyer-Haywood-Pettibone frame-up. He had made all these suggestions to the SLP.

He called the SLP publishing house, at 28 City Hall Place "...a millstone around the neck of the party." The six-story building, rented by the publishing company, was located in the expensive rent area near the Brooklyn Bridge. Three floors lay idle. It should be moved to New Jersey, he proposed, where rents were cheaper. Furthermore, "The jobbing department... is practically at a standstill, though the pure and simple union employees draw their pay with most praiseworthy regularity." Subs to the *People* were falling off, he reported. All of this could be rectified by "an energetic management and a revolutionary party."

The response to these suggestions, he said, had earned him the name of "traitor" or "*Daily People* killer" and "disruptionist."[21] He had repeatedly been called a Jesuit by those attacking him. In concluding his appeal against the actions of the NEC, Connolly had bitterly referred to this: "The chief argument, indeed," he said, "was the glib and constant use of the phrase, 'Jesuit,' 'Jesuit,' 'Jesuit' and 'hireling of the Catholic Church.' The talk of 'Jesuit' comes very badly from his [De Leon's] lips." The Jesuits were more likely to choose as their best leaders, "the aristocrats whose

[20]Connolly Archives, Letter, Connolly to Matheson, January 30, 1908.
[21]*Ibid.*

instincts and training were already on their side than to trust the plebian whose interests were antagonistic to aristocracy, and when I listen to all this attempt of our editor to raise the howl of 'Jesuit,' I think of the thief who shouts to stop thief the loudest when he is nearest being caught."[22]

There is no doubt that Connolly suffered painful wounds from the continuing personal attacks against him. Occasionally, as in the latter instance, he permitted himself to answer in kind. More objective is a statement in which he alluded to De Leon's articles attacking him in the *People* as: "Chiefly valuable as illustrating that comrade's present state of mind and depths of misrepresentation to which a man of genius can descend when he allows personal prejudices to overshadow principle."[23]

He had resigned, formally, as New Jersey NEC delegate, but regretted it a little later, when he learned that the De Leonites had decided on a referendum to demand his recall. "I wish to go on record as declaring that had I known of this bluster before... I would certainly not have resigned. I am at all times ready to meet my opponents either in another convention or in an appeal to the Sections," he wrote to those to whom he had sent the letter of resignation. This letter revealed, in passing, that the Pennsylvania State Executive Committee, meeting on April 28th, had supported Connolly, in connection with discussions on the powers of the subcommittee, "which is the real crux of the whole controversy."[24]

Connolly wrote Matheson: "My friend, Dan, made a great effort to destroy me at general party meetings here in New York after the July NEC meeting but he was routed, horse, foot, and artillery."[25]

The appeal of the Transvaal Independent Labor Party and Bohn's reply appeared in the *Weekly People* four months after the exchange of communications, on January 26, under the heading "Two Letters." The same issue contained a blistering attack on "Transvaal Socialism," an editorial by Daniel De Leon. In comparison, the reply of the subcommittee to the vicious racism of the Transvaal letter was clearly inadequate. There is only part of a sentence alluding to its racism. Although De Leon's editorial had its shortcomings, it excoriated the racism of the Transvaal ILP as anti-working-class and pro-capitalist. The principal plank of the

[22]*Ibid.,* Undated Statement, Ms. 13930.
[23]*Ibid.,* Letter, Connolly to William Teichlauf, Secretary, Investigation Committee. Here Connolly attacked again the violation of SLP appeal procedures and changing the Minutes by the De Leonites, as well as the unconstitutionality of the activities of the rump committee, composed of De Leon supporters in New Jersey.
[24]Connolly Archives, Undated three page letter, Connolly to "Dear Comrade."
[25]*Ibid.,* Letter, Connolly to Matheson, September 27, 1907.

ILP's campaign, the exclusion of Chinese labor, De Leon charged, was an "agitation so anti-Marxian as to tend, instead of uniting the proletariat of all countries, to play into the capitalist's hands, of rupturing the world-wide Nation of the Proletariat by race distinction."[26]

Racism in the Transvaal was compared by De Leon to the racism displayed by the blatantly anti-Black Senator Tillman, of South Carolina, who "has been disputing the fitness of Northern Senators to discuss the question of Negro lynching...".

He added, however, that without doubt, "exceptional" cases of "criminal activity," on the part of Blacks (and Chinese) were used to attack an entire people and excuse lynching. De Leon, as other socialist leaders of the time, did not comprehend the basic racism of wide-spread persecution of Blacks through the method of frame-up--charging them with crimes they did not commit, particularly those who fought against their oppression. He did explain, however, that racism furthers "the bourgeois instilled spirit of competition between race and race, creed and creed, nationality and nationality--man and man."[27]

Championing of non-whites--Blacks, Japanese and Chinese--appeared many times in De Leon's articles and editorials. The action of the American Socialist Party delegation, led by Hillquit, in offering an anti-immigration resolution in the Amsterdam Congress of 1904 was again attacked by De Leon in his editorial. The resolution, written by Hillquit, at the Amsterdam Congress, contained the clause: "In further consideration of the fact that workingmen of backward races (Chinese, Negroes, etc.) are often imported by capitalists in order to keep down the native workingmen by means of cheap labor..." The resolution was signed by Morris Hillquit, Algernon Lee and H. Schluter, of the American Socialist Party, two delegates from Holland and one from Australia. Hillquit had inserted an introductory clause which stated there was no objection to immigration, in general. The objection, in the first draft, was to "inferior" races, but this term was withdrawn in favor of the word "backward."

The resolution was withdrawn in committee, without coming to a vote, because of the opposition of the international left wing that included De Leon. His book, *Flashlights of the Amsterdam Congress,* delivers hard blows against the Hillquit-Berger leadership of the SPA, which was working with Samuel Gompers to turn the American unions towards racism.[28] His conclusion was eloquent: "Where is the line that separates

---

[26]*Weekly People,* January 26, 1907.
[27]Reeve, pp. 125-136.
[28]Daniel De Leon, *Flashlights of the Amsterdam Congress,* pp. 115-118.

'inferior' from 'superior' races... Socialism knows not such insulting, iniquitous distinctions as 'inferior' and 'superior' races among the proletariat. It is for capitalism to fan the fires of such sentiments in its scheme to keep the proletariat divided."[29]

Defeated at Amsterdam, Hillquit stubbornly carried the anti-immigration position into the 1907 Stuttgart Congress, as the official point of view of the SPA. The National Executive Committee of his party had passed an anti-immigration resolution in March, 1907, written by Hillquit. At Stuttgart, the resolution went down to defeat. The 1908 convention of the SPA also passed anti-immigration resolutions.[30] In the 1910 convention of the SPA, after a debate, Hillquit's "substitute" anti-immigration resolution was carried by a vote of 55 to 50.[31]

Connolly's position against racial prejudice was demonstrated in his articles in the *Harp* a number of times--on India, for instance, a little later. Nevertheless he underestimated the dangerous racism of the immigration policy of the right-wing SPA leaders. He did not see the importance of attacking Hillquit's role as a racist in his early days in the Socialist Party.

In a letter written to Matheson November 8, 1908, Connolly at some length criticized De Leon's activities in the current election campaign. From Duquesne, Pennsylvania, on tour for the *Harp,* he answered Matheson's questions about Hillquit's candidacy for the Socialist Party: "You ask me about the probable effect of Dan's campaign upon Hillquit... Dan's whole campaign was directed against Hillquit. I am informed that he scarcely ever referred to the capitalist candidate."

The SLP vote fell off in the 1908 election. "How could it be otherwise when the very few men they did have were withdrawn from the work of attacking capitalism to the work of knifing Hillquit. Let Hillquit be what he may, and I do not know him at all, he was at least the representative of Socialism fighting capitalism."

Connolly emphasized the importance of the large vote of Eugene V. Debs, the SPA's left-wing standard bearer and candidate for President. "Debs' vote will probably roll up very close to a million... I think it is an exceedingly good showing. Debs talked good industrial unionism in every large center he was in."

Connolly, who had suffered unfair political blows at the hands of De Leon, now was moved to deal one of his own: "The belief is slowly forming

---

[29]*Ibid.,* p. 118.
[30]Reeve, pp. 132, 133.
[31]*Ibid.,* p. 134.

in my mind that Dan has fooled me all along and that he really is purposely doing the work of the capitalist class. It is hard to believe that any Socialist really thinks that the immigration question is serious enough to justify a Socialist in doing the dirty work of the capitalist class as De Leon has done in his campaign against Hillquit, when the latter was engaged in fighting to wrest a seat from Tammany Hall..."[32]

Connolly's lack of awareness of the importance of the fight against the anti-immigrationists in the 1908 elections seems to confirm the validity of Matheson's rebuke that he had become too subjective about De Leon. This is particularly true since the immigration question was of such great importance to the foreign-born workers whom he consistently championed.

On the other hand, Connolly was a strong supporter of IWW principles, and an organizer who carried out its program -- the most clear-cut of its time against discrimination.

[32]Connolly Archives, Letter, Connolly to Matheson, November 8, 1908.
Additional References
For additional background information on the period see the following: William Z. Foster, *History of the Three Internationals,* pp. 200-208; David Herreshoff, Chapter 5, "Reformism and Revolution - De Leon"; Eric Hass, *The SLP and the Internationals,* pp. 48, 80; Ira Kipnis, p. 278; Hass, *Capitalism, Breeder of Race Prejudice,* p. 30; David Shannon, *The Socialist Party of America; American Socialism,* pp. 71-80.

CHAPTER IX

IN THE IWW, DE LEON'S OPPOSITION AGAIN

In 1907, Connolly and De Leon had battled on several important theoretical fronts. Before the year ended, the confrontation between the two men on wages again came to life. This time, the outcome meant the survival of the IWW. Connolly, now the full-time organizer of the New York District Council of the IWW, defended a position which was to decide, to a great extent, whether the IWW would be confined to an educational, revolutionary union whose sole aim would be to' seek to hasten the socialist revolution (in line with SLP policy) or whether the organization would struggle militantly to raise living standards of workers and organize the unorganized into mass unions for their immediate needs, in addition to revolutionary educational work.

The IWW and James Connolly, at this point, felt compelled to fight De Leon's stand to a conclusion. Fred Thompson, an IWW historian, described the battles with De Leon:[1] "The conflict grew hotter in the fall of 1907 over a question of economic theory: Does a rise in wages cause a rise in price such that workers achieve no real gain? De Leon said it did... The argument to the contrary [was] by James P. Thompson[2] and James Connolly... They supported their position by the practical consideration that employers oppose wage boosts, while they would profit by them if De Leon's position were correct. It may have been theory, but it probed deeply into the question whether workers should consider unions worthwhile...".

The IWW had been organized in 1905, in Chicago, in the midst of an onslaught against the workers by industry. By 1907, the country faced the worst financial and economic crisis ever experienced in the United States. The years 1902 to 1910 -- Connolly's stay in the United States--were marked by widespread unemployment.

He arrived the first time four years after the outbreak of the Spanish-American War, which brought the United States on the world scene as a

---

[1]Fred Thompson, pp. 37, 38.
[2]James P. Thompson was a leading organizer of the IWW.

full-blown imperialist power. It was an era of burgeoning trustification and acquisition of colonies by finance capital. The Trusts were being built on the ruins of smaller businesses. J.P. Morgan & Co. dominated the American financial scene. The Republican Party, on behalf of the banks and trusts, administered the government, headed by President William McKinley (his mentor, Senator Mark Hanna) during the period of the Spanish-American War; President Theodore Roosevelt, from 1901 to 1908; and President William Howard Taft, from 1908 to 1912.

The United States, in only a few years, forcibly gained control of Hawaii and parts of the Samoan Islands, including the harbor at Tutuila, Puerto Rico, Cuba and the Phillipines. Carrying out the Monroe Doctrine, it consolidated its hold on the Latin-American countries. Exports soared. Railroads were thrust across the continent. By 1900, 193,000 miles of track had been laid and five transcontinental lines established. J.P. Morgan & Co., buying out Carnegie interests, organized U.S. Steel Co., the first billion dollar corporation. Large trusts, including the Beef Trust were built. The monopolies expanded production on a vast scale but the immensity of the new productivity could not be absorbed into the economy. The capitalists could not find adequate markets to meet projected gains. The inability of the population to buy what was offered drew capital towards economic downfall, in a period of acute international rivalry.

Laboring in shops and on farms was a minimum of 1,700,000 children--a source of cheap labor. It is recorded that in Southern cotton mills, children were kept awake at night by throwing cold water in their faces.[3]

In the 19th century, many workers still hoped they might change their status by moving westward to the frontier and farming the land. Others attempted to extricate themselves from the working class by developing their own small businesses. Now the frontier had disappeared. Finance Capital dominated the basic industries. The Trusts had become giants which threatened the existence of small business. The banks controlled the farms, through mortgages and ownership of the railroads and large grain elevators.

---

[3]*American History,* p. 599. The *People* provides a vivid picture of general working-class misery in the early years of the century--unemployment, hunger, strikes, suicides, child labor, prevalent industrial accidents, fires and terror. Random issues here listed give such examples: *Daily People,* May 9, 22; *Weekly People,* May 10, 24, 1902; *Daily People,* August 5, 6, 7, 8, 11, 14, 20, 1902; *Weekly People,* August 2, 9, 1902; *Daily People,* September 16, 1902, October 8, 17, 22, 23, 28, 1902; *Weekly People,* October 5, 1902; *Daily People,* November 27, 1903; *Weekly People,* November 28, 1903; *Daily People,* December 7, 1903; *Weekly People,* December 5, 1903; *Daily People,* April 15, 1904; *Weekly People,* March 26, 1904.

Economic upheaval and fierce attacks on their organizations threatened the workers and farmers. Large armies of unemployed became a fact of daily life and breadlines and demonstrations of the unemployed were common. Bitter strike struggles against wage-cuts and lay-offs were the order of the day. Hundreds of workers were being killed, for lack of safety devices on the job. Workers were shot down, clubbed, and jailed frequently by the National Guard, to break up picket lines.

AFL union leaders followed the class conciliation policies of Samuel Gompers, its President and John Mitchell, head of the United Mine Workers of America. Both men functioned in the National Civic Federation, an organization of capitalists and labor leaders which had been formed by Mark Hanna, "to settle disputes between capital and labor."[4] In the Civic Federation, the AFL leaders conferred with such financiers and industrialists as J.P. Morgan and August Belmont. For service in its efforts, the labor leaders were given gifts, flattery, and substantial salaries.

In March, 1904, workers of the Interborough Rapid Transit System of New York, owned by Belmont, went on strike. At this time, Belmont was President of the Civic Federation and sat in conference with the union leaders. The result was that the strikers were sent back to work and, subsequently, more than one-half of the striking employees were fired, many being blacklisted.

The Civic Federation was loathed by militant trade-unionists, both inside and outside the AFL.[5] Daniel De Leon exposed the handsome salaries paid by the Civic Federation to the corrupt labor leaders for carrying out strikebreaking activities against the trade union membership they were supposed to represent. He called these labor officials "labor lieutenants of the capitalist class," a phrase which became internationally famous.[6]

It was the corruption of the AFL officialdom and their association with the National Civic Federation which turned many of the outstanding socialists of the day towards dual unionism and led to the formation of the IWW. Debs, De Leon, Haywood and other SLP and Socialist Party leaders and syndicalists took the position that the AFL had proved to be a

---

[4]Reeve, pp. 70-74.

[5]Philip S. Foner, *History of the Labor Movement in the United States,* Vol. 3, pp. 61-110. Foner cites correspondence exposing strike-breaking activities of labor leaders working with financial and industrial leaders in the National Civic Federation, including personal letters of J.P. Morgan to labor leaders. Reeve, pp. 69-77.

[6]Reeve, pp. 70-74.

purely capitalist institution. Not only was its class collaboration policies under attack but also the craft form of organization, high initiation fees and the exclusion of all but skilled, native-born workers. In the opposition to the AFL, no differentiation was made between the rank and file AFL unionists and the policy-making leadership.

In his speech at the Founding Convention in Chicago, Bill Haywood, chairman, stressed the aim of the new organization: to organize all the workers.

He declared: "There are at least twenty million unorganized workers in the USA... This Industrial Union movement is broad enough to take in all of them...". From the beginning, the organization fought against all discrimination against workers. He summarized: "It does not make a bit of difference whether he is a Negro or a white man -- it does not make any difference whether he is an American or a foreigner... The organization that has been launched in your city recognizes neither race, creed, color, sex...". Regarding the unskilled: "We are going down in the gutter to get at the mass of the workers and bring them up to a decent plane of living."[7]

The Preamble to the Constitution condemned the craft unionism of the AFL and pointed to Socialism as the only solution for the workers. Around the IWW's program of industrial unionism, class struggle orientation and no discrimination, such diverse leaders as Daniel De Leon, Eugene Debs, "Big Bill" Haywood, James Connolly, William Trautmann and Vincent St. John with their diverging theories, could unite -- if only for a few years.

In October, 1907, the stock market crashed. For the workers, there was general misery. On the job, wages were cut 15 to 20 percent. Early in 1908, 184,000 jobless were counted in New York City alone and 75,000 in Chicago.[8]

Neither Connolly's work nor the welfare of his family were exempt from the disaster. At the onset of the "Panic," Ina Connolly saw the first dramatic manifestations of crisis. On her way to school, on an October morning, she "saw a large crowd gathered outside one of the banks and people were crying. There was a terrible commotion and great distress." Police were called out to attempt to "control the mass of depositors who were threatening to pull down the building if the doors were not opened to them... Shops were closed down in every street... The staffs were dismissed for no customers meant no wages."

---

[7]*The Founding Convention of the IWW*, pp. 575-577.
[8]Foner, p. 100.

Ina recounted: "Organized workers who refused a reduction in wages and went on strike were replaced by non-union men... However, the scab did not have an easy time of it."[9]

Connolly wrote Matheson: "...the misery and hunger now in New York are dreadful. I am simply frightened at the immediate outlook for the family and myself..."[10].

The crisis was felt to the greatest degree by the unskilled and semi-skilled workers, by the foreign-born and the Blacks. Trautmann, Secretary of the IWW, commented: "...The misery following in the wake of that collapse was mostly felt in places where the IWW had established a stronghold."[11]

In Philadelphia, 500 destitute people ate left-overs from the Reading Terminal market sales. In Birmingham, Alabama, 12,000 coal miners struck in July 1908 and the city contracted to offer "able-bodied persons" to the mines for $10 a month, using prisoners. A month later, a reign of terror and lynchings was unleashed. Lynchings took place, also, in Texas, Georgia and Florida. Seven Blacks were killed in a race riot in Illinois. In Coney Island, New York, a line formed, to eat the food left on the beach by picnickers.[12]

By December, 1907, IWW revenue had already fallen off by half, forcing it to curtail much of its strike activity. It turned to campaigns for the shorter work-week and demonstrations for the unemployed.[13]

"The only danger confronting the IWW is this almost universal bankruptcy through unemployment of its members..." wrote Connolly to Matheson on April 8, 1908.[14]

The lack of funds is apparent in expense accounts of the IWW organizers of the period, found in the IWW Minute Book.[15] The expense account of William Trautmann for the months of January and February, 1910, when the economic situation was only slightly better than 1907 and 1908, shows that he spent twenty-five cents for meals away from Chicago. Hotels cost fifty cents a night. The largest portion of expense money was used for fares for himself and other speakers at meetings. In December, 1909, Trautmann took only wages and no expense money.

The expense account of Vincent St. John for December 13, 1909 to

---

[9]Ina Connolly Heron, *Liberty,* April, 1966, pp. 20, 21.
[10]Connolly Archives, Letter, Connolly to Matheson, April 8, 1908.
[11]Foner, p. 100.
[12]New York Evening Call, August 3, 4, 5, 14, 16, 17, 21, 24, 1908.
[13]Foner, op. cit.
[14]Connolly Archives, Letter, Connolly to Matheson, April 8, 1908.
[15]*Minute Book,* IWW Archives.

January 6, 1910 showed a total of $150.05, of which $104.75 was railroad fare. For twenty-five days, St. John was reimbursed $9.50 for hotels and rooms.[16]

In 1907, Connolly had only recently been appointed an IWW organizer when he was faced with the revived discussion on wages and immediate demands and the Marxist role of the trade unions. He explained to Matheson on September 27, 1907: "They asked me to take the job when the fight between Dan and I was at its height and when I believed I was utterly discredited in the party. Instead, I found to my surprise that they had come to the conclusion that I had the real grasp of the revolutionary situation... I have now been about three months in their pay. 'Tis a world of surprises."[17]

The question was a very immediate and practical one now. There were increasing numbers of militant, working-class leaders who were trying to organize unorganized workers into the IWW and to secure relief benefits for the unemployed. De Leon was increasingly frustrated by the position of Connolly and the IWW leaders who favored fighting for "partial," immediate demands.

The wages question was raised in the IWW by De Leon's followers. In an article printed in the official organ of the IWW, the *Industrial Union Bulletin,* June 15, 1907, Frank Reed, a De Leonite, wrote: "A raise in wages virtually means a 'cut-down.' If the cost of production is 20 percent greater, the price of the product will usually be 30 percent greater. A forced rise in wages means increased cost of living."

James Thompson, one of the leading IWW organizers, answered him, under the heading: "Marx or Reed. Which?" Connolly once more addressed himself to the issue. "Realizing the importance of this discussion to the path which the American labor movement should follow," he began the wages debate where he left off in 1904.

"Few economic questions," Connolly wrote, "are of such great practical importance to the labor movement as this one and it is quite conceivable how a wrong stand upon this point might easily eliminate from us large numbers of our fellow workers...".[18]

The *Industrial Union Bulletin* readers were reminded of his argument on wages in 1904: "Some years ago, I brought up this question before the Socialist Trades and Labor Alliance, as I was then convinced that some of the speeches of that body were at sea upon the matter, with the result that

---

[16]*Minute Book,* p. 209. St. John's accounting was opposite p. 208.
[17]Connolly Archives, Letter, Connolly to Matheson, September 27, 1907.
[18]*Industrial Union Bulletin,* October 26, 1907.

they were fast reducing their organization to a negligible quantity as an economic force...". He wanted to support and amplify James Thompson's position, in order that "the IWW might not fall into the same pitfall, might not make the same mistake of confounding revolutionary phraseology with true revolutionary teaching." Connolly made the same Marxist analysis as in 1904. This time, with the support of the IWW press, his arguments in the controversy could be heard. Once more Marx's *Value, Price and Profit* was a central point in the discussion.

Connolly emphasized that the question was not whether the capitalist can recover from the workers what he lost by a rise in wages. He eventually recovers his losses "by speeding up, by new machinery, by improved methods, by the levelling process of economic crises, reducing wages again below the former level and by many other means...". He developed this theme. The majority of workers in the United States are not engaged in producing articles of food, clothing, coal or furniture. The followers of Reed argued as if the workers produced nothing which they did not consume. "Be it noted," he pointed out, "that these trades whose products workers do purchase and consume...are the lowest paid in the country and the most sweated, proving conclusively that the wages paid are not the determining factor in causing high prices...Let me remind our readers... prices invariably to up first, and wages slowly climb after them."

Finally, Connolly wrote: "Our common, every-day experience is in striking confirmation of the theory of Marx in *Value, Price and Profit*, viz., that the market price of labor (wages) is determined by the value (price) of the necessities of life.

"On the other hand, the contentions of our opponents on this matter, that a rise in wages is offset by a rise in prices, is best crystallized in the formula that wages determine prices, a theory that Marx, at the beginning of the fifth chapter of the book in question calls 'antiquated and exploded'...".

Connolly's article was the last straw for De Leon. He considered it a personal betrayal and treason to the SLP.

Fred Thompson attempted to analyze De Leon's position: "He was inclined toward such a conclusion [that a rise in wages causes a rise in prices] as it focused attention on the abolition of the wage system rather than on union demands, and support for the conclusion can be obtained by misinterpreting the experience that in periods of rising prices workers are most moved to demand wage boosts... James P. Thompson and James Connolly, who was here from Ireland and helping the IWW... supported their position by the practical consideration that employers oppose wage boosts, while they would profit by them, if De Leon's position were correct."[19]

The IWW leaders, James and Fred Thompson, unlike Connolly, did not believe that immediate demands could be related to the political struggles for socialism. Marx and Engels, as well as Lenin, always supported struggles for the immediate necessities of the workers. These would strengthen the working-class and unify it for higher levels of struggle. According to the syndicalists, a choice had to be made between immediate demands on an anti-political basis, or socialist politics, which, in their view, dropped the struggle for day-to-day needs.

William Z. Foster's position, four years after 1907, offered a plan to build the unions and avoid inter-union warfare. He proposed the building of mass unions out of existing AFL unions, as well as organization of the unorganized into the IWW. But the syndicalists and dual unionists rejected Foster's plan.

Two months after Connolly had repeated his stand on wages, Daniel De Leon rushed into a meeting of the General Executive Board of the IWW, with a series of personal and political charges against Connolly. It was a significant meeting and shall be described more fully in another chapter. De Leon now completely reverted to the position reached by him many years earlier that any program or campaign for immediate demands was wrong.[20] The attack on Connolly's position on wages was but one part of his over-all formula against all immediate demands and complete concentration on education towards socialism.

This was stated as early as April 16, 1902, in a major speech, "The Warning of the Gracchi" and repeated throughout the years.[21] His attitude was, of course, contrary to the warnings of Marx and Engels against the formation of "sects" divorced from the immediate struggles of the workers.[22]

---

[19]Fred Thompson, pp. 34-39.

[20]Reeve, pp. 62-67.

[21]Daniel De Leon, *Warning of the Gracchi*, p. 85. Here he declares: "The characteristic weakness of the proletariat renders it prone to lures... short of the abolition of wage slavery, all 'improvements' either accrue to capitalism or are the merest moonshine... There is but *one* demand of the working class -- the unconditional surrender of the social felon... Capitalism, as the usurpation, must be overthrown."

[22]For more on this divergence from Marx, see: Karl Marx and Frederick Engels, *Correspondence, 1846-1895*, Letter No. 91, p. 21; Letter 209, p. 466; Letter 207, p. 460; Letter 156, p. 315 ff. These letters present a strong position against sectarianism. The several volumes of "Documents of the First International, Minutes" are replete with statements by Marx and Engels supporting efforts and movements by workers for their immediate needs, in many countries, including the United States. To the contrary, De Leon, in *Socialist*

Eight months before Connolly's important article on wages in the Industrial Union Bulletin, De Leon wrote a surprising editorial. In the *Weekly People* of February 23, 1907, he responded to a letter by B.S. Frayne, of the Vehicle Workers Local of the IWW. Frayne reported on an open meeting at West End Turner Hall in Cincinnati, Ohio. He revealed the extent of the turmoil brought about in the IWW locals by the De Leonites. SLP members, even before the appearance of Connolly's article, were discussing the theory of wages in meetings.

The "splendid revolutionary"speech of the IWW speaker, Frayne wrote, was entirely wasted because the speech spread the illusion that by striking, the workers could win higher wages. "In the minds of these poor slaves was deeply imbedded that old time fallacy that the workers could force an increase from the capitalist class." Frayne chided the IWW speaker for not explaining, "At the monopoly stage, which we have reached, increase in wages forced from the capitalist class, is simply added by that class to the selling price of the commodity." After the meeting, he chided the IWW speaker, a "big, good-natured, brawny giant." "Look here," he said, "you don't want to fall into that old time error of striking for an increase; there is nothing in it; it is a waste of energy...".

De Leon's editorial was complicated. Students of his career have more than once commented on his inconsistency, which was again exhibited here. His new approach was to divorce theory from practice. He complimented Frayne on not adhering to "abstract" Marxism, which did not, he conceded, bear out his argument that prices rose with wages. Under monopoly capitalism, Marxian, or "economic" laws do not always apply, he wrote. In this editorial, De Leon concluded, the IWW *should* try to win higher wages.

"Our correspondent," he wrote, "furnishes a praiseworthy illustration of that well-balanced poise of mind which will not be thrown off its base by an abstract principle, regardless of the facts as they are experienced in practice." According to Marx, De Leon wrote, "a rise in wages, of itself, need not increase prices of goods; all it would do would be to reduce the

---

Economics in Dialogue, pp. 25, 23-74, presented the theory that wages must go down steadily under capitalism, until the socialist system takes its place. In the later, more developed stages of capitalism, De Leon claimed, strikes were useless and could not win higher wages or other partial demands. Reflecting this is "What Means This Strike?", an address delivered February 11, 1898 to New Bedford textile strikers. (Reprinted in *Socialist Landmarks,* p. 104.) In 1904, De Leon described the mass unions as "worthless." The "pure and simple" union could not keep wages from falling. ("The Burning Question of Trade Unionism," included in *Socialist Landmarks,* pp. 137-150.)

margin of profit." The "abstract principle" laid down by Marx, admittedly, did not stand in the way of winning higher wages, according to this editorial. "In.. the monopoly stage of capitalism... *at this stage, strict or one-time economic laws of capitalism are frequently found to be inapplicable.*" (Our emphasis.)

"Our correspondent," continued De Leon, "showed the practical sense in calling attention... to the fact of the towering price of living hand in hand with any rise in wages. This is a point, theoretical and practical, that the SLP ever insists on." Frayne, therefore, was right! Now, giving a perfect example of speaking for two opposing positions at once, De Leon said the IWW *should* strive for higher wages. The correspondent, though right, was also wrong!

"The IWW," concluded De Leon, "for the very reason of being a revolutionary body, has the duty to counteract the monopolistic practices and tendencies of capitalism. It should strike a blow whenever feasible, for better conditions--higher wages as well as lower hours, while ever intent upon its goal, the overthrow of the capitalist system."

These frequent discussions in the *People* concerning IWW policy irked the IWW leaders, causing them to determine, as Fred Thompson put it, that the SLP was attempting "to make the IWW tail to De Leon's kite."

In 1907, the second time around for the wages controversy, the decision was that Connolly's position on struggle for wage increases was the policy accepted by the IWW and, unlike 1904, De Leon suffered defeat.[23]

---

[23]In Volumes 2 and 3 of *Capital,* Marx emphasized his position that prices do not go up automatically after a wage increase. Note Manus O'Riordan thesis, *James Connolly in America,* pp. 47, 48.

CHAPTER X

AN IWW ORGANIZER IN NEW YORK

Connolly's organizing work for the IWW District Council of New York marked a particularly fulfilling and productive period of his life. This was what he most wanted to do -- to be involved in the fight of the workers for their needs, to bring them into an industrial organization which, he felt, by reason of its concept and form, could effectively, through struggle, win their demands and eventually bring about the social revolution. He was where he liked to be -- among workers, coping with their economic problems and devising strategy for fulfillment of their needs.

The fundamental differences in approach between Connolly and De Leon were no more clearly in evidence than here. Both men were scholars and writers, steeped in labor history and students of the class struggle. De Leon, however, was basically an editor, publisher and lecturer, who seldom participated in actual labor struggles "at the point of production," where Connolly found the focus of his activities and where he felt completely at home. Until this time, in the United States, Connolly had been a worker, as he had been in his youth in Scotland and, for a large part of the time, in Ireland. Now, speaking, organizing, touring and writing, he was able completely to devote his energy and time to the objectives of the working-class.

The years 1907 and 1908 for Connolly were a time of development and growth, in which he gained rich experience in trade union work and strike strategy. This was a strong influence on his effective trade-union leadership in Ireland, after his return there in 1910. R.M. Fox, one of Connolly's biographers, summed up the dimension gained by Connolly during this period. He said: "Probably the biggest single contribution which the American years brought was to give him a complete grasp of the theory and practice of industrial unionism in its early militant phase."[1] As to Connolly's return to Ireland: "He had gone away from Ireland a propagandist; he was returning as a leader of men."[2] It could be added that he was tempered and strengthened in the fire of the De Leon controversies.

Connolly's union recruiting efforts involved a variety of trades in New York -- harbor workers, painters, members of the building trades -- carpenters, bricklayers, masons -- milk distribution employees, etc. His

---

[1]R.M. Fox, p. 6.
[2]*Ibid.*, p. 83.

attempts to organize them into the IWW met with the opposition of both employers and the AFL. The minutes of the General Executive Board meeting of December 23, 1907, where De Leon appeared to challenge Connolly, described these activities, in part. Ben Williams, IWW organizer and member of the General Executive Board, was convinced that De Leon was antagonized by Connolly's intensive organizing work and that this was the basic reason for the hostility he displayed against Connolly at the GEB meeting.[3] De Leon, undoubtedly, looked askance at admitting numbers of non-revolutionary workers into the IWW, a revolutionary organization, as he saw it.

The situation in the New York building trades was described in the "Notes from New York" column, written by Connolly in the *Industrial Union Bulletin,* in December. The AFL craft unions were very active in the building trades. In the New York District, Connolly frequently came face to face with AFL leaders. Often the struggle ended with the employer accepting the class-collaborationist AFL union as the lesser of two evils. There was jurisdictional rivalry also among the craft unions, as well as corruption and bribery.

Connolly wrote: "We have all heard so much about the strong and impregnable position of the building trades, especially in New York, that we-have almost come to believe in it...".[4] But on the contrary, "...Things are looking ominous for the pure and simplers in the building trades of this city...". Employers had refused to renew the contract with the Brotherhood of Carpenters, due to expire on December thirty-first, a few days following the publication of Connolly's article.

..."It is expected that the Brotherhood will call out its men on the first day of the year," continued Connolly. "The bosses wish to force a reduction of fifty cents a day." The craft form of their organization was at the root of the carpenters' crisis, he wrote. "Whilst the carpenters fight, the other crafts will work and sympathize." he predicted, "... Even in their direst extremity, these leaders repudiate and denounce the only practical proposal by which a fight could be made, viz. the industrial unionizing of the trade."

The Board of Walking Delegates of the Brotherhood of Carpenters attended a meeting called by Connolly, under the auspices of the IWW, to debate conditions of the carpenters, as described by him. Connolly presented figures from their own *Journal* on speed-up and wages. Their so-

---

[3]Ben Williams, pp. 34-37.
[4]*Industrial Union Bulletin,* December 28, 1907, "Notes from New York."

called top wages position did not exist for most of the membership. The
AFL carpenters' publication verified that the actual yearly wage was low,
due to seasonal weather conditions.

A survey by Local Union 309, which gathered data for the 26 week
period ending September 4, 1907, indicated that of the 885 members
answering the questionnaire, only 206 worked full time for the entire
period. The average wage for highly skilled work was $19.16 per week,
because of lost time. "I gave them a short exposition of Industrial
Unionism," declared Connolly.

He had told the delegates that the figures proved conclusively that the
pure and simple form of organization was a failure. The so-called standard
wage of five dollars a day did not exist. In addition, the figures for the six
months survey included the good-weather months of May, June, July and
August. What would be the figures for the six months which included
winter?[5]

The work of Connolly in the building trades reflected the difficult
situation in which the IWW organizers found themselves. On the one
hand, there was the problem that the AFL was split into many crafts.
Leadership, often corrupt, had a no-strike, class collaborationist ideology
and worked against the industrial union. On the other hand, the IWW,
since its founding convention, was committed to dual unionism -- as was
Connolly at this time--and against working within the AFL. Everywhere
he turned, in organization of the building trades, Connolly was confronted
with craft union leaders who were determined to block industrial
organization, as an enemy. The Socialist Party's national apparatus, right-
wing, had no disagreement with the AFL bureaucracy and collaborated
with it. The SPA left-wing, led by Eugene Debs and "Big Bill" Haywood in
the trade-union field, differed, and felt that the AFL was hopeless.

In Ireland, when Connolly returned, he did not find the strong class-
collaborationist apparatus in the trade unions which opposed industrial
organization in the United States. The Transport and General Workers
Union in Ireland did not have to face such an intrenched craft union
bureaucracy as the Gompers machine presented in the United States.

It was after Connolly had left the United States, that Haywood, then
leader of the IWW, agreed "in principle" with William Z. Foster's proposal
that in certain industries the dual unions be dissolved and work be done
inside the old unions. Haywood agreed to pursue this policy only in the
building and printing industries.[6] The question had not yet arisen in

[5]*Ibid.*
[6]William Z. Foster, *From Bryan to Stalin,* p. 56.

Connolly's time.

The articles by Connolly in the *Industrial Union Bulletin* set forth highly developed principles of effective strike strategy. The workers should strike before the bosses had time to prepare. They should strike at the beginning of a busy season, not at the beginning of the slack season with its lay-offs. The carpenters, however, he pointed out, were being "called on to strike at the worst period of the year when thousands of the men will be idle necessarily as a result of climatic conditions... This unfortunate tactical mistake has been foisted upon the workers as a result of the trade union contract with the bosses..."

The trade union contract called on the men to give months of warning before a strike. Connolly mourned: "This is what is euphemistically called great leadership..." In terms of "another army... they are lions led by asses...".[7]

AFL painter's union officials converged upon one of Connolly's meetings which had been called to explain "the principles and purposes of the IWW" to the painters. They demonstratively asked questions and made statements in the meeting--"to intimidate the rank and file workers present," commented Connolly.

"Is it not a fact," queried one official, "that at the second convention of the IWW, Gompers and De Leon stayed in the same hotel?"

Connolly answered: "I did not care if they had slept in the one bed. We were not concerned about men, but about principles, and if they could not show something against our principles, he would do well to drop such childish talk." According to Connolly's report, the meeting ended "without any practical results."

An unexpected strike situation, however, came to Connolly's attention through the painters' meeting. Connolly was approached by a group of strikers from a teddy-bear factory in the Brownsville area. The strikers were members of a small, independent union. They had listened to IWW speakers and liked what they heard. They felt Connolly could help them. An official of the painters' union, who had attended Connolly's meeting entered the picture. He approached the employer, a right-wing Socialist, and asked him to "hold out." This was not the first time that Connolly had encountered an employer who was a right-wing socialist.

"This was, in itself, a complication," he declared. "But we could realize that any employer, even if a Socialist, will have trouble with his employees..." The strike came as the result of the employer firing workers

---

[7]*Industrial Union Bulletin,* December 28, 1907, "Notes from New York."

who had attempted to form a union, "though an active and progressing Socialist," Connolly added wryly.[8] The employer was a member of the publishing company which issued the Socialist Party's Jewish newspaper, the *Vorwaerts,* the editor of which refused to print a statement of the strikers against the employer.

This type of situation for many months influenced Connolly to stay within the anti-reformist SLP. This also illuminated the heterogenous character of the Socialist Party--where in its leading echelons were professionals--petty-bourgeois lawyers, ministers, business men, etc., -- most of whom were far removed from labor struggles.

Connolly wrote: "The IWW stands for the economic organization and for the political as the reflex thereof; the pure and simple political Socialist fires his employees for belonging to an economic organization."

But there were other working-class Socialists: "It is time the honest rank and file of the Socialist Party did something to clear the name of their party from the smirch these unclean actions cast upon it."[9]

His "Notes from New York" in the *Industrial Union Bulletin,* which were filled with information on union struggles, attacked the leadership of the Bricklayers and Mason's International Union, which advised its membership that the bosses had refused to sign the upcoming contract and were proceeding to downgrade the workers' conditions. The employers were demanding an anti-strike clause and threatened to "fill every job in New York City with non-union men." The Committee "made no reply." All concessions in the old contract were "ruthlessly swept aside," and the leadership quietly accepted.

Here, Connolly felt, the divisiveness of the craft form of organization was clearly demonstrated. With this, the collaborationist policies of union leadership lay at the root of the workers' weakened position. The Union leadership had called for termination of the contract at the beginning of the *slack* season, he pointed out.

Connolly admonished the building trades workers: "Surely it does not need the wisdom of Solomon to see that if all the workers in that industry were united in one union and that union refused to sign a contract, but instead bided its time, and at the opening of the busy season, or at its height, represented to the bosses the collective demands of all the workers, with the intimation that refusal to accede to any one of these demands would mean a strike of the entire body, then the chances of victory would

---

[8]*Ibid.*
[9]*Ibid.*

be a million times greater than they are under the present criminally stupid division of forces...".[10]

Not every industrial union branch was operating in conformity with Connolly's high aspirations for industrially organized workers. He made no attempt to hide the fact in "New York Notes." A branch of Building Trades Industrial Union No. 95 had to be expelled for pursuing the same discriminatory practices as the AFL craft unions. "We lost them," he commented, "but we also lost the odium of their actions."[11]

In Yonkers, New York, unorganized trolley workers struck and completely tied up the city. As Connolly described it: "...The spontaneous instinct of the workers had achieved a complete stoppage of industry." "Pure and simple" leadership could never have achieved such solidarity. On the first day of the strike, a trolley worker, who was a member of the IWW, sent for Connolly. He took a train for Yonkers "at once" and quickly faced a confrontation with AFL leaders.

He reached there just before the arrival of an AFL organizer sent by the Teamsters Union. Connolly presented his IWW credentials and was given the floor. In accordance with an IWW principle, he did not attempt to organize the workers into the IWW, since they had not been educated in the concepts of industrial organization as yet.

In his "New York Notes," he wrote: "I am not in favor of organizing into the IWW, men who are on strike, who, at the moment of organizing are talking strike." The advantages of industrial unionism was the theme of Connolly's speech. He urged the strikers to "besiege the power-house employees with deputations, not only in their work, but at their homes, and to keep at them night and day until they left their positions and joined the men on strike." He complimented the strikers "upon the spirit and method of their strike, especially in refusing to give warning to the bosses." He concluded by comparing their wisdom to the course of action generally pursued by "pure and simpledom."

Connolly was informed, however, that the men had already voted to join the AFL. An official of the Teamsters Union rose to speak. His speech consisted of "invective against the IWW and all its works... vials of wrath upon... De Leon, Eugene Debs, Haywood, Trautmann and all our real or supposed leaders." The Teamsters Union official guaranteed the "unequivocal support of his union" and that of the Amalgamated Street Railway Employees, and the entire AFL.

---

[10]*Ibid.*
[11]*Ibid.*

Connolly rose and asked the Teamster official "how it was that he could promise the support of his unions to a strike in which they were only indirectly interested whilst in the case of the longshoremen's strike in the Port of New York, his union continued to work and handle the goods loaded or unloaded by... scabs." Jennings, the union leader, replied smoothly that apparently the longshoremen did not feel it was necessary for the teamsters to strike. Connolly replied, emphatically, that the teamsters had, in fact, been asked to come out on strike but had replied that "they must stand by their contracts... as AF of L members they could do no less."

Connolly ascertained that once again the craft union had aided the employer. Although the trolley workers made a determined effort, the electricians and engineers, whose separate unions had operating contracts, remained at work and refused to turn off the power. The men were returned to work by the AFL leaders, pending negotiations and arbitration. "Henceforth," wrote Connolly, "if the Yonkers trolley men strike, they will first give the boss a few months' notice and due time to procure scabs."[12]

Correct strike strategy was a science that should be studied by the working-class, Connolly believed. It should be based on the theory, he expounded, that the workers' interests were opposed to that of the employers.

He returned to this theme in an article in the *Socialist Review* of February, 1910, in which he polemicized against AFL craft union leadership, which limited its agreements with the employers to a craft-wide basis, at the same time binding the workers to iron-clad, no-strike contracts. He lamented: "Our unfortunate brothers in the AFL are tied hand and foot, handicapped and hobbled...".

Connolly praised the example set by Rose Pastor Stokes, a member of the left-wing of the Socialist Party, in the New York City shirt-waist workers' strike. She had urgently called for a strike, to take place during the busy season of Philadelphia shirt-waist makers.

"Our Comrade... according to our Socialist press," he wrote, "was continually urging... the wisdom of striking before Christmas and during the busy season. No more sensible advice could have been given. It was of the very essence of industrialist philosophy. Industrialism [Industrial Unionism] is more than a method of organization... It is a science of

---

[12]*Industrial Union Bulletin,* December 14, 1907.

fighting. It says to the worker: fight only at the time you select, never when the boss wants a fight. Fight at the height of the busy season and... when the workers are in the thousands upon the sidewalk, absolutely refuse to be drawn into the battle... take it lying down in the slack season, but... when work is rushing and master capitalist is pressed for orders, squeeze him... till the most sensitive portion of his anatomy, his pocket-book, yells with pain...".

To the contrary, Connolly pointed to the contracts of the United Mine Workers, which expired in the early summer, "when they have before them a long, hot season, with a minimum demand for coal. The expiration of the contract finds the coal operators spoiling for a fight and the union secretly dreading it."

Contracts of the New York City carpenters usually expired in January, "...in the middle of a northern winter, when all work in their vicinity is suspended, owing to the rigors of the climate."[13]

One aspect of the framework within which Connolly worked at this time was his ever-recurring poverty. At the General Executive Board Meeting held at the end of December, 1907, the General Secretary-Treasurer of the IWW, William Trautmann, announced that he could no longer guarantee payment of salary to any organizer, since one-third of the IWW membership, "if not more" was unemployed.[14]

Connolly did not consider giving up but, characteristically, continued working.

---

[13]*International Socialist Review,* "Industrialism and the Trade Unions," by James Connolly, February, 1910.
[14]*Industrial Union Bulletin,* February 1, 1908.

CHAPTER XI

A STORMY G.E.B. MEETING

The IWW, in the face of the economic crisis, was struggling to organize important industries: textile, shoe, harbor workers, building-trades, and the lumber workers, metal miners and migratory agricultural workers of the West. It was also campaigning actively among the unemployed. Many of the members of the SLP and left-wing Socialists, working together toward these goals, continued to speak of organizational unity of the socialist parties.

However, Connolly's attitude on this subject changed, as the SLP declined. Still attached to the SLP, a "Unity Resolution," passed by the National Executive Committee of his party, was opposed by him. It called for a joint convention of the SPA and SLP to nominate common candidates for election.

He wrote Matheson at the end of January, 1908: "They have about 30,000 members; we have about 1500 (at most). So you can understand which wing of the movement the candidate will represent. The proposal simply means that the SLP wants the SP, for Christ's sake, to take them in out of the wet, but to leave them the right to exist as a propagandist body and cooperative publishing association... A number of Dan's enemies in the SLP are... for unity, in the hope that... it will be possible to leave him on the outside."

Connolly refused to go along. "I do not wish to swallow the S.P. policies, in order to get rid of even such a malevolent old scoundrel as Dan. I never was much of a believer in trickery, anyway...".[1]

Three months earlier, during the 1907 convention of the IWW, a surface truce prevailed between De Leon and the syndicalists, although the latter had objected to De Leon's series of articles, "As To Politics." On the other hand, De Leon balked at the articles on wages in the *Industrial Union Bulletin,* which contradicted his theories. However, the SLP and the IWW leadership maintained unity.

---

[1]Connolly Archives, Letter, Connolly to Matheson, January 30, 1908.

Reacting against the bureaucracy and corruption of the regime of Charles O. Sherman, who had been ousted as IWW President in the convention held a year before, the convention's mood had been to attack every semblance of those evils which existed or might exist in the IWW. Connolly supported this anti-bureaucratic drive. There had been dissatisfaction at "the retention of the label, the resurrection of the office of the President, under the thinly disguised name of 'general organizer' and the voting down of every attempt to exercise a firm control over the paid organizers." Connolly, to whom salary meant only the means to keep body and soul together, agreed with the rank and file. "The idea of charging wages for seven days in the week sticks in our throttle," he told Matheson.

The convention saw the defeat of the "anti-political crowd," which Connolly termed "a good thing." Further, "The tendency of the central officers to hold themselves above the orders of the rank and file is to be regretted and must be controlled."

Charges of bossism were beginning to be levelled against De Leon. Connolly's letter to Matheson, written after the convention, reflects this. "Most of us here in New York think that the election of so many SLP men to the Executive Board...tends to foster the suspicion that we [the SLP] control and 'boss' the IWW... But that is De Leon's method; he can't trust the revolutionary working-class movement, unless it is in the control of his creatures."[2]

The constant "theoretical" arguments, which were taking place within the SLP and the IWW locals upset him. He protested against the hair-splitting in his "Notes from New York," December 7, 1907. "What is needed...," he declared, "is not a fiery zeal to blow your own trumpet, but a calm determination to build and build correctly. The motive power of the IWW is not hot air, but a clear conception of industrial organization... The work that counts longest is often the longest in doing, and... an excessive multiplication of charters issued is no real criterion of the spread of industrial ideas."[3]

Two weeks later, De Leon angrily appeared at a special meeting of the General Executive Board of the IWW with an all-out blast against Connolly.

The meeting had been called by IWW Secretary William Trautmann, with the approval of Vincent St. John, national organizer, at the request of Connolly. Its purpose was not to discuss Connolly versus De Leon, but the

---

[2]*Ibid.,* Letter, Connolly to Matheson, September 27, 1907.
[3]*Industrial Union Bulletin,* December 7, 1907, "Notes from New York."

opportunities for organizing, particularly the harbor workers in the New York vicinity, among whom Connolly had made considerable headway. The longshoremen had been brought to a point where they appointed a committee to confer with Connolly on "the question of entering the IWW as a body, 10,000 strong" as Connolly later described it to Matheson. He requested information from the IWW on the application fee for a body so large. Trautmann arranged for the GEB to meet in New York, instead of Chicago, to discuss the matter.[4]

Trautmann informed the Board members: "It is evident that the waterfront workers of New York City...and surrounding ports can be organized in the IWW, providing the matter of dues and department organizers can be arranged." He explained that IWW speakers and volunteers had given material help to the strike a year before of harbor workers of New York, Hoboken and Jersey City. Another matter to be considered at the special GEB meeting was a convention of boot and shoe workers, as suggested by James Thompson.

Trautmann concluded: "I believe, and so does St. John, that the suggestions involved in the affairs of transportation and shoe workers, with the culmination brought about by three years propaganda among these workers, is the most important matter that ever confronted the IWW since its inception."[5]

The meeting, which began December 22, 1907, lasted several days. Ben H. Williams, chairman of the sessions, had been called to the meeting from a speaking tour. The question of the Harbor Workers was discussed on the first day. Connolly reported that of the 40,000 harbor workers in the area, 12,000 were organized into independent unions, unaffiliated with the AFL. Among the workers, large numbers were Irish, German or Italian. By this time, Connolly spoke the two foreign languages fluently. The Irish workers, of course, looked on him as their own.

These workers, Connolly informed the GEB, had been influenced towards the IWW through education carried on by "vigilant organizers and committees and by the distribution of leaflets." Eighteen branches of the harbor workers' organization had passed a motion to find out under what conditions they could unite with the IWW. They wanted one charter for an industrial union "embracing all waterfront workers of New York, Hoboken and Brooklyn." The Freight Teamsters Local, although in the AFL, also promised to "join such a union."

[4]Connoly Archives, Letter, Connolly to Matheson, January 30, 1908.
[5]*Industrial Union Bulletin,* February 1, 1908. Minutes.

It was agreed that the harbor workers be taken into the IWW and the technical questions of organization were also settled. Towards the end of the morning, Connolly was excused from the meeting, in order to present the decisions reached to the Harbor Workers' Central Committe.

In the meeting, Connolly had answered a series of questions by Board members to confirm that the harbor workers actually understood the principles of the IWW. Connolly, answering a question of Board member Cole, declared that the movement to become part of the IWW came from the rank and file, and the Central Committee of the organization acted as the result of the demands of the branches.[6]

Connolly reported back on the second day of the meeting. According to the Minutes, he had gone before the Harbor Workers' Central Committee and presented the decisions of the GEB, "but as the organization had... other very pressing business... including election of officers... the Central Committee could not consider the proposition at this meeting, but he, Connolly, had been assured that the subject matter would be taken up in the first meeting in January," less than two weeks away.

The issue never became active again, in part because of the demoralizing disruptive effects of the political bombshell injected by De Leon into the IWW at this Board meeting.

At the end of the morning session, on the second day, December 23, Rudolph Katz, GEB member from Paterson, New Jersey, and De Leon's chief lieutenant in the IWW, asked for a point of personal privilege.[7]

"Fellow Worker De Leon" wished to be heard by the GEB "on a very important matter..."

Connolly had again left the meeting early. As he later wrote to Matheson: "my sickness was just getting the better of me."[8]

Williams, as Chairman, declared: "Fellow Worker De Leon, as well as any other member of the IWW has the privilege to present matters to the GEB."

In the afternoon session, Katz requested that De Leon be heard in Executive Session. At this point, the door-keeper left the room. De Leon then took the floor. His first words made it clear that he was determined to bring matters to a head. He immediately stated his opposition to Connolly's work in organizing the Harbor Workers. He had intended to proceed to Chicago, he said, when he heard of the negotiations. The

---

[6]*Ibid.*
[7]*Ibid.*
[8]Connolly Archives, Letter, Connolly to Matheson, January 30, 1908.

Minutes described his position: "He deemed his knowledge of things important enough to entertain the fear that injury may result from misdirected moves."

"De Leon intimated that there was a 'police spy' at work in IWW affairs," stated the Minutes, "and proceeded with the outline of his theory, until he had established sufficient grounds to bring out open charges against James Connolly, the organizer of the Industrial District Council of New York City."[9]

T.J. Cole rose and protested. Any star chamber proceedings would destroy the unions in the New York City Industrial District Council. Interrupted by De Leon, Cole said he would leave the convention and go home, "if the Executive Board would stand for such a mode of procedure." Trautmann, though he had no vote, insisted on recording in the Minutes his own protest against "continuation of star chamber proceedings, at which the most serious and grave charges are presented against another member of the IWW, without the accused having a chance to hear the charges, or to defend himself."

Chairman Williams, too, joined the protest and wanted it recorded. He ordered that the doors be thrown open before proceedings continued. He later wrote: "The 'secret' session adjourned, with the chairman meeting a baleful eye from his majesty of the SLP." De Leon had, "in a round-about manner" warned against "hasty action, in view of this man, Connolly, who was unreliable," and, moreover, who "had been trying to break up the SLP."[10]

De Leon proceeded with his charges. He professed his sincere wish to keep "party wranglings" out of the IWW. He charged Connolly with conspiracy in an attempt to "drag the Connolly affair into the IWW."

Cole, once more on his feet, moved that the charges by De Leon against Connolly be postponed until the Industrial District Council of New York City be given the opportunity "to have defendant and witnesses summoned... to present their side of the case." The motion was carried. Katz moved, with Cole seconding, that the "De Leon - Connolly matter be taken up at 9 o'clock a.m. next morning, so that the board may dispose of all other matters before them."[11]

Connolly, ill, at home, was informed of the Board's decision. "That night I was in the anxious seat," he wrote Matheson. "Word was brought

[9]*Industrial Union Bulletin,* February 1, 1908.
[10]Ben H. Williams, Chapter 6, "The Fight with De Leonism."
[11]*Industrial Union Bulletin,* February 1, 1908.

to me about 9 o'clock of Dan's appearance, but no one knew then what his charges were."

Trautmann and Cole "were furious" with De Leon, for "tricking them into holding a secret session for such a purpose. Cole had suffered under Sherman by such despicable methods, and he was wild *with rage.*" Williams had been an SLP organizer for a long time and, initially, was prejudiced against Connolly, but De Leon's actions at the Board meeting "converted him," according to Connolly.[12]

On the morning of the 24th, with Connolly present, De Leon presented formal charges. According to Board Minutes, De Leon started by "explaining the situation of a man who is with one foot in the SLP and with the other in the IWW... the injury done to one foot must... also affect the other, that consequently the mischievous acts of one man in the SLP must cast their reflex in the doings of the IWW."

De Leon revealed that of major importance to him was Connolly's stand on wages. He attacked his "Wages and Prices" article in the *Industrial Union Bulletin* of October 26th, as having a "destructive effect." The Minutes described De Leon's charges: "...Connolly uses the *Bulletin* to assail the record of the Socialist Trades and Labor Alliance, by asserting that said Alliance had taught false economics, whilst in reality, the claim of Connolly that prices go up first before wages are increased is absurd and a false doctrine...". Connolly's article, he said, was "interjecting... SLP disputes into the IWW."

De Leon had written to Trautmann demanding an explanation, he said, but none had been forthcoming. He condemned the career of James Connolly in Ireland, calling him "a destroyer and wrecker of any movement he had been connected with." Connolly had "ruined the SLP in Ireland."

At this point, T.J. Cole took the floor on a point of order. Would the chair permit the "injection of matters with which the IWW had nothing to do?" The chariman responded by ruling that such matters were out of order and the parties to the controversy "would have to go through the regular channels."[13] Only after all other means had been exhausted, could the GEB rule.

Williams attempted to make his position clear, over the objections of Katz. Connolly's article in the *Bulletin* could not "be construed as an attempt to inject SLP matters into the IWW, inasmuch as the Socialist

---

[12]Connolly Archives, Letter, Connolly to Matheson, January 30, 1908.
[13]*Industrial Union Bulletin,* February 1, 1908.

Trades and Labor Alliance was considered an economic organization."

On roll-call vote, Cole, Yates and Williams moved to sustain; Katz was against. Also brought to a conclusion in the GEB was the Lancaster matter, in which, on the first day of the GEB meeting, Katz brought charges against Connolly that he had spoken to two young silk strikers, in such a manner that resulted in breaking the strike, which Katz led. Connolly had denied the words attributed to him. The Minutes of the GEB reported: "Fellow Worker Campbell" had overheard the discussion and "corroborated the statement of Connolly."[14]

Though not apparent through the Minutes, De Leon in the Board had repeated the charge that he was an agent of the Jesuits and of the Catholic Church. The IWW was not convinced, since Connolly, in speeches and articles, answered every attack on labor by the Catholic hierarchy.

A remarkable aspect of the discussion in the General Exeuctive Board was the fact that Connolly did not speak in his own defense. In the Board meeting, and afterward at the 1908 convention, it was obvious that he was trusted and respected by the IWW leaders.

His letter to Matheson, written January 30, 1908, after the Board meeting was concluded, reflected several additional details, not included in the Minutes. De Leon had said: "Conolly's purpose in bringing in the longshoremen was to carry out the wishes of the Jesuit order, as the majority of the longshoremen were Irish Catholics." There was a secret agreement, he charged, between Connolly, the longshoremen and the Jesuits, to "demoralize the IWW."

Connolly continued: "He then dropped his voice, and in a melodramatic manner... asked the members, 'What would you do if you knew you had a police spy in your midst? What would you do if one of your organizers was a Jesuit agent, working to destroy you?'"

Connolly offered further illumination on why Cole objected to the proceedings. "Cole had to go to the toilet," Connolly wrote his friend. "Dan tried to proceed in his absence, but was ordered to stop. When Cole got out, he found... to use his own words to me 'that he was sitting on a volcano.' He was surrounded by a number of the most active members, all white with rage and they told him they could guess what Dan wanted a secret session for, and if this Star Chamber proceedings was to go on, they might put the IWW in New York up their ----.' If it was known that Dan could control the GEB then all was up with the hope of the IWW growing in this district. Cole went back, and as soon as Dan began to speak, he rose

---

[14]*Ibid.*

and declared that he would not tolerate any more such star chamber proceedings, and if Dan said another word, he would demand his fare back to Chicago..."

And: "Of course, nobody took the charges [by De Leon] seriously. They only served to illustrate the depth of malevolence to which De Leon had sunk... These are the charges continually insinuated against me in the SLP, but I have never yet got a body to insist upon De Leon... either preferring charges or shutting up... At the last party meeting, I took occasion to openly brand De Leon and some of his crew... as liars and slanderers and challenging them to bring charges against me for saying so as I was now a member of section New York."[15]

It was at this time that Connolly, surprisingly, received an invitation from the SLP to lecture in New York City. He declined.

De Leon's fireworks in the GEB sharpened the differences between the IWW and the SLP leader. "Trautmann and the GEB" Connolly wrote, "are now preparing for the attack which they know he [De Leon] will launch upon them sooner or later..." The IWW, he continued, believed "it is destined to wipe out both so-called political parties, and erect a political party in its proper place, viz., as an expression of the economic organization." The difference in opinion held by the two camps--"those who believe in the IWW and the organization of the present as well as the future; and those who regard it as a recruiting ground for the SLP only... is growing tense all over the country...

"For myself, I think I told you over a year ago that I did not believe that the SLP had any future. Its future is all behind it...".[16]

Between the Board meeting at the end of 1907 and the Fourth Convention of the IWW, in September, 1908, the locals of the IWW in the New York district were thrown into turmoil by charges and counter-charges, growing out of De Leon's attack. Katz, avowedly speaking for De Leon, demanded that the Minutes of the Board meeting be suppressed. The De Leonites realized that De Leon had gone too far with the charges of "Jesuit" and "spy". No doubt De Leon and Katz were shocked by the adverse reaction to De Leon's performance at the Board meeting. The De Leonites alleged that the Minutes had falsified De Leon's position. However, in accordance with IWW procedure, they were published in the *Industrial Union Bulletin* of February 1, 1908.

Fred Thompson, who recorded that De Leon's demand for the secret

---

[15]Connolly Archives, Letter, Connolly to Matheson, January 30, 1908.
[16]*Ibid.*

session was based on his evaluation that Connolly's "articles on economics constituted heresy," related that De Leon's charges at the meeting, "brought the quarrel with De Leon to a head all over the country--and for that matter, in the industrial union clubs that had been formed in Britain and Australia."[17]

In view of the situation, Ben Williams was assigned to stay on in New York for the national office of the IWW, until the 1908 convention. He was appalled at the dissension which had been brought into the IWW locals.

"At street and hall meetings, [I] witnessed the bizarre antics of the SLP fanatics in our local union meetings. I made a couple of speeches before SLP gatherings, emphasizing the oneness of the IWW -- a oneness De Leon himself had expressed in the Third Convention, when he stated 'the IWW is a way out of which all else would proceed.' Now, however, De Leon branded the Executive Board of the IWW, with one or two exceptions, a bunch of anarchists, repudiating political action and preaching the gospel of physical force exclusively."[18]

Katz wrote again and again to the *Bulletin,* charging that the Minutes were garbled, and threatening that SLP funds would be cut off. Trautmann then went on the offensive. He charged both De Leon and Katz with "misleading quotations," and called for Katz to resign from the SLP, since by IWW rules, "organizers or officers of the IWW should not mix IWW matters with either SLP or SP affairs."

William Yates, a member of the SLP and an IWW Board member, in a letter published in the *Industrial Union Bulletin,* February 29, 1908, in what appeared an attempt to protect the SLP and its leader, also opposed publication of the "De Leon - Connolly affair." A month earlier, he had also expressed reservations to publishing the minutes in full. "De Leon made the assertion," he wrote, "that there was a police spy in the New York Industrial Council and the people would be liable to jump at the conclusion that Connolly was meant. I do not think so... We did a wise thing in cutting out this matter...".[19]

A lengthy letter in the April 25th *Industrial Union Bulletin,* by Samuel A. Stodel, described how the controversy had stopped organizing work at a special meeting of the SLP held in Arlington Hall, New York, on March 11th. Called to hear Ben Williams discuss organizing the shoe, textile, harbor and building trades workers into the IWW, the purpose of the

[17]Fred Thompson, pp. 38-40.
[18]Ben H. Williams, p. 34.
[19]*Industrial Union Bulletin,* January 15, 1908.

meeting was sidetracked by De Leon, who spoke for over 50 minutes, "most of which grossly misrepresented Williams and some of which distorted economic history." Undoubtedly adding salt to De Leon's wounds, Stodel added: "...this latter was straightened out for him by Connolly."[20]

Another angry letter from Katz, resurrecting the charges against Connolly's role in the Lancaster strike brought Trautmann's decisive action. This time he brought charges against Katz. De Leon's fight against Connolly in this period, overlooked in labor histories, was, undoubtedly, an important factor in the deteriorating relationship with the IWW leadership.[21]

A letter, unpublished until after De Leon's death, addressed to Katz on November 4, 1907, indicated that De Leon was already incensed at the IWW leadership for printing Connolly's article on wages in the *Bulletin*. Of Trautmann, he wrote: "His conduct is reprehensible."[22] Two days later, on November 6th, in another letter to Katz, De Leon returned to the subject. He did not want to "wound the sensibilities" of the IUB editor by "a spontaneous answer by me." He wanted Katz to request Edwards, the editor, to ask him to answer Connolly's article. De Leon commented: "An unseemly clapperclaw in the *Bulletin* may be avoided by a stiff article, written academically, yet without mincing matters...".[23]

At this point, however, the IWW repudiated De Leon and his theories.

Connolly's disenchantment with the Socialist Labor Party as a revolutionary organization was reflected in the letter he wrote to Matheson on January 30, 1908. He wrote: "Indeed John, I have been reluctantly driven to the conclusion that as a revolutionary proposition, the SLP is a great piece of bluff, with nothing to it... A Socialist Party that holds no meetings except during election times, that repeats like a parrot whatever is said by one man, whose sections go for years without entering a new name upon its books, that in a number of the largest cities in the

---

[20]*Ibid.*, April 25, 1908.
[21]In *Symposium*, published by the National Executive Committee of the SLP, in commemoration of Daniel De Leon (who died in 1914) Rudolph Katz wrote: "All the efforts of De Leon to preserve harmony in the IWW were unavailing. St. John, Trautmann, Edwards (editor of the IUB) and the majority of the five members of the General Executive Board turned overnight... against the fundamental principles of industrialism as laid down in the IWW preamble... At a special session of the General Executive Board... in New York City, De Leon appeared and endeavored to enlighten those who gave signs of being in need of enlightment. Such examples of wisdom as Trautmann, Williams and Cole would take no advice from De Leon...". (p. 137)
[22]*Symposium*, p. 146.
[23]*Ibid.*, pp. 145, 146.

country was not able to put up a ticket after twenty years of activity (thought it previously polled large votes in the same places in recent years) that has a daily paper that after seven years existence has less than 2,000 readers... such a party, John, is in my opinion a fraud and a disgrace to the revolutionary movement..."[24] He was to leave the SLP in four months, in April, 1908.

In May, in the letter to Matheson, in which he announced his resignation from the SLP, he wrote: "You people cannot understand the situation of a man surrounded by enemies, and with a man so unscrupulous as De Leon in complete control of the chief source from which the rank and file derive their information; you cannot understand how it is to feel that after giving about twenty years of your life to the Socialist movement and always deliberately lining up with the most revolutionary side, and therefore the poorest side, you should yet be in danger of being damned forever in the eyes of the revolutionary working-class as a disrupter and spy."[25]

---

[24]Connolly Archives, Letter, Connolly to Matheson, January 30, 1908.
[25]*Ibid.*, Letter, Connolly to Matheson, May 7, 1908.

CHAPTER XII

THE IWW PARTS COMPANY WITH DE LEON

The fourth convention of the IWW, in Chicago in September, 1908, marked a turning point in its history. The convention dropped the controversial "Political Clause" from the Preamble of the IWW Constitution, thus severing itself, organizationally, from the socialist parties and declaring against all politics. De Leon was denied a seat, signalling a split between the IWW and the SLP. The organization's attention was directed westward -- to the migratory agricultural workers, lumber workers and metal miners. Later crucial battles would see the IWW also in confrontation with the Eastern textile industry.

James Connolly was a fraternal delegate from the Propaganda Leagues, which he had promoted, initially in New York City. Not too successfully, they spread to the West, possibly as a result of Connolly's contacts with western delegates at the convention. Through the Leagues, Connolly was again trying to break a militant organization out of a sectarian rut. He hoped to broaden the propaganda of the IWW, by an auxiliary organization which would accept non-wage workers. The rigid rule that only wage workers could belong to the IWW, barred wives of members, as well as non-working class sympathizers.

The respect paid Connolly at the convention made clear that the IWW membership did not, for a moment, believe De Leon's charges and insinuations in the General Executive Board meeting. Had there been a shred of belief that Connolly might be a "police spy" or "agent of the Catholic Church," he would have been refused admittance to the hall.

Vincent St. John, chairman of the convention, agreed with Connolly on the usefulness of the Propaganda Leagues but wanted to avoid a controversial matter. He tried to keep the formal question of accepting the credentials of Connolly and other fraternal delegates off the convention floor until disposition had been made of the De Leon question and the Political Clause debates.

Connolly asked for the floor, without his status having been clarified. Being recognized, he asked why the credentials of the fraternal delegates from the New York Propaganda League had not been accepted. Delegate

Axelson responded that it was thought that the seating of delegates from bodies outside the IWW would "tangle up" matters too much. However, at any time, Connolly could have free access to the floor and would have all the rights of a fraternal delegate, without first being formally seated.[1] The Propaganda Leagues were finally approved by the Convention.

St. John, in the *Industrial Union Bulletin,* gave the Leagues his blessing, after the convention. He wrote: "The resolution passed by the convention... now opens the door for the wives of wage workers to assist in the propaganda work. It also makes possible for the chartering of many foreign nationalities, clubs and associations, which carry on revolutionary propaganda work... and who, in the past, could not be chartered under the old constitution of the IWW."

First organized in April, 1908, the Leagues, before and after the convention, vigorously campaigned for unemployment relief and public works funded by the city government. The large open air meetings featured speakers such as Elizabeth Gurley Flynn, Connolly and many other IWW members and Socialists. Included were those who could address the foreign-born in their own languages.[2]

At the outset, De Leon immediately protested against the Propaganda Leagues. His charges against Connolly and the occurrences in the GEB were taken up in the same session of the convention in which Connolly spoke for the Propaganda Leagues. The ensuing debate proved that the delegates supported Connolly.

In accordance with policy, the GEB had referred De Leon's charges to Connolly's local union. Connolly made counter charges in De Leon's local union -- Mixed Local No. 58 (which had elected De Leon as a convention delegate). This local refused to consider Connolly's charges and he appealed to the National Convention.

Connolly took the floor and asked for consideration of "Document 16." The convention Minutes reported: "Appeal of James Connolly against refusal of Local #58 to entertain charges against a member, Daniel De Leon. Majority report of Committee recommends that De Leon must be compelled to either bring evidence of the assertions made that Connolly is a police spy or stand exposed to the world as a traducer and traitor to the working class."[3] The minority report recommended that the local investigate the charge. The convention adopted the minority report. The documents were referred to Local 58 for decision.

[1]*Industrial Union Bulletin,* November 7, 1908.
[2]Philip S. Foner, Vol. 4, pp. 101, 134.
[3]*Industrial Union Bulletin,* December 12, 1908.

The aim was to sidetrack discussion on the convention floor, in view of the plan to exclude De Leon. However, the controversy could not be kept under wraps. A vigorous discussion followed.

F.W. Heslewood, for years a close friend and follower of De Leon and who only recently had broken with him, claimed: "The appellant would not get better consideration by local 58 as when he brought the case before them the first time."[4]

Williams backed Connolly's appeal. He addressed the delegates: "Someone in the IWW is slandered by De Leon by his constant reference to a police spy. The organization has a right to know who he is and the local should make De Leon name the spy." He felt sure that De Leon meant Connolly, he said. But "An injury has been done by De Leon to the organization...".[5]

De Leon's followers took the position that they did not believe that De Leon's accusations were directed against Connolly. William Yates, member of the GEB, an SLP member, was given the floor on a point of special privilege. He disagreed with Williams and Connolly that De Leon meant Connolly, when he referred to the police spy.

The convention unseated De Leon on a technicality; he was representing the wrong local -- he should have come from the printing local, not a mixed local. In addition to his attacks on Connolly, the majority of delegates had three principle motives for denying De Leon a seat: (1) Opposing his position, they wanted to organize the workers and fight for a higher living standard; (2) the avowed syndicalists were determined to sever all ties with both socialist parties--political activities were fruitless and further caused dissension within the IWW; (3) De Leon confused mass force with individual, anarchist acts. He emphasized that the ballot was the only legal, peaceful step toward revolution. All who were in favor of any kind of force--not only individual violent acts but mass action in free-speech fights--were lumped together by him as "bummery."

In his unpublished manuscript, Ben Williams, writing on the history of the IWW, divulged that St. John, before the fourth convention, was still willing to compromise with De Leon. Williams declared that before the convention, en masse, the SLP members of the IWW paid back dues and "packed" the New York Mixed Local, in order to insure that De Leonites would be delegates to the convention.[6]

---

[4]*Ibid.*
[5]*Ibid.*
[6]Ben H. Williams, p. 35.

"Arriving in Chicago," [as New York GEB representative] he revealed, "I found St. John, in particular, a bit uncertain about bringing the controversy before the convention. He thought it might be confined to New York. I insisted that this was impossible, as I knew the SLP the country over, in its fanatical adherence to the De Leon cult. I argued that we should bring the whole New York mess before the Credentials Committee. As chairman, St. John finally agreed."[7] The technicality which unseated De Leon dodged the basic differences between De Leon and the majority of the IWW. Nonetheless, the differences emerged in the discussion.

Rudolph Katz made a fervent plea for the seating of De Leon, on the basis of his important role in the past history of the IWW and the workers' movement. Katz conceded: "The conduct of the protestee [De Leon] is far from perfect and he would not hesitate to criticize him on that account, but that it should be remembered De Leon has done marvelous work for the international labor movement... that through his writings many have been led on the right track, that it should not be forgotten that mostly due to De Leon's teaching... prior to the formation of the IWW, the brilliant chance of constructive work on the lines of industrial unionism is made possible; that it should not be forgotten that De Leon's name is a stench in the nostrils of every labor faker and that he is the most hated man among enemies of the industrial union movement and of working class organizations."

De Leon, he continued, had made valuable contributions, as a leader in the defense of Moyer, Haywood and Pettibone, "was the first to raise his mighty pen in behalf of the persecuted revolutionist exiles from Russia [in the 1905 revolution]". De Leon had exposed Sherman's corruption in the first days of the IWW, "and he deserves the admiration of every man and woman who are in the struggle of the working class for the emancipation of the proletariat."[8]

It is a curious fact, illuminating Katz's plea for De Leon, that two months after De Leon was rebuffed at the GEB meeting, the February, 1908 issue of the *Industrial Union Bulletin* carried large display ads, signed by Secretary William Trautmann, advertising De Leon's pamphlets, along with Marxian classics, many of which De Leon had translated.

Delegate Hertz, in supporting the unseating of De Leon, "objected... on constitutional grounds, that the *Daily People* had dragged the Connolly

---

[7]*Ibid.*
[8]*Industrial Union Bulletin,* October 10, 1908.

controversy into the IWW and wherever the paper is circulated, its attack
on officers of the IWW has hampered the propaganda work of the IWW."

De Leon defended himself. He contended the organization of the
industrial union was based on the tool used, in his case, the pen. Since there
was no local based on this tool (writers) therefore he was correctly in a
mixed local. St. John answered that the industrial union must be based not
upon the tool used, but upon the *workshop* and therefore De Leon should
have been in the printers' local. The shop, he said, was the foundation of
the industrial union.

De Leon recalled: At the Founding Convention, "I was clasping hands
over the 'bloody chasm' with Eugene Debs." From the start, he said, he saw
the necessity of political as well as industrial unity. He had twice saved the
organization -- "at the first convention, when it was sound reasoning of the
delegates of the STLA that saved the organization from falling in the
pitfall of compromise, the second time when the *People* came to the rescue
after the brutal assault [of the Sherman forces] of October 4, 1906, and sent
the first $100 received by your chairman of the convention."

Bitterly, De Leon cried out: "Instead of sticking the knife in me, it should
stick the knife in Trautmann and Williams."[9] He charged that "anarchist
methods are being advocated by the present officers of the IWW and such
tendencies inevitably lead to disruption and chaotic conditions."

The convention, on its tenth day, passed a motion, presented by
Elizabeth Gurley Flynn and four other delegates, condemning an article in
the *Weekly People,* describing IWW members as "slum proletariat."

De Leon was denied a seat by a roll call vote of 40 to 21. With De Leon
unseated, the other major question in the convention, which involved the
Socialist Labor Party, was the elimination of the "Political Clause".

It had been included in the IWW Preamble by the Founding Convention
in 1905. It read: "Between these two classes [capitalist and the working
class] a struggle must go on until all toilers come together on the political as
well as the industrial field, and take, and hold that which they produce by
their labor, through an economic organization of the working class,
without affiliation to any political party."

St. John's appraisal, in his history of the IWW, was that the IWW was
formed by a coalition of dual unionist militants, including four main
trends: "Parliamentary socialists -- two types--impossibilists and
opportunists, Marxian and reformist; anarchist; industrial unionist; labor
fakers.

[9]*Ibid.*

"The task of combining these conflicting elements was attempted by the convention. A knowledge of this task makes it easier to understand the seeming contradictions in the original preamble."[10]

The 1906 second convention had been stormy. The reformist and thoroughly corrupt Charles O. Sherman, President of the IWW, supported by right-wingers in the Western Federation of Miners and right-wing socialists, attempted to seize absolute control of the organization. During his Presidency, he had spent the IWW's funds freely to line his own pockets. He demanded, at the convention, the abolition of all political agitation in the local unions, including literature, "bearing on any complexion of a political nature..." St. John commented: "This convention demonstrated that the administration of the IWW was in the hands of men who were not in accord with the revolutionary program of the organization."

De Leon, before the convention, had used the *People* to campaign against Sherman. At the convention, a coalition of De Leon, St. John and Trautmann succeeded in defeating Sherman. However, the Second Convention, with De Leon's agreement, watered down the Political Clause further, by adding: "Therefore, without endorsing or desiring the endorsement of any political party, we unite," etc.

In the Third Convention, in 1907, the leadership, apparently, demonstrated unity.[11] Differences on policy, nevertheless, sharpened in the interim between the third and fourth conventions. In the 1908 convention, the boiling point was reached. Now the demand was for complete elimination of the Political Clause. It was the general opinion in the IWW that the threat of domination by the SLP would in this way come to an end.

The *Daily* and *Weekly People* had been calling for the retention of the Political Clause. The officials of the IWW, largely syndicalist, were irked at De Leon because of these extended discussions in the SLP publications. De Leon, however, continued attacking the syndicalists' advocacy of the dropping of the clause.

Under the title *As To Politics,* reprinted in pamphlet form, was a series of questions and answers which appeared in the *People* in 1906 and 1907. It was widely distributed in the IWW and became a point of contention between De Leon and the syndicalists, as well as the anarchists in the IWW. Although in conciliation, De Leon emphasized the subordinate

---

[10]Vincent St. John, p. 6.
[11]*Ibid.,* pp. 7, 8. Foner, Vol. 4, pp. 71 ff. Brissenden, pp. 136-153. Reeve, pp. 105-118.

position of the party to the industrial union, the pamphlet failed to win the IWW to his policy. Its theme was that political agitation in elections by a political party was the only peaceful road to Socialism. "...The organization that rejects this method," he wrote, "and organizes for force only reads itself out of the pale of civilization...".[12]

Many IWW members participated in the discussion in the *People*. One writer put it: "Bread and butter now, our emancipation as soon as we are well enough organized."[13]

In the 1908 convention, the delegates were almost evenly divided on retention or rejection of the Political Clause. Heslewood pleaded against changing the Preamble," as he did not care to be called a dynamiter." The IWW might be denounced as an anarchist organization.[14]

Like William Z. Foster, at that time leaning towards syndicalism, "Delegate Flynn spoke in favor of the change. The present preamble, with its contradictions had been the cause of much dissension and confusion..."

The resolution passed by the convention declared: "The IWW refuses all alliances, direct or indirect, with existing political parties or anti-political sects, and disclaims responsibility for any individual opinion or act which may be at variance with the purposes herein expressed." The anarcho-syndicalists felt the necessity of supporting the resolution, which indicated that the IWW, by changing the Preamble, in no way favored terrorism.[15]

After the Convention, Connolly was asked how he stood on the rejection of political action. He responded: "It will be impossible to prevent the workers taking it."[16]

Connolly informed Matheson in a letter written during the convention, on September 27th: "Convention has just settled De Leon and De Leonism for good... St. John gave him the worst drubbing ever I saw a man get. Even his chief supporter, GEB member Yates (an honest man nevertheless) admitted that De Leon had 'shown ignorance of industrial unionism.' "[17]

The convention had demonstrated the growth of the IWW in the West. St. John had reported: "In proportion to population, the West has by far purchased and distributed more IWW literature, furnished more readers of the *Bulletin* and contributed more to the financial support of the

---

[12]Daniel De Leon, *As To Politics.*

[13]*Ibid.,* See letter from J.A. LaBille, pp. 20, ff. Also letters of J. Wagner and Leon Vasilio, pp. 28, 55. For anarchist position, see letter of Arturo Giovannitti, pp. 42, ff.

[14]*Industrial Union Bulletin,* November 7, 1908.

[15]Foner, Vol. 4, p. 112.

[16]Greaves, p. 218.

[17]Connolly Archives, Letter, Connolly to Matheson, September 27, 1908.

organization, than the entire section east of the Rocky Mountains."[18] It was the Western delegates, who had been marshalled to the convention by riding the freights, by James H. Walsh, Western IWW organizer, who tipped the scales against De Leon. From 1908 on, De Leon always referred to the IWW as "the bummery," "physical forcists," and "anarchists," all of which terms he used particularly against the Western delegates at the convention.

After De Leon was unseated, the De Leonite delegates walked out of the convention. A new "IWW" was set up in Detroit, "over the protest of De Leon," according to Olive Johnson. She reported him as saying: "...The IWW had strangled itself and should be allowed to die."[19]

De Leon's approach to mass activities was once again described in a letter to Olive Johnson dated April 13, 1908. Referring to the free speech demonstrations as "riots," he admitted that he feared the IWW members in Spokane would "throw a bomb" or that a bomb might be thrown by a police agent to discredit the labor movement. "I have been trying to keep the SLP skirts clean against such an eventuality," he wrote. He added: "I notice with pleasure that some of the Spokane capitalist sheets are quoting the *People* on Spokane. So that they know there are Socialists who spurn I-am-a-bummism and all that thereby hangs."[20]

Connolly took a different attitude towards the western workers. He discussed the popularizing of the IWW song, "Halleluia, I'm a Bum," in a letter to Matheson in December, 1908: "I have always insisted upon a due recognition of the *dignity* of our movement as a necessary prerequisite to its development, and have no sympathy with such a degradation of our cause from whatsoever causes it emanates... But the tactics of the SLP in setting this 'bum' talk in such livid light is the old game of seizing upon some trivial unimportant slip of an opponent and magnifying it... in order to obsure the real principles at stake. It is thoroughly Danite. But it cannot hide the fact that these Danites refused to allow the action of the Convention to be voted upon by the rank and file before they seceded; that they ran away from the referendum vote of the membership and tried to wreck an organization because De Leon could not control its officers."[21]

Replying to Matheson's inquiry about the truth of De Leon's charges of "bummery" and anarchism against the IWW leadership, he replied: "As to

[18]*Industrial Union Bulletin,* November 7, 1908, February 27, 1909.
[19]Olive Johnson, pp. 80-82.
[20]*Symposium,* "Daniel De Leon, Our Comrade," Olive M. Johnson, p. 107.
[21]Connolly Archives, Letter, Connolly to Matheson, December 20, 1908.

the convention... I think your definition of 'slum proletariat' would be the same as mine and I do not think you would include in that definition men who gave up their work and in order to save expense to their locals, risked their lives jumping on trains and beating their way half across a continent to attend a convention in the interest of the working class, as many of the Western delegates undoubtedly did. Nor yet, were they anti-political, as a whole. They held that the reference to political action in the old preamble had tended to confuse the workers, by all sorts of suppositions as to what political party they favored, and that it was best to cast that reference out, and amend the preamble accordingly. Then they proceeded to define their attitude as an organization, neither committed to political parties nor anti-political sects.

"I would have been as well pleased had the old preamble stood, but I do know that the wording of the old preamble did cause confusion."

He again berated the Scottish SLP for its dependence on De Leon: "Of course, you may elect to keep the prospects and hopes of a real revolutionary cause in Great Britain fettered to the cause of a discredited and discreditable slanderer and wrecker in America, and thus prevent the workers getting an opportunity of judging your cause on its own merits, but if you do, I would not like to have your responsibility. I most fervently trust that you will not make that mistake but that, as you ever have done, you will line up for the *revolution* and not for a man. Especially such a man."[22]

After many years, minutes of a secret meeting of the General Executive Board, held during the 1908 convention, have come to light. It is probable that these minutes were kept from the public, as the result of an agreement of all concerned. The meeting, held September 25, 1908, considered serious charges against Rudolph Katz.

The Minutes state: "This is to certify that the following is the record of transactions in the matter of Rudolph Katz.

"Executive Board was called to order by Secretary Trautmann. Cole acted as Chairman. St. John stated the reason he wanted the Board together was to consider the matter of charges against executive board member, Katz... The organization was and is in a most critical position. The fight that it has had to make for existence has strained the resources of the organization to the breaking point... To, at this time, thrash out the charges against Katz was, in the opinion of St. John, to furnish a fresh

[22]*Ibid.,* Letter, Connolly to Matheson, November 8, 1908.

supply of ammunition to those enemies that would, under the conditions existing, seriously hamper the work of organization for some time to come... and it might be used to entirely wreck the organization. In view of these conditions, St. John had two propositions to make to Katz.

"(1) That Katz resign from the Executive Board forthwith and get out of the movement entirely, so far as the economic movement is concerned. If Katz would do so, St. John would agree to allow him to resign on those terms without prejudice and the incident would be closed, so far as the IWW was concerned and no attempt would be made to use this action against him in any other field he might choose to become active in, so long as Katz did not, in any way, attempt to injure the IWW.

"(2) If Katz failed to accept these terms, St. John would proceed at once to draw up charges against Katz and push the matter to a full investigation, as he, St. John, was of the opinion that the information in his possession called for such action on his part for the good of the movement."

"Katz stated that as he did not think he would get a fair consideration from the convention, he would accept the first proposition. None of the Executive Board members objecting, it was then ratified."[23]

Connolly clarified the reasons behind this mutual agreement. He told Matheson: "Katz resigned from the movement today [September 27, 1908] on an agreement that if he did so, his case would be quietly dropped. He was accused of having trafficked in the label [union label] and of having exploited the IWW for personal purposes. The understanding is that in order to avoid giving material to the enemy, no reference is to be made to Katz, as long as he makes no war in the future on the IWW."[24]

Katz turned his back on Proposition No. 1, which he had agreed to follow in the secret GEB meeting. Immediately after the convention, he was the driving force in organizing the rival IWW in Detroit, called, at first, the "Detroit IWW" and later, the "Workers International Industrial Union." In 1924, this endeavor expired.

---

[23]Minutes, GEB meeting, September 25, 1908. Minutes were pasted in Minute Book "October 4, 1906-September 15, 1911," p. 196.

[24]Connolly Archives, Letter, Connolly to Matheson, September 27, 1908.

CHAPTER XIII

POLITICS VS SYNDICALISM

During the time Connolly was most active in the IWW, he was constantly confronted with many members' deep distrust of politics. Probing the reasons, Connolly wrote in the *Harp:* "Perhaps...there has been far too much theorizing...too great a fondness for philosophical disquisitions, and hence too great a proneness to forget that, in the last analysis, the whole concern of Socialism in the immediate present is with the workshop and the struggles of the men and women therein."[1]

Marxist theory never ceased to concern Connolly. The wordy, "spittoon" philosophers, who were completely alien to the problems of labor, were his target. He was surfeited with abstract, random theories, divorced from practice.

"I am wearied unto death listening to Socialist speeches and reading Socialist literature about materialism and philosophy, ethics, sex, embryology, monogamy, physiology," he wrote. "...from men to whom the more immediately important question of unionism is a sealed book...the organization of labor in the workshop, the robbery of labor here and now, and not the question of what influence the social organism of the future will have upon the minds, morals or theology of the race of the future, are what the Irish worker is interested in. And I am inclined to think that in that respect he is not so different, after all, from the workingmen of other races...".[2]

How to convince the workers that their goal must be Socialism? He advocated a change in agitiation methods. "Personally, I believe that the fact that we still have long platforms and programs," he wrote in December, 1908, is "one of the signs of the comparatively backward state of the Socialist movement, of our unripeness for Social Revolution... Express our whole fighting principle in one simple phrase, capable of being remembered by the average school boy, we will then... cease to be a

---

[1] *Harp,* May, 1909.
[2] *Ibid.*

propagandist association and become a revolutionary army."[3]

He had met Charles H. Kerr at the time of the IWW convention in Chicago, where he had arrived during the course of a tour for the *Harp.* Kerr was the head of the cooperative publishing house, Charles H. Kerr & Co., around which gathered the loose left wing of the Socialist Party. The *International Socialist Review* also originated in this publishing house.

Articles on the workers' struggles, industrial unionism and socialist principles, written in 1907 and 1908 by Connolly, which appeared in the *Industrial Union Bulletin,* the *International Socialist Review,* the *Harp,* and socialist papers from abroad, formed the basis of a pamphlet, *Socialism Made Easy,* published early in 1909 by the Kerr Co.

The pamphlet was Connolly's first widely-read work. Thousands of copies were sold in the United States and Canada and it was widely distributed in Australia, England, Scotland and Ireland. The small pamphlet influenced men and women and socialist movements throughout the world. In Australia, it was issued in numerous editions, under the title, *Axe to the Root.* In later years, the Irish Transport & General Workers Union reissued it several times, including editions in 1921 and 1934.[4]

Frank Bohn, while he was still National Secretary of the SLP, visited Connolly during the time he was preparing the material for the pamphlet. Bohn described his visit in an article which appeared in May, 1916, in the *New York Post,* after the Easter Rising. He erroneously believed that Connolly was still alive. The purpose for Bohn's visit was "to urge him to make his peace with a labor editor [Daniel De Leon] who had deeply wronged him.

"I found him sick in bed," wrote Bohn, "surrounded by his wife and six small children. They were actually suffering from lack of food and the rent was overdue. The white face of Connolly lay back on the pillow and his voice was weak." Bohn was amazed to find that sick as he was, Connolly was busy on *Socialism Made Easy.*

"I shall never make peace with that man!' he said, 'I know he can drive me from my job and ruin me temporarily! He has his paper and I have no means of redress, but he is wrong and I am right.'

"Amid such surroundings, some men might wish to die," wrote Bohn. "Connolly spent this season in writing poems and a booklet on Socialism,

---

[3]*Harp,* December, 1908.
[4]The second section of the pamphlet was printed by the union as *Axe to the Root.* Included also was Connolly's *Old Wine in New Bottles,* printed in 1914, in the *New Age.*

of which 40,000 copies later were sold."[5]

Bohn's impression was of an unhappy, somber man. Another Connolly was seen by Ralph Chaplin, who, in his early years, was an IWW poet and artist. He was asked by Kerr to meet Connolly and discuss the art work for *Socialism Made Easy.* Chaplin described Connolly's "spicy humor and fine, friendly manner." He asked him whether there was any suggestion in connection with the cover design. " 'None at all, my boy,' " Connolly chuckled. " 'Just so it's plenty Irish.' "

Chaplin designed a cover "full of runic decorations, shamrocks and the Irish harp... Connolly was... delighted... He left a lasting impression on me and everyone else with whom he had associated. It was a sad day for all of us, a few years later, when we read of him strapped in a chair to face a British firing squad, after the Easter Rebellion, in Dublin."[6]

Socialism Made Easy is divided into two parts: (1) "Workshop Talks," written in the form of questions and answers, and (2) "Political Action of Labor," which represents his thinking in connection with the relationship of industrial unionism to political parties. In part, this latter theoretical section was printed in the *Harp,* December, 1908. The chapter on "The Future of Labor," included in the second section, was based on a lecture he delivered and which was printed in the *Industrial Union Bulletin,* April 18, 1908, on its front page.[7]

Section one opens with a question posed to the worker: "You unite industrially, why then do you divide politically... Why not unite at the ballot box as you unite at the workshop?"

The question, said Connolly, was based on a "flagrant misstatement." On the contrary, the workers are not united, even in industry, but are "most hopelessly divided," due to the craft union form of organization in the AFL. He gave examples of craft unions scabbing against one another.

Striking at American arrogance, he contrasted the craft union situation in the United States with the solidarity of industrial unions led by socialists in Copenhagen, where the boycott, as well as the strike were working class weapons.[8] He drew on the history of the Land League in Ireland for a lesson in internationalism for American socialists: "The historic example of their Land League bequeaths to us a precious legacy of wisdom, both practical and revolutionary...".

When a tenant was evicted from a farm, "practically the whole country

[5]Reprinted in *Solidarity,* May 27, 1916.
[6]Ralph Chaplin, p. 105.
[7]Connolly, *Socialism Made Easy.*
[8]*Ibid.,* pp. 36 ff.

united to help him in his fight." When the farm where the eviction took place was rented by the landlord to another tenant, "a landgrabber or 'scab' every person in the countryside shunned him as a leper.

"...How great a lesson for the American workers is to be found in this record of a class struggle in Ireland!"[9]

In America, the Socialist Party "should strive to realize the industrial union as the solid foundation upon which alone the political unity of the workers can be built up and directed towards a revolutionary end."

The industrial unions were to be built up for "the practical purposes of today," advised Connolly. This position differed from that of De Leon. But, at the same time, they would be "preparing the framework of the society of the future." This was pure De Leonism.

Socialism Made Easy, which championed industrial unionism, was published and distributed by left-wing forces of the Socialist Party. Later, the dominant "Right-Center coalition" entered upon a series of purges of pro-IWW Socialists. Debs was attacked by Victor Berger but the influence of his huge following made punitive action impossible. Trautmann and others were expelled for "treasonable conduct." The anti-industrial union activity of the right-wing culminated with the removal of "Big Bill" Haywood from the National Executive Committee of the SPA.[10]

In his pamphlet, Connolly's description of the state is this: "Political institutions of today are simply the coercive forces of capitalist society."[11] Omitted is the Marxist theory of the leading role of the political party of Socialism, which with the initiation of a socialist society, sets up a "dictatorship of the proletariat," as Marx and Engels called it, to protect and lead it. Such a political state, as a transition to a classless society, is replaced in the pamphlet by: "The administrative force of the Socialist Republic of the future will function through unions, industrially organized." However, of prime importance was contemporary enrollment of workers into industrial unions -- "the swiftest, safest, and most peaceful form of constructive work the Socialists can engage in. It prepares within the framework of capitalist society, the working forms of the Socialist Republic."[12]

Connolly, again reflecting his De Leonite schooling, often repeated the statement which appeared in *Socialism Made Easy:* "The fight for the

[9]*Ibid.,* p. 41.
[10]Reeve, p. 116.
[11]*Socialism Made Easy,* p. 44.
[12]*Ibid.,* p. 47.

conquest of the political state is not the battle; it is only the echo of the battle." The *real* battle is in the workshop.

It is apparent, however, that even at that early time, he attached importance to the position of the political party in the working class struggle. It was necessary to bring the "workers as a class into direct conflict with the possessing class *as a class* -- and keeping them there... Nothing can do that so readily as action at the ballot box."[13]

And, with Connolly's emphasis: "...ACTION AT THE BALLOT BOX SHOULD ACCOMPANY ACTION IN THE WORKSHOP."

Connolly at this time was a semi-syndicalist. Orthodox syndicalism would have had no use at all for the political party of socialism. Later, after his return to Ireland, Connolly moved rapidly away from his early syndicalism.

Socialism Made Easy asserted that while the industrial union was gaining strength and the workers were becoming class conscious, "the Socialist Party will carry on an independent campaign of education and attack.upon the political field, and as a consequence will remain the sole representative of the Socialist idea in politics."

He warned against premature moves to bring "these two wings of labor"--the economic and the political together. "Two things must be kept in mind," he declared, "viz., that a Socialist political party not emanating from the ranks of organized labor is, as Karl Marx phrased it, simply a Socialist sect, ineffective for the final revolutionary act, but that also the attempt of craft organized unions to create political unity before they have laid the foundation of industrial unity... would be an instance of putting the cart before the horse. But when that foundation of industrial union is finally secured, then nothing can prevent the union of the economic and political forces of labor."

This pamphlet repeated his admonitions to the IWW: "I look forward to the time when every economic organization will have its political committee, just as it has its organizational committee or its strike committee, and when it will be considered to be as great... an act of scabbery, to act against the former as against any of the latter."[14]

Elizabeth Gurley Flynn, reflecting on this period of American socialist history, examined the reasons for the prevalence of syndicalist theory. In a handwritten manuscript, obviously the notes for a lecture, she commented: "Once when I was lecturing at a Workers' School... on my Socialist

---

[13]*Ibid.*, p. 55.
[14]*Ibid.*, pp. 56, 57.

generation, before 1910, and how we moved around so undecidedly from anarchist to Socialist Party, to Socialist Labor Party, to IWW, and thus to anarcho-syndicalism, a young student burst out, excitedly: 'But I can't understand how people as smart as Comrade Foster and you could make so many mistakes.' "

Her reply: "Forty years hence, the mistakes of our present generation may meet with a sterner criticism. 'Why did you put up with capitalism so long?' "

"My youth was truly a period of confusion in the American Socialist movement...," she wrote."The lines of organizational and theoretical demarcation were not yet drawn nor ideas tested by experience." From 1860 to 1914, she noted in her memorandum, more than 53,000,000 immigrants came to the United States. Non-English speaking workers, in large numbers, found it difficult to become naturalized American citizens. They formed the great majority of workers in the basic industries of coal, oil, steel, textile, meat-packing. "They were politically a negligible quantity." They could not become part of the political process; they could not vote. Women were denied the right to vote until 1920.

She observed: "The migration of Negro workers to Northern industrial areas was still slight and the vast working-class Negro population of the South was deprived of the right to vote, even more than today. Nor did the Socialist movement conceive of the workers having political allies such as farmers, professionals and middle-class, and the 'white collar' elements."[15]

A general distrust of politics resulted. This was made more acute by brazen political corruption, vote-stealing and bribery. Many workers adopted a syndicalist attitude as a reaction to the opportunism and class collaboration displayed by Socialist Party right-wing leaders. The sectarianism of the De Leonite Socialist Labor Party also played a role.

Elizabeth Flynn and her father were caught on the horns of this dilemma. She had already had her fill of opportunism in the Socialist Party. It was only at the 1908 IWW convention that her split with the SLP became final.

William Z. Foster, discussing the same subject in relation to his early years in the labor movement, said: "It was an easy step for me to conclude from the paralyzing reformism of the Socialist Party that political action in general was fruitless and that the way to working class emancipation was through militant trade union action, culminating in the general strike..."[16]

---

[15]Elizabeth Gurley Flynn Papers.
[16]William Z. Foster, American Trade Unionism, p. 15.

Both Connolly and De Leon borrowed substantially from the anarchists, Pierre Joseph Proudhon and Michael Bakunin, in considering the state, particularly the transition dictatorship of the proletariat.[17]

In 1875, Marx wrote a criticism of the Gotha Program of the German Social Democratic Party, which was first translated by Daniel De Leon into English and printed in the *Daily People* on January 7th, 1900. "Between the capitalist and communist society, there lies a period of revolutionary transformation from the former to the latter. A stage of political transition corresponds to this period, and the State during this period can be none other than the revolutionary dictatorship of the proletariat."[18] Neither De Leon nor Connolly fully understood this. Nor were they familiar with the letter which Marx sent to Joseph Weydemeyer on March 5, 1852, in which he described his additions to socialist thought as follows:

"(1) That the existence of classes is connected only with certain historical struggles which are characteristic of the development of production; (2) That the class war inevitably leads to the dictatorship of the proletariat; (3) That this dictatorship is only a transition to the destruction of all classes and to a society without classes."[19]

In 1920 and 1921, a Marxist position on the relation of the Socialist political party to the trade unions was argued in the Soviet Union. A "Workers' Opposition", and other factions, led by Trotsky and Bukharin, proposed unions must "coalesce" with the workers' state and run the country, the Communist Party to be subordinated. Lenin held that this was a syndicalist deviation.

"The organization of the management of national economy," declared the Workers' Opposition, "is the function of the All-Russian Congress of Producers, organized in industrial unions..." Lenin maintained that the dictatorship of the proletariat was necessary before a classless society is run by a "Union of Producers:" "The trade unions are not state organizations, not organizations for coercion," he insisted, "they are educational organizations that enlist and that train; they are schools, schools of administration, schools of management, schools of Communism."

---

[17]Reeve, pp. 138, ff. "De Leon and the Theory of the State."
[18]Karl Marx, *The Gotha Program,* p. 48.
[19]Marx and Engels, *Selected Correspondence,* p. 57. Marx's defense of the Paris Commune, published in English by the SLP, in 1902, also covered the functioning of the workers' dictatorship. See Marx, *Civil War in France, The Paris Commune,* pp. 70, 78, and V.I. Lenin, *The State and Revolution.*

Lenin argued that the unions were organizations of the entire class. "The proletariat is still so split up, so degraded, so corrupted in some places (by imperialism, in certain countries) that the organizations which embrace the whole class cannot directly effect the proletarian dictatorship." The vanguard of the class, said Lenin, the Communist Party, can effect the proletarian dictatorship. Lenin's position was upheld and the question of the unions leading the party and the state did not arise again in the Soviet Union.[20]

On the positive side, both the IWW itself and Connolly's leadership of industrial union movements (sometimes called amalgamations in Great Britain) were a significant influence in the development of the labor movement in Europe as well as in the United States. Labor historians, particularly in Great Britain, have paid attention to this fact. Tom Bell recognized the debt to the industrial unionists of the pre-World War I era: "The foundations of many of our large national trade union organizations in England of today were laid in those days (1910-1912) of severe criticism of the weakness of having a multiplicity of unions in a given industry."[21]

Walter Kendall, English labor historian, speaking of this influence in connection with the De Leonite Connolly-led Scottish SLP, stresses: "It was De Leon's elevation of industrial unionism to a cardinal feature of policy which provided the basis for the influence which the SLP [of Scotland] subsequently gained in Great Britain... Industrial unionism was highly relevant to the industrial situation of the pre-war years."[22]

Kendall overlooks the fact that although De Leon did emphasize industrial unionism, he was no proponent of mass struggle, as was Connolly, whose contribution, he said, was the "fountainhead of the rank and file movement known as the Shop Stewards Movement" in the period of large strikes during World War I. The leaders of this movement "were greatly influenced by James Connolly. MacManus, Bell, and the supporters of the SLP, revered him, not only as a socialist but also as a founder and first chairman of their own party. Murphy [one of the shop steward leaders] found Connolly's views 'even more precise than anything I had read or heard from other socialists.' It was Connolly's conception of

[20]V.I. Lenin, *Selected Works,* Vol. IX, "Party Unity and the Anarcho-Syndicalist Deviation," pp. 124, 40; *Selected Works,* Vol. X., "Left-Wing Communism, an Infantile Disorder," p. 55.
[21]Bell, p. 78.
[22]Kendall, pp. 67, 142, ff, "The Shop Stewards' Movement."

the role of the industrial union in the struggle for socialism that constituted the mainspring of the shop stewards' thought."[23]

Tom Mann, left wing British labor leader, who had led the historic dock strike of 1889, lived for almost a decade in Australia and New Zealand. There he agitated for industrial organization and socialism. He returned to England in May, 1910, at a time when labor militancy was at a boiling point and strikes were proliferating.

Kendall relates: "Mann's experiences... coupled with a reading of James Connolly's *Socialism Made Easy,* convinced him that industrial unionism was the answer to the problems facing the working class." The pamphlet expressed Mann's line of thinking so completely that he dropped a plan to write his own work on industrial unionism and socialism.[24] Later he led huge strikes and opposed dual unionism. In 1913, he attempted to convert the IWW in the United States to work within existing mass unions.[25]

The theory of industrial unionism in the United States grew beyond the confines of the IWW. In 1914, Socialists led in forming the Amalgamated Clothing Workers, an industrial union. In 1919, for the first time, numerous craft unions of the steel industry were organized by William Z. Foster to strike unitedly. The militant socialists of those early years who popularized industrial unionism included, in addition to Bill Haywood, Elizabeth Gurley Flynn, "Mother" Ella Reeve Bloor, Rose Pastor Stokes and others. "Mother" Bloor was a full-time organizer for the International Association of Machinists (AFL) many leaders of which firmly advocated industrial unionism. She also organized in the needle-trades. Foster raised "Amalgamation" as a slogan in AFL unions. Later, as leader of the Trade Union Educational League and the Trade Union Unity League, he brought policies of industrial unionism into mining, textile, etc.

The leaders of the IWW steered toward total syndicalism. Connolly and Ben Williams, though they publicly expressed their differences on politics, maintained a close relationship. In March, 1908, Williams wrote in the *Industrial Union Bulletin,* addressing himself to the two socialist parties: "Hands Off: whether... individuals belong to one or the other of the two Socialist Parties...".[26] In April, Connolly lectured on "The Future of Labor," which was to become a part of *Socialism Made Easy.* He sent a copy of th's speech, reprinted in the IUB, to Matheson, concerned with

---

[23]*Ibid.,* p. 162. See Gallacher, *Revolt on the Clyde.* He was the first Communist member of the British Parliament.
[24]Greaves, p. 229.
[25]Kendall, pp. 145, 146.
[26]*Industrial Union Bulletin,* March 14, 1908.

clarifying his stand on the necessity for socialist political action. [27]

"It is not the theorists who make history," he said in this article, "it is history, in its evolution, that makes the theorists... In the workshop has been and will be fought out these battles between the new and the old methods of production." Action by the IWW at the ballot box, "will be action coming straight from a working class economic orgainization, and strained, so to speak, from the loins of the class struggle."

Writing to Matheson, five months before the IWW convention, Connolly mentioned Williams' anti-political ideas. Connolly did not". want to be ranked as a supporter of his *entire* position." He explained: "... he and I differ on one cardinal point... I believe that political action *at the ballot box* must be taken by the IWW, hand in hand with the economic action; he insists that it *may* be so taken, but most probably *will not* ... Williams, in my estimation, commits the mistake of under-estimating the necessity of fully utilizing the political structure of capitalism as a propagandist basis."

Connolly ended this letter with a wry comment: "You once asked me to write a pamphlet for the SLP of Great Britain, on the basis of an impromptu speech of mine in Edinburgh, and I have used the basis... here, in the hopes that you might find room for it in the *Socialist*. Unless your National Executive Committee wish it to be endorsed by the National Executive Committee of the SLP of America, a la the *Harp*."

Connolly asked: " By the way, what answer, if any, did they get to that request?"[28]

On May 7th, Connolly wrote Matheson: "Of course you will have seen the lecture in the *Bulletin* and now you, at least, know that I am not an 'anti-political' nor in any danger of becoming so. But I am not a fossil, and still capable of learning, even from those who differ from me."

In this letter, Connolly again drove against sectarianism in the Scottish SLP. He proved that he clearly recongnized opportunism, even if displayed by an old friend. Matheson and the other Scottish SLPers had rebuked Connolly for his friendly attitude to Keir Hardie, founder of the Independent Labor Party. Hardie had befriended Connolly in the early movements of the late 1800s. He was now a centrist and pacifist who concentrated on bringing union men and women into his organization. Connolly made clear to Matheson that he recognized Hardie's opportunism. However socialists could learn from Hardie how to avoid

[27]*Ibid.,* April 18, 1908.
[28]Connolly Archives, Letter, Connolly to Matheson, April 18, 1908.

sectarianism.

"I have come to the belief," he wrote, "that Keir Hardie was wise in his generation when he worked to form the Labor Representation Committee." [The L.R.C. was a committee set up by trade unionists within the S.D.F. and was the forerunner of the Labor Party of Great Britain.] Connolly continued: "His readiness to compromise, his truckling to certain prejudices, his watering down of the revolutionary program, unfit him or his party ever to rise to the real heights of revolutionary effectiveness. But he has demonstrated to us the real method of building a Socialist Labor Party. What we want to do is to show that the same method can be utilized in building a revolutionary party, free of the faults and shunning the compromises of the L.R.C.

"If that body was dominated by industrial unionists instead of by pure and simplers; if it was elected by the industrial unions and controlled entirely by them, and capable *at any moment* of having its delegates recalled by the unions, and had also its mandate directly from the rank and file organized in the workshops, it would be just the party we want...".[29]

The sectarianism in the Scottish SLP which Connolly was arguing against in the May, 1908 letter, was referred to by Thomas Bell, several years later. "It was considered a virtue amongst many of the Marxist students to remain not only 'independent' but aloof from party politics."[30]

The paralleling of Connolly's approach to Lenin's is demonstrated here. Lenin, after the formation of the Communist Party of Great Britain, proposed to its membership, that it should work within the Labor Party, as well as the mass unions, in spite of reformist leadership. At an earlier time, Connolly was evolving an approach along the same lines.[31]

In the Spring of 1908, several developments took place in the socialist movement which made an impression on Connolly. The Socialist Party gave him permission to preside over a table in the lobby of its convention hall to sell the *Harp*. This was an influence on Connolly's softening attitude on the SPA. Justus Ebert, in the April 18 issue of the *Industrial Union Bulletin*, wrote an open letter of resignation from the SLP and urged other active members to do the same. Ebert characterized the SLP as "at best a noble tradition; at worst a dangerous delusion."

In September, Connolly again attempted to clarify his postition on

[29]*Ibid.*, Letter, May 7, 1908.
[30]Bell, p. 84. Note p. 44, Bell's description of sectarianism within the Scottish SLP.
[31]Lenin, *Left-Wing Communism,* Chapters 6, 7, 9. Also Gallacher, pp. 248, ff. in Chapter 11.

politics and syndicalism for Matheson. Written during the IWW convention, the letter contained Connolly's appraisal of the Socialist Party. It also revealed that he had become a member.

He wrote: "I am still, as ever, an IWW man... I believe in the necessity of an uncompromising political party of Socialists and I do not believe that the Socialist Party, of which I am a member, is *yet* such a body. But I believe that the conduct of De Leon has rendered impossible any clear cut movement *in America...*".

He urged that the Scottish SLP display more tolerance toward the idea of working with other organizations: "My only criticism of the SLP of Great Britain is that it wastes too much time in picking holes in the candidates and platforms of the other parties without strengthening our own. A vigorous and relentless criticism of craft unionism, and exposition of the wisdom and necessity of a straightforward revolutionary policy, and at the same time, a due recognition of the fact that those other parties are also a part, even if an unclear part, of the working class movement, is in my mind, the need of the hour for *your* movement...

As to his joining the Socialist Party: "Now, if before joining the SP," he argued, " I had to accept the compromising elements and their political faith, I would never have joined it. But it is not necessary to do so. In the SP there are revolutionary clear-cut elements (43 votes in the last convention) and there are also compromising elements. Neither claim the right to be the Socialist Party. I have read SP papers which branded Berger, Carl Thompson, et al., as tricksters and compromisers and other papers which sneered at their opponents as 'impossibilists,' but both are loyal members of the party and fight out their differences at their convention. Neither attempts to expel the other. Now it was a long time before I felt that it was better to be one of the revolutionary minority inside the party than a mere discontented grumbler out of political life entirely."

Connolly summarized his position: "I would rather have the IWW undertake *both* political and economic activity now, but as the great majority of the workers in the movement are against me in that matter, I do not propose to make my desires a stumbling block in the way of my cooperation with my fellow revolutionists. Would you? I think not."[32]

Matheson had misunderstood Connolly's approach to his membership in the Socialist Party. In December, Connolly attempted to correct this: "I never meant, when I asked you to declare yourself, that you should eulogize the SP... There has to be a lot of development in the SP before it

---

[32]Connolly Archives, Letter, Connolly to Matheson, September 27, 1908.

will be at all our ideal of a revolutionary party. But your criticism of it is not exactly just.

"In order to estimate the success of its policy, it would be necessary to compare its compromising, wobbly speeches, and actions of five or six years ago with its increasingly revolutionary and uncompromising policy towards all other [capitalist] parties. And also to point out that since it came into existence, it has built up a Socialist sentiment in the country that is but feebly reflected in the vote allowed it by the old parties. I am certain that the SP polled over a million votes [in the November 1908 election] even if the official vote is not perhaps over 500,000."[33]

Connolly had differed with De Leon's constant criticism of Debs as early as 1906. In June of that year, he wrote Matheson: "As to Debs, I think Debs is thoroughly honest and I base my belief upon the fact that although he has changed his position several times in the past, that every change was a move forward...".[34]

Connolly, the teetotaler, wrote Matheson, the teetotaler, that he had heard rumors that Debs was too fond of his "wee drappie." He very much approved of Debs' politics, however, and warmed to his support to the IWW. "He is in a strange fix, his instincts are all revolutionary; but he balks at swallowing De Leon and the latter's followers insist that to accept the IWW in its entirety is to accept Dan."[35]

Connolly continued to keep Matheson apprized of developements in the SLP. He informed Matheson, in his December, 1908 letter: "Practically all the active men and women here have left the SLP. Among the latest, Timothy Walsh, who used to write the 'Claudius' Stock Exchange articles, his wife, 'Aunt Annetta,' of the Sunday *People*, Tom Flynn, who so recently denounced me as 'trafficking in Irish Flesh and Blood,' Miss Jane Roulston, from California (at the general party meetings, last year, she nearly went into hysterics of rage when she heard us daring to criticize De Leon; now she weeps as she tells of the fifteen years of her life spent in building up a party which he tore down as quickly), all the 34th Assembly District, the whole Paterson section of the SLP and the whole of the Yonkers comrades, except one."[36]

An important addition to Connolly's writings on industrial unionism was *Old Wine in New Bottles,* which appeared in *The New Age*, in April, 1914, after the desperately fought strike and lockout of 1913 in Dublin.

[33]*Ibid.,* December 20, 1908.
[34]*Ibid.,* June 10, 1906.
[35]Samuel Levenson, p. 120.
[36]Connolly Archives, Letter, Connolly to Matheson, December 20, 1908.

Connolly, with Jim Larkin, applied at that time the principles of industrial unionism which Connolly had developed in the United States. It marked a turning point in the Irish labor movement. *Old Wine in New Bottles*, reprinted many times, related, in part, to Connolly's experiences in the IWW. His emphasis here was that the perfect industrial *form* of organization was not sufficient to insure militant action. "The militant spirit, the fighting character of the organization was of the first importance. I believe that the development of the fighting spirit is of more importance than the creation of the theoretically perfect organization." He credited the American IWW with furthering the European industrial unions.

Insisting that the perfect organization could become " the greatest possible danger to the revolutionary movement," if it repressed the rank and file's fighting spirit, he cited the English seamen's strike of 1911. Other unions in the strike, according to Connolly, though industrial unions, reverted to the craft union spirit. They handled "tainted" goods, rejecting solidarity. The union officials, "destitute of the revolutionary spirit" were responsible. "Into the new bottles of industrial organization is being poured the old, cold wine of Craft Unionism," he wrote.

However, still in the United States, as late as 1910, in an article in the *International Socialist Review*, Connolly refuted the anti-political actions of the 1908 IWW Convention, also attacking anti-IWW bias in the SPA.

"All objections which my comrades make to industrial unionism on the grounds of the supposedly, or truly anti-political bias of many members of the IWW is quite beside the mark," he wrote. "...If at any time the conditions of a struggle in shop, factory, railroad or mine necessitate the employment of political action, those workers so organized will use it, all theories and theorists to the contrary notwithstanding. In their march to freedom, the workers will use every weapon they find necessary."[37]

This latter statement once more represented Connolly's most basic theory of struggle and revolution. All means -- none excluded except methods of individual terror -- would be used by the working class to attain its goals, each chosen in the circumstances which would call them forth.

Politics, syndicalism, theories and practice, the struggle for survival of himself and his family -- these grim problems did not represent the only side of James Connolly's life during this period. There were interspersed some joyous moments of family life.

---

[37]*International Socialist Review*, February, 1910.

The memoirs of Ina Connolly, at the time a very small girl, give her picture of Connolly with his family.

"We saw little of father, for he was travelling full time, helping to organize trade unions and lecturing about the country. Once in a while his work brought him to the city, and we had grand weekends. He often took us to large public meetings and it was a treat to hear him speak...

"Upon occasions, during these brief reunions, father took us on outings of the Socialist Party. Father was popular, not only for his organizing activities, but also because he was founder and editor of... the *Harp*. The catering at these affairs was done by the Party members. There were sandwiches, sweet cakes, ice cream, soda pop, and for the men, beer out of the barrel.

"Father didn't drink. He was not partial to it, and if he were, he used to say, he would not have been able to afford it. Nevertheless, in organizing the men, he often had to make contact with them in saloons. He used to complain to mother: 'What with the quantities of ginger beer I've drunk, my stomach is in worse condition than any toper's.'

"There were grand speeches at the outings, and the band played with gusto. We danced and sang to our heart's content. Mother did not share our enthusiasm, however; travelling with a young family in a New York summer was a trial. I can understand her remark when we returned from one such picnic: 'I'd rather do two days' washing than ever again face such a day's pleasure.' "[38]

---

[38]Ina Connolly Heron, *Liberty,* April, 1966, p. 19.

CHAPTER XIV

CONNOLLY ISSUES *THE HARP*

With the publication of the *Harp,* first issued in January, 1908, James Connolly at last had a vehicle of his own, free from De Leonite SLP sectarianism, by which he could speak to the Socialists and militant trade unionists, particularly the Irish Americans. As editor of the organ of the Irish Socialist Federation, he was in a position to present theoretical articles and comments that were uniquely his own -- forceful, eloquent, bitingly satiric and penetrating observations of life around him and the movement toward socialism.

Students of Connolly's life agree that the *Harp* contained some of his finest writing. Desmond Ryan, in his early, brief biography of Connolly, summarizing the importance of the paper, paid tribute to Connolly's "brilliant and penetrating judgments."

"In his genial and trenchant manner," Ryan commented, "he expresses in the *Harp,* the best criticisms of American society, Irish-American politicians (once described by him as descendants of the serpents St. Patrick banished from Ireland), his complete political and social ideals, as well as his practical policy for Irish workers."[1]

Notwithstanding Ryan's tribute, much of Connolly's writings in the *Harp* are still virtually unknown.

The booth publicizing the *Harp* which Connolly presided over at the National Convention of the Socialist Party in May, 1908 in Chicago, brought the publication and its editor to the attention of Socialists throughout the United States. A number of SPA leaders, including J.O. Bentall, organizer from Illinois, immediately became supporters.

Bernard McMahon, active member of the Socialist Party in the Chicago area, also greeted the *Harp's* appearance at the Socialist Party Convention. He wrote an article for the *Harp* on the convention, which appeared in its August issue: "For the first time in the history of the American movement, an appeal was seen and heard from a new element,

---

[1]Desmond Ryan, p. 32.

the Irish, and the *Harp,* the organ of the Irish Socialist Federation, made
its initial bow in a National Convention, with a stand well-stocked with
printed matter, directly appealing to the sons and daughters of the Green
Isles."

The convention, McMahon noted, showed that the Western states were
"more gallant than the Atlantic ones, in the matter of women delegates."
The California delegation was "unique", in that it sent the only Black,
Reverend George W. Woodbey, from San Diego, to the convention.[2]

The November issue displayed a picture of the *Harp* booth,
accompanying a report by Connolly. The selection of Eugene Debs and
Ben Hanford as national candidates in the coming elections "was a popular
one," he wrote, and the ratification meeting at Orchestra Hall was crowded
and enthusiastic. "Haywood, the 'undesirable' citizen of Colorado and
Idaho, presided," he observed.[3]

McMahon, who worked in the Chicago Collector's office, became
Connolly's friend. After Connolly's execution in the Easter Rising, he
described the impact of the *Harp* on him, in the *New York Evening Call*:

"Some comrade... mailed me a copy of the *Harp*... Looking it over
casually, I saw that it was a Socialist paper with a special appeal to the Irish
race and that its editor was James Connolly, of whom I had heard. I read
every line of it and concluded... that it was worthy of Bronterre O'Brien,
Fintan Lalor or John Mitchel, three of Ireland's greatest writers on
economic subjects...".

A committee of three, Mary O'Reilly, Patrick Reardon and McMahon
appeared before the National Executive Committee of the Socialist Party,
in session in Chicago, where Connolly, touring for the *Harp,* had arrived.
The three urged the NEC to make use of Connolly's talents in a national
lecture tour for the Socialist Party. The NEC approved the proposal and a
national tour was slated for Connolly for May, 1909.[4] Contributing to the
decision was the warmth with which many Socialist Party branches had
received him.

---

[2]*The Harp,* August, 1908.

[3]*Ibid.,* November, 1908.

[4]*New York Evening Call,* May 27, 1916. In his eulogy, McMahon recalled: "One of the
most generous tributes to his ability was from the late Thomas Morgan, who said he could sit
at the feet of Connolly and look up to him cheerfully for instruction." Morgan played an
important role in trade union struggles in Chicago at the turn of the century. He left the SLP
in 1896, defying De Leon's order to leave the AFL to join the STLA. He organized united
front conferences of unions and later joined the Socialist Party.(Reeve, pp. 52, 56, 64, 100,
103.)

On April 13, 1908, three months after the *Harp* first appeared, and possibly in the very week when Connolly formally resigned from the SLP, a letter from the New York County SLP, addressed to Connolly by Joseph Scheuerer, "organizer pro tem," almost hesitatingly invited him to speak at the May Day meeting in New York City. Scheuerer was evidently instructed for the second time by the New York General Committee "to request you to speak at Webster Hall meeting May 1st. I hereby ask you to let me know if you are in a position to accept the invitation, as the handbills must be gotten out as soon as possible."[5] Connolly declined.

A major article in the first issue of the *Harp* warned that isolation of Irish-American socialists from Irish non-Socialist workers was a serious danger. In the article, "Our Purpose and Function," he wrote: "The present writer has been in the socialist movement more years than he cares to enumerate, and... has noted with regret the adoption by Irishmen, as soon as they become Socialists, of a line of conduct fatal to the best interests of the Socialist cause amongst our people."

The Irish Socialist in the United States "should become a medium for... translating Socialist ideas into terms of Irish thought... But this he could only do as long as his Socialism did not cause him to raise barriers betwixt him and his fellow countrymen and women..." With the adoption of the Socialism, many Irishmen "...often ended by ceasing to mix in Irish gatherings or to maintain Irish connections."

Connolly summarized the aims of the Irish Socialist Federation in simple words, showing the relationship of nationalism and socialism:

"We propose to show all the workers of our fighting race that Socialism will make them better fighters for freedom, without being less Irish; we propose to advise the Irish who are Socialists now to organize their forces as Irish and get again into touch with the organized bodies of literary, educational and revolutionary Irish... imparting to them a correct interpretation of Irish history, past and present... to take control of the Irish vote out of the hands of the slimy [illegible] who use it to boost their political and business interests to the undoing of the Irish as well as the American toilers.

"...After 700 years battling against a mighty oppressor... we raise the idea of the legions of our unforgotten dead: 'Ireland for the Irish' on the higher plane of the nobler: 'The World for the Workers.' "[6]

---

[5]Connolly Archives, Letter, Jos. Scheuerer, Org. pro tem, SLP, Section New York County, to Connolly, April 13, 1908.

[6]*Harp*, January, 1908.

Connolly had studied the Irish in American history with the same zeal he had brought to his research of labor in Irish history. This the *Harp* reflected. Two penetrating articles analyzed the "Know Nothing" movement of the 1830s and '40s, which was directed against the foreign-born, particularly Irish immigrants. By inference, Connolly placed De Leon, *the People,* and their SLP followers, who attacked him and the Irish Socialist Federation as "Jesuits," in the same category.

Introducing the articles, he declared: "In order that this characteristic attempt to revive the spirit of Know Nothingism may not entirely lack of its educational value, we propose to publish... a short history of the ... movement in America."[7] He emphasized the need for solidarity, as one lesson to be learned from the articles, which appeared in the March and April, 1908 issues: "...The Irish had in their day of weakness in this country, to suffer all the insults, abuse and ignominy now poured so freely upon the Italian, the Pole, the Hungarian, the Slav and the Jew... The Irish should be the first to protest against this senseless vilification and discrimination, instead of being an actual agent therein, as he too often is today."[8]

The contribution of the Irish to independence of the United States was another important theme. Connolly contended that historians "quietly ignored" the fact that the men who gathered to defend the American Revolution in the Continental Army were not only Anglo Saxons. They came from Irish, Dutch, French and German settlements. Washington's adopted son had declared that to every soldier from another foreign country, Ireland had contributed ten soldiers. In the roster of officers of Washington's army, in the records of the states, he wrote,"...the number of Irish names proclaims emphatically not only the nationality of their owners, but also the estimation in which the race was held by the soldiers of freedom." The following officers were Irishmen, according to Connolly: General William Irvine; Major-General Henry Knox; General William Thompson; General Walter Stewart; Major-General Anthony Wayne; General Edward Hand; Brigadier-General Stephen Moylan; Major-General Zebulon Butler; General Richard Montgomery; General John Stark.[9] Irishmen, too, played an outstanding role in the American Navy --

---

[7]*Ibid.*, February, 1908.
[8]*Harp*, March and April, 1908.
[9]Dirk Struik became interested in Connolly's list of Irishmen who had fought in the American Revolution. All of the names did not appear to be of Irish extraction. He commented, in a letter to us, July 5, 1976: "I looked up... Stark. He hailed from Londonderry, N.H. and thus was Scotch-Irish. Although descendants of Scotch-English colonists were

Commodore John Barry, for instance. "The first British port captured... was captured by an Irishman, John Sullivan... at the Harbor of Portsmouth, N.H. in 1774...".

During an investigation in the House of Commons, to place responsibility for the failure of the British armies, Connolly recorded, Edmund Burke asked the witness, Major-General Robertson: "How are American armies composed...?" Robertson answered: "General Lee informed me that half the Continental Rebel Army were from Ireland."[10]

The second installment traced the means by which Irish-Americans were robbed of civil rights. In 1839, in Louisiana, the Native American Association published an "Address," in which "every effort was made to arouse hatred, to urge an exclusion of foreign-born... from political rights, more especially from the right to hold office..." The foreign-born were described as: "destitute of any intellectual aspirations... criminal... offal of society--the pauper, the vagrant and the convict...".

In the North, "tales of Jesuit conspiracies" were widely spread. Mobs in Boston and Philadelphia, in 1844, burned Catholic institutions to the ground -- libraries, schools and churches. In Massachusetts, Connecticut and New Hampshire, anti-Catholics ran for office on an anti-foreign-born program.

But, related Connolly: "In a few years, these same native American states were begging the despised immigrants from Europe to take up arms to defend the union, and the 'hordes and hecatombs of beings in human form' were the only effective barriers between that union and disruption."

Here Connolly referred to De Leon's accusations that the attempts to get the longshoremen into the IWW was a Jesuit plot. "Did we not rightly characterize it as a recrudescence of Know Nothingism. Know Nothingism is dead but its ghost walks in the most unexpected places."[11]

Connolly returned to the subject of American chauvinism more than once in the *Harp*. An article entitled "Europe and America" was particularly explicit. He commented: "One of the salient characteristics of American life [is]... the intense chauvinism, the exaggerated patriotism of

---

settled by the British to subdue the Irish, many of these Protestants were pro-American in the Revolution. I looked up Aptheker's book on the American Revolution. He writes that during the early 1770s 'the first major wave of Irish immigration came to America; from 1770 to 1775 about 50,000 Irish arrived.' These Irish were overwhelmingly pro-American... I conclude that Connolly was right in mentioning these many names of fighting Irish on the side of the Americans."

[10]*Harp,* March, 1908.
[11]*Ibid.,* April, 1908.

its inhabitants." Labor, under attack by the trusts and the government, was in retreat. Yet American smugness and superiority towards the labor and socialist movements in Europe was apparent. This chauvinism, he suggested, interfered with a real international spirit... The American nation, "so young, so new, so unformed," he said, exhibited "an abnormal degree of satisfaction with itself."[12]

The proclaimed right of asylum in the United States for victims of the struggle against imperialism was emphasizd by Connolly. The words chiseled on the Statue of Liberty: "Give me your tired, your poor... your huddled masses, yearning to be free..." was a beacon for revolutionists and democrats, whose lives were threatened by tyrants of their native lands.

Many American socialists and progressives supported the demand for the right of asylum for revolutionists, in Connolly's time.[13] He wrote on Gomper's fight to restrict immigration, and repression of the foreign-born in the past, citing the Chinese Exclusion Act of 1882 and laws restricting foreign-born immigration, passed in 1888, 1891, 1903 and 1907.[14] He protested against "the present attempt to extradite the Russian and Mexican political refugees and hand them over to the hangman of their respective countries."

He appealed to his Irish readers on the basis of their history: "What attitude should the Irish workers take?... Irishmen, who remember the long list of Irish patriots who sought refuge on these shores from the clutches of the English tyrant, will surely not hesitate and waver in their choice of action here.

"Would you have voted to surrender John Mitchel, or John Boyle O'Reilly on their arriving here after being rescued from the penal colonies of England, or John Stephens, on his escape from Richmond prison, or Kelly and Deasy [Fenians] to rescue whom three brave Irish workingmen gave up their lives on the scaffold at Manchester? I know you would not, and I know also that you will not willingly see the revolutionists of other countries given up."[15]

---

[12]*Ibid.*, February, 1908.

[13]Charles and Mary Beard, pp. 416-422.

[14]On August 30, 1909, Gompers reaffirmed his chauvinist position in a speech at the International Socialist Congress in Paris, in which he refused to pledge the affiliation of the AFL "unless Americans were given the right to self-government." Riled by the free immigration stand of Congress, Gompers declared: "American labor unions will never submit to rule by men who are ignorant of conditions in America." (*New York Evening Call,* August 31, 1909.)

[15]*Harp,* February 1909. The *New York Call,* August 24, 1909, reported that refugees from

Through the bitterly ironic picture of an Irish immigrant, searching, vainly, for Liberty, Connolly, in December, 1908, presented a panorama of class struggle in the United States. "The only Liberty we know of today," he began, "outside the Liberty to go hungry, stands in New York Bay, where it has been placed, I am told, in order that immigrants from Europe may get their first and last look at it, before setting foot on American soil. Some ignorant, discontented unit of the hordes of Europe... might feel tempted to go nosing around in this great country in search of Liberty, and his search might take him into the most awkward places."

In his article, Connolly takes the "greenhorn" (Connolly's word) South, where he can see "little white American children of seven, eight and nine years of age, working in our cotton mills, enjoying their liberty to work for a boss...". Connolly turned to Alabama, where Black workers, as well as white, were on strike. The "greenhorn" might have gone to "Alabama and seen American citizens out on strike, driven out of their homes by the capitalist mine-owners, and when they erected tents upon private land... he might have seen a Democratic governor order in the state militia, to cut down the tents and drive the American workers back to the mine at the point of the bayonet." (At this time, 40,000 Blacks were members of the United Mine Workers Union.)

The construction camps of Florida was the next stop for the searcher for liberty. Here men were kept at starvation's door and beaten and cursed, in virtual peonage. If they attempted to escape these conditions, they were arrested and returned to the camps in handcuffs. Though not so described, the majority here were Blacks.

"The pilgrim in search of liberty might have learned from the coal miners of Pennsylvania that their state is dotted over... with localities where union miners were shot down like dogs, whilst peacefully parading the streets or roads in time of strikes; he might have learned that practically every industrial center in the country, from Albany, New York to San Francisco, California; from New Orleans to Minnesota, has the same tale to tell of the spilliing of workmen's blood by the hirelings of the master class."

In Union Square, New York, the searcher, attending an unemployment demonstration, might have seen "free American citizens rapped on the head for daring to ask for a job collectively, instead of begging for it individually."

---

the Mexican democratic revolution had been arrested and held incommunicado, on behalf of the Diaz government. They were "labor organizers and liberal leaders." This issue also protested attempted extradition of Russian revolutionists, who had fled Czarist terror after the unsuccessful 1905 uprising.

The condition of the New York longshoremen, many of whom were Irish-Americans, exemplified the crisis. "This greenhorn might have strolled along West Street and interviewed some Irish longshoreman, who could tell him that in contrast to Ireland, since he became a participant in the freedom of America, he has to turn out to his work, rain or shine, winter and summer, and be ready to stand in line to be picked out of a gang, as he used to pick out pigs at a fair at home; only that the pigs got fed, whereas he and his family are likely to go hungry, if he does not keep on the soft side of the boss and get picked; and if he does get picked for a job, he has to stand worse driving and foul abuse than an Irish ass ever received from its driver."

Connolly's pilgrim then interrupted a Fourth of July orator, demanding "to be shown where this American liberty is." The orator might have answered: "Liberty is to be found outside in the Bay of New York." Thus, liberty "is placed upon a pedestal, out of the reach of the multitudes... it has a lamp to enlighten the world, but the lamp is never lit, and it smiles upon us as we approach America, but when we are once in the country, we never see anything but its back."[16]

In the foregoing article, Connolly wrote about Blacks, without designating them as such. Child labor in Southern cotton mills was white, because Black children were not permitted to work in the mills. Even as late as 1929, in Gastonia, North Carolina, Black adults were relegated to the "waste mill" and to menial porter jobs. Black child labor worked in the cotton fields.

In the *Harp,* June, 1908, Connolly quoted an article on peonage in the cotton fields. The story, printed in the *Chicago Socialist,* began: "Little children five years old have to go out and hoe cotton in May, June and July." Afterward they could attend school for a few weeks. "In September, the cotton picking begins," and children, with their parents, were driven back to the fields.

Connolly passionately protested against these conditions. The officials of the capitalist government, he charged, while demanding the building of 48 additional battleships, demonstrated "at least cold neglect or a passive indifference to every suggestion for the preservation and ennobling of the lives of the workers" who labored under "awful conditions."[17]

Why did Connolly fail to emphasize the *super* exploitation and social

---

[16]*Harp,* December, 1908.
[17]*Ibid.,* June, 1908.

discrimination imposed on the Blacks? Why did he not set forth their specific needs and demands? In the *Harp*, consistently, no distinction is made between black and white Americans. His approach is typical of the Socialist movement, even the left wing, in the years in which Connolly was in the United States. Following the example of Debs and De Leon, while protesting against Jim Crow, he adopted the idea that no demands should be raised for any particular segment of the working class.

In historical perspective, it is inevitable to come to the conclusion that lack of energetic championing of Blacks actually was more deeply rooted in the socialist leaders than sectarianism. They lived in an environment of pervasive white chauvinism and were affected by it. Burgeoning American imperialism engendered white chauvinism. The Government, North and South, the press, the AFL leadership, the capitalist political parties, the bourgeois organizations, all fostered white chauvinism.

There was relatively a small number of Black workers in the industries of the North, as compared to the foreign-born, at the time. The white progressives, on the whole, took the line of least resistance and did not join with the Blacks, in fighting for their rights. The employed Blacks, in the most menial and lowest-paid jobs, found it next to impossible to get into AFL unions in the North.[18] In the South, disenfranchised Blacks were forced into peonage in the cotton fields and in the lumber and turpentine camps. They were subject to arrest on petty charges. Local governments sold prisoners to employers for a pittance a day. Whippings and murders of Blacks were frequent occurrences. Not only individual lynchings, as well as rapes of black women, were commonplace, but massacres and wholesale lynchings took place.[19]

There were attempts made by Blacks to seek unity and support for their struggles from white socialists. Several newspapers proposed an alliance with Debs and the left-wing Socialists. The response of the Socialists was apathetic.

True, articles had appeared in the *International Socialist Review* against segregated SPA locals in the South.[20] The SLP's *People*, also, strongly condemned the SPA practice of segrated locals. In spite of this, Robert Hunter, in the *New York Call*, asked the Black: "to fight his own battles and win his own victories." Debs, in the course of speaking against Jim Crow, inconsistently said: "We have nothing special to offer the Negro and

---

[18]The documents in Herbert Aptheker's *A Documentary History of the Negro People in the United States* describe militant struggles of Northern and Southern Blacks, pp. 827-915.

[19]*Ibid.,* pp. 832-839, 853-856, 866.

[20]*Ibid.,* p. 856. See Oakley C. Johnson, Chapter 5, pp. 68 ff.

we cannot make special appeals to all the races." The story, in the August 27, 1908 *Call,* carried a four column headline: "NOT RACIAL BUT CLASS DISTINCTION, LAST ANALYSIS OF NEGRO PROBLEM -- DEBS."[21]

In the 1908 convention of the SPA, those attending, including one Black delegate, heard Ernest Untermann, a theoretician of the right-center leadership, say: "I am determined that my race shall be supreme in this country and in the world." This reaffirmed the position of Victor Berger in 1907 when he stated that Canada and the United States should be "white man's country."[22]

Although Debs vigorously opposed such racism and responded sharply in the *International Socialist Review* to its expression in the 1910 convention,[23] the lack of energetic campaigns against lynching, disenfranchisement, union and job discrimination, southern peonage, etc., was a basic reason for the small number of Blacks in the socialist organizations of the day.

There were individual left-wing Socialists who understood the mistake. Dr. I.M. Rubinow, using the pseudonym of I.M. Robbins, wrote a series of fifteen articles during 1909 and 1910, in the *International Socialist Review,* criticizing the Socialist Party's policy. He demanded an "actively aggressive" struggle for the rights of Negroes.[24]

The *Harp,* however, reflected the failure of the socialists to struggle against racism.[25] Connolly had, in his publication, fought Gompers' racist policy excluding immigration. He charged: "American and Canadian workers vehemently oppose Hindu immigration on the ground that the Hindu is not up to the American standard... Yet in their own country, these Hindus are putting up a desperate fight for freedom against the forces of a tyrannical and absolute government, whilst the American workingman, living amid free political institutions, is doubly submitting to the imposition of fresh economic chains."[26]

---

[21]*New York Evening Call,* August 27, 1908.

[22]Reeve, p. 134.

[23]*Ibid.,* pp. 134, 135.

[24]Johnson, p. 77.

[25]An indication of the obtuseness of the Socialists towards the Blacks can be seen in a leading front prage editorial, July 2, 1908, in the *New York Evening Call:* "What Socialism Has to Offer the Negro." Answering a query by Blacks living in Boston on an article in the *Guardian,* a Negro paper, which suggested a "revolt" against domination by the Republican Party, the *Call* stated: "directly the Socialist Party is doing *nothing* to secure the Negro vote." Socialism offers the Negro "exactly what it offers any other member of society." Only Socialism would make discrimination impossible.

[26]*Harp,* August, 1909.

In the June, 1908 issue, he criticized Socialist Party leaders who were aloof from the worker's struggles: "...We must not be a sect standing apart from the general labor movement, but be instead... that part which comprehends the whole line of march in the midst of the interests of the moment... As you all know by this time," he wrote, " 'Spailpin' [the pseudonym he used on occasion] is unequivocally a proletarian socialist and would rather depend upon the class instincts of the man in the workshop than upon the knowledge of these estimable Socialist men and women who belong to the classes who live upon our labor. Indeed the wisest of these 'intellectuals' are of a similar mind."

By "intellectual," Connolly meant the petty-bourgeois opportunists and Utopians, who wrote and spoke, in varying eloquence, about the class struggle, which was foreign to them. He, himself was a highly accomplished, self-educated worker-intellectual. Nor was he, in fact, anti-intellectual. He made close relationships with many progressive intellectuals, in the United States and in Ireland. One of these, William E. Bohn, one of the editors of the *International Socialist Review,* a college librarian, was amazed to discover the depth of Connolly's scholarship. Writing in the *International Socialist Review,* just after Connolly's execution, Bohn recalled a speech by Connolly at a western university, where he first met him. Connolly, as usual, was suffering financially. "He had abundant debts and little hope. But he made a wonderful speech. As a combination of simple logic and commanding emotional power, that speech stands out in my mind as the best I ever heard."

They strolled across the campus. Connolly was watching the students. He remarked, contemplatively: "I went to a university once...".

"Did you?" asked Bohn, surprised.

"Yes," said Connolly. "I carried cement."

The next day the two went to the university library. "When we came to the section devoted to Irish history, I had a revelation. This hod-carrier ran his eye over the shelves, with the eye of a trained scholar. His commentary on authors, books and historical characters would be valuable to me now, if I were able to reproduce it. One volume after another he took down. With unerring memory, he turned to chapter and page, to point out something applicable to the argument we had been having... To one who had spent years trying to teach students to use books, this man's mastery was astounding." Bohn continued that he was not surprised at the outstanding quality of Connolly's *Labor in Irish History.* Connolly had written, he said, "some of our best pamphlets... he kept his paper going under all but impossible conditions."[27]

As Connolly saw current American life, at the time he was editing the *Harp*, a basic feature was the starving jobless, whose condition was completely without alleviation. He wrote: "Our great American institution today is the bread line. Every night in New York, thousands of men and women stand in line in the public streets, waiting for their turn to receive a few crusts of bread to keep body and soul together. The same in every other city and town from East to West. The breadline is a great American institution. But I do not think I would shoulder a rifle in defense of it."[28]

In his inimitable style, he attacked the savagery inflicted upon the unemployed. He dreamed, he recounted, that he was back in Dublin, demonstrating against British rule. Mounted police were charging and "hordes of policemen on foot, with clubs drawn, were swoopng upon unoffending crowds and smashing in heads." When he awoke, he became aware that he was not in Dublin. "I was in New York during an Unemployment Demonstration. Those smashed heads did not belong to Irish rebel patriots but to American out-of-works, and those club-waving cops were not hirelings of England... they were the paid, freely elected servants of the men whose heads they were smashing."[29]

In August, 1909, in the *Harp,* he again criticized the trends in the Socialist movement of the day. He had been a member of the SPA for a little over a year. "The tendency in America," he wrote, "seems to be largely away from the labor movement." He was appalled at the proposal of a number of Socialists that they remain "neutral" in all trade union matters. The right-wing socialists had stated they would not attack "pure and simple AFL union leadership."

"I confess," he wrote, "that the poor revolting slaves at Philadelphia, McKees Rocks, New Castle, etc., seem to me to be better harbingers of the new era than most of those rose-water revolutionists who look complacently upon the martyrdom of organized labor and tell us that the economic organizations must fight out their own battles...

"None of our duty to help save our brothers and sisters from social destruction?" he asked, "Then, for heaven's sake, what are we here for, if it is not our business to stand by our class in its peril, to bring our superior knowledge of the organization of capital to bear in helping them and in instructing them to perfect organizations of labor."[30]

[27]*International Socialist Review,* July, 1916.
[28]*Harp,* May, 1908.
[29]*Ibid.,* March, 1908.
[30]There were strikes in Pennsylvania in the McKees Rocks steel mills, in the New Castle tin-plate mills and in the needle-trades in Philadelphia.

Connolly, like De Leon, frequently attacked the class collaboration policies of Gompers. The latter had visited the Republican and Democratic nominating conventions in Chicago and Denver. He went, accused Connolly, "begging for crumbs of comfort from the capitalist leaders... instead of giving them the long overdue notice of dismissal. If, when they heard these whining accents, they really heard the voice of labor, they might truly draw a long sigh of satisfaction." Gompers and his crew and especially his tactfulness in dealing with such delicate questions as treachery and betrayal." The workers' alternative was to vote for Debs and the Socialist Party ticket.

The young paper had its financial problems from the beginning. Less than six months after the *Harp* was established, Connolly found it necessary to plan for his second tour in the United States, in the industrial centers of the East and in the Middle West. The papers of William O'Brien contain a number of letters showing the support of SPA branches and IWW locals for the tour, which was announced in the June, 1908 issue. Letters were sent out asking that dates be arranged, "in order to help forward the work of spreading Socialism amongst the Irish in America, and to push the sale of our journal during the presidential year..." The tour, financially, was based entirely on the sale of the newspaper and subscriptions. If one hundred issues of the paper were purchased at retail rates, Connolly would deliver one lecture. Five hundred issues of the *Harp* would entitle the local organization to a week of lectures.[31]

By late summer, the *Harp* announced some eight dates in Massachusetts and Connecticut. Meetings were to be held in Vermont, Maine and New Hampshire.[32] Fourteen meetings were scheduled in the Pottsville, Pennsylvania area, and subsequently Michigan and Illinois were added to the tour.

The tour covered 3,000 miles. As he described it, Connolly spoke "at hundreds of meetings and addressed many thousands of Irish workers on the question of Socialism." He campaigned at every meeting on behalf of Debs.[33]

In accepting the August third date for Malden, Massachusetts, J.D. Williams described the lack of cooperation of local conservative organizations: "The 'Celtic' people refused to rent their hall, claiming it was a social club and their members refused to give it up for any purpose

---

[31]Connolly Archives.
[32]*Harp*, August, 1908.
[33]*Ibid.*, November, 1908.

whatsoever. The 'Hibernian Hall' wanted $10, which price is scandalous. We are now negotiating for an open lot, and failing in that will get a hall in the center of the city."[34]

The Hibernians of Quincy, Massachusetts, however, offered their hall for the Connolly meeting and, according to James F. Foy, "they promise us a crowd of Irishmen, if we can get Comrade Connolly."[35]

In July, letters began to arrive on official stationery of Socialist Party branches. "The Socialist Party Club of Boston," confirmed their date of August 21. They wished to have Connolly give an address "in South Boston... where the vast majority of the people are Irish."[36]

Late in 1908, J.E.C. Donnelly, the *Harp's* manager, reported the results of the tour up to the end of the election campaign in November: "The tour has already been successfully completed in Massachusetts, Maine, New Hampshire, Pennsylvania and Illinois... The national office [of the SPA] has received from all those states the most glowing reports of his abilities, and especially his tactfulness in dealing with such delicate questions as religion." The success of the *Harp* in dealing with the Irish "has been sorrowfully admitted by Catholic papers throughout the country. He is, however, equally entertaining and convincing on the broad question of Socialism in general." Constant education, Donnelly emphasized, even after the election campaign was needed. Connolly's availability for further dates was announced. This time, terms for the lectures were different from before. The fee now would be "five dollars flat per lecture."[37]

By the Spring of 1909, the *Harp* had increased in subscriptions to 3,000.

In November, 1908, Connolly wrote his friend, Matheson about the *Harp* tour and the *People's* campaign against his work: "An evidence of the truthfulness of the *People,* you might have seen in a letter from Philadelphia about two months ago...stating that they had learnt that I had been in Philadelphia for a week and if they had only known it, what they would not have done to me. Would you believe that I began my campaign there by a meeting of about a thousand persons at the City Hall Plaza, and the SLP were out in full force, and asked a lot of questions of

---

[34]The Connolly Archives contain numerous letters making arrangements for the tour. Only a few are quoted here. The J.D. Williams letter to Manager, The Harp, is dated July 26, 1908.

[35]*Ibid.,* Letter, James F. Foy to Comrade Carey, August 19, 1908.

[36]*Ibid.,* Letter, John F. Molloy, Corresponding Secretary, Socialist Party Club of Boston, to Manager, The Harp, August 6, 1908. Another letter on Socialist Party stationery, Local Bridgeport, Branch No. 10, is from Fred Cederholm.

[37]*Ibid.,* Notice headed "Lecture Tour of James Connolly, Editor of 'Harp.' " Signed "Manager, The Harp."

the speaker who got up after me. And although I was a week in the city
after that, they never came near my meetings...".[38]

An echo of the 1902 SLP tour came in a letter from William Brown, a
former Minneapolis member. He recalled the attack on Connolly by "some
fanatical De Leonites" for "a few simple verses... which were published in
the *Workers Republic*... Good luck to you, Connolly, and success to the
Harp," Brown concluded. In the letter was a plan for placing the
publication on Minneapolis newsstands.[39]

In the issue of March, 1909, as a typical instance, letters of support,
enclosing subscriptions came from more than twenty states and industrial
centers, and from Ireland. A Detroit reader, Mrs. Wallace, ordered all
back issues. She wrote: "I would like to study your movement from the
beginning as we found Mr. James Connolly's lecture... extremely
interesting, along lines with which we are not so familiar as we would like
to be." A glowing tribute came from W.P. Ryan, editor of the *Nation,* in
Dublin. Subscriptions came from the South and far West and from
Canada.

Nevertheless, in the July, 1909 issue, Donnelly found it necessary again
to review the *Harp's* finances. There had been no issue the month before.
An appeal for funds in May had not brought the desired response.
Undoubtedly, the fact that Connolly was by this time a full-time, national
organizer for the Socialist Party, made circulation problems more dificult
for the publisher. His article continued in a more cheerful mood: "Now,
however, the readers have helped and the publication will go forward
regularly." This time, news of the poor financial health of the paper
brought responses from all over the country.[40]

Although Connolly was responsible for most of the material appearing
in the *Harp,* by 1909 there were numerous other contributions. Anna
Maley, SPA national organizer for women,wrote on the women's rights
movement, in the September, 1909 issue, the same in which A.M. Simons,
editor of the *Chicago Socialist,* noted the "effectiveness of the *Harp.*"
Justus Ebert and Patrick Quinlan were also contributors.[41] Elizabeth
Gurley Flynn sent news of her tours.

In spite of differences, Connolly had established friendly relations with
the *Gaelic American* and its editor, the old Fenian, John Devoy. The

[38]*Ibid.,* Letter, Connolly to Matheson, November 8, 1908.
[39]*Ibid.,* Letter, William Brown to Manager, Harp, September 28, 1908.
[40]*Harp,* August, 1909.
[41]*Harp,* September, 1909.

Gaelic American was the publication of the Irish-American nationalist Clan na Gael, which was supported by the secret organization, the Irish Republican Brotherhood. Here was established the basis for future cooperation of Devoy, the Brotherhood members, the Irish Volunteers and Connolly, representing labor and the socialists, in 1916 in organizing the Easter Rising in Ireland.

The February, 1908 issue of the *Harp* referred to the *Gaelic American* in an editorial note: "This widely circulated and influential weekly Irish paper, reprinted, with acknowledgment, one of the articles in our January number." Also cited in that issue of the *Harp* was the *Evening Tribune,* of Seattle, which also "published a few compliments about us."

By January, 1909, even wider recognition was given the publication. William Mailly, one of the editors of the *New York Evening Call,* wrote an article for the *Harp,* which included a tribute to Connolly's paper. He also became a member of the Irish Socialist Federation. The *World,* of Oakland, California, announced: "The *Harp...* holds a unique position in Socialist journalism."[42]

A piece which Connolly published in the *Harp* of August, 1908, is notable as a deeply personal expression of his innermost aspriations, which made his own difficulties seem unimportant and incidental:

"In the Dark Ages of Europe, the Irish Race carried the torch of learning and civilization to the benighted races of Europe; may we not hope that Irish apostles of Socialism will ere long be privileged to carry the message of that grander civilization of the future to the masses lost in the dark ages of capitalist bondage?

"May we not hope that another race of Irish missionaries will carry the torch of a sweeter, purer faith of freedom and humanity to a world dying for want of it. If we can leave to our children the knowledge that we, their sires, helped to achieve such a consummation, will we not have won a heritage of honor for the Irish race, such as shall make the generations of the future rise up and call us blessed!"[43]

The young "Rebel Girl," Elizabeth Gurley Flynn commented on Connolly's devotion to his paper: "He performed the 'Jimmy Higgins' tasks with no false pride, and encouraged others to do likewise.

"It was a pathetic sight to see him standing, poorly clad, at the door of Cooper Union, or some East Side Hall, selling his little paper. None of the

---

[42]*Ibid.*
[43]*Harp,* August, 1908.

prosperous, professional Irish, who shouted their admiration for him after
his death, lent him a helping hand at that time. Jim Connolly was an-
athema to them because he was a 'So-cialist.' "[44]

[44]Elizabeth Gurley Flynn, p. 60.

CHAPTER XV

"JOYOUS, DEFIANT SINGING"

Particularly during 1903 and 1904, but frequently throughout his career, James Connolly, to express his devotion to the struggles of the working class and the ultimate objective -- the Workers' Republic -- turned to writing poetry. In 1907, J.E.C. Donnelly, who published the *Harp,* printed a little booklet, entitled *Songs of Freedom by Irish Authors.* Most of the material, and the Introduction, were written by Connolly. Subtitled "The 'Take and Hold' Song Book," it was dedicated "to the industrial and political movement for the emancipation of the working class." The accompanying music to each lyric, consisted of traditional Scotch and Irish airs.

Connolly wrote in his Introduction: "No revolutionary movement is complete without its poetical expression. If such a movement has caught hold of the imagination of the masses, they will seek a vent in song for the aspirations, the fears and the hopes, the loves and the hatreds engendered by the struggle. Until the movement is marked by the joyous, defiant singing of revolutionary songs, it lacks one of the most distinctive marks of a popular revolutionary movement...".[1]

The "Rebel Song," his first attempt, appeared in 1903, in Scotland, when he was the first organizer of the Scottish SLP, which was being born out of the upheaval in the Social Democratic Federation.

Set to music by Gerald Crawford, a young composer of the group, its final stanza declared:

> "Our army marches onward,
>   its face toward the dawn.
> Its trust secure in that one thing
>   the slave may lean upon--

---

[1]Connolly, *Songs of Freedom by Irish Authors.* Copy was made available to us by Internationaal Instituut voor Sociale Geschiedenis,, Amsterdam, Holland. We have since learned that there is also a copy in Villanova University.

The might within the arm of him
who, knowing Freedom's worth
Strikes home to banish tyranny
from off the face of earth."[2]

Connolly's recurring theme was "Freedom," -- freedom of the worker
from capitalist exploitation. Among his poems were: "Hymn to Freedom,"
"Freedom's Sun," "Freedom's Pioneers," "Human Freedom," "Freedom
Our Own," etc. A poem entitled "A Love Song" extolled love for freedom.

"Lift the Flag" appeared in the *Weekly People,* October 3, 1903. It
admonished: "Lift that flag and tenderly guard it; Guard it as lover would
guard his love..." This was the "Flag that beckons to Liberty."[3]

At Christmas, 1903, alone in the United States, homesick for his wife
and children in Ireland, he wrote one of the infrequent poems which
reflected personal feelings.

" 'Tis Christmas Day in Ireland, and I, my lot bewailing
    Am fretting in this western land, so cold
Where the throbbings of the human heart are weak and
unavailing.
    And human souls are reckoned less than gold..."

The "heart-sick Irish exile" turns his face "To that land where love and
poverty can wander hand in hand...".

"The Watchword," which originated during Connolly's stay in the
United States, has been reprinted more often than any other Connolly
poem. It is the first song in the pages of the songbook; it was reprinted in
the *Irish Worker* in 1913 and reissued by the Socialist Party of Ireland in
1914. As the "Watchword of Labor," it was a particular favorite of singers
at the Connolly Commemoration meetings, held by the Transport
Workers Union of Greater New York (C.I.O.) from 1941 to 1952.[4]

---

[2]Bell, p. 48. He wrote: "The 'Rebel Song' is a fine example of his work, and there are many
others, which ought to take their place in a section of our literature, at present woefully
deficient."

[3]Connolly apparently revised his original lines for subsequent publication. Comparison of
his poems, as they appeared later, to the original, showed his efforts to make improvements.
Here, in the earlier edition of this poem in the *People,* such minor differences appear.

[4]Gabriel Fallon answered Sean O'Casey's criticism of "The Watchword of Labor" as too
sentimental, by saying: "Well, there was nothing particularly sentimental about a badly
wounded man, strapped to a stretcher, boldly facing a British firing-squad in the yard of
Kilmainham Gaol." *(Sean O'Casey, The Man I knew,* p. 74.)

It began with the words, "Take and hold," (the De Leonite slogan):

> "O, hear ye the watchword of Labor
> The slogan of they who'd be free.
> That no more to any enslaver
> Must Labor bend suppliant knee...".

Its many stanzas carried the chorus:

> "Then send it afar on the breeze, boys,
>   That watchword, the grandest we've known,
> That Labor must rise from its knees, boys
> And take the broad earth as its own."

"Be Moderate," which first appeared in 1904, is an echo of another Connolly, teasing and satirical. It declared: "Our demands most moderate are. We only want the earth."

One of his most moving poems is "The Legacy" written during what obviously was a low point in his life, probably when he was ill, penniless and desperately at odds with De Leon. The poem is one of the clippings that is in the scrapbook of Eugene V. Debs in the Tamiment Library of New York University.[5]

In the poem, the worker tells his son:

> "...Treasure in your heart this legacy of hate
>   For those who on the poor man's back
> Have climbed to high estate...
>   "...To speed the day... when Labor long opprest
> Shall rise and strike... and from the tyrants wrest
>   The power they have abused so long...".

---

[5]The February, 1908 *Harp* carried Connolly's note: "Since writing my notes for the January *Harp,* I have been down in the Valley of the Shadow, whilst the angels of life and death fought for my poor carcass. Today I am breathing a little freer, but I ask the reader, if he finds my notes a little in the plaintive key, to remember that they came from the sickbed." It is highly conceivable that this poem was written at that time.

Dorothy Swanson, Tamamint Librarian, New York University, wrote us March 7, 1973: "The Connolly poem is in the Debs scrapbooks which, according to library records, were assembled by Debs and indexed by his brother, Theodore."

In February, 1909, "The Festive Song" appeared in the *Harp,* and in the *New York Evening Call* a month later. Connolly, who did not drink, wrote a drinking song for drinking men, of whom he knew many. His toast: "Then fill the cup with liquor up. Pledge every man his neighbor, That in the light of Truth he'll fight. To win the world for Labor."

Several songs, apparently written after Connolly returned to Ireland, were uncovered in the Connolly Archives of the William O'Brien Collection. They have a unique feeling of urgency. "Arouse" calls:

> "Then arouse! ye workers all,
>   Braving scaffold, sword, and ball
> And at Labor's trumpet call
>   Quick appear...
> "For the day we long have sought
>   For which our fathers fought--
> The day with Freedom fraught
>   Now is here!"[6]

Forthright, unsubtle poetry, perhaps, to the ears of the critic. But Connolly's poems represented "joyous, defiant singing" for the rhythmic step of the workers' march to freedom toward the Worker's Republic. To Connolly, these were no empty words, but the fibre of his bones and the consistency of his blood.

---

[6]This song came from the Connolly Archives and probably was written after Connolly's return to Ireland. With the same note of immediacy is "Shake Out Your Banners," also provided by the National Library, which houses the Archives. One stanza declaims: "Joy, joy to our heart that this day, we have seen; When the war-flags of Labor, saluting the light, Of Freedom for mankind, around us doth stream."

CHAPTER XVI

LONGING FOR IRELAND —
A TRYING SPA TOUR

The Socialist Party made use of Connolly's abilities prior to his national tour. On December 20, 1908, he lectured at Brevoort Hall in New York City on "The Labor Movement in Ireland and in America." William Mailley, one of the editors of the *Call* was chairman. Several days later, the *New York Socialist Call* announced that Connolly would tour New York State for the Party.[1]

On the first of the month, Connolly had received a letter from J. Mahlon Barnes, National Secretary, informing him that he had been "placed in nomination as a candidate for member of the National Executive Committee..." The letter asked for acceptance or declination.[2] Connolly involved with his various tours and his writings, did not accept.

The New York State tour proceeded, with the *Call* publicizing and reporting it. A meeting in Poughkeepsie, New York, near the Vassar campus, was held in Odd Fellows Hall, on March third. "There were more men present at the meeting than usual and it was essentially a workingmen's gathering, although there were a large number of Vassar students... as well," the account stated.[3] The tour was successful.

Barnes wrote Connolly in April, to finalize arrangements for the forthcoming extensive national tour. Copies of letters which had been mailed to state secretaries in New Jersey, Pennsylvania, Ohio, Indiana and Illinois were enclosed. These requested that "possibilities of assignment" be examined. Barnes asked Connolly for biographical material and "a cut of yourself, which we may use in getting out proper advertising." He hoped to start the tour early in May.[4]

In many ways, the year ahead was to be the busiest and most diverse year he had yet spent in the United States. It was basically a painful year for

---

[1] *New York Evening Call,* December 15, 1908.
[2] Connolly Archives, Letter, J. Mahlon Barnes to Connolly, December 1, 1908.
[3] *New York Call,* March 11, 1909.
[4] Connolly Archives, Letter, Barnes to Connolly, April 9, 1909.

Connolly; most important to him then was to convert into reality his dream to return to Ireland.

Barnes sent several hundred letters to locals on April 14, 1909. It was Connolly's desire, he wrote, to visit places with a large Irish population. He added: "There is much prejudice against socialism among the Irish and especially among the Irish Catholics and Comrade Connolly is perhaps better fitted to break down this feeling than any other man we have." Terms were five dollars for one meeting, twelve dollars for three. Advertising matter would be furnished free of charge.[5]

The *Call*, in addition to carrying news of the tour, from time to time reprinted excerpts from the *Harp*. A short article by Connolly appeared in June, on the use of opium by the British government as a means of demoralizing the people of India.[6]

Connolly was to be away from home for eleven months. The extent of his travels can be seen from the cities from which he corresponded with William O'Brien, in Ireland, during that time: Washington, D.C., May 24, 1909; Crooksville, Ohio, June 10, 1909; Brazil, Indiana, July 9, 1909; Springfield, Missouri, September 12, 1909; Keystone, Iowa, October 3, 1909; Rock Rapids, Iowa, October 26, 1909; Denver, Colorado, November 2, 1909; El Paso, Texas, December 6, 1909; Tucson, Arizona, December 18 and 20, 1909; Butte, Montana, March 7, 1910 and then on to California. May third, 1910, Connolly wrote O'Brien from his home in New York City.

Connolly now was one of six national organizers for the SPA, a leader in a large socialist organization, with a strong apparatus, including a number of newspapers. Connolly had substantial support. His pamphlet, *Socialism Made Easy,* was becoming increasingly popular. *Erin's Hope,* and other pamphlets which he had written, were being distributed, also, by the Socialist Party.

Financial difficulties, this time, were absent. He received the respectable sum of three dollars a day, plus all expenses, seven days a week, as well as all proceeds from sale of socialist literature.

Nevertheless, his tour was to be carried out under trying circumstances. Touring the middle and far West, Connolly's responsibilities for editing and providing copy for the *Harp* continued, in addition to the daily duties of the tour -- traveling, preparing his lectures, and the constant meetings and interchanges with people, socialist and non-socialist.

5 *Ibid.*, Letter to Locals from Barnes, April 14, 1909.
6 *New York Call*, June 5, 1909.

Added to this, he was increasingly involving himself in Irish problems, through letters and articles, written for Irish and Scottish left-wing publications, on issues of Irish labor, nationalism and Socialism. He was also putting the finishing touches on *Labor in Irish History.*

The small socialist movement in Ireland was growing. There was, however, a lack of skilled leadership. William O'Brien was active in the Dublin Trades Council, but could not be considered a socialist mass leader. James Larkin, the head of the Transport Union, was not yet a full-fledged member of the Socialist Party of Ireland, although he cooperated with it. The organization had no newspaper of its own. This, Connolly had always felt, was basic to the growth of a socialist party. The *Nation,* distributed among the Socialists, was run by the liberal Sinn Feiner, W.P. Ryan. There was no national party. Dublin was the stronghold, with, by far, the largest membership. Connolly began to hope, deeply, that he might help build a strong, effective Irish movement.

During the Socialist Party national tour, weighing on his mind, was the decision he had reached that he must again become part of the struggles in Ireland and that at all costs he must return.

Connolly's longing for the Irish movement, from which he had come, was an old story. In 1909, his eagerness to return, was fanned by exploratory letters from William O'Brien. Their correspondence -- a remarkable series of letters, written during his national tour in 1909 and in 1910 -- came to light after O'Brien's death.

He had already concluded an agreement with the Socialist Party of Ireland that it print and jointly distribute with the Irish Socialist Federation, a number of pamphlets, several written by Connolly. These continuing arrangements and the association of the ISF with the Socialist Party of Ireland went a long way toward healing the wounds of 1903. The Irish Socialists, subsequently, offered to make Connolly their delegate to the coming Second International Congress. Connolly declined, but added: "The offer of your party gave me more pleasure than anything I have experienced since the unfortunate day we had our disagreement."[7]

A letter to Matheson in April, 1908, again revealed Connolly's hunger for Ireland: "Last week I received a letter from Dublin, from a young comrade who, in addition to being in the ISRP, had also been with me in New York... whilst my family were in Troy. He says that a number of comrades have asked him *whether I would be willing to return to Dublin* if

---

[7] Connolly Archives, Letter, Connolly to O'Brien, April 15, 1907.

some provision could be made for my upkeep. They suggested some kind of business... Now, in a letter you sent me, you also suggest that it would be good if I could get home... I wrote to my Dublin comrade, saying that I had all the will and all the desire in the world to get home out of this cursed country, but I can't...

"Give me your opinion on this matter, so that I may either finally abandon hope of repatriating myself or else get something to hope for... I have a hunger to get back among the parties I *disrupted.*" Connolly's friend, undoubtedly, understood the pain and irony of the derogatory word, used by De Leon to describe Connolly's work in the ISRP. Connolly concluded: "If you take any interest in this matter and care to write to my Dublin correspondent, his name and address are John Mulray, 55 Jones Road, Dublin... Do not be afraid that the truth will hurt my feelings, or rather tell it, whether it does or not."[8]

Permeating the Connolly - O'Brien correspondence, are his motives, his ideas, his feelings, ideals. There are expressions of his love for his family and his deep regret for the years of poverty to which he felt he had subjected them, but above all, his bond with his native land -- not Ireland's scenery, but love for its struggle for freedom.

The lengthy, and now very serious, seesawing negotiations with O'Brien began in May, 1909. O'Brien notified Connolly that the Dublin Trades and Labor Council was seeking an editor for a weekly paper. He asked Connolly how much money was required by him as salary.

The letter reached Connolly in Philadelphia, from where he cabled at once: "Fifty shillings."[9] The next day, Connolly wrote O'Brien from Washington, D.C.: "I wish to thank you very much for your thoughtfulness and to express the same feeling for the other comrades who are associated with you... I am more than willing to be repatriated; I am exceedingly desirous for that end.

"I may confess to you," he continued, "that I regard my emigration to America as the great mistake of my life, and as Jack Mulray can tell you, I have never ceased to regret it. Of late I have been studying very attentively the situation in Ireland... and I am very much impressed with the belief that all the conditions are favorable for a forward move in our direction. The thought has filled me with a burning desire to get back, but as an individual, the position was hopeless.

"My family are growing and their needs are pressing." Connolly

---

[8] *Ibid.*, Letter, Connolly to Matheson, April 8, 1908. Emphasis in this letter is Connolly's.
[9] *Ibid.*, Cable, Connolly to O'Brien, May 23, 1909.

informed O'Brien that he was on tour and might, in about six months, collect "some money to spare... but just now I am only painfully recovering from the long financial depression of the winter. If, by any possibility, you get that job for me, the task of raising the money for the passage would fall entirely upon the comrades in Ireland."

Connolly, for the first time in his letters, referred to the tragic accidental death of his daughter, Mona: "Owing to the terrible accident which blighted our last separation, my wife would never consent to make the trip without me accompanying her. *So that if I go to Ireland, I have to bring my family along with me.*" He continued: "To do that would require about two hundred dollars... and I do not see how in heaven that money is to be raised."

Characteristically, changing the somber mood of the letter, he added: "If you get me appointed and can break into the Bank of Ireland when the cashier is not looking, please cable me that amount and I will set out for Ireland in a week or two."

Even what seemed a small chance, called forth a flood of longing: "I am vain enough to believe that I could do good work in Ireland. I am ardent enough to believe that the times are propitious and that our propaganda in the past has borne fruit which could be reaped today--but I am not in Ireland. And I am, as ever, or more than ever, convinced that the propaganda of Socialism amongst the Irish in this country, will wait upon Socialist success in Ireland... You wanted a letter of my position. Here it is. I am dying to go to Ireland. But how? If you can answer that question, future generations (of little Connollys) will rise up and call you blessed."[10]

In July, Connolly wrote again, from Brazil, Indiana. He had been informed by O'Brien that P.T. Daly, Sinn Fein member of the Dublin Trades Council, had been given the editorship. Connolly was deeply disappointed. He wrote: "I wish to thank you all for the comradeship and interest shown in me by your effort to get me that position. It makes me feel that I had not lived in vain, and that you all apparently shared with myself the wish that our unfortunate disagreements should be forgotten, for the sake of our... comradeship and our future hopes. We have at least the consolation that a much worse man than Daly might easily have got the place--one less susceptible to advanced ideas. I am not ashamed to confess that I was moved when I read in your letter that Tom Lyng appeared as my representative. It reminded me of the many fights in which Tom and I

---

[10] *Ibid.*, Letter, Connolly to O'Brien, May 24, 1909.

stood shoulder to shoulder before our cussed hot-headedness made us mistake and misrepresent each other."

Through the years of hardship and controversy with De Leon, Connolly had managed to maintain an outward poise. But his desire to return to his home land was a different matter. "You say in your letter that you hope the matter 'has not knocked me about in any way.' Well, it has. It has upset me entirely. It has aroused the call of Erin in my blood until I am always dreaming of Ireland, dreaming of going back to the fight at home. Now you know, I have a way of trying to realize my dreams. I think I will try to realize this one."

He formulated a new plan, conceding that he would pay his passage. He wrote: "I see my way, by the time this tour is ended, if not before to raise my passage money. But I do not see my way to live after I once more set foot on Irish soil, and that part of the problem is the hardest, as, of course, I could not go into the Dublin slums again to live. One experience of that is enough for a lifetime... My children are now growing up, and it is a part of my creed that when I have climbed any part of the ladder towards social comfort, I must never descend it again. So the problem of repatriating myself is difficult."

In spite of his regular and adequate salary from the SPA, he wrote, "I am not-satisfied here; have not even the enthusiasm for the fight that I had in Ireland and want to get amongst people with whom I feel I have more in common."[11]

A letter from O'Brien, in August, again explored the possibilities. But the Irish Transport Union was in a slump period "since the Dublin strike last December." Perhaps there would be an opening in the union, "if the Cork strike turned out anyway well."

At Trades Hall, in Dublin, a mass meeting had been held to launch a national Socialist Party. In September, 1909, Connolly reported in the *Harp*: "Some months ago, the editor... urged upon our comrades in Ireland, the advisability and necessity of establishing an organization of Socialists in Ireland which would embrace all who accept the Socialist ideal, and leave questions of tactics, etc., to be settled by the conventions and discussions of the party afterward... The advice has been acted upon."[12] This was an important first step.

O'Brien believed Connolly could weld all the socialists into a party that was united, and double the membership. "And I know of no one," he

---

[11] *Ibid.*, Letter, Connolly to O'Brien, July 9,1909.
[12] *Harp*, September, 1909.

wrote, "who would more likely succeed than yourself. For this reason, I intend to do all I can to enable you to come back here." If Connolly could organize a party of four or five hundred, it would solve the financial problem... "but the difficulty is to arrange matters at the start." He thought it might be possible that a *reliable* guarantee of Connolly's salary could be arranged.

For the first time, O'Brien raised the possibility of moving the *Harp* to Dublin. "I was thinking that if you could keep the *Harp* afloat and that you transferred it to Dublin, when coming yourself, it would be a good idea."

Connolly wrote from Springfield, Missouri, in September, congratulating O'Brien on the formation of the new party, giving his thoughts on its scope and principles and repeating his concern for his family's welfare.

"Unless I can see my way to satisfactorily settle that, I would scarcely venture my family upon the chance... It makes me shudder even yet when I think of... those poverty-stricken years, of the hunger and wretchedness we endured to build up a party in Ireland. And you know the outcome."

The SPA planned to continue his tour through the winter, though "National organizers are generally laid off in December, at least they are laid off in November, first Tuesday, and paid up till the end of the year. But I am to be kept on through the winter, and to be brought right through to the Pacific Coast for a trip through Washington, Montana, etc., and back through San Francisco and California... It is the purpose of the national committee to keep me permanently in the field, but although it is the best job I ever had in my life, I am willing to resign it, if I can get a living at *tradesman's wages* in Ireland. But can I?" He declared that he could save money, taken in during the winter, until April, to apply to the purchase of passage. What he had considered impossible, he would attempt to make possible, in order to get to Ireland.

As to the new party! "All that is necessary for your future," he wrote, in part, "is... a resolve to subordinate all purely individual opinions to the general welfare. Comrades should realize that it is better that differences of opinion should be discussed within the party, rather than form a number of small parties, in which to ventilate said differences. This is quite different from the 'broad platform' theory of the politicians. They... refuse absolutely to define their *ultimate goal*... you, on the other hand are precise... about your ultimate goal and only allow differences of opinion to exist as to the manner of realizing it."[13]

---

[13] Connolly Archives, Letter, Connolly to O'Brien, September 12, 1909.

This long letter answered questions raised by O'Brien several months earlier. It was difficult to correspond, under the circumstances. Connolly was constantly on the move. It often took weeks for mail to catch up with him. He expressed skepticism about the "guarantee" proposed by O'Brien. "We had some experience of those guarantees that did not guarantee. But go ahead. See what you can do. I am sure you will realize the seriousness of the step we are discussing. I could get home to Dublin for the opening of the summer season, 1910."[14]

He and O'Brien agreed completely on the necessity of forming a socialist party, united nationally. "I have confidence enough in the Irish workers and in myself to believe that I could succeed in uniting all the Socialist elements in Ireland and help in making them a formidable factor in the life of our country."

He was engrossed with the problems of the socialists in Ireland. They must work out their own destiny, Connolly advised O'Brien. It became clearer later that he had in mind, not only separation from the influence of De Leon, but especially the opportunism of the I.L.P. of England and the SLP of Scotland, still, to an extent, following the sectarian policies of De Leon. "I do agree," commented Connolly, "that the less we interest ourselves in what other socialist parties think of us, the better for the movement in Ireland." There should be no affiliations.

Not for a minute did Conolly forget that Ireland was a country oppressed by a foreign nation. He believed that the English did not recognize the importance of the independence of the Irish Socialist and labor movement. He continued: "Indeed, I have formed a fairly well-developed plan of action for Ireland, and I am afraid many non-Irish Socialists would not understand it, and I am certain that their failure to do so would not cause my soul any uneasiness."

He suggested the printing by the Irish Socialists of *Labor in Irish History,* for distribution both in Ireland and America. His articles had been running serially in the *Harp.*

"I presume you have been reading my articles on 'Labor in Irish History,' " he wrote, and added, "Well, I have finished them." He wanted them issued by a publisher "who could reach the Irish public in Ireland and also in Great Britain." Sheehy-Skeffington, he noted, was a member of the SPI. He asked O'Brien to ask him to approach a London publisher. "His introduction would go a long way to secure a reading, and perhaps acceptance." The book, published "on your side of the water," would "make a sensation, help to arouse attention to the Socialist position, and... help to solve the economic problems of yours truly."[15]

Almost a month later, writing from Keystone, Iowa, he seized on O'Brien's earlier suggestion that they look into the idea of moving the *Harp* to Dublin.

Connolly had been away from New York for many months. It was increasingly difficult to handle the *Harp* from a distance. Donnelly, its Manager, was showing signs of discouragement. Connolly felt that in Dublin, the *Harp* might have more support than in New York City. There were obstacles to the move. The *Harp* was losing money.

He requested estimates on the cost of printing in Ireland, "and send the figure to me at once...The next step would be to fix a date for its publication in Dublin (which need not wait upon my return) and the circulating of *all* Socialist bodies in Ireland and Great Britain... You see, I am proceeding upon the idea that I am going back to Dublin." He added, somberly: "Perhaps I am doomed to disappointment. It would break me up completely if I was."[16]

As it turned out, the timing of the move was fatal to the *Harp*.

From Rock Rapids, Iowa, Connolly replied to O'Brien's letter, informing him that publication of *Labor in Irish History* had been arranged. His focus on returning to Ireland is reflected in the casual manner in which he accepted this important news. Connolly wrote, simply: "Will send on the manuscript as soon as it is out of the hand of the typewriter." But O'Brien's silence regarding Connolly's return seemed ominous. "You say not one word about the other matter, my getting to Ireland. Have you abandoned it or found the SPI was not sympathetic? *Please* let me know as it will have a great effect upon my plans to know whether I am destined for exile or for Ireland. Yours anxiously."

A postscript emphasized: "Do not hesitate to tell me the truth about the outlook, and forgive my impatience."[17]

While Connolly was touring the West, meetings of the Irish Socialist Federation continued to be held in New York. In August, a meeting was held to ratify Edward F. Cassidy's nomination for Mayor on the Socialist Party ticket.[18] An article by John Wall, in the *Call*, reported frequent open-

---

[15] *Ibid.*

[16] Connolly Archives, Letter, Connolly to O'Brien, October 3, 1909.

[17] *Ibid.*, Postal, Connolly to O'Brien, October 20, 1909.

[18] *New York Call*, August 5, 1909.

air meetings. "Who has not seen the great, green banner that bombards the crowds at 38th Street and 125th twice a week?"[19]

One meeting, reported in early November, bore an augury for Ireland's future. It strengthened the growing bond which brought nationalists, socialists and union members to fight shoulder to shoulder in the 1916 Easter uprising. The main speaker at the ISF meeting was the old Fenian, O'Donovan Rossa, called by Devoy, "The Unconquerable Rebel."[20] Imprisoned in England in 1865, he had come to the United States many years ago, great protests having forced his release.

Gladstone's "Liberal" government had suppressed the fact that a number of the Fenian prisoners in England had been tortured to death or driven insane. The First International, led by Karl Marx, initiated a successful world-wide campaign for the release of the Fenians. Marx's daughter, Jenny, in a series of articles in the French newspaper, *Marsellaise* (reprinted around the world) broke the conspiracy of silence, exposed atrocities against O'Donovan Rossa and shamed Gladstone before world opinion.[21] When Rossa spoke for the Irish Socialist Federation, he had been in exile 38 years. In spite of his erratic theories, his unquenchable, rebellious spirit against British imperialism, won the esteem of Irish militants.[22]

Rossa warned, at the meeting, that British imperialism could never be trusted. "The English Parliament," he said, "is forever promising Home Rule to Ireland -- tommorrow. But tomorrow never comes." According to the *Call*, the meeting in Codington's Sixth Avenue Restaurant in New York City, was attended by "half a hundred members of the Irish Socialist Federation." Justus Ebert was one of the Socialist speakers. Timothy Walsh and Patrick Quinlan joined him on the rostrum.[23]

Connolly now reached Denver, Colorado. Unaware that a letter from O'Brien was on the way, with the bad news that the SPI had rejected Connolly's terms for his return, Connolly wrote him, November 2, 1909, in connection with publication of the *Harp*: "I was glad to see that the

[19] *Ibid.*, August 28, 1909.
[20] *Ibid.*, November 1, 1909.
[21] Marx and Engels, *Ireland and the Irish Question*, pp. 379-403; for Jenny Marx's articles, pp. 275-299 for articles and letters on Rossa. Also pp. 155-164, 166, 323-325.
[22] An example of Rossa's position was his lack of understanding of the Paris Commune. For Marx's comment on Rossa's political line, see *Ireland and the Irish Question*, p. 299 and Note 301, p. 469. For the attitude of Marx and Engels on mistakes of the Fenians, including their conspiratorial methods, p. 441, Note 134 and p. 145. John Devoy, pp. 328, 331, 342. For more on Rossa, Connolly, *Labor and Easter Week*, 1916, p. 69. See also pp. 71, 75.
[23] *New York Call*, November 1, 1909.

Nation's estimate made it possible for me to give them the order...I propose issuing from Dublin with the January issue." He did not wish the Irish socialists to completely bear the burden of the *Harp*. He continued: "As during our unpleasantness in Dublin, it was freely stated that the paper was a drag upon the party, and as that feeling may still exist, I propose shouldering the responsibility for the paper myself. If the party in Ireland wish otherwise, the initiation for another arrangement must come from them. Some comrades in America will help me as individuals. When I get back to Dublin, if I do get back, we can take stock anew."

He offered to pay one pound a month, "to any person the party in Dublin likes to name, who will undertake to act as sub-editor and manager of the paper, including posting the copies to subscribers." Referring once more to *Labor in Irish History*, Connolly added: "Will send Sheehy-Skeffington copy of book, as soon as it is out of the hands of the stenographer."[24]

The next day, from Montrose, Colorado, he gave O'Brien further suggestions on the *Harp*. Donnelly was unwilling, or no longer able, to sustain its financial burdens. This would make it necessary for Connolly to handle both American and Irish editions, "but if you in Ireland will cordially cooperate with me in securing an Irish sale, and also a sale in Great Britain, perhaps we will win out..." He added: "I am certainly rushed to catch trains and make connections and ride on stage coaches, and up here in the Rocky Mountains, it leaves me no time to do anything. I hope you will get someone to accept the post of manager and make things move."[25]

November 19,1909, from Durango, Colorado, he alluded, somewhat testily, to the unacknowledged one hundred copies of *Socialism Made Easy* and the hundred copies of *Songs of Freedom*, which he had contributed to the SPI, at his own expense, at an "expenditure of at least ten dollars on my part, and as I have to earn my money pretty hard, I want to know if the books reached the party." The letter also referred to distribution of *Erin's Hope* in Ireland, and, with obvious frustration at the length of time it took mail to reach him on his travels, he asked that letters be sent him "*please* [underlined several times] care of Mahlon Barnes, at the national office of the Socialist Party in Chicago. "It saves a week in time."[26]

[24] Connolly Archives, Letter, Connolly to O'Brien, November 2, 1909.
[25] *Ibid.*, Letter, Connolly to O'Brien, November 3, 1909.
[26] *Ibid.*, Letter, Connolly to O'Brien, November 19, 1909.

From El Paso, Texas, O'Brien was notified by Connolly that copy for
the first issue of the *Harp* to appear in Dublin, had been sent to the *Nation*.
He still had not received O'Brien's pessimistic letter, containing the adverse
decision of the SPI. Nevertheless, Connolly was uneasy.

"In a recent letter...you said that I supposed that the matter of arranging
for me in Ireland was 'easy'. I don't know where you got such an idea, but I
wonder at you writing it to me. I had thought earnestly and seriously that
you and I and all of us had got lessons enough upon the folly of judging or
guessing what were another man's thought -- that way has all kinds of
quarrels as in the past. Let us avoid them in the future. Remember that I
am absolutely in the dark not only as to what opinion, if any, the Dublin
comrades entertain of me, but even as to the personnel of the Dublin
comrades, and still more as to the method by which you proposed to
broach the subject. My *last* recollections of the Dublin comrades are not
happy ones. Please do not revive them. I only know that I would rather
work in Ireland than anywhere else, *for the cause.* Apart from the cause,
Ireland has no attractions for me."[27]

Connolly's hopes for repatriation were once more shattered by O'Brien's
letter dated November 30, 1909, which finally caught up with him in
Tucson, Arizona, in December. It was a sharp and painful blow. The whole
matter of Connolly working as an SPI organizer "has fallen through", at
least for a year, O'Brien informed him. O'Brien depicted a party of only
eighty members, most of whom did not know Connolly personally. As to
the *Harp*, O'Brien had based his suggestion that Connolly move to Dublin
on the basis that Connolly was coming with it. Without Connolly,
everyone was opposed to the move. They all felt that the *Nation* met their
needs.[28]

O'Brien, despite all this, had not given up and was still looking for a way
out. Connolly himself, he wrote, could tip the scales. "If it were only
possible for you to be on the spot and discuss the matter of your coming
here with the members, I feel sure all difficulties would be overcome, but
the idea of taking you out of a good job, and bringing yourself and family
3,000 miles frightens the most of the members." He suggested a short tour
of about a month, during Connolly's "idle" period, "but I suppose this is
out of the question?"

[27] *Ibid.*, Letter, Connolly to O'Brien, December 6, 1909.
[28] Greaves, p. 234. He states that the Sinn Feiners around the *Nation*, though inclined
toward socialism, were uninclined to identify with it, since they wanted no split with Arthur
Griffith, leader of Sinn Fein, who was, at that time. opposed to any alliance with labor or the
socialists.

Connolly was dismayed at this letter, and another which rejected all responsibility for the *Harp*. He wrote O'Brien: "Received your two letters, and to say that their contents surprised me is stating the matter faintly." The *Harp* would be printed in Dublin, Connolly reiterated, whether or not the Dublin comrades participated. He repeated arrangements made with the *Nation*. He simply needed someone to handle the details in Dublin. That person would only need to give three days a month to the job, and Connolly would pay him. "If the Socialist Party in Ireland does not want to touch the paper, I don't care," he wrote. He had transferred the publication to Dublin, "becuase printing is cheaper and it would appeal more coming from Ireland."

His chagrin at the rejection by the Dublin Socialists evoked the most emotional and subjective response up to this time in his letters. "You tell me that the comrades say I will lose money on it. What the devil do they know about it? Do they know how many subscriptions I get per month or anything else about the matter? I am old enough to know what I am doing and my days for guileless trust on the *comradeship* of Socialists is long since over."

Concerning the suggestion of an exploratory short tour, Connolly sharply criticized O'Brien for not carrying out his request to send notices to the British Socialist press. "If you had, I could, I am certain, maintain myself between the two countries, until things were ripe enough in Ireland. But to take a trip to Ireland to *beg* the comrades there to help me to come back permanently -- excuse me, friend, I ate that bread once and it was made very bitter.

"When I go to Ireland, my family will go with me, or I do not go. Please help me to get the paper published in Dublin, irrespective of whether I return or not and I will forever remember you in my prayers."[29]

It took Connolly two days to cool off, doubtlessly after agonizing hours of reevaluation and reconsideration. He wrote from Tucson again: "I now write to you again, in the dread that my last letter was misunderstood and that you might think that it was your failure to obtain a *guarantee* I was surprised at. This was not the case." His hurt still showing, he bitterly commented, "although I did wonder at your misconception of the attitude of your comrades. I can only take it that their refusal to *tell how far they could go* in this direction of your proposals is as delicate a hint as I could get."

In connection with his relationship to O'Brien: "I want to thank you for

[29] Connolly Archives, Letter, Connolly to O'Brien, December 18, 1909.

your offer, and assure you that I deeply appreciate your kindness, and regret that you and I seem always fated to misunderstand each other. But I always admired your steadfastness to principle and believe that you are really anxious to help me, in the belief that thereby you are helping the cause."

Once more, what had seemed impossible before, again became a possibility, by reason of the depth of his need to return. Connolly's opposition to a trip to Ireland, in advance of his family, was weakening: "I would cheerfully go if my Irish comrades *asked* me, but for me to ask them is another proposition."[30]

An interval of nearly three months elapsed in the correspondence, while Connolly continued the long tour as SPA national organizer. In March, 1910, from Butte, Montana, Connolly again established communication with O'Brien, who had supplied him with several Dublin newspapers. The letter begins: "Although your efforts on my behalf fell through, you must not think that I am no longer desirous of keeping up our correspondence. I am anxious that you shall, now and then, as your position permits, drop me a few words upon the state of affairs socialistic in Dublin. I received your papers and thank you now for same."

He inquired about the circulation and reception of the January *Harp*, and asked for news of old friends. He remarked that he had been invited to tour Canada. In the meantime, he had discovered that three chapters of *Labor in Irish History*, which he had sent to be typewritten, had been lost in the mails. "I am afraid I will have to write it all over again, which will mean a great loss of time, and possibly not be able to locate the sources from which I quoted before."

He was now faced with the undeniable fact that there was no choice, but to leave his family in America for a time, and go to Ireland alone, to arrange for his future there -- or give up his return entirely. He decided, however reluctantly, in favor of the former. He continued his letter: "Since my last letter to you, I have been considering that there might be more practical wisdom in your suggestion that I take a trip home [home, in his mind, defined now, forever, as Ireland] to look the ground over than I thought at the time. If upon more consideration, I resolve to do so, would your offer hold good and would anybody else be interested enough to aid in the same manner? I understand this is nothing definite, no haste required. I could not dream of such a *mere experimental trip* or trip of exploration, before the end of the summer *possibly*."[31]

30 *Ibid.*, December 20, 1909.
31*Ibid.*, March 7, 1910.

He again faced the question of financial security for himself and his family, versus a shaky financial situation in Ireland, when he was offered backing by Socialist Party left-wingers to start a new Socalist paper in the United States. He wrote O'Brien: "They have promised a great deal of help all over the country...but I replied that if once I became moored into a constant job of that kind, I might bid farewell forever to my dreams of returning to Ireland. The work would be too engrossing. So I asked for time to consider, and in the considering, your suggestion cropped up again. Write me freely." A postscript added: "Just received a letter from J.W. O'Beirne that Larkin has accepted the position of manager of the *Harp*. Good."[32]

O'Brien replied a month later. He had put the matter before the Dublin party. Out of 21 members present, only Lyng, Mulray and McManus knew Connolly personally. However the meeting officially voted to agree to a tour by Connolly. O'Brien established a Connolly Tour Committee and arranged to establish a guarantee fund for the purpose, presuming that Connolly would also tour England and Scotland. He requested a prompt reply.

The Western tour completed, Connolly was with his family in New York when he received the letter, which, as usual, had followed him from city to city.

Early in May, 1910, Connolly cast the die and agreed to go to Ireland. In the interim, he, apparently, had written a rather negative letter to Larkin, which again spoke of his dilemma.

"I suppose," he wrote O'Brien, "after you saw my letter to Larkin, you' are inclined to swear." He confessed: "Well, the fact is that I am torn between desire and fear. I am letting 'I dare not' wait upon 'I would.' But in order to put the matter to a final issue, my wife and myself had a Committee of Ways and Means, with the understanding that its decision should be final. So we have decided to inform you that *I will be in Dublin on the last week in July*. This is *definite*. So go ahead."[33]

Having made the decision, Connolly enthusiastically planned details of the tour with O'Brien. Answering O'Brien's question as to where he wanted to go, he replied as a disciplined "party man." He declared: "Well, I want to go where I can do the most good. And men and women in Ireland are the best judge." He had also made clear in his letter to the *Nation* that the SPI should be consulted regarding the contents of the *Harp*. He did not intend

---

[32]*Ibid.*
[33]*Ibid.*, Letter, Connolly to O'Brien, May 3, 1910.

to act independently.

"I would suggest that your Committee should inform the Socialist Party that the Committee is bringing me to Ireland, but that it wishes to place my services at the disposal of the SPI, as say, national organizer, whilst I am in the country." The party could arrange meetings for him as they desired. "I think a week in Belfast will be well spent." He wanted to spend at least a month in Ireland, then to tour Great Britain, appearing also at Independent Labor Party branches in Scotland, as well as in meetings for the Socialist Labor Party in Glasgow.

Connolly requested that O'Brien ask the Manchester and Liverpool branches of the ILP to undertake to arrange the tour of England, providing that Jim Larkin was not available to do so. Otherwise Larkin, who had made the offer, should take care of this. This tour should be so organized, Connolly suggested, as to facilitate his permanent move to Ireland.

In conclusion, he made a firm commitment: "Have no fear of any change in my intentions."[34]

A week later, at the request of the Socialist Party, Connolly undertook the last position he held in the United States. He went to New Castle, Pennsylvania, to act as Managing Editor of the *New Castle Free Press*. This last assignment for the Socialist Party of America took him into the heart of the American industrial scene -- the Pittsburgh steel area, where foreign-born workers, led by Socialists and IWW members, were responding to an important challenge by the Steel Trust.

[34]*Ibid.*

CHAPTER XVII

CONFRONTING THE STEEL TRUST

When the steel workers of the Pittsburgh area went on strike in 1909, they confronted a formidable adversary -- the U.S. Steel Trust. In New Castle, Pennsylvania, 30 miles from Pittsburgh, leadership was provided by two radical newspapers: the Socialist weekly, *The Free Press,* and the IWW paper, *Solidarity.* In the course of the strike, editors of both papers were jailed on fabricated charges, and Connolly, in the Spring of 1910, was called upon to become temporary Managing Editor of *The Free Press.* It was his final rehearsal in the United States for coming union struggles in Ireland.

Connolly, in lectures and in the *Harp*, had paid close attention to the strike. [1] Its main issue, he wrote, was the right of workers to organize; "The Steel Trust has declared that it will not tolerate a trade union in the steel industry." He agitated for industrial unionism as the strategy for the strike.

Two strikes began in the middle of the summer in 1909: one in the Pressed Steel Car Company, at McKees Rocks; the other in the American Sheet and Tin Plate Company, in eleven mills throughout the area. While Robert Hunter urged the Socialist Party's National Convention to remain neutral in trade-union problems, Connolly used the lesson of McKees Rocks to preach the absolute necessity for forming industrial unions to achieve victory. [2]

The workers of the Pressed Steel Car Co., a subsidiary of U.S.Steel, in McKees Rocks, struck, in July, 1909, in reaction to the declaration by the company that it would cease dealing with the union and institute the "open shop".

On June 1, 1909, the American Sheet and Tin Plate Company, also owned by U.S.Steel, notified the American Association of Iron, Steel and Tin Workers (AFL) that first there would no longer be union recognition, that its contract would not be renewed and the "open shop" would prevail; and, second there would be a three percent wage cut. On June 30th, 11,000

---

[1] *Harp,* August, 1909.
[2] *Call,* February 12, 1910.

workers walked out in Western Pennsylvania. The majority were foreign-born and unorganized by the union. The AAIST remained leader of this strike, the AFL union representing the interests of the skilled, native-born workers.

Three thousand tin mill workers went on strike in New Castle, The strike lasted into the middle of 1910. The IWW local cooperated with members of the AFL union, but not without criticism of its leadership. The strike formally ended in defeat on August 23,1910. The McKees Rocks struggle, under the leadership of the IWW, was victorious.

The New Castle Socialist Party members, who were also members of the IWW, distributed thousands of copies of *The Free Press*, house by house in McKees Rocks. Charles McKeever, editor of the paper, was elected, in the heat of the struggle, on the Socialist ticket, to City Council of New Castle. He and the other leading Socialists of the area who were involved in the New Castle strike, also acted in an advisory capacity in McKees Rocks, meeting with strike committees regularly.[3]

Connolly had visited the area several times, during the tours for the *Harp* and for the Socialist Party. On the occasion of a two-day visit to New Castle on October 31 and November 1,1908, he lectured on "Industrial Unionism" at Socialist Hall. *The Free Press* announced his visit under a front page headline: "*Very Special.*" A second front page story challenged Rev. Father Joseph V. Sharp, "or any other preacher or politician" to publicly debate with Connolly on the question of Socialism.[4] A week later, the publication printed an article from the *Harp*, by Connolly, on "Socialism and the Catholics."[5]

The situation of the steel workers, described in surveys by colleges and social foundations, was reported and commented upon Connolly in the *Harp*. "Systematic overwork, pushed to the point of manifest cruelty, especially in the steel mills...where the working schedule is a twelve-hour shift for seven days a week...Wages...adjusted to the needs of a single man in a lodging house," were several hardships to which he pointed. And the family? "Family life is destroyed, not in any imaginary way, but by the appalling number of preventable accidents, and a typhoid fever rate that has already been commented upon throughout the civilized world as a disgrace to the American people."[6]

---

[3]Foner, Vol. 4, p. 288.
[4]*The Free Press*, October 31, 1908.
[5]*Ibid.*, November 7, 1908.
[6]*Harp*, August and September, 1909. Included was a survey by Professor John R. Commons, Labor Reports, University of Wisconsin; quoted were Florence Kelley; E.B. Butler, Sage Foundation; and Crystal Eastman of the New York Bar.

Father A.F. Toner, pastor of St. Mary's Roman Catholic Church of McKees Rocks, was horrified by treatment of workers in the Pressed Steel Car Company. "Men are persecuted, robbed and slaughtered," the priest accused. They "...are forced to sacrifice their wives or daughters to the villainous foremen and little bosses, to be allowed to work...Scores of men were being killed and no record made of their deaths," Connolly quoted the priest.[7]

When accosted by citizens who responded to the exposure of the conditions which caused the strike, President Hoffstat of U.S. Steel, declared: "We buy labor in the cheapest market."[8]

One of the grievances of the McKees Rocks men was the gang or pool system, under which their pay was decided from week to week, with no accounting made on the method of determination. Some men were given $1.00 a day for a twelve and a half hour day. Others were given $1.00 for three days work.

The steel magnates were living like kings. In September, 1908, *The Free Press* reported that William H. Singer, a director of U.S. Steel, gave a dinner on the occasion of his golden wedding anniversary. Beside the plate of each of his two sons and two daughters lay an envelope containing a "favor" of four million dollars. To the steel workers, the lesson was clear. Their poverty had provided this enormous gift.[9]

Sixteen nationalities were involved in the Pressed Steel Car Co. strike at McKees Rocks. A committee, representing all the nationalities, which included the IWW - Socialist members, soon assumed leadership.

The Trust utilized hundreds of company thugs, deputy sheriffs, state constabulary, etc., against the strikers, who armed in self defense. An attempt to evict the strikers from their shacks was launched. The strikers and their wives answered by mass picketing. Nearly one hundred strikers were injured in the battle which ensued. Twenty-five steel workers were arrested and charged with inciting to riot. Refusing to meet with an elected committee of strikers, the President of the mill declared: "There is no strike."

Friends of the strikers distributed twenty wagon loads of food on July 24th. On November 11th, Steve Howat, a striker, was killed on the picket line. Thousands of workers and their families attended his funeral. The strike committee issued the unadorned warning: "For every man you kill,

---

[7]*Harp,* August, 1909.
[8]Foner, Vol. 4, p. 288.
[9]*The Free Press,* September 19, 1908. See Foner, pp. 282-295.

we will kill one of you."

By August 15th,1909, the IWW, openly, had taken over the strike, under the auspices of its Car Builders Industrial Union. William Trautmann spoke to a meeting of 8,000 people. Connolly's friend, Ben Williams, was stationed in New Castle and, with Charles McKeever, became an active leader of the McKees Rocks strike.

On Sunday, August 22, pickets ordered a notorious strike-breaking sheriff, Harry Exler, off a trolley headed to the mill. Exler drew his gun, and was felled in the exchange of shots. State troopers attacked the picket line and eight strikers were killed; in addition, many were wounded. Also killed were two scabs and a mounted trooper.

Arrests by the score followed. *The Pittsburgh Post Dispatch* admitted: "Exler's own actions and his very profane reply to the strikers was the cause of his death and the terrific battle that waged afterward."[10] The *Chicago Tribune*, on the contrary, editorially demanded: "For rioters of this type, the order issued to the troops, 'Fire to Kill' is the only proper treatment."[11]

Frank Morrison, Secretary-Treasurer of the AFL, summarized the attitude of the craft union leaders. The strike was caused, he said, by "ignorant and foreign labor, aliens who do not speak *our* language, or understand our institutions."[12]

On September 8, 1909, the McKees Rocks strikers, victorious, marched back to work in a body. However, after some months, the Steel Trust again moved to take away the benefits they had won. They failed to discharge the scabs as promised, and reduced the wages of the screw boys. The entire plant again downed tools. The American flag was invoked in attempts to divide the native-born workers in the craft union from the bulk of the industrial union workers who were, on the whole, foreign-born. The native-born Americans were called upon by the company to become strikebreakers, after the second walk-out.

As Connolly described it: "After the foreign-born workers had won the strike, by organizing upon the industrial plan and drawing out on strike all the employees whom the foolish craft unionism of the Amalgamated Association of Iron and Tin Workers had refused to organize, the company...proceeded to violate their pledges...Whereupon the men struck again. But the American workingmen decided to break faith with their

---

[10]*Industrial Union Bulletin,* September 2, 1909.
[11]*Ibid.*
[12]*Ibid.*

fellow workers and to march back with the American flag flying at their head, asserting that they would 'shoot to kill,' anyone who dared to 'desecrate the flag.' ...as dastardly a piece of treachery as Benedict Arnold was ever guilty of, betraying their brothers in the hour of conflict... Oh, Patriotism, what crimes are committed in thy name!"[13]

The IWW was finally able to announce the terms of victory for "Industrial Union No. 209 of the IWW at McKees Rocks." Included in the agreement was establishment of a five and a half day week and discharge of any foreman accepting a "bribe" for awarding work. Connolly observed, in the *Harp*: "There is now a union to enforce this demand." Other terms included abolition of the pooling system, an over-all wage increase of five percent and restoration of wages from the 1907 wage-cut.[14]

In the Tin Plate strike, although the Socialists within the craft unions exerted influence, the leadership remained in the hands of the AFL craft union machine. Despite this, there were occasional auxiliary strikes. In the face of threatened terror, the mechanical department of the large Shenango Mill walked out in a body, in response to the firing of leaders of the anti-strikebreaking movement in the mill. The action was attributed to IWW members within the Amalgamated Association who were agitating against importation of scabs.[15]

The Free Press made constant suggestions for strengthening the strike. A week after the victory at McKees Rocks, the publication hailed the achievement of the 6,000 "foreigners." In the New Castle Tin Plate strike, by contrast, it reported, the Amalgamated strikers "sit around in their little picket tents, watching scabs go in and out, morning and evening, big as life, in automobiles with salaried chauffeurs."[16] The "independent" Tin Plate mills, as everyone knew, were also owned by U.S. Steel. The New Castle city government, accommodating to Steel Trust interests, called out the state constabulary early.[17] Police and private thugs arrested every striker found in the vicinity of the plants. As late as December, 1909, when the strike was six months old, 24 strikers were jailed because they refused to get off the streets near the main mill on strike.[18]

The can factory, in the seventh ward, struck two weeks before Connolly arrived in New Castle. The workers were unorganized, yet everyone joined

---

[13]*Harp*, October, 1909.
[14]*Ibid.*, November, 1909.
[15]*The Free Press*, July 31, 1909.
[16]*Ibid.*,September 11, 1909.
[17]*Ibid.*, August 14, 1909.
[18]*Ibid.*, December 18, 1909.

the strike -- press hands, slitters, feeders -- all. In this mill, very small children were working from 7 A.M. until 6 P.M. The main grievances were speed-up and long hours. On Monday morning, 75 girls and 75 boys walked out. On Tuesday, the workers were able to return. Their demands had been granted. Hours were reduced by one-half hour and wages increased $.88 to $1.05 a day. The strikers were taken back in a body.[19]

When the strike began, the girl assorters told the strikers: "We'd like to go out on strike too."[20] The AA turned down the girls' pleas and refused to admit them into the union.

The Steel Trust was granted an injunction against the Tin Plate strikers. By October, 1909, destitution of the New Castle workers was extreme. Children could not attend school, since they had no shoes nor clothing. *The Free Press* called for a march to demand food and clothing from the Poor Commissioner.[21]

In the Spring of 1910, with the Tin Plate mill strike still dragging, the Steel Trust decided to wipe out the troublesome socialists and *The Free Press*. A series of arrests and indictments was initiated. The Mayor and other city officials cooperated. Eleven socialists were arrested, charged with non-compliance with a minor law concerning publications, which called for publishing the names of "all its owners, management and editors -- which in practice is not observed by Pennsylvania papers,"[22] as *The Free Press* commented.

Those arrested were charged with being connected with *The Free Press* and *Solidarity*. The employees of the latter, throughout the persecutions, used the example of the Spokane Free Speech fights as their model. They refused to give bail or hire lawyers and remained in jail.

The militant labor and socialist movement sprang to the defense of the New Castle Socialists. Bill Haywood rode in, to speak at a mass meeting. Justus Ebert, Connolly's friend, helped to organize the defense. Charles Ervin, editor of the Amalgamated Clothing Workers' Journal, "Advance," wrote about the frame-up in the *New York Call*.

At the municipal hearing, the Socialists filed a list of Pennsylvania publications which ignored the technicalities which caused the arrests. The Steel Trust *New Castle News* had violated the same law, they charged, but was found "Not Guilty." This, on the very day the workers of *The Free*

---

[19]*Ibid.*, April 30, 1910.
[20]*Ibid.*, July 17, 1909.
[21]*Ibid.*, October 23, 1909.
[22]*Ibid.*, March 1, 1910.

Press and *Solidarity* were sent to jail.

A few days later, a more serious charge was levied. Four men were rearrested, charged by Chief of Police Gilmore with being "wicked, malicious, *seditious* and evil-disposed persons," and held for a jury trial. Aimed principally against McKeever, the charges were based on old English "common law" of several centuries past and revived the "alien and sedition" laws, which Thomas Jefferson had fought.

A third charge was also developed against McKeever. On the statement of a stool-pigeon, he was charged with conspiring to blackmail a Catholic priest, "by means of menace and force." The case was dropped, since the priest renounced the statement he had been prevailed upon to sign.[23] The Socialist Party, particularly the industrial unionist left-wingers, felt action had to be taken to assure the continued publication of *The Free Press*. They requested that Connolly move into the situation. He agreed to take over editorship of the paper, temporarily, and kept the post until he departed for Ireland. The May 14, 1910 edition of *The Free Press* bore Connolly's name as Managing Editor and McKeever's as Owner.

The issues of May 14th, 21st and 28th carried Connolly's exposures of red-baiting by the small businessmen. Organized into the Business Men's Exchange, they worked hand-in-glove with the Steel Trust, and threatened to deny credit to all strikers.[24] Connolly described them as acting as "jackal to the capitalist lion in the hunting of Labor."[25]

While many columns of *The Free Press,* necessarily, were devoted to the defense, the court hearings and trials, Connolly issued a lively and well-rounded paper. The issue of May 14, 1910 contained an article headed, "Labor War in Ireland," which reported on the strike of longshoremen in Cork, led by "James Larkin, national organizer of the Transport Workers Union, who is also sub-editor of the *Harp,* the only Socialist paper published in Ireland." Larkin, also, had been arrested on trumped up charges and there were other similarities to the New Castle strike -- government oppression, terror, use of strikebreaking thugs and the courts.

The issue prior to Connolly's becoming editor had printed a racist article which implied that Blacks, mainly, were involved in the prostitution racket.[26] He undoubtedly remembered the controversy over the Transvaal

---

[23]*Ibid.,* May 14, 1910.
[24]*The Free Press,* May 14, 20, 28, 1910, contained articles by Connolly protesting the business men's activities in the strike.
[25]*The Free Press,* May 14, 1910.
[26]*Ibid.,* May 7, 1910.

Labor Party letter to the SLP, and the reply of the NEC, which De Leon, correctly, criticized as too weak. His answer to the blatant racism of the previous issue of the paper was to print a letter from Tom Mann, dated March 4, 1910 and sent to him from Johannesburg, South Africa.

Connolly described Mann as "so long and favorably known as a Socialist labor leader in England." The letter, he stated, described "some of the conditions which attend the martyrdom of labor in South Africa." Mann's letter discussed the racism of whites in the Rand gold mines near Johannesburg, where 50 companies owned 130 mines. The "natives" outnumbered whites "about nine to one." The white bosses left the worst work to the Blacks. "Of the 30,000 white 'workers'... only 4,000 were organized", and "none of the 'natives'."

The white "workers" made the contract and hired "natives" to do the work. "To be quite frank," wrote Mann, "many of the whites... whilst holding the natives in contempt and treating them accordingly, are quite willing that the native should do the hard, the heavy and the dirty work and this for about two shillings a day." Under the circumstances, both whites and blacks got dust in their lungs, but the latter "survive only one year, compared to the average life of the white miner working with the drill -- no more than eight years." Mann concluded his letter: "The workers have no power here."[27]

Guidelines for the conduct of SPA industrial unionists in the forthcoming Socialist Party convention were presented in an editorial written by Connolly: "Never has capital been so fiercely aggressive," but "never has labor shown a... greater readiness to follow revolutionary instincts." The industrial unionists, he advised, should not insist that the convention pass a resolution endorsing the IWW or industrial organization, as opposed to craft unionism. The development of the SPA towards industrial unionism should proceed "from the bottom up." He explained: "The only endorsement that is of value is to be found in the action of its members joining it and helping it."[28]

After observing the situation in New Castle for two weeks, in the May 28th issue, Connolly discussed strike strategy in a major editorial, "The

[27]*Ibid.,* May 14, 1910.
[28]*Ibid.* The 1910 SPA convention was marked by entrenchment and control by the right wing. Hillquit's anti-immigration stand was adopted by a vote of 55 to 50, demonstrating the strength of the left-wing. It was also at this convention that Mother Ella Reeve Bloor's resolution, calling for the SPA to participate in the suffrage movement, was defeated. She, Rose Pastor Stokes and other socialist women set up their own committees for participation in the suffrage movement. Reeve, pp. 132-137; Kipnis, pp. 287 ff.

Tactics of Labor." In the face of certain defeat, the lack of leadership by the AFL, the complete impoverishment of the strikers and the cooperation of the Steel Trust, the police and city officialdom in waging open terror, he called for an organized retreat. The editorial was an outstanding exposition of his already noted mastery of strike strategy. Connolly later used the organized retreat policy in Belfast, when he led a strike of the "mill girls," and in Dublin, during the 1913 general strike and lockout. In both instances, he was able to turn defeat into partial victory and to preserve the union.

"At this stage of the game," he wrote in *The Free Press*, "a few remarks upon the art and science of fighting the battles of labor may not be amiss." A strike is no mere endurance contest, he commented, "simply a trial of strength between a full purse and an empty stomach." Socialists did not invent the "class war." But that phrase "will not seem in the least an exaggeration," to anyone who has been involved in a strike. Nor is a strike a mere "misunderstanding," as many workers think, said Connolly. The bosses know better. "They employ spies in war; they mass armed forces, with orders to shoot to kill, they capture and imprision pickets." Under industrial unionism, the workers are strengthened.

In the current situation, Connolly advised, the struggle "should not be fought out until our last battalion is decimated. This is a common error of union men... As a result, when defeat can no longer be denied, the union has been wrecked and long years of discouragement follows." To the steel strikers, he gave the advice he had given other workers before. To be most effective, he wrote: "Strikes would be ordered at the moment the boss was least able to meet them; would be refused, no matter what the provocation, when it was apparent the boss desired or expected them; and when strikes were on and... would entail much suffering without great certainty of victory, the strikers would march back to work and bide their time for another strike at a more propitious moment.

"A general in command of an army does not consider it a point of duty to expend his last cartridge and lose his last man... if his experienced eye tells him that for the time being the position is untentable. No, he retires at the first opportunity... and rearranges his forces for another battle. So will the battles of labor be fought when labor studies its position, and ceases to follow leaders who cling to old fashioned methods and principles of action."[29]

---

[29] *The Free Press*, May 28, 1910.

In the face of nationwide protest, the Steel Trust halted its terror against the Socialist leadership in New Castle and settled the court cases. Connolly was enabled to return to New York and complete preparations to leave America forever.

Connolly was, virtually, two men in one, during the steel strike. Half of him was immersed in the strike. The other half was in Ireland. He was giving advice on union and party matters to the Dublin Socialists and planning his tour. He was also trying to stabilize publication of the *Harp* in Dublin.

On May 14, 1910, enclosing sixty-four dollars for the *Harp,* he wrote O'Brien: "Nobody in Ireland seems to think it worth their while to render me an accounting of sales, expenses or anything else. And the manner in which the paper has *not* been delivered to American subscribers has practically killed the hope of new subscribers... *I have not yet got a receipt for the last 64 dollars I sent in.* I will send no more money until I get an account of how things stand financially... subs expired, total amount remaining, etc. The cash pays for May and June."

Two postscripts added: "No May *Harps* have arrived in New York yet," and "I am acting editor of *The Free Press* and they want me to take it permanently, but I have told them I can not answer until I go to Ireland."[30] Another letter, dated May 29, again carried the complaint that he had received no news from Ireland of the *Harp.*[31]

Connolly had great respect and sympathy for Jim Larkin, the leader of the Irish Transport Workers Union, since he was applying principles of industrial unionism. He wrote O'Brien, in July, 1909: "Tell comrade Larkin that I believe his union to be the most promising sign in Ireland that if things were properly handled on those lines, the whole situation... might be revolutionized." He added as a postscript: "If I were in Ireland now, one of the first things I would do would be to start an *Irish* Workers Union, to combine all Irish unions gradually into one body... I would aim at using the present bodies as far as possible. That is why I say that Larkin's union is the most promising sign, because it is already founded on the lines others should follow."[32]

Three weeks before he sailed for Ireland, learning that Larkin had been sentenced, in Dublin, to a year's hard labor, he wrote that the news "completely unnerves me. Poor fellow, he has to suffer hard for his cause.

---

[30]Connolly Archives, Letter, Connolly to O'Brien, May 14, 1910.
[31]*Ibid.,* May 29, 1910.
[32]*Ibid.,* July 9, 1909.

What will become of the Union? Has it men enough to fill the breach? Is he married and with a family? The union and the socialists owe it to Larkin that the flag be kept flying whilst he is in prison."[33]

Even before his arrival in Ireland, Connolly believed that the problems of Northern Ireland, particularly the heavily industrial city of Belfast, needed special attention. Several independent "socialist" branches existed in the latter city, theoretically at variance, and ranging from sectarian to reformist. A basic factor was the strong influence of Great Britain, even on the "socialists" in the northern counties. Connolly advised O'Brien that he did not want to speak under the auspices of a particular ILP branch in Belfast, headed by William Walker, since it was against even Home Rule for Ireland, let alone complete independence, yet considered itself socialist.

"I am not wanting to go to Ireland to speak for a party that is against political freedom," he wrote, "If I were asked upon their platform what my view upon [Home Rule] were, I would state frankly that I am a Separatist and do not believe that the English government has any right in Ireland... Imagine the mess that would make of an ILP meeting in Belfast." His alternative was to have meetings arranged under the auspices of the Socialist Party, one at the start of the Belfast stay and one at the end. He suggested that the ILP be asked to arrange for a meeting of its members and supporters where he would speak in favor "of a Socialist Party for Ireland. At this meeting, the ILP and our side could fight out our differences."

He hoped to meet with other organizations, industrial unionists, etc. "A night or two of personal visiting and discussion. That is often as fruitful as any other piece of organizing--sometimes more... I do not mean to attack or fight the ILP in any way other than by a statement of our reasons for a separate Socialist Party for Ireland...".[34]

Connolly, also in connection with the tour, reassured O'Brien, in his lengthy letter about Larkin. "I make no stipulations," he wrote, "I only make suggestions." He again expressed concern with providing for his family while in Ireland. An English tour would be important to help solve these problems, he wrote. He would be sailing on the cheapest steamship line. "I will leave New York on the 16th of July by the Anchor Liner, Furnessia. It is scheduled to reach Londonderry on Monday morning, July 25th." He would proceed to Dublin the next day.[35]

----

[33]*Ibid.*, June 24, 1910.
[34]*Ibid.*, June 6, 1910.
[35]*Ibid.*, June 24, 1910.

The family's reactions are recounted by Ina Connolly Heron:
"Mother had known for some time that father was eager to return to Ireland... She was not surprised then, when he told her he had been invited to lecture for the Socialist Party of Ireland. This meant nothing to us children, any more than if he were going to Canada, but it was of much more significance to mother."[36]

Nora Connolly O'Brien also recalled the discussion of his trip. "It's only for a few months, Lillie," James Connolly told his wife. "Things are beginning to stir once more over there and I'd like to help. I'd like to see Dublin again, Lillie."

Lillie reminded: "Think of all the misery we had there. How can you want to go back?"

Connolly answered: "I love Dublin, Lillie. I'd rather be poor there than a millionaire here."[37]

The night before his departure, Connolly's socialist associates and the members of the Irish Socialist Federation gave him a farewell dinner at a downtown hotel. The entire family were honored guests. In a number of speeches, Connolly was warmly praised by his comrades for his work in the United States.

Two days before, Connolly felt it was necessary to cheer O'Brien, who, apparently, was reacting to some of the tour's difficulties.

"Cheer up, my boy," wrote Connolly. "We never died of a winter yet. Be assured whatever happens, no blame is put upon you for not being master of circumstances... But -- in self preservation, in view of earlier experiences... you know that agreement to talk six days a week does not mean to talk twice in one day. I am not made of cast iron, nor yet of India rubber."[38]

On July 26, 1910, O'Brien received a telegram from Connolly, posted at Londonderry: "Just landed. Arrive Dublin on Tuesday."[39] Connolly was back forever on his native soil.

[36]Ina Connolly Heron, *Liberty,* April, 1966, p. 24.
[37]Nora Connolly O'Brien, pp. 108, 109.
[38]Connolly Archives, Note, Connolly to O'Brien, July 14, 1910.
[39]*Ibid.,* Telegram, Connolly to O'Brien, July 26, 1910.

CHAPTER XVIII

HOME AGAIN TO ERIN

Connolly knew what he wanted to accomplish in Ireland. He was determined: (1) to bind together the heterogenous branches and sympathetic individuals, with varying socialist philosophies, into a national Irish socialist party; (2) to give impetus to the industrial union movement, through strong support of the Transport and General Workers Union, led by Jim Larkin; and (3) to build a broad Irish Labor Party, independent of the English ILP. All of these objectives were accomplished.

There were highly important additional dimensions to his activity. He became the center of an effective anti-war, anti-recruitment campaign, after the outbreak of World War I. He made an alliance with the anti-imperialist Irish Republicans, and with them prepared for the Rising against Great Britain. Regarded as the leading Socialist and labor leader in Ireland, he also became an outstanding leader of the 1916 Easter Rising itself.

When Connolly arrived in Ireland, British imperialism was experiencing a deepening economic and political crisis. In Dublin, thousands of unskilled workers were crowded together in unsanitary slums -- many families living in a single room. Food prices were high. Child labor was widespread. Disease spread rapidly. The city's death rate was the highest in Europe.

In England, the Tories, challenged by the Liberals, were going down to defeat. A sizable bloc of Labor members won places in Parliament. There were strikes in the cities. The question of democractic rights, especially "Votes for Women," was stirring the workers and middle-class and militantly challenging the status quo. In Dublin and Belfast, it was the "sweated," unskilled workers who rallied to the leadership of Larkin, and of Connolly, a little later.[1]

Nora, shortly after the family joined Connolly, early in December, 1910, reacted sharply to the Dublin slums. She volunteered to electioneer for the

---

[1]Greaves, pp. 246-263.

socialist candidate and went to a street in the heart of the slums. She told her father: "...It was awful, awful. How can people bear to live in such places... I went up pitch black stairs, my feet squelching and slipping in the filth... That awful, miserable, heartbreaking street."

Connolly answered: "That is what we are working for, Nono -- to change all that." His daughter murmured: "It's too slow, daddy..."[2]

Almost immediately upon his arrival, Connolly visited Larkin at Mountjoy Prison in Dublin. He had been arrested in the course of the industrial union strikes. Connolly was soon speaking at large defense meetings. At Cork, 2,000 attended. He demanded Larkin's release before large audiences in Belfast and Dublin. In Belfast, also, on August 7, 1910, he established the Belfast branch of the Socialist Party of Ireland.

In mid-September, Connolly and his comrades organized a national delegated conference in Dublin, which formed a national Socialist organization. Francis Sheehy Skeffington was chairman of the gathering. A unity program stressed amelioration of the immediate needs of the workers. The document, with its limitation, succeeded in uniting such men as Skeffington, P.T. Daly, etc., with the old-time Socialists. Connolly was prepared to straighten out theoretical shortcomings in the course of struggle.

In Queenstown (now Cobh) when Connolly attempted to hold meetings, opposition by reactionaries came to the surface. The hoodlums of the Ancient Order of Hibernians organized mobs to interfere. Connolly dubbed them: "The foulest brood that ever spawned in Ireland."

The first mass campaign conducted by Connolly in Ireland -- for feeding impoverished children -- was close to his heart. Articles which he had written in the United States had condemned the Irish Parliamentarians, led by Redmond, for allowing, without protest, the House of Commons to eliminate Irish children from the benefits of the "Act for the Feeding of Necessitious Children."[3] Connolly called on Maud Gonne, the Women's Franchise League and Inghinidhe na h'Eireann (Women of Erin) for a joint campaign. The Trades Council also backed the effort. Larkin, who was in and out of prison frequently in these years, added his voice.

The Mayor of Dublin, moved to act by this united pressure, called a meeting for December 12, 1910 in the Mansion House. Connolly presented demands also, on behalf of the children, before the Belfast City Council.

---

[2]Nora Connolly O'Brien, pp. 119, 120.
[3]*Harp*, April, 1908.

His efforts culminated in having the Act for feeding the children extended to Ireland.[4]

In the early months of his return, Connolly was faced with the prospect of the bleak poverty he had endured so often in the past. He wrote O'Brien from Belfast: "In re. your offer to me of an organizership in Ireland at a wage of about thirty-five or thirty-six shillings per week for six months in the year, I regret to be compelled to decline... It has been a struggle with me to come to this decision... but a man with my responsibilities could not maintain life on less than two pounds per week, unless I went into the slums, which I will not do.

"...As you cannot raise any more, and I cannot accept what you propose,I am afraid that I will have to bid a final adieu to Erin on this occasion. Unless some other plan can be conceived and worked out."[5] A week later, he wrote O'Brien, explaining the amount he and his family would need to live on, and the cost of bringing his family to Ireland. [6] On tour in Glasgow, on September 20th, he wrote suggesting that final meetings be arranged for him in Belfast and Dublin before he returned to America.[7]

The required two pounds a week "guarantee" being agreed upon, however, and steps being taken to raise money, Connolly prepared to bring his family to Dublin.

A painful blow, which Connolly had to face upon his arrival in Ireland, was the fact that the *Harp* had died. He used his meagre personal funds to pay some of the paper's debts. To Matheson, he wrote, after the paper's demise: "The *Harp* ceased publication since June. There were four libel actions instituted against it over its last issue, and as the whole thing has been mismanaged since its transfer to Dublin, I did not feel able to lose any more money upon it. I return your sub." He blamed Larkin's poor administrative ability, in part, for the collapse.[8]

Scottish followers of De Leon sniped at Connolly with charges that he reverted to reformism in organizing the Socialist Party of Ireland. The foregoing letter was one of a series of letters to Matheson, in early 1911, which refuted these assertions, and, in addition, revealed Connolly's tactics and approach toward building a strong socialist movement as an

---

[4]Desmond Ryan, p. 59.
[5]Connolly Archives, Letter, Connolly to O'Brien, September 9, 1910.
[6]*Ibid.,* Letter, Connolly to O'Brien, September 16, 1910.
[7]*Ibid.,* Letter, Connolly to O'Brien, September 20, 1910.
[8]*Ibid.,* Letter, Connolly to Matheson, January 9, 1911.

important factor in Irish struggles and establishing united fronts with non-socialists.

The activities of Farrell, the local agent of the *Socialist* (of which Matheson was still editor) provoked one of the discussions against sectarianism. The paper, now being published in Edinburgh, remained, to an extent, under the influence of De Leonite policies.

"A very nasty thing occurred here last night," wrote Connolly, in part. "The man who handles the *Socialist* here insisted on coming into our election meeting to peddle the paper... and as he has been making himself obnoxious generally to the party here, I forbade him peddling the paper *except to those who were his usual purchasers*... This fellow regards me, or professes to, as a compromiser, because I refused to break up the party when I came home. He objected to members of other parties being in ours. So did and so do I, but I held and hold that the real way to settle that question was not by a full dress debate upon a theory...

"I hold that it is the logic of the battle which must shape and build a party and shape its policy... But these men of the type of your agent wanted a fight over a theory quo theory. I wouldn't; hence I was a traitor." Connolly emphasized the results vindicated his approach. "When we entered the fight, the members of our party who had also been members of other parties took sides *with us* to fight their other organizations, and the so-called revolutionists refused to help and do all they can to discourage and discredit the membership...".[9]

Matheson's good opinion was important to him and two days later, he again referred to Farrell. "Re. the Farrell episode..." he wrote, "fact is I am not over-solicitous about the good opinion of the SLP. It was solely your opinion I was thinking about. You apparently misapprehend the situation when you speak of us making a martyr of Farrell by *firing* him. He is not a member. That was one of the main grounds of my objection to his use of our meetings. I could not stomach the idea of a non-member, who was not even a friend, coming in to our meetings to peddle anything."[10]

Several months later, Matheson received another lesson in tactics for unity. Connolly chided him that the Scottish SLP had provoked unfriendly relations with other socialist and labor parties. He, himself, had earnestly been trying to influence members of the ILP and the SDF in Belfast--which looked to England for guidance--to work with the SPI, or better still, to join it.

---

[9]*Ibid.*
[10]*Ibid.*, Letter, Connolly to Matheson, January 11, 1911.

"Your paper," he wrote, "never mentions the ILP or SDP except to denounce them as fakers and frauds, and then you pout when they do not return the compliment by exhibiting an excess of zeal to record your good deeds. Be reasonable, John, and when you go into a fight, expect to get as good as you give... For myself, I want to keep out of the melee in Britain. I am greatly in love with none of your bodies, but am willing to help anything or anybody that tends to draw the British worker on to a 'class position'... The Labor Party is not much, the Labor man in Lanarkshire was perhaps 'a poor devil' as you say, but both are an enormous step in advance on what was in their places twenty years ago...

"Perhaps that is the difference between us, John. I fancy that you are forever comparing the actual with the conceivable, and hence tend to impatience, and I am prone to contrast the actual present of the movement with its actual near past, and am rather solaced by viewing the result... How could I find fault with the backward political or social ideas of the Britishers when the people among whom I am working are a generation behind the brutal Saxon in *their* concepts of politics and social order?"[11] Connolly's work was in the Belfast area.

In the summer of 1911, the "guaranteed" salary not having been forthcoming from a party unable to provide it, it was decided it would be wise for Connolly to move his family to Belfast to join him.

The extent of Connolly's need at this time is shown in a letter written by him from Dundee to Richard J. Hoskins, a Dublin party member, through whom he had made a bank loan.

"Mrs. Connolly is under the impression, " he complained, "that when the Dublin comrades got us out of Dublin, they left us to starve, as she has already been three days in Belfast, a strange town, without a penny to buy food, and I away in Scotland. Such an impression... makes my work in the movement rather difficult."[12]

The situation changed when Larkin and his union came to Connolly's rescue a month later. In July, Jim Larkin named Connolly secretary and Belfast organizer of the union, placed him on the union payroll and gave him two weeks' pay. Connolly opened union offices in Corporation Street, and almost immediately set to work with an organizing drive. Union funds were small but a regular salary was forthcoming.

Three days after he became organizer, he was at the docks, meeting the workers and talking with them about their grievances. Three hundred

[11]*Ibid.,* Letter, Connolly to Matheson, April 18, 1911.
[12]*Ibid.,* Letter, Connolly to Richard J. Hoskins, June 14, 1911.

dockers came out on strike in sympathy with demands of the seamen. The waterfront workers were engaged in the first militant struggle since the strike of 1907 under the leadership of Larkin. In the tradition established at that time, the workers of Belfast were united in the union, despite religious differences. Prominent in strike activities was the "Non-Sectarian Labor Band," composed of Catholics and Protestants, organized by Connolly. It paraded through Belfast streets, organizing support and collecting funds for the striking workers.

In the two years that Connolly worked in Belfast, in spite of reaction in Ulster, he organized hundreds of dock workers, secured union recognition, rebuilt the Transport and General Workers Union, and won economic concessions for the workers from the shipping magnates. He emerged as an outstanding leader of Irish labor.

Several months earlier, Connolly introduced a resolution in the Belfast branch of the Transport Union for the organization of an Irish Labor Party.[13] Connolly's resolution was brought before the Irish Trade Union Congress in May. William Walker, member of the Belfast branch of the ILP (affiliated with the British ILP) moved for an amendment, calling for support of the British Labor Party. Connolly's resolution was defeated by three votes -- 32 to 29.

Walker's position reflected the ongoing campaign by Great Britain to influence industrial Northern Ireland. It reflected also the domination which British capitalism maintained in Ulster. Walker equated public ownership of utilities with socialism. He was against Home Rule. C. Desmond Greaves describes his orientation as being for the "Protestant succession... a 'socialist' monarchy."[14]

Connolly debated Walker in meetings and polemicized against Walker's attacks on the Socialist   position on national independence, as being based on a false concept of "internationalism." Quoting Marx on the need for English workers to struggle for Irish independence, Connolly emphasized in the *Forward* that real internationalism meant "a free federation of free peoples." Walker subsequently left the movement and went to work for the British government.[15]

Connolly again introduced the resolution for the formation of an Irish Labor Party in 1912, at Clonmel, at the Irish Trade Union Conference.

---

[13]Greaves, p. 259.

[14]*Ibid.,* pp. 259, 260.

[15]For more on the Connolly-Walker controversy, see William McMullen's Introduction to *The Workers' Republic. A Selection from the Writings of James Connolly.*

This time it passed, by a vote of 49 to 18.[16] The Irish Labor Party was formed at a conference at the Antient Concert Rooms in Dublin, on Easter. It included ILP branches, SPI branches, unions, miscellaneous working-class and middle-class organizations, and individuals.

Although Connolly was based in Belfast, the national office of the union called on him at various times. In January, 1912, Connolly was summoned to go to Wexford, where three large foundries had been on strike since August. The employers, who had brought in scabs, had committed themselves publicly never to recognize the Transport Union. Connolly engineered union recognition and concessions from the employers by changing the name of the local union to Foundry Workers Union, affiliated with the national office of the Transport Workers Union.

In Belfast, the political situation was becoming increasingly reactionary. The Home Rule Bill, which passed the House of Commons on April 11, 1912, provided that England should retain control of all important functions of government. Nevertheless, this almost meaningless Home Rule Bill was opposed by the Ulster leaders, the Protestant Orangemen, headed by Sir Edward Carson, their leader in Parliament.

The Liberal Party, now in power in England, was ostensibly for Home Rule. Connolly did not trust their protestations and raised Socialist demands on the contingency of their selling out. He felt that the Irish Labor Party, representing independent political activity of the working class, would play an important role as opposition in the new Irish Parliament, should Home Rule pass.

In this period, Connolly gave a series of lectures on "The Re-Conquest of Ireland," which were combined into a pamphlet, in 1915. In a Foreword, he explained: "The Labor Movement of Ireland must set itself the Re-Conquest of Ireland as its final aim." That reconquest involved the establishment of a socialist Ireland, "taking possession of the entire country, all its power of wealth, production and all its natural resources, and organizing these... for the good of all."[17]

The Ulster "Unionists" were splitting the Irish people, by using religion, in an old strategy of "divide and conquer," he stated. They were anti-labor, anti-nationalist, anti-socialist and anti-civil rights. These loyalists to England were polluting the life of Ulster. Under the Orange Flag, they physically forced thousands of Catholics out of the shipyards, in response to incendiary speeches of the Carsonites. Their objective was to split the

---

[16]Greaves, p. 282.
[17]Connolly, *The Re-Conquest of Ireland.*

Ulster Counties away from Ireland, he charged, and form a closer bond with England.

The Director of the Workman Clark Shipyard, George Clark, was a member of the Unionist Council -- one example of its composition. Shipyard owners ruled that Catholics, Socialists and all Irish nationalists, even if these should be Protestants, must leave. Trade-union agreements then in existence were cancelled.

On September 28, 1912, a "Solemn League and Covenant," was entered into by Ulster Loyalists. They swore "to use all means which may be found necessary to defeat the present conspiracy to set up a Home Rule Parliament... and to refuse to recognize its authority."[18]

The Belfast ILP surrendered and stopped campaigning for Home Rule. In December, 1912, the Carsonites began to enroll men into the Ulster Volunteers. Behind the scenes, English Tories--capitalists, retired generals, etc., supplied money and arms.

In spite of this situation, Connolly entered the January, 1913 municipal elections in Belfast. He ran for Councilman "in an Orange ward," as he wrote O'Brien on January third.[19] "...The ILP has given up its Sunday meetings here and I have taken over the hall for election work. Hence no regular Sunday lectures are being held by the party. I am up to the neck in trade union, insurance and other allied work..."

Connolly conducted a vigorous campaign in the Dock Ward. His candidacy was endorsed by the Transport Union local and, unanimously, by the Belfast Trades and Labor Council. "It is time," his election literature proclaimed, "that Belfast City Council was interesting itself more about... "matters of minimum wages, health insurance and child feeding, "and less about the perpetuation of the religious discords that make Belfast a by-word among civilized nations."[20] His program endorsed Home Rule and advocated socialism, in order to "secure the abolition of destitution and all the misery, crime and immorality which flow from that unnecessary evil."

Connolly urged his supporters to persevere against the Ulster reaction. In spite of Unionist attacks, he demanded that: "Ireland should be ruled, governed, and owned by the people of Ireland." He called for equal rights for women, "the same political rights for all... I stand for the class to which I belong."[21]

---

[18]Greaves, p. 293.
[19]Connolly Archives, Letter, Connolly to O'Brien, January 3, 1913.
[20]Connolly, *Workers' Republic,* "Belfast Municipal Elections, January, 1913," p. 99.
[21]*Ibid.*

In March, 1914, Prime Minister Asquith proposed partition of Ireland. Consenting were the "so-called Nationalist politicians," as Connolly called the Redmonites. He responded in the *Irish Worker* of March 14, accusing them of treachery. He called on labor to fight partition, "even to the death, if necessary, as our fathers fought before us."[22]

British policy made an economic impact on Protestant and Catholic workers alike. In Belfast both were sweated, undernourished and diseased. Sir Edward Carson and his followers in the British Parliament consistently voted against pro-labor and progressive legislation. They had voted against the Right to Work Bill, the Minimum Wage for Miners, the Minimum Wage for Railwaymen, etc. He characterized them as "...true blue loyalist leaders, who on every platform assert their unquenchable enthusiasm for the cause of Protestant liberty," yet were "the slimiest enemies of the social advancement of the Protestant working class."[23]

The difficulties in his union work, caused by the increasing Orange loyalist attacks, were described in a letter to O'Brien, in July, one month before Connolly left Belfast for Dublin, to take over the national office of the union: "The feeling of the city is so violently Orange and anti-Irish at present that our task has been a hard one all along. But we have gained... more substantial advantages than even the Dublin men have gained... Our fight is a fight not only against the bosses, but against the political and religious bigotry which destroys all feeling of loyalty to a trade union."[24]

In August, 1913, Connolly, in spite of growing reaction around him, negotiated with the G. & G. Burns, Ltd. Shipyards of Belfast. He wrote the company, in part: "We are instructed by your employees on the Belfast docks, members of our organization, to bring under your notice their desire for an improvement in the conditions governing their labor and to request... that we should be granted an interview for the purpose of discussing the new conditions they propose." The workers' demands included a 60 hour week, the day's labor to start at 6:30 A.M., and two full meal hours. Connolly wrote in brackets: "A ten hour day any time between 6 A.M. and 7 P.M." The proposed agreement included set standards for the various trades, overtime pay after 10 hours of work, double time on Sundays and holidays, a four hour minimum period of labor each day. The

22Connolly Archives, *Irish Worker,* March 14, 1914, "Labor and the Proposed Partition of Ireland," by Connolly.

23*Workers' Republic,* "Sweatshops Behind the Orange Flag," from *Forward,* March 11, 1911, pp. 93-97. See p. 103.

24Connolly Archives, Letter, Connolly to O'Brien, July 29, 1913.

last demand was: "Recognition of the above Union and free access to shed and ship of Union officials."[25]

Three days later, receipt of a reply from the employers was acknowledged and anti-union propaganda on the job protested.[26] On August 26, 1913, Connolly was able to report that an agreement had been reached which was a definite victory for the Union. Seven major demands had been met and two were tabled for further negotiation.

Three days after this victory, Connolly was called to Dublin, to assume national leadership of the Union, Larkin once more having been arrested.

Several weeks later, in *Forward* of August 23, 1913, Connolly called on the socialists and the unions, particularly those in Northern Ireland, to keep fighting, even though times were difficult. "A real socialist movement," he admonished, "can only be born of struggle, of uncompromising affirmation of the faith that is in us. Such a movement infallibly gathers to it every element of rebellion and of progress, and in the midst of the storm and stress of the struggle solidifies into a real revolutionary force."[27]

[25]*Ibid.*, Letter, Transport Union to the G. & G. Burns, Ltd., Co., August 2, 1913.

[26]*Ibid.*, Letter, Connolly to Manager, Messrs. G. & G. Burns, Ltd., August 5, 1913.

[27]*Socialism and Nationalism. A Selection from the Writings of James Connolly*, quoting Forward, August 23, 1913, p. 107. Also p. 101. The Connolly Archives also contain an appeal issued by Connolly: "Ireland and Ulster. An Appeal to the Working Class, April 4, 1914."

CHAPTER XIX

GENERAL STRIKE AND LOCKOUT -- DUBLIN, 1913

Jim Larkin and the Irish Transport and General Workers Union represented hope for the Dublin workers living in the slums, and the thousands of unskilled laborers of the city. After 1911, the union grew steadily, with their belief that organization could alleviate their unspeakable conditions.

The smoldering discontent of the workers throughout Dublin was ignited in January, 1913, when the quay porters at the North Wall struck for higher wages and shorter hours. The great Dublin strike had begun, and spread rapidly. The employers responded by city-wide lock-outs. The events of 1913 brought the Dublin workers to a higher level of unity than ever before. They displayed a high degree of heroism, militancy, fierce determination and devotion to the union, in spite of great personal suffering, and drew support from a large segment of middle-class intellectuals.

Such solidarity and strength greatly alarmed the employers. William Martin Murphy, richest Irish capitalist in Dublin, who owned the tramway system and many other enterprises, including a large Dublin newspaper, the *Independent,* hotels, etc., took the lead in declaring war on the unions. Under his leadership, 400 employers presented an ultimatum against "Larkinism" to the workers of Dublin. It declared they they must pledge that they would neither belong to nor help the ITGWU, nor any union.[1]

Workers by the thousands were dismissed when they refused. Soon more than one-third of the population of Dublin was involved in the greatest labor struggle Ireland had yet seen.

British soldiers and Dublin police savagely attacked and injured hundreds of workers. An army of paid thugs fought beside them. Larkin was arrested again, and at the same time an onslaught was made on people massed on the street. James Nolan, a striker, was clubbed to death. Twenty-thousand people marched in his funeral procession. Two other

---

[1] W.P. Ryan, "The Struggle of 1913," from *1913, Jim Larkin and the Dublin Lock-Out* p. 11.

workers, James Byrne and Alice Brady, died as the result of their injuries. Police did not dare interfere with the mourners. The British Trades Union Congress, meeting in Manchester, condemned the "Castle" for the brutality and pledged food, money and strike support for the workers.

In this situation, with Larkin and other trade-union leaders in jail, and 37 unions involved in strikes and lockouts, Connolly became Acting National Secretary and led the union in the most critical stages of the 1913 struggle.[2] The training which he had received in working class movements in the United States was very important.

Connolly, campaigning for the release of Larkin, was also jailed, charged with holding a meeting prohibited by the English military. During his imprisonment, he carried on the first hunger strike in Ireland.

An unpublished manuscript of Ina Connolly Heron, which she made available to us, tells the story:[3]

"There were baton charges... My father was arrested and when he wrote to my mother from Mountjoy Prison, he said, 'It was not entirely unexpected, and it is not as bad as it might have been... there is not much chance of getting my head broken here, as many poor fellows are getting outside!" Ina commented that her father always "put on a bold front" to his family, to mask difficult situations. A week later, word came that their father was on a hunger strike.

"He was the first man in Ireland, or the British Isles, who adopted this method of fighting for his rights and free speech. 'What was good enough for the Suffragettes to use,' he said, 'is good enough for us.' "

Lillie went to Dublin with Ina. Nora remained in Belfast to look after the rest of the family. Ina observed that the jailings, brutal attacks and murders brought together people "from all branches of political thought and literary clubs, in fact, the best men of our times came out and backed my father in his attempt to fight for... the Dublin workers..."

William O'Brien and Eamonn Martin, another friend, joined Lillie and Ina in the visit to Mountjoy. Connolly was sick in bed. Ina recalled: "We saw father, lying... with a feverish, red face and glassy eyes. He looked so ill that we did not know whether to run to the bed or walk on our tip-toes, in case of upsetting him. Then I remembered finding myself in his arms and realizing he wasn't dead. He intended to let everybody know they could not kill his spirit."[4]

---

[2]Connolly Archives, "Copy of the Charges Against the Strike Leaders, August 28, 1913."
[3]Ina Connolly Heron, Unpublished Manuscript.
[4]*Ibid.*

In the campaign for Connolly's release, labor delegations confronted the British authorities and appeared at numerous organizations -- wherever support might be expected. Lillie was informed by K.M. Shannon of some of the activities. "There is to be a meeting outside the prison tonight and if he is not released -- one tomorrow also. Mrs. Skeffington saw him on Tuesday and said he was quite cheerful. I'm sure he'll be released tomorrow for we're worrying everyone about him...".[5]

Pressure in England, as well as Ireland, forced Connolly's release. Ina tells of the welcoming reception in Belfast on his return -- a reception in contrast to previous mobbings of socialists by Carsonites.

"The dockers all turned out to a man, and all the mill girls in their shawls," declared Ina. "The Fianna Boys and Girls [members of the Republican youth movement] were there in strength. The train came in. There was a roar of greeting and a shout of song. The band played and through the struggling throng, we managed to get father to the entrance of the station and he was put on a side car with myself beside him and mother on the other side."

They drove through the city to the steps of the Custom House, the crowd swelling all the way. Connolly, weakened from the hunger strike, was too fatigued to speak. He turned to Ina and told her to thank the crowd "for their glorious welcome." She promised them for him that he would speak in several days. Driving home, bonfires greeted them, "...outside our own home, which was at the top of the Falls Road. In the space outside the city cemetery, the biggest bonfire of all was flaming...".[6]

Returned to Dublin, and again leading the strike, Conolly wrote a warm letter to John Matheson. The old friendship had a very personal meaning, in spite of political disagreements. He wrote:"...Since I came out of prison, I have learned that you wrote to me whilst I was in. I did not receive the letter, but fortunately, comrade O'Brien had made a copy of it, which he has given me. Now that I have about five minutes to spare, I wish to thank you for your expressions of sympathy, as well as for your fine appreciation of our fight. It is always encouraging to know that an old comrade is with one still. So many allow petty distinctions of doctrine, and still pettier beliefs that there is a vital distinction of doctrine, to warp their judgment and estrange their sympathies from those who are on the firing line. But, as

---

[5]Connolly Archives, Letter, K.M. Shannon to Mrs. J. Connolly, September 11, 1913.
[6]Ina Connolly Heron, Unpublished Manuscript.

we say in Ireland, 'I never doubted you.'."[7]

Connolly and Larkin toured England together to get the support of British trade unionists for the Dublin workers. At a huge meeting in Albert Hall, in London, Connolly referred to "A Citizen Army of locked-out men." The term, "Citizen Army" caught the imagination of those present. Larkin spoke, as did George Bernard Shaw, George Lansbury, Labor member of Parliament and Sylvia Pankhurst, the Socialist and Suffragette. "Big Bill" Haywood came from France with a check for one thousand francs, from the Confederation of Labor, and continued on to Dublin, to encourage the strikers.[8] Another speaker was G.W. Russell (A.E.), Irish poet, who wrote his famous "Open Letter to the Masters of Dublin," published in the *Irish Times,* October 7, 1913. This letter placed upon the shoulders of the employers, responsibility for all the starvation and other inhuman evils of the lockout. "You may succeed in your policy and ensure your own damnation by your victory," he wrote. "The men whose manhood you have broken will loathe you and will always be brooding and scheming to strike a fresh blow. The children will be taught to curse you...".[9]

October found Larkin back in jail and again Connolly's first order of business, as Acting Secretary, was to win his freedom. On November 13, Connolly announced Larkin's release: "Dublin has won the first great victory in its great dispute," he announced. "At one o'clock Wednesday, all hands on Cross Channel boats downed tools and in a quarter of an hour the whole port was closed... In eighteen and a half hours, Larkin was at liberty."

The strike was greatly weakened by the refusal of the British Trade Union Congress to sanction further sympathetic strikes, which Connolly felt was the key to victory. When Larkin and Connolly appeared before it on December ninth, J. Thomas, and other reformist leaders, rebuffed them. The sympathetic strikes then taking place were ordered terminated. Later, on February 10, 1914, the TUC officials stopped donations to the Dublin workers.[10]

According to Connolly, by the end of 1913 and at the beginning of 1914,

[7]Connolly Archives, Letter, Connolly to Matheson, October 13, 1913; *Forward,* October 4, 1913. *Workers' Republic,* "Glorious Dublin," p. 122. Also pp. 111-113, 114-116, 127-131. Articles beginning on pp. 132, 134, 138, 140, 147, 168, 175, 185 supply additional information on the strike.
[8]William D. Haywood, pp. 272-274.
[9]R.M. Fox, pp. 149-151.
[10]Greaves, pp. 330-337. R.M. Fox, pp. 157-167. See also *1913. Jim Larkin,* etc., p. 101.

the situation was a "draw." To safeguard the unions, which the employers had not succeeded in smashing, and to prevent blacklisting, it was necessary to prepare an organized retreat.

A letter addressed to Guiness & Co., James Gate, dated December 12, 1913, showed confidence and dignity -- and held out the olive branch to the company. It made clear that the union, after almost a year of lockout and strikes, was still a powerful force, which could not be ignored. He wrote: "I have been instructed by the General Committee of the... Union to inform you that in view of the efforts at present being made to end the unfortunate dispute in Dublin, and as an evidence of our desire to cooperate in that direction, we have resolved to handle goods consigned as well as coming from your firm... which we have for some time refused... as the result of the dismissal of a few of your men.

"Without at all making it a condition of our action, we desire to suggest to you that if your firm could see their way to the reinstatement of the six men in question, the act would help greatly to straighten out the tangle on the Quays, and thus clear the way for the final greater settlement now being sought by all parties concerned." A postscript gave the names of the blacklisted workers.[11]

From a sickbed, in Belfast, early in January, 1914, Connolly wrote O'Brien in Dublin, advising how a compromise settlement might be secured, to protect the workers, in the weakened position of the ITGWU. It is apparent that Connolly was the architect of the settlement which safeguarded the union. Connolly suggested that it be announced that in view of the scabbing by the British unions, which had begun to handle "tainted" goods, "as these unions were now handling all sorts of traffic loaded in Dublin by scabs... We are now prepared to advise a general resumption of work and the handling of all goods, *pending a more general acceptance of the doctrine of tainted goods by the trade union world.*

"But having completely foiled the attempt of the employers to crush our union or to dictate to us our union affiliations, we reserve to ourselves the right to refuse to work with non-union labor where such labor has not formerly been employed, or to withdraw our labor again, if within a reasonable period, varying according to the nature of our work, we find that any of our members have been victimized, or left unemployed without a satisfactory reason." With this strategy, he continued, "I do not believe

---

[11]Connolly Archives, Letter, from Connolly, Acting General Secretary, to Guiness & Co., December 12, 1913.

that the Murphy gang would be able to hold them [the employers] in any longer [from settlement.] It would also save us from the danger of being compelled to sign an unsatisfactory *general* settlement..."[12]

In answer to the terror against the strikers by the military and the police, as well as company thugs, defense corps of union members had been organized. These became the Irish Citizen Army, labor's army, which was to play an important role in the coming struggle for Irish independence.

In Dublin, the employers formally gave up their demand that workers sign the anti-union pledges. The strike and lockout gradually ended.

Connolly always refused to countenance attempts by employers and reformist British trade union leaders to separate him from Jim Larkin for he saw it as an attempt to weaken the union. When English labor leaders praised him, in contrast to Larkin, in order to sow dissension between the two, Connolly recalled: "At last I could stand it no longer. I told them that though we spoke with different accents, we spoke with the one voice and that they could not split the Transport Union."[13]

Nevertheless, Larkin sometimes made him extremely impatient. He was exasperated at Larkin's failure to audit and settle insurance accounts, which Connolly was handling in Belfast. This violated government regulations, he wrote Larkin, and left the Belfast office without funds. It disrupted the staff. After sharply criticizing him, Connolly concluded his letter: "I propose absenting myself from the offices from Wednesday, July 16. Whether I ever resume office or not will depend upon the report of your agent."[14] Larkin came around. The required report was prepared. He called Connolly into the national office and they made peace. They remained an effective team.

In the middle of 1914, only a few weeks before the outbreak of World War I, Larkin announced that because of his weakened health and the terrible mental strain he had undergone, he would go to America to lecture and would vacate his union position. In private conversations, he favored P.T. Daly to take his place and Connolly to take the subordinate position of head of the insurance department. Connolly, in a series of letters to O'Brien, made it clear that he would not accept this decision. He did not want to see Larkin leave Ireland and felt there might be some hope of reviving his spirits by involving him in the forthcoming Trade Union Congress.[15] However, as the result of a phone conversation with Larkin, he

———————

[12]*Ibid.*, Letter, Connolly to O'Brien, January 15, 1914.
[13]*1913, Jim Larkin, etc.*, p. 109, from *Forward*, June 27, 1914.
[14]Connolly Archives, Letter, Connolly to Larkin, July 15, 1913.
[15]*Ibid.*, Letter, Connolly to O'Brien, June 8, 1914.

was forced to come to the conclusion: "He seems bent upon a tour [of America]."[16]

Four months later, at the beginning of October, the question of Larkin's replacement had not yet been settled. Connolly "hated the insurance work,"[17] and the possible choice of Daly made him uneasy, since Daly, he felt, would be unacceptable to the nationalists.[18] Right or wrong, Connolly's reservations about Daly remained with him. He would express them again, privately, to his daughter, Nora, a day before the British executed him.

Connolly wrote to Larkin in October: "His leadership means the loss of all power and prestige to the Transport Union amongst the outside public..." At stake, Connolly reminded Larkin, was not only the critical stage of the union, but the position of Ireland itself, a World War having existed for two months. "During the very critical period of last year's fight," Connolly declared, "you placed me in charge." Putting Daly in as head of the union would be a vote of no confidence.[19]

Larkin, when it came time to render a decision, named Connolly, under pressure also of the other trade-union leaders. At a huge meeting, Larkin delivered his farewell message: "Jim Connolly is in command of the Union, the Citizen Army, *Irish Worker*, and general propaganda work; P.T. Daly is taking over the work of the Insurance."[20]

Larkin departed for America on October 25, 1914. He was to become a charter member of the Communist Party of the U.S.A., serve a prison sentence, because of his opposition to the war and, finally, was to be deported to Ireland in 1923.

After the defeat of the Easter Rising, Larkin paid tribute to Connolly's leadership of Dublin's workers, at a time when reactionaries had mobilized to destroy the union: "Connolly never failed us, even in that hour of our trial."[21]

Elizabeth Gurley Flynn knew both men. In her autobiography, she wrote: "In Connolly and Larkin was a remarkably effective combination for the struggle for Irish freedom, the building of an Irish labor movement and the establishment of a Socialist movement. They complemented each

---

[16]*Ibid.*, June 15, 1914.
[17]*Ibid.*, October 6, 1914.
[18]*Ibid.*
[19]Connolly Archives, Letter, Connolly to Larkin, October 9, 1914. Letters to O'Brien from Connolly, July 23 and August 22, 1914, reflect this position.
[20]*The Workers' Union of Ireland.*
[21]James Larkin, "The Irish Rebellion," *New Masses,* July, 1916.

other...".[22]

With Larkin's departure, Connolly and the union faced a new world situation -- British imperialism in crisis and in a world war.

---

[22]Elizabeth Gurley Flynn, p. 174. Thomas Johnson, a co-worker, characterized the two men in *Memories,* printed in Dublin, p. 238. "Larkin was... daring, reckless, defiant, dramatic... Connolly was a cool, level-headed analyst, precise, careful and accustomed to weighing evidence and words." In his *Re-Conquest of Ireland,* Connolly fiercely refuted a savage attack on Larkin by the *Irish Times.* "Larkinism is a revolt against intolerable conditions... the general effect... has been to raise wages and improve conditions...".

CHAPTER XX

WORLD WAR I. IRELAND'S OPPORTUNITY!

The World War, which began August 5th, 1914, soon involved millions of British, French and Russian soldiers -- the "Allies -- in deadly combat with soldiers of Germany and Austria-Hungary, on a vast, blood-sodden European battlefield. It was increasingly obvious that President Woodrow Wilson of the United States supported the Allies, although he had issued a "Proclamation of Neutrality." The U.S. became the arsenal for the Allies. Huge war orders poured into the country. Loans by American banks to foreign industries to pay for these orders were sanctioned by the American President. American finance capital took the first steps to win a dominant position in British economy.

The large anti-war sentiment in the United States, in which many Socialists, the IWWs, the pacifists and a large section of the foreign-born workers played an important part, strongly influenced Wilson to delay taking the country actively into the war. He found it prudent, in 1916, to run for re-election under the slogan: "He Kept Us Out of War." Nevertheless, six months after his election, the United States was fully involved.

The World War was the deepest crisis of world capitalism thus far and, as Connolly saw it, changed everything.[1] The Socialist Party of Ireland (particularly in Dublin) the Transport and General Workers Union and the Irish Citizen Army, all now led by Connolly, formed the cornerstone of the anti-imperialist, anti-war movement in Ireland. Almost daily, Connolly directed passionate onslaughts against England and the imperialist war -- editorials, articles and speeches. He condemned the virtual collapse of the international socialist majority in the Second International, which refused to oppose the war. With all their prestige and their members in Parliament, Connolly wrote, the Socialist Party leaders

---

[1] *Labor and Easter Week 1916. A Selection from the Writings of James Connolly*, p. 1.
[2] *Ibid.*, pp. 38-42, from *Forward*, August 15, 1914.

of the Second International betrayed the international working class by supporting their own governments.[2]

He saw the solution as civil war and immediately began organizing an anti-recruitment movement against conscripting the young men of Ireland. Connolly addressed the socialists of other countries: "If these men [the international socialists] must die... would it not be better to die in their own country, fighting for freedom for their class and the abolition of war, than to go forth to strange countries and die, slaughtering and being slaughtered by their brothers, that tyrants and profiteers might live?"[3] As to "patriotism," reminiscent of Lenin's writings, Connolly concluded: "To me, the socialist of another country is a fellow patriot, as the capitalist of my own country is an enemy."[4]

The statement that the war was for the protection of small nations, using "little Belgium" as an example, evoked a bitter response. Citing the position of the Russian Bolsheviks, Connolly wrote: "The Russian Socialists have issued a strong Manifesto denouncing the war," and are "pouring contempt upon the professions of the Czar in favor of oppressed races." The Russian Czar and the English government, he noted, are for the rights of small nations, "everywhere, except in those countries now under Russian and British Rule."[5]

The Ulster loyalist movement, Carson's followers, totally supported England's war. William Devlin, head of the Ancient Order of Hibernians, and John Redmond were vigorous recruiters for England in Ireland. The testament to their betrayal of the cause of Ireland were the numbers of Irish youth, dead in an English war, their remains, "...twisted, blown and gashed by inconceivable wounds... each of them, in all their ghastly horror, crying out to Heaven for vengeance upon the political tricksters who lured them to their fate...".[6]

Asquith came to Dublin, together with Redmond, to hold a recruiting meeting. The Citizen Army marched through the streets in protest, with ten thousand Dubliners cheering them. The meeting failed in its purpose. Only six recruits were secured, despite Redmond's fanfare.[7]

Redmond's National Volunteers began to dwindle as his unpopular position became clear. The numbers of Irish Volunteers, led by the secret

[3]*Ibid.*
[4]*Ibid.*
[5]*Socialism and Nationalism,* p. 148, from *Irish Worker,* September 12, 1914.
[6]*Ibid.,* pp. 136, 137, from *Irish Worker,* August 29, 1914.
[7]*Labor and Easter Week,* p. 91, from *Workers' Republic,* October 30, 1915.

Irish Republican Brotherhood, increased. Joint actions between this organization and the Irish Citizen Army were stepped up. On October 25th, a giant mass meeting was called by the two organizations. Padraic Pearse, representing the Irish Volunteers, and James Connolly, representing the Irish Citizen Army, shared the platform.

Connolly reiterated the position that the war had its origin in economics. "... This war is not a war upon German militarism, but upon the industrial activity of the German nation," he said. Great Britain had dominated the commercial life of the world for decades. Germany's rising industrial challenge was met by the mobilization of the powerful British fleet, the largest in the world. At this point, Conolly described capitalist governments as: "...committees of the rich to manage the affairs of the capitalist class...".[8]

With William O'Brien and other labor and socialist leaders, Connolly organized an anti-war united front with the middle-class nationalists, many of whom found that here they could unite with the socialists. The anti-labor Griffith found himself now aligned with them and with labor, in opposition to England's war. The "Irish Neutrality League" was organized. Signed by Connolly, as President, the initial statement carried the names of a number of unionists and nationalists.[9] It pledged to watch "Ireland's interests at every phase of the war, preventing employers from coercing men to enlist, inculcating the view that true patriotism requires Irishmen to remain at home, and taking steps to preserve the food supplies of Ireland for the people of Ireland...". The League did not attract mass membership, but it added to the influence of the anti-war forces and intensified the campaign against recruiting and conscription.

Shortly before the organization of the League, Connolly forwarded a draft circular to O'Brien, with his notations. Its theme was one which Connolly repeated often. The war provided the opportunity for Ireland to strike for independence. If the Irish should wait until the war ended, Britain could turn its entire army against her. "...If Ireland's position can be strengthened, it must be done during the war."[10]

One of Connolly's articles refuted statements by the English and pro-war Irish press that the American people were eager to get into the war. He

---

[8]*Socialism and Nationalism*, pp. 136-142, from *Irish Worker*, August 29, 1914.

[9]Connolly Archives, Statement, "Irish Neutrality League," October 5, 1914.

[10]*Ibid.*, Note, Connolly to O'Brien, written on draft circular, an invitation to attend "a small meeting... to discuss the position of Ireland in view of the European War." September, 1914.

declared: "Ten minutes calm reflection upon the history of immigration into America would show that the Anglo-Saxon in that country represents a very small drop in a very big ocean of races." He believed the foreign-born workers in the United States would not support the war nor would the Irish-American and German-American population. The Poles and Hungarian-Americans, the Scandinavians, of whom there were many thousands in basic industry, the Finns and peoples from the Baltic provinces, he reasoned, all hated the Czarist government, ally of England.

The Jewish population in America, he continued, would not, willingly, support the Czarist government. Many thousands had fled Russia because of pogroms against them, organized by the Czar's government agents. "And now, this same Czar, addressing the unfortunate survivors, calls them his 'beloved Jews,' " declared Connolly.[11]

The effective movement against recruiting in Ireland alarmed the British military. In mid-November, 1914, they began arresting key figures. Captain Robert Monteith, a skilled drill-master for the Irish Volunteers, was dismissed from his job and ordered deported from Dublin. Indignantly, Connolly called a protest meeting under the auspices of the Citizen Army.[12]

Like Lenin, Connolly rejected slogans without working-class substance, such as "anti-militarism," and "peace at any price." He maintained: "The war of a subject nation for independence, for the right to live out its own life in its own way, may and can be justified as holy and righteous. The war of a subject class to free itself from the debasing conditions of economic and political slavery should at all times choose its own weapons; and hold and esteem all as sacred instruments of righteousness. But the war of nation against nation, in the interest of royal freebooters and cosmopolitan thieves, is a thing accursed."[13]

A mass meeting, held by the union at the end of August, 1914, honored the three martyrs of the 1913 strike and lockout. Connolly demanded that the workers make their armed stand in Ireland. "Make up your mind to strike before your opportunity goes," he told the assembled workers.[14]

In December, three newspapers fell victim to the campaign by the British military to suppress the republican press. *Irish Freedom, Sinn Fein,* and

---

[11]*Ibid., Irish Worker,* October 22, 1914, "America and Europe."
[12]R.M. Fox, p. 178.
[13]*Labor and Easter Week,* p. 46, from *Forward,* August 22, 1914.
[14]*Ibid.,* p. 49, from *Irish Worker,* September 5, 1914. Also p. 87, from *Workers' Republic,* October 30, 1915.

the *Irish Worker,* the latter edited by Connolly, were shut down. Tom Bell, Arthur MacManus and other friends of Connolly, in and around Glasgow, were called upon for help. It was arranged that MacManus should see to the printing of the paper in Scotland. The next few issues were also smuggled into Ireland by him. He was determined to keep his pledge to Connolly, despite, at one point, suffering from a broken collarbone.[15]

The February 20, 1915 issue was seized by police. Three months later, Connolly issued the *Workers' Republic,* printed, this time, at Liberty Hall, in Dublin.

Throughout 1914 and 1915, with the prodigious energy that characterized him, Connolly fought battles on many fronts. Solely to preserve living standards, let alone to improve them, serious struggles had to be waged. While in the center of the anti-recruiting campaign and working for the independence of Ireland, Connolly tackled the problem of securing from the employers the every day needs of the workers. He wrote that England, "in the name of freedom from militarism, establishes militarism in Ireland; battling for progress, it abolishes trial by jury; and waging war for enlightened rule, it tramples the freedom of the press under the heel of a military despot...".

Using the slogan, "The War for Civilization," as his title, he declared: "...there is another war for civilization... waged by the forces of organized labor... We here in Ireland, particularly those who follow the example of the ITGWU have been battling to preserve those rights which others have surrendered; we have fought to keep up our standards of life... to better our conditions..."[16] While he was organizing for revolt against England, the union which he led recorded substantial gains for the workers, including the boatmen and workers in the coal association, employees of the shipping companies, the stevedores, the deep sea dockers, the cross channel dockers, the "contact" men, the dock-yard laborers and other trades.[17] A hard fought railway strike, which extended the union's resources to the limit, resulted in an agreement for the strikers.

By mid-1915, recruiting had fallen off drastically. Daily casualty lists grew longer every day. Bodies of the dead and the seriously maimed men and boys were being returned home by the thousands. Civil liberties had been almost obliterated by the English occupation. In this situation, and moved by the agitation of the union, led by Connolly, the rank and file

---

[15]Bell, p. 49.
[16]*Labor and Easter Week,* pp. 87-90, from *Workers' Republic,* October 30, 1915.
[17]Greaves, p. 370.

Irish Volunteers became increasingly militant.

Connolly placed revolution on the order of business. "Revolution is no more unthinkable in Europe; its shadow already looms upon the horizon."[18] Four months earlier, he concluded, according to a report in the *Workers' Republic,* that although he had spent a "good deal of his life in decrying force between man and man... if force was to be the sole arbiter, then let those who have right on their side gather all the forces they can to help them."[19]

In September, Connolly paid tribute to the accomplishments of the union in the face of its great difficulties. By its fight against recruitment and conscription, it had, "saved the lives of thousands, held together thousands of homes, and amid all the welter and turmoil of a gigantic and unparalleled national betrayal, we presented to the world, the spectacle of the organized Irish working class, standing steadfastly by the highest ideals of freedom, so that the flag of labor became one with the standard of national liberty."[20]

The Socialist Party members in Ireland, with few exceptions, stood firmly against the war. Hyndman and the Social Democratic Federation in England, like most of the leaders of the Second International, supported their own governments. Exceptions included William Gallacher, in the minority in the English Socialist Party, who took a strong anti-war position. He later became a Member of Parliament from Scotland, representing the Communist Party. Thomas Bell, Arthur MacManus in Scotland and the majority of the Scottish SLP worked with Connolly.

The Independent Labor Party, led by Keir Hardie and Ramsay MacDonald, issued a manifesto on August 13, 1914, in opposition to the war, along pacifist lines. Their position was "centrist" and weak. Six months later, on February 14, 1915, Hardie chaired a conference in London held by the International Socialist Bureau and the Independent Labor Party. To this conference, initiated by Emil Vandervelde, only pro-war Socialists, from countries supporting the Allies, were invited.

M. Litvinov, a permanent member of the International Socialist Bureau, representing the R.S.D.L.P. (Bolshevik) Party, an exile from Russia, was not invited, although he resided in London. He attempted to read an anti-war declaration but Keir Hardie stopped him.[21]

---

[18]*Labor and Easter Week,* p. 42, from *Workers' Republic,* October 16, 1915.
[19]*Ibid.,* p. 63, from *Workers' Republic,* June 5, 1915.
[20]*Ibid.,* p. 82, from *Workers' Republic,* September 18, 1915.
[21]Lenin, Collected Works, Vol. XVIII, *The Imperialist War, The Struggle Against Social-*

Lenin demanded that Vandervelde of Belgium and Guesde and Sembat of France, leave their positions in the War Cabinets of their countries, as Socialists, but they did not do so.

Connolly's position took him on the road to Easter Week, 1916.

Chauvinism and Social Pacifism, 1914-1915, p. 428. See Letter from Litvinov, printed March 3, 1915, pp. 140, 141. Also "Declaration," printed March 29, 1915 in *Sotsial Demokrat*, pp. 142, 143, 144, 157. Lenin stated, October 17, 1914: "The proletarian slogan must be civil war." (*Ibid.*, p. 75.) Two weeks later, he issued the call: "Turn the Imperialist War into Civil War" as "the only correct proletarian slogan... it follows from all the conditions of an imperialist war among highly developed bourgeois countries." (*Ibid.*, pp. 82, 83, November 1, 1914, "The War and Russian Social Democracy.") See also p. 197, July 26, 1915, "Defeat of 'Our' Government in the Imperialist War," and p. 225, August 1915. Also p. 248 Note, "Marxism is not pacifism. It is necessary to *fight* for a speedy end of the war. But only through a call to revolutionary struggle, will the 'peace' demand gain proletarian content."

CHAPTER XXI

PREPARATIONS FOR REBELLION

The Minutes of the Royal Commission of Inquiry, which was convened a month after the Easter Rising, in May, 1916, confirmed the effectiveness of the anti-war campaign, led by Connolly.[1] Major Price, head of Intelligence at Irish Military Headquarters in Dublin, reported: "The army lost 50,000 men as the result of the 'Sinn Fein' activity in Ireland." All Republicans were "Sinn Feiners," in the Commission's Minutes, obscuring Labor's role in the Rising. Price mourned the attitude of the farmers. "They looked down upon the army... recruiting among them was not satisfactory." Many members of the church, he said, "acted as an anti-recruiting league."

Maurice Dockrell, who headed the Dublin City and County Recruiting Committee, used his office as a center for informer activities. His testimony recorded that after June, 1915, recruiting "fell off, owing to the efforts made to undermine the Committee's work, by anti-recruiting methods."

J.C. Percy, Honorary Recruiting Officer, reported work so futile that the Minutes noted "laughter," at several points. He could neither organize recruiting meetings nor suppress anti-recruiting activity. He singled out the *Irish Worker*. He declared: "They were signing on the people not to fight for England at Fairs, markets, etc. Especially many farmers' sons were against recruiting."

The chairman of the Royal Commission, Lord Hardinge, asked: "How are you getting on now? Are you still recruiting?" The answer: "No, I have returned to private life and given up recruiting. (Laughter)". Percy confirmed that he had reported anti-recruiting articles in "seditious" newspapers to Scotland Yard, among them the *Irish Worker*. This must have involved no small effort. From the Fall of 1915, until the Rising on Easter Monday, 1916, almost every article and speech by Connolly was a call for armed resistance to England.[2]

---

[1]*Sinn Fein Rebellion Handbook*. Minutes of the Royal Commission of Inquiry.

[2]Connolly, *Workers' Republic,* November 20, 1915, p. 106; p. 71, July 31, 1915; p. 75, August 7, 1915.

It was during 1915 that Connolly's ideas on the workers' state crystallized. In January, he made clear he had dropped the old formula of semi-syndicalist take-over. He now concluded that the road to socialism was through armed insurrection. He decided that, "nothing less than superior force will ever induce them [the ruling class] to abandon their throttling grasp upon the lives and liberties of mankind." The two-fold force which was available to the working class for this purpose was industrial and political. The latter "includes military organizations to protect political and industrial rights."

Connolly quoted the Scriptures: " 'Those who live by the sword shall perish by the sword.' ...and it may well be that in the progress of events, the working class of Ireland may be called upon to face the stern necessity of taking the sword (or rifle) against the class whose rule has brought upon them and upon the world the hellish horror of the present European war."[3]

In December, 1915, he directed the attention of the Irish people to the vacillation of those middle-class leaders of the Irish Volunteers who supported Eoin MacNeill as President. The latter was widely known to be anti-labor and had consistently opposed a Rising taking place during the war. Members of the Military Council of the Irish Republican Brotherhood put it on the agenda but they kept their aims hidden. They were handicapped by what they considered the necessity of retaining him. The situation, Connolly believed, was hindering preparations for the Rising.

Connolly named the MacNeill - Bulmer Hobson wing of the Irish. Volunteers, the "Not Yet leaders." He brought to the rank and file of the Volunteers the working class principles of mass agitation and mass organization. "We are raising our voice... to insist upon taking the military leaders of the Irish people [the Irish Volunteers] into our confidence; to ask our leaders to insist... if the rank and file must obey, so also is it true that the leaders must listen...". He criticized the Irish Volunteer leaders for grappling "a revolutionary situation with the weapons of a constitutional agitation. ...We believe in constitutional action in normal times; we believe in revolutionary action in exceptional times. These are exceptional times."[4] He had already made it clear that the Irish Citizen Army would not be held back, in spite of delay or equivocation on the part of the Volunteer leaders.[5]

---

[3]*Labor and Easter Week*, p. 50, from *The Worker*, January 30, 1915.
[4]*Ibid.*, pp. 114-119, from *Workers' Republic*, December 4, 1915. Greaves, p. 383.
[5]*Labor and Easter Week*, p. 91, from *Workers' Republic*, October 30, 1915.

Connolly had regretfully refused an invitation from his friends of the Scottish SLP to speak at an anti-conscription meeting. He wrote Arthur MacManus: "Every moment in Dublin just now is full of tragic possibilities, as our beneficent Government is becoming daily more high-handed in its methods and my presence is required here in constant watchfulness..." He sent a message to "all the Comrades who refuse to be led astray to fight the battles of the ruling capitalist class.

"Tell them that we in Ireland will not have conscription, let the law say what it likes... we know... that no force in their possession can decide for us *where* we will fight. *That* remains for us to decide; and we have no intention of shedding our blood abroad for our masters. Rather will we elect to shed it, if need be, for the conquest of our freedom at home."[6]

The Irish employers had imposed "Economic Conscription" on the workers. In January, 1916, William Martin Murphy and more than 400 employers heard the appeal of the Lord Lieutenant to "facilitate enlistment." As a result of this meeting, dismissals of workers of military age increased daily. "The meanest and cruelest form of conscription is already in active operation in this country," Connolly charged. He called for "Economic Conscription" by the working class, in its own interests. In two articles in the *Workers' Republic,* he set forth the need for revolution and presented the Socialist concept of an organized society. He wrote: "We want and must have economic conscription in Ireland, for Ireland... the conscription by an Irish nation of all the resources of the nation... *and* its men and women, all cooperating under one common direction, that Ireland may live and bear upon her fruitful bosom, the greatest number of the freest people she has ever known."[7] A month later, he again spoke of socialism as the solution. The productive powers of the conscripted resources should be "applied to the services of the community loyal to Ireland and to the army in its service." Ireland must be reconquered from those who stole it. "If the arms of the Irish Volunteers and Irish Citizen Army is the military weapon *of,* the economic conscription of its lands and wealth is the basis *for* that reconquest."[8]

Connolly did not use Lenin's term, "dictatorship of the proletariat," but he made it clear that he was aiming at a workers' state in a free Ireland. "Recognizing that the proper utilization of the nation's energies requires control of political power, we propose to conquer that political power

---

[6]Connolly Archives, Letter, Connolly to Arthur MacManus, November 23, 1915.
[7]*Labor and Easter Week,* pp. 120-124, from *Workers' Republic,* December 18, 1915.
[8]*Ibid.,* pp. 125-128, January 15, 1916.

through a working class political party and recognizing that the full development of national powers requires complete national freedom, we are frankly and unreservedly prepared for whatever struggle may be necessary to conquer for Ireland her place among the nations of the earth."[9]

On March 26, 1916, a new play, "Under Which Flag?" was presented by the Workers' Dramatic Company at Liberty Hall. It was again performed a second time, a week and one day before the Easter Rising. Its author was James Connolly.[10] The play carried a double message: the imminence of the Rising, and a sharp warning of the need for secrecy. Set in the period of the Fenian revolt, in 1867, it called for loyalty to the cause of Irish Independence and hatred of the detestable role of the informer.

In the first act, the mother expresses Connolly's working class approach. She says to her son, who has announced he is leaving for America, since Ireland is only fit for slaves: "Far off hills are always green... Always other people, always going hungry that others may be fed, naked that others may be clothed, badly housed that others may live in palaces. 'Tis the way of the world in America as well as in Ireland...".

Francis Sheehy Skeffington reviewed Connolly's play in the *Workers' Republic,* April 8, 1916. Both playwright and critic were dead a few weeks later, with Skeffington, in custody of British troops, shot in the back by an officer. In the review, the pacifist wrote:' "Under Which Flag?"... breathes the true spirit of patriotism; and at the present time, nothing could be healthier for the youth of Ireland than the lesson it teaches."[11] Fifty-three years later, on May 13, 1969, the Abbey Players again presented "Under Which Flag?" to raise funds for a memorial to Skeffington.

In view of Connolly's play, a portion of the transcript of the Royal Commission of Inquiry is of interest. Sir Mackenzie Chalmers interrogated Lord Wimborne, Lord Lieutenant and Viceroy of Ireland: "Q. You think with an efficient detective force you ought to have had rather more information than you had? A. Yes, but the problem was a difficult one. The secret was kept in a very few hands."[12]

The Right Honorable Augustine Birrell, Chief Secretary in Ireland, testified: "I always felt I was very ignorant of what was actually going on...".[13] There had been no informers and the secret of the Rising had been

---

[9] *Workers' Republic,* pp. 188-190.
[10] Connolly Archives, Mss. 13,945.
[11] *Ibid.,* Program, "Under Which Flag?" issued by The Abbey Players for performance of May 13, 1969 at Liberty Hall.
[12] *Sinn Fein Rebellion Handbook;* p. 123.
[13] *Ibid.,* p. 117. Also *Leaders and Men of the Easter Rising,* Chapter I, Leon O'Broin,

kept.

In January, 1916, Connolly appealed particularly to the Irish Volunteers to "Strengthen the hand of those leaders who are for action, as against those who are playing into the hands of the enemy... The time for Ireland's battle is NOW; the place for Ireland's battle is HERE."[14] Connolly lectured regularly to the Citizen Army on the strategy and tactics of street fighting.[15] In January, he disappeared. After four days, in which his family and friends had no word, he walked into Surrey House, the residence of Madame Markievicz. In answer to questions as to where he had been, he said: "I have been in Hell, but I conquered my conquerors." Connolly had gotten agreement from the Military Council. Now the Irish Citizen Army and the Irish Volunteers set the date for the joint Rising for Easter Sunday. Connolly had become a member of the Military Council of the Volunteers.[16]

Time was running out. A police raid had taken place at Surrey House only three hours before Connolly returned from his mission. Arrests and deportations had increased and anti-British newspapers destroyed. On February 12, 1916, Pearse communicated secretly with John Devoy, in New York City, through Joseph McGarrity, of Philadelphia, indicating that it was expected that British soldiers were about to take action against the leaders of the Rising. The message, in code, which mainly pertained to German arms, pleaded: "Send rifles to Limerick between Good Friday and Easter Sunday. May have to strike before then, but in any case cannot delay longer. Men would be imprisoned. Answer."[17]

The British military machine confirmed, after the Rising, that suppression of the Republican movement was to have taken place. In the Inquiry of the Royal Commission, one after another British official testified that for months they had been planning military occupation of Ireland by British troops. A police network had been spread over Ireland. Lord Wimbourne testified: "Ireland was under a microscope." Colonel E. Johnstone, Cheif Commissioner of the Dublin Metropolitan Police, testified that on April 23d, he had proposed a comprehensive plan which all English officials accepted, including Sir Neville Chamberlain, Inspector General of the Royal Irish Constabulary. It included "suppression of

---

"Birrell, Nathan and the Men of Dublin Castle," p. 10.

[14]*Labor and Easter Week,* p. 136, from *Workers' Republic,* January 22, 1916.

[15]His lectures were printed as articles in the *Workers' Republic.* These were printed in 1968 as a pamphlet, *Revolutionary Warfare.*

[16]Jacqueline Van Voris, p. 162.

[17]Sean Cronin, p. 153.

seditious newspapers," simultaneous arrests at 2 A.M. of Republican leaders, meanwhile their "strongholds" would be occupied, "so that the rank and file... would not be able to mobilize and arm." This was to be followed by "house to house search and all known Sinn Feiners disarmed."

Sir Matthew Nathan told of the conclusion of a meeting held on Easter Monday, 1916 at the Viceroyal Lodge where Johnstone's plan had finally been agreed upon. In the midst of the discussions, "...shots rang out at the Gates..." The Rising was taking place. It was too late to stop it.[18]

John Devoy and the Irish Republican Brotherhood, in the United States, had arranged for the shipment of German arms to Ireland, in cooperation with the Irish IRB. The German ship, "Aud," failed to make contact with the Volunteers, as it made its way into Cork Harbor. The ship was scuttled by the crew, to avoid discovery by the British fleet. Roger Casement, in charge of the project, went ashore from a German submarine. He was arrested and, later, hanged in England.

MacNeill, although not having been made aware of the plans for the Rising, learned the date and called an immediate meeting with Griffith and Hobson to head it off. On Saturday, MacNeill, as President of the Irish Volunteers, inserted into the press throughout Ireland, notices that: "Owing to the very critical position, all orders given to Irish Volunteers for tomorrow, Easter Sunday, are hereby rescinded, and no parades, marches or other movements of Irish Volunteers will take place. Each individual Volunteer will obey this order strictly in every particular."

This was a major blow to the Rising, especially sabotaging the movement outside Dublin. MacNeill gave as his excuse that he would not be responsible for the death of Irish men and women.

Connolly had never relied on Germany for Ireland's revolt, although he welcomed help. The Irish people must conduct their own revolution with their own resources, he believed. The leaders of the Citizen Army were faced with a difficult decision. They could continue with the uprising or accept military occupation without a struggle. The date for the Rising was changed to Easter Monday and attempts were made to inform the Volunteers outside Dublin. Nora and Ina Connolly were among those sent North as messengers. The situation was one of extreme confusion and there was little chance to mend the damage.

Madame Markievicz recalled that Connolly said to her, in connection

---

[18]*Sinn Fein Rebellion Handbook,* p. 133. The Royal Commission discussed the role of the Citizen Army and reported: "The leader was James Connolly... a man of great energy and ability."

with MacNeill's countermanding of the Easter Sunday mobilization: "There is only one sort of responsibility I am afraid of, and that is preventing the men and women of Ireland fighting and dying for Ireland, if they are so minded."[19]

He realized that MacNeill had dealt a telling blow and that the movement had been split and weakened. He is reported to have told his friend, William O'Brien: "We are going out to be slaughtered."

Monday morning, April 24th, the battalions of the Army, now named the Irish Republican Army, marched out and took over the buildings assigned to them. Connolly, Commandant General for Dublin, led his men to the General Post Office and captured it. The other officers, which included Padraic Pearse, Commander in Chief, Eamon de Valera and Madame Markievicz, as captains, took their places.

The first act of Pearse and Connolly, after taking over the Central Post Office, was to proclaim the Provisional Government of the Irish Republic. Pearse read the Proclamation, which he had written and Connolly had edited, from the Post Office steps. The document contained Connolly's socialist approach that Ireland belonged to all the Irish people. It began: "IRISHMEN AND IRISHWOMEN: In the name of God and of the dead generations from which she receives her old tradition of nationhood, Ireland, through us, summons her children to her flag and strikes for her freedom... We declare the right of the people of Ireland to the ownership of Ireland and to the unfettered control of Irish destinies to be sovereign and indefeasible...".

It proclaimed woman suffrage and pledged that religious and civil liberty, "equal rights and equal opportunities," would prevail. It anounced its "resolve to pursue the happiness and prosperity of the whole nation and of all its parts, cherishing all the children of the nation equally and oblivious of the differences carefully fostered by an alien government...".

The document was signed by Thomas J. Clarke, Sean MacDiarmada, Thomas MacDonagh, Eamonn Ceannt, Joseph Plunkett, and Pearse and Connolly.[20]

[19]Van Voris, p. 186.
[20]*Sinn Fein Rebellion Handbook,* p. 28.

CHAPTER XXII

DIALOGUE WITH THE CATHOLICS

To Connolly, finding the means of reaching Catholic workers with the program of socialism was a constant, driving force, in his activities in the United States. More than any other Socialist of his day, he was successful in achieving a dialogue between socialism and the Catholics -- intellectuals as well as workers, and a segment of socially oriented Catholic priests.

From the beginning of World War I, in 1914, to the time of the Easter Rising, in 1916, in Ireland, this bore rich fruit. The Minutes of the Royal Commission of Inquiry into the Rising found that the Irish Catholic Church, except its hierarchy, joined in the anti-war, anti-recruiting and anti-conscription campaigns of labor, the socialists and nationalists.

Connolly's most profound writings on religion were completed in the United States. In the *Harp,* moving towards achieving detente with the Catholics, he stimulated discussions between the socialists and the Catholic world. The approach toward religion in his letter to the *People,* on "Wages, Marriage and the Church," in 1904, while it caused "professional atheists" to heap abuse on him, served the important purpose of initiating a discussion in the SLP, and later in the SPA, which led to the building of a corps of Irish American Socialists, around the Irish Socialist Federation and the *Harp.*

One phase of sectarianism in the SLP, which Connolly rejected, was the emphasis and glorification of anti-religious sentiments in its propaganda. He charged, in his much discussed letter: "It is scarcely possible to take up a copy of the *Weekly People* of late, without realizing from its contents that it and the party are becoming distinctly anti-religious. If a clergyman anywhere attacks socialism, the tendency is to hit back, not at his economic absurdities, but at his theology, with which we have nothing to do."[1]

He criticized the space devoted to an "absurd" article on the Catholic Church, written by the Belgian Social-Democrat class collaborationist, Emile Vandervelde.

---

[1] *Weekly People,* April 9, 1904.

Connolly commented: "M. Vandervelde is a middle-class doctrinaire, who, on every question of tactics, has proven himself unsafe as a guide... His general Kangerooism is recognized by every thinking student of the European Socialist movement, but he speaks against the Catholic Church, and, presto, he becomes an oracle. But I refuse to worship at this Delphic shrine." This was not "a reasoned appeal to the working class," said Connolly,"...but an appeal to the free-thinker to look to the Socialists to fight their battles for them...".

Connolly's attempt to improve the relationship of the socialists to the Catholic workers was a new tactic to the SLP. He concluded: "If we but pause to think, we will see in the anti-religious tone of our papers and speakers how the ground here is being unwittingly prepared for... confusion." He believed attacks against religion obscured existing economic and political questions. "I shall certainly do my share toward repelling every such tendency, as strongly as I would fight to prevent the movement being identified... with the tenets of the Catholic Church, the Protestant, the Shinto, or the Jew."

In his lengthy answer, De Leon pointed to attacks by the Catholic Church against Belgian Socialists. He repeated a statement made in a speech and a pamphlet on Anarchism, printed in 1901, in connection with the assassination of President William McKinley by Leon Czolgosz, identified by him as a Catholic. Nine assassins of history, stated De Leon, were Catholics -- his conclusion, the Catholic Church bred assassination.[2]

Connolly believed that portraying the Catholic Church as causing anarchism and terrorism was a distortion of Marxism. Individualism, terrorism and anarchism were considered by Marx, Engels, and later Lenin, as petty-bourgeois ideologies, growing out of class differences, and detrimental to the working class. De Leon omitted the class basis of the assassinations, Connolly charged. In his "Reply to the Editor of the Daily People," (which De Leon refused to print) submitted to Troy Section, New York, Connolly made no attempt to spare his antagonist, emphasizing that De Leon had held no consistent position. Almost concurrently with his Czolgosz speech and the pamphlet, De Leon had replied in the *People* of October 5, 1901, to a Providence, Rhode Island reader, that although Czolgosz and four other assassins were Catholics, "...not for that is there any reason to impute assassination by reason of them to the Roman Catholic Creed".

---

[2]Daniel De Leon, *Socialism vs. Anarchism.*

Connolly concluded: "So that, in October 5, 1901, our comrade declares a man would be 'off his base,' if he attributed the acts of the assassins mentioned to their religion, and in his lecture on Socialism and Anarchism, he apparently goes off his base on that very point."[3]

It is not inconceivable that De Leon might have been influenced by the polemics with Connolly. Immediately following the 1904 controversy, in August, 1904, he attended the Amsterdam Congress of the Second International. There he fought against the opportunism of Vandervelde and others. In his *Flashlights of the Amsterdam Congress,* De Leon devoted a chapter to severely criticizing Vandervelde's opportunist policies.[4]

In the United States, during Connolly's stay, especially in the working class districts, where there was a large proportion of foreign-born Catholics, there was increasing concern with social problems by the Catholic clergy. Rising imperialism had taken its toll of the foreign-born parishioners particularly. The *Harp* was soon peppered with discussions for and against socialism by Catholic leaders, with Connolly's thoughtful comments. Step by step, guidance for socialist work among Catholics was spelled out.

Speaking for the Irish Socialist Federation, he advised Irish socialists to avoid entanglements in purely theological speculations. "As long as the priest speaks to us as priest upon religious matters," he admonished in the *Harp,* "we will listen to him, with all the reverence and attention his sacred calling deserves, but the moment he steps upon the political platform, or worse still, uses the altar from which to tell us what to do with our political freedom, then in our sight, he will cease to be a priest and be simply a politician."[5]

"Christian Socialism" had become popular within the Socialist Party in 1908 and 1909. SPA members of the clergy related socialism to the morality of the Christian religion. They discussed this in articles and lectures. Connolly made the point: "Every time we approach a Catholic worker with a talk about 'Christian Socialism,' we make this a religious question, and on such a question, his religion teaches him that the clergy must say the final word. Why should we go out of our way to give the clergy the right to interfere in our politics, by giving a religious name to an

---

[3]Connolly Archives, "Reply by James Connolly to the Editor of the *Daily People.*" Also from the Archives, *The Socialist,* June, 1904, "Wages and Other Things," by Connolly.
[4]De Leon, *Flashlights of the Amsterdam Congress.*
[5]*Harp,* October, 1908.

economic and political movement?"[6]

For years there has been speculation on the part of labor historians as to whether James Connolly was an "orthodox" Catholic. His legacy of a body of definitive writing, both in America and Ireland, leaves his position on religion and religious workers very clear. As for his personal beliefs, a letter came to light in the William O'Brien papers which offers additional clarity. Dated January 30, 1908, this letter was written to John Matheson, in answer to his direct question. Connolly informed his friend: "For myself, though I have usually posed as a Catholic, I have not gone to my duty for 15 years, and have not the slightest tincture of faith left. I only assumed the Catholic pose in order to quiz the raw freethinkers, whose ridiculous dogmatism did and does dismay me, as much as the dogmatism of the Archbishop. In fact, I respect the good Catholic more than the average free-thinker."[7] He observed along these lines many times that atheists were not, per se, Socialists; on the other hand, many were upholders of imperialism.

The letter to Matheson should be considered in conjunction with his writings on religion. A statement to Tom Bell, at the time member of the SLP in Scotland, offers further information on Connolly's position. Bell, an admirer of Connolly, was considered a "skeptic" by the Catholics. In his autobiography, he wrote that on the question of religion, he thought that De Leon had been correct, in the controversy with Connolly. He recounted a revealing discussion.

"Connolly," he wrote, "...never failed, too, in his denunciation of the Church, to make clear he was a Catholic. This was rather disquieting to me... One night, following a meeting... where the straight question was asked 'Was he a Catholic?' and the straight reply given, 'Yes,' I tackled him on this. 'How is it possible,' I asked, 'to reconcile the Catholicism of Rome with the materialist conception of history?'

" 'Well,' he replied, '...in Ireland, all the Protestants are Orangemen and howling jingoes. If the children go to the Protestant schools, they get taught to wave the Union Jack and worship the English King. If they go to the Catholic Church, they become rebels. Which would you sooner have?"[8]

In his articles and in the pamphlet, *Labor, Nationality and Religion,* Connolly went beyond the Erfurt program of the Second International, which considered religion a private matter. While claiming that religion

[6]*Ibid.,* April, 1909.
[7]Connolly Archives, Letter, Connolly to Matheson, January 30, 1908.
[8]Bell, p. 51.

had nothing to do with economics or politics, Connolly, here, and in subsequent writing, stated clearly the Marxist, historical materialist approach to the history and philosophy of religion. He did attack the basic idealistic philosophy of religion but at the same time, in the foreground of his tactics, was achievement of the united front with religious workers, as the objective.

He wrote: "The passionate adherence of the Irish to Catholicity in Reformation times was, no doubt, largely due to the fact that the English Government had embraced Protestantism."

Religion reflected the conditions under which it existed: "The Reformation was the capitalist idea appearing in the religious field. As capitalism teaches that the social salvation of man depends solely upon his own individual effort... it created its reflex in the religious world, and that reflex, proclaiming individual belief was the sole necessity of salvation, appears in history as the Protestant Reformation. Now, the [Catholic] Church curses the Protestant Reformation -- the child, and blesses capitalism -- its parent."[9]

Perhaps the most probing writing of Connolly on religion appeared in the *Harp* of September, 1908. Entitled "Roman Catholicism and Socialism," this article presented a study of the history of religion in Ireland and its role in the class struggle. Connolly described a pamphlet, written by Patrick J. Cooney, of Bridgeport, Connecticut, a practicing Catholic and a militant socialist, as "refreshing as an oasis in the desert to the tired and thirsty traveller." Although he recognized that a sound materialist approach to history was lacking, Connolly considered Cooney's pamphlet important in developing a dialogue with the Irish-American and Irish workers.

"Here and there," noted Connolly, "his loyalty to the Church seems to betray him into statements regarding her position which... would hardly stand the test of modern criticism and historical research." Softening the blow, he added: "But we confess that, in that respect, his attitude is a refreshing change from that of the crudely superficial thinkers (?) and scribblers who so commonly discredit the Socialist ranks by their dogmatism on that subject."

The Catholic Church in Ireland, historically, adapted its policies to expediency, he wrote. It "always accepts the established order, even if it had warred upon those who had striven to establish such order." He cited

---

[9]Connolly, *Labor, Nationality and Religion,* in *The Workers' Republic,* pp. 262, ff.

the Irish revolutionary movements of 1798, 1848 and 1867. Each time the Catholic Church had supported the counter-revolutionary, pro-English government forces and denounced the revolutionists. But in later years, when the Irish people honored their martyrdom, the clergy also accorded them honor.

When the church "realizes that the cause of capitalism is a lost cause," he argued, "it will find excuse enough to forget the anti-socialist encyclicals and then approve of the position of those lowly priests who want to grant freedom of speech and embrace social ideas." The dreams of the Freethinkers, of a major confrontation with the Catholic Church, "are not the product of modern socialist philosophy, but a survival from the obsolete philosophy of the days preceding the French Revolution." Though they had tried to bring their petty-bourgeois ideas into the camp of Socialism, such ideas "are also held by an even greater number of enemies of Socialism... their first progenitors, both in England and France were also the first great exponents of the capitalist doctrines of free trade, free competition, free contract and free labor.

"Such conceptions of religion are entirely opposed to the modern doctrine that the intellectual conceptions of men are the product of their material conditions... In... this modern conception of... historical progress, religion appears as the outcome of the efforts of mankind to interpret the workings of the forces of nature, and to translate its phenomena into the terms of a language which could be understood... that which the cultured man of the twentieth century would explain and understand as 'a natural process,' the mental vision of our forefathers could only see as the result of the good or ill-will of some beneficient or evil spirit -- some God or Devil." This accounted for the development of fairy and leprechaun beliefs in Ireland.

The development of religious thought in Ireland was a progression. "The different stages of development of the human mind in its attitude toward the forces of nature," he continued, "created different priesthoods to interpret them, and the mental conceptions of mankind as interpreted by those priesthoods, became systematized religion...".[10]

The Catholic hierarchy in Ireland maintained it position by its subservience to the English government and its dominant Anglican Protestant Church. Its history was one of support of British and Irish capitalism and intrigue against people's movements. The lower category of priests and Catholic laymen, however, often were rebellious and gave

---

[10]*Harp*, September, 1908.

support to Irish nationalist movements. The *Harp* reprinted an article from the monthly publication, *Sinn Fein*. Written by an Irish priest, it described the pro-British bias of the Irish Catholic hierarchy during the American Revolution. The Bishop of Ossery, Ireland, had called on his flock to pray and fast for the victory of England. He referred to the fighters for American independence as "seduced by the specious notions of liberty and other illusive expectations of sovereignty." The Americans, he said, "disclaim any dependence on Great Britain and endeavor, by force of arms, to distress their mother country, which has cherished and protected them." The *Sinn Fein* writer charged that the Church's political policy had been "one long crime against human progress." The priest demanded "an unconditional surrender by the Papacy of its political alliance with capitalist society."[11]

As an example of anti-working class interference by the church hierarchy, Connolly focused on its tyrannical control of education in Ireland. "This system," he charged, "is the direct result of an understanding, or as the Americans would say, a 'deal' between the Vatican and the English government in Ireland -- a direct outcome of the secular policy of the Papacy. Every revolutionist in Ireland realizes that this compact is the source of the unflinching opposition of the higher Catholic clergy to every real revolutionary movement in our country... I had always a sympathetic feeling towards the saying attributed to Thomas Francis Meagher, to wit: 'If the altar stands between man and his freedom, I would say 'Down with the altar.' "[12]

Practically every issue of the *Harp*, from 1908 to 1910, contained material on religion, which reflected the growing success of Connolly in developing a responsive communication with the Catholic world. An article by Dr. Cassertelli, quoted from the *Labor Leader*, admitted that the socialists were trying to win social reforms for the people. But what, he asked, if social reforms win material things and a man lose his soul? Connolly suggested that only the souls of poor people concerned him and these the Doctor hoped to save by depriving them of security.[13]

In the same issue of the *Harp*, Connolly described the palace in Killarney, where the Bishop of Kerry lived amid huge stone and marble Catholic institutions. In the rear of these buildings were the workers, in

---

[11]*Harp*, March, 1909.
[12]*Ibid.*, May, 1908. This article is also quoted by Manus O'Riordan, in his thesis, "Connolly in America."
[13]*Harp*, October, 1908.

shabby and degrading slums. Connolly recognized, "a certain amount of justice in the complaint that the Church put into stone and lime and pictures and statuary what would be better invested in food and clothing and education for those in need."[14]

Not always was the dialogue friendly. With biting sarcasm, he responded to the attempt of the *New World,* a Catholic newspaper, to incite a riot against a meeting of the Irish Socialist Federation in Chicago. Irish heroes of the past, he wrote, had been stoned by the priests. "Does the clergy wish to raise all those hateful memories?" he asked. He dubbed Mr. O'Malley, the editor, who proposed to rotten-egg Connolly's meeting, "a foul-mouthed scribbler." Said Connolly: "Let Mr. O'Malley lay in his supply of rotten eggs, for that meeting will be held." The *Chicago Citizen* made a similar incitation to riot.

The Irish Cardinal Logue, in the Spring of 1908, in a well-publicized visit to the United States, called upon John D. Rockefeller at his home. Connolly denounced the Cardinal for using his influence to suppress the progressive Irish newspaper, *Irish Peasant.* "The time has long since gone by," he warned the Cardinal, "when Irish men and women can be kept from thinking by hurling priestly thunder at their heads. We may still kneel to the Servant of God, but when he speaks as the Servant of our Oppressor, he must not wonder if he receives from slaves in revolt, the same measure as his earthly masters. His Eminence... cannot act the despot and throttle the press in Ireland, and act the patron of free institutions in America... It is well, above all, to let all the clerical ranters (Protestant and Catholic) against Socialism realize that it is not Socialism that is on trial before the Bar of Civilization, but they and theirs. Socialism is today in the role of public prosecutor, and all its enemies are on trial for treason to freedom and humanity."[15]

He was quick to emphasize instances of leading Catholics who were discussing differences with the socialists with increasing friendliness. He reported, for example, an article in the *Catholic Fortnightly Review* of December 15, 1908, which called attention to increased discussions of Socialism in many Catholic circles. The *Review* admitted that Connolly had been correct in charging that many Catholic writers lacked even a rudimentary knowledge of socialism. It quoted, with disapproval, the *St. Louis Church Progress,* which presented the attitude: "Between the Church and Socialism, there can be no compromise."

---

[14]*Ibid.*
[15]*Harp,* May, 1908.

The *Catholic Fortnightly* commented: "Sympathy for the downtrodden masses, suffering from the undeniable abuses of our capitalist economic system, are driving not a few Catholics out of the Church."[16]

The following month, the *Harp* quoted the *Catholic Register,* which carried an address by the pastor of St. Aloysius Church, Rev. M.P. Dowling, J.J. "Why should people die of hunger in the midst of plenty?" asked the Catholic newspaper. "Socialists have some right on their side." This fact, "...cannot be met by abuse or by making light of existing evils and wrongs... It behooves us, then, to see what there is good in Socialism, which of its recommendations and tenets can be accepted and adopted by loyal Catholics."[17]

During this period, an attack by a priest, writing in the *Catholic Union and Times,* brought this admonition from Connolly: "We are now entering a period when a knowledge of theology will not excuse ignorance on social questions."

The best known work of Connolly on religion, *Labor, Nationality, and Religion,* was written in the United States and printed in Ireland, after his return in 1910. This work answered a series of Lenten lectures attacking Socialism, by Father Kane, S.J. of the Gardiner St. Church, in Dublin. Connolly wrote his pamphlet at the request of the Irish socialists,[18] taking much of his material from his writings in the *Harp.* Enlarging on his September, 1908 article in the *Harp,* he depicted the role of the Catholic Church in Ireland from the twelfth century. He listed in detail the crimes of the Popes and Bishops against the Irish people.

Historically, said Connolly, "The instincts of the reformers and revolutionists have been right, the political theories of the Vatican and the clergy unquestionably wrong..."[19]

Kane had preached that the workers, if they were born in poverty, should accept Divine Will. This was "blasphemy," to Connolly. "In the degree in which we support them [the gross injustices of the system] we become participators in the crimes upon which they were built." To the charge that socialism is against freedom and the rights of the individual, Connolly responded: "How can a person, or a class, be free, when its means of life are in the grasp of another? How can the working class be free, when the sole chance of existence of its individual members depends upon their

---

[16]*Harp,* January, 1909.
[17]*Harp,* February, 1909.
[18]*Labor, Nationality and Religion,* pp. 191-264.
[19]*Ibid.,* p. 203.

ability to make a profit for others?"

Under socialism, Father Kane accused, "the will of the people would be nothing more than the whim of the tyrant mob -- blindly led by blind leaders." Connolly commented: "Spoken like a good Tory and staunch friend of despotism."[20]

In his sixth lecture, Father Kane depicted the socialists as anarchistic bomb-throwing believers in brute force. This brought forth the following: "The fact that some Socialists believed that force may be used to inaugurate the new social order only indicated their conviction that the criminal capitalist and ruling classes will not peacefully abide by the verdict of the ballot but will strive by violence to perpetuate their robber rule, in spite of the declared will of the majority of the people." This belief was borne out by every revolution in history, he added.

The conclusion of Father Kane was that his church, "teaches both men and masters that for their own sake, they should be friends, not foes..." His final word: "Have pity on the poor... There is no need, no excuse for socialism. But there is sore need of social reform."

Connolly denounced the priest's approach, bitterly criticized the church's performance and called for the end of capitalism. "After again and again admitting the tyranny, the extortions, the frauds, the injustices perpetrated... by those who control and own our means of existence," he said, "he has no remedy to offer but pity... Professing to denounce Mammon, he yet shrinks from leading the forces of righteousness against it, and by so shrinking, shows all his professed solicitude for justice, all his vaunted hatred of tyranny were 'mere sound and fury signifying nothing.' Is not this attitude symbolic of the attitude of the Church for hundreds of years? Ever counselling humility, but sitting in the seats of the mighty; ever patching up the diseased and broken wrecks of an unjust social system, but blessing the system which made the wrecks and spread the disease... The day has passed for patching up the capitalist system; it must go."[21]

As the 1916 rebellion approached in Ireland, in the midst of the hardship, suffering and death imposed on the Irish people by "England's War," Catholic priests, in increasing numbers, turned toward labor. Only three months before the Rising, Connolly praised "the splendid speech delivered under the auspices of the Dublin Trades Council, Tuesday, January 15, by Father Laurence, O.F.M., Cap." Connolly declared: "Here we had a great meeting of workingmen and women, overwhelmingly

---

[20]*Ibid.*, p. 230.
[21]*Ibid.*, pp. 256, 257, 263, 264.

Catholic in their religious faith, gathering together to discuss problems of social life and national aspirations with a priest whom they held in affectionate esteem, but insisting upon discussing these problems in the spirit of comradeship and equality." His article illustrated the working unity of priests, labor and the socialists. As spokesman for the most militant wing of the labor movement, Connolly said he "could see no fundamental difference between the views expressed by Father Laurence and ourselves." He noted only differences in names and definitions.[22]

It is reported that Connolly, badly wounded and about to be executed, took the last rites of the Catholic Church, before he was taken to his death. Desmond Ryan, in his biography of Connolly, wrote that this was at the earnest request of Padraic Pearse, Connolly's fellow fighter for Ireland's freedom, his friend, and a devout Catholic.

It does not seem strange that Connolly took this step. His writings indicate clearly his tremendous sensitivity to the Catholic's feeling for his creed. It is impossible to believe that at this time, when he felt he represented the deepest hopes of Irish men and women, the majority of whom were Catholic, that he would affront the people he led, and refuse the last rites for the dying -- a most sacred sacrament -- whatever his personal beliefs.

Herbert Apthekier's *The Urgency of Marxist-Christian Dialogue,* is a discussion of the need for dialogue between Marxists and Christians and all followers of religion, in a time when coexistence and peace betwwen vast socialist populations and capitalist countries are on the order of business.

One cannot read Aptheker's book without failing to note the similarity of Connolly's position on religion with that of Marx, Engels and Lenin.[23] The discourse indicates that Marx, Engels and Lenin pointed out basic differences in fundamental philosophy between historic materialism and religion. They examined religions historically and explained the causes of their growth. Lenin attacked institutionalized religion in Russia, a staunch supporter of the tyrannical suppression of the workers and peasants under Czarism. Aptheker, referring to Lenin's article on religion: "The Attitude of the Workers' Party to Religion," written in 1909, explains: "Lenin emphasizes that the struggle against religion [in Russia] must in no case be marked by the prohibition of religious practice and belief. It must, on the contrary, be one of argument, persuasion and education, and above all, of

---

[22] *Workers' Republic,* pp. 188-190, January 19, 1916.
[23] Herbert Aptheker, *Marxist-Christian Dialogue,* pp. 14, 15.

active struggle against those abominable social conditions whose existence is at the root of religious tendency." A private matter, so far as the state is concerned, religion has serious differences with the party and Marxism. "Prohibition of religion, he emphasizes -- as did Marx and Engels -- is wrong and, in any case, ineffective." The "social roots of religion" must be eliminated -- and Lenin points to : "ruin, destruction, pauperism, prostitution, death from starvation...".

The program of the Russian Communist Party, in March, 1919, was consistent with this. It announced its support for the separation of the Church and State and Church and the schools. The role of the Czarist church, in helping Russian imperialism exploit the workers, would be the subject of an educational campaign. The Russian Communist Party emphasized: "While doing this, we must carefully avoid anything that can wound the feelings of believers, for such a method can only lead to the strengthening of religious fanaticism." Lenin requested that believers, who were honest and devoted to the working class, be admitted to the Communist Party.[24]

Many miles away from the Russian Bolsheviks, and some years earlier, the majority of the workers to whom Connolly addressed himself, in the United States and Ireland, were followers of religion, mainly the Catholic Church. Connolly's efforts to achieve their understanding of Socialist objectives were fervent, tactful, patient, brilliant, and very clearly, in his time, effective.[25]

---

[24]*Ibid.,* p. 18.

[25]Constance de Markievicz. She quotes Rev. P. Coffey, Ph.D., Maynooth College, from the *Catholic Bulletin* of 1920. He seriously discussed socialism and approved of much of Connolly's teachings. Countess Markievicz, a Catholic, was a devoted follower of James Connolly.

CHAPTER XXIII

"THE MOST THOROUGH-GOING FEMINIST--"

When Connolly wrote his preliminary letter to the *People,* in 1904, on Wages, Marriage and the Church,[1] the portion of his letter on marriage represented but a small part of his concern with the woman question. During his life-time, he was to go far beyond most Socialists of his day, in attempting to remedy the bitter inequities, indignities and super-exploitation borne by women -- particularly those of the Irish working class.

It is a fact that the Proclamation of the short-lived Provisional Irish Republic was the first political document that wrote equality of suffrage into the life of a nation. This statement was not only edited by him but was largely influenced by his ideas.

- In 1904, his brief presentation, defending monogamy in marriage, in the De Leon controversy, displayed his serious concern with bringing working class women to Socialism. He had become impatient with constant discussions of sex relationships, in the SLP, and the promotion of promiscuity by some SLP members, as a Socialist attitude. The Catholic Church constantly used the "free love" spectre, in its attempt to alienate Catholics from Socialism.

Connolly's letter criticized a section of August Bebel's *Woman Under Socialism,* translated by De Leon and running, serially, in the *People.* The work, exhaustive insofar as it presented woman's status in succeeding systems of society, devoted few pages to women under Socialism. It was introduced by De Leon in a Preface, March 30, 1903, which, in part, declared: "There can be no emancipation of humanity without the social independence and equality of the sexes. Up to this point, all socialists are likely to agree... The moment the field of the known is abandoned, and one launches out into pictures of future forms, a wide field is opened for speculation. Differences of opinion start over that which is probable or not probable."[2]

---

[1] *Weekly People,* April 9, 1904.
[2] Daily People, March 30, 1904.

The discussion which followed found many SLP members declaring for promiscuity as an acceptable sex relationship under Socialism. To Connolly, the space allotted to Bebel's book was a waste; the material was useless as propaganda and, in some part, "prurient." He thought De Leon's failure to take a stand for monogamy was losing working class women for socialism and the SLP.

Bebel wrote that under Socialism, all women must have the same right as the "great souls" of the past and present, to fulfill their love and sexual needs, as they arose. "The woman of future society," he wrote, "is socially and economically independent; she is no longer subject to even a vestige of dominion and exploitation... In the choice of love, she is, like man, free and unhampered. She woos or is wooed and closes the bond from no considerations other than her own inclinations... The satisfaction of the sexual instinct is as much a private concern as the satisfaction of any other natural instinct...".[3]

Lenin, later, in discussions with Inessa Armand on free love, was to describe her point of view, which subscribed to promiscuity, as "bourgeois." In conversations with Clara Zetkin, German woman Communist, he commented: "Dissoluteness in sexual life... is a phenomenon of decay."[4]

Considering the youth who were building the new society, he reiterated this stand: "The revolution demands concentration, increase of forces. From the masses, from individuals. It cannot tolerate orgiastic conditions such as are normal for the decadent heroes and heroines of D'Annunzio... The proletariat is a rising class. It doesn't need intoxication as a narcotic or a stimulus. Intoxication as little by sexual exaggeration as by alcohol... Self-control, self-discipline is not slavery, not even in love."[5]

James Connolly wrote to the *People,* in his letter of 1904: "When touring this country in 1902, I met in Indianapolis an esteemed comrade who almost lost his temper with me because I expressed my belief in monogamic marriage, and because I said, as I still hold, that the tendency of civilization is towards its perfection and completion, instead of towards its destruction. My comrade's views, especially since the publication in the *People* of Bebel's *Woman,* are held by a very large number of members, but I hold... that such works and such publications are an excrescence upon the movement."

---

[3]August Bebel, p. 343.
[4]*The Woman Question,* pp. 80, 76. Reeve, pp. 165-175.
[5]*The Woman Question,* pp. 80, 81.

He concluded: "I question if you can find in the whole world one woman who was led to Socialism by it, but you can find hundreds who were repelled from studying Socialism by judicious extracts from its pages."[6]

As bitterly as De Leon denounced Connolly for his letter, it was a fact that he changed his position to support of monogamy, as a result of Connolly's strong position. He remained unmoved, however, by Connolly's thrust against sectarianism and never understood this aspect of his views on marriage and Bebel. De Leon did not criticize promiscuity until his translation of *Woman Under Socialism* was printed in book form in 1904. Five years after the discussion, in 1909, De Leon returned to his earlier position: "Socialism plants itself exclusively upon the economic question... What concern is it of Socialists as to whether monogamy will or will not continue?"[7]

De Leon's translator's preface to *Woman Under Socialism* the book read, in part: "The moral, as well as the material accretions of the race's intellect, since it uncoiled out of early Communism, bar to my mind, all prospect--I would say danger, moral and hygienic, of promiscuity, or of anything remotely approaching that... For one, I hold that the monogamous family--bruised and wounded in the cruel rough-and-tumble of modern society... will have its wounds staunched, its bruises healed and... bloom under Socialism into a lever of mighty power for the moral and physical elevation of the race."[8]

In his "Reply by James Connolly to the Editor of the *Daily People*," which he presented to the Troy Section, which tried and exonerated him, he wrote on Marriage: "The question of marriage, as treated by me, is in its last analysis, the question of the wisdom of publishing Bebel's book... I stated that I believed in monogamic marriage and disagreed with Bebel who taught otherwise... It has been said that his work is based upon that of Morgan's [Lewis H. Morgan's *Ancient Society*] but the most delicate minded could read Morgan without a blush, and the same cannot be said of Bebel... Bebel declares openly and avowedly that under Socialism, the modern Monogamic Marriage will collapse and yet, his book, we are told, is based upon that of Morgan, and Morgan declares, as unreservedly, his belief in the beauty and permanency of the modern marriage."

He commented wryly: "Comrade De Leon also believes that the Monogamic Marriage will remain, yet he declares that the book he disagrees with is the 'best aimed shot at the existing social system.' Either

---

[6]*Weekly People*, April 9, 1904.
[7]*Ibid.*, June 22, 1901. Daniel De Leon, *Watson on the Gridiron*.
[8]*Woman Under Socialism*, Translator's Preface by Daniel De Leon.

De Leon has not much faith in his own markmanship or else he believes that the best aimed shot is that which proceeds from correct premises to wrong conclusions."

As a result of the discussion, it appeared that there was agreement on the ability of monogamy under Socialism to survive. Connolly, in a conciliatory mood, after reiterating his belief in the future for monogamy, wrote: "...I believe that no matter what may have been the force which gave birth to any institution, its permanency will and must be tested not by its origin but by its adaptability to the... economic institutions of the future."[9]

Connolly disagreed with De Leon's position that it was reformist to struggle for the special needs of women workers. De Leon opposed campaigns for suffrage, equal pay for equal work, for special legislation protecting women workers. The Socialist Revolution was the one viable demand for working class women.[10]

Karl Marx, on the other hand, in a letter to Dr. Ludwig Kugelmann, written December 12, 1868, stated his belief that the status of women's rights revealed the level of social progress. His letter praised the American Labor Union, which, in its Congress had treated working women with equality. [11] Marx and Engels never wrote against monogamy but exposed its hypocrisy under capitalism. The abolition of capitalism would bring "full freedom of marriage," according to Engels, "for there is no other motive left, except mutual inclination. And as sexual love is by its very nature exclusive--although at present this exclusiveness is fully recognized only in the woman--the marriage based on sexual love is, by its nature, individual marriage."

Under Socialism, Engels predicted, "the equality of woman thereby achieved, will tend infinitely more to make men really monogamous than to make women polyandrous... But what will certainly disappear from monogamy are all the features stamped upon it through its origin in property relationships--supremacy of the man... and... indissolubility."[12]

Connolly's attention to the condition of Irish working class women was evident in the *Harp*. In the issue of September, 1908, he reviewed an article in the *Boston Pilot* on the life of an imaginary Irish princess, as reconstructed from a study of gold and silver ornaments found in the bogs

[9]Connolly Archives, "Reply by James Connolly to the Editor of the Daily People."
[10]Reeve, pp. 165-175.
[11]Marx and Engels, *Correspondence,* Letter, Marx to Kugelmann, p. 255.
[12]Frederick Engels, *Origin of the Family, Private Property and the State,* pp. 25-75. *The Woman Question,* pp. 74-76.

of Ireland. "To me," he wrote, "it was especially interesting as illustrative of the curious effect modern property relations have upon the mind of even the most gifted amongst us."

The princess was attended by slave women. "What appeared to my Socialistic mind," commented Connolly, "was that the writer... treated the princess as a typical 'colleen' of ancient Ireland, and utterly neglected to recognize in the slave women any right to be regarded as Irish types at all."

Connolly admonished the writer: "Shake up for us the dry bones of history and tell us about the wives and mothers and daughters of the producing classes of our native country." The princess was part of a class "whose predatory proclivities hindered the free development of the nation and prepared the way for its subjection." Connolly wanted to read about the women of the people--"those Irish girls, who in the recent dock strike in Belfast, joined their fathers and brothers and sweethearts in the streets, to battle against the English troops, imported in the interests of Irish capitalism." To his mind, they were "a thousand times more admirable 'types of Irish colleens.' "[13]

Connolly levied a particularly forceful indictment against Judge Tuthill, of the Circuit Court of Cook County, Illinois, who upheld the "right" of women to work overtime. The Judge said of the law limiting the workday of women factory workers to ten hours: "Such a law would put women back 100 years... It deprives her of the right to exercise the right of contract which is given her by the constitution." This law had been won by intensive campaigning by working women, supported by the labor unions .

Connolly editorialized: "The pretense that a woman wage worker, owning nothing but her labor power and an empty stomach, was able to make a free contract with the capitalist owner of the means by which alone that labor could be employed... has been abandoned for half a century by every jurist in the world."

But a Judge in America, "needs only to be possessed of a pliant conscience, a smooth tongue and a willingness to prostitute all talents to the service of those who control the moneybags...".[14]

The young girls who came to the United States from Ireland were the least equipped members of their families, according to Connolly, to face the hardships of survival in a new land. The country girls had no future on their household farms, the oldest son, by law of primogeniture,inheriting. These untrained girls were set adrift in the United States, to exist as best

---

[13]*Harp,* September, 1908.
[14]*Harp,* October, 1909.

they could, on the basis of physical endurance and native intelligence. Many did not overcome the odds against them.

The general assault against the working class was accompanied by attempts to extend prostitution among young working class women, by organized crime rings, many of which were in collusion with "respectable" politicians. Connolly alluded to this frequently in the *Harp* and in his later writings. This state of affairs was dramatized in the case of Ella Gingles, a beautiful 18 year old girl, the daughter of Irish lace-makers. On the night of February 16, 1909, she was seized and carried to the Wellington Hotel in Chicago, where she was gagged, drugged and assaulted. The trial of the perpetrators, in view of their political connections, caused a national sensation. It was revealed that the plan was to install the girl in a brothel hotel, the Everleigh Club, frequented by Chicago politicians, including Mayor Busse.

The *New York Call* and the *Chicago Socialist,* as well as the *Harp,* closely followed the matter. The politicians attempted to counter the unfavorable publicity by counter-charging that Ella was a thief. Tom Taggart, ex-chairman of the Democratic National Committee and his friend, John Kern, Democratic candidate for Vice-president, were accused of being involved in the "white slave" traffic.[15]

To Connolly, Ella Gingles was: "...another poor Irish immigrant in this land... under this system which Irishmen are asked to grow enthusiastic about." Exonerated, Ella Gingles went back to Ireland, with the support of the *Harp,* the *Call* and other Irish organizations. The Chicago authorities, as Connolly charged, displayed "absolute refusal to arrest those whom she accused of a crime more revolting than murder."[16]

"Votes for Women" was the chief political demand of militant women in the United States and Europe during these years. The growing movement met with scathing derision, often in high places, both in England and the United States. In December, 1908, Lloyd George, M.P. declared he would not speak at any session where women were present.[17] Woodrow Wilson, President of Princeton University, in December, 1908, attacked "Votes for Women," at the Southern Society's annual dinner, at the Waldorf Astoria, New York.

"Women are so much more illogical than men," he declared. The reasoning of women is entirely... false."[18]

---

[15]*New York Evening Call,* August 12, 1909.
[16]*Harp,* August, 1909.
[17]*New York Call,* December 4, 1908.
[18]*Ibid.,* December 10,1908.

In March, 1909, in the *Harp,* Connolly criticized the convention of the United Irish League, in Dublin, for ignoring the women's movement. It "recognized... the rights of a dead language," but "denied the rights of living women."

Women must strengthen their own organizations, he advised. "What politician ever allowed a great principle to weigh so much with him as the fear of losing cash and votes? The Irish politician will respect the woman's movement when it is strong enough to kick them, not before. Until then, they will talk about the beauties of the daughters of Erin and continue telling [them] to stay home and mend shoes... whilst their lord and masters are settling the fate of Ireland."[19]

Connolly always tried to involve his family in the struggle for women's rights. Ina Connolly recalled: "The Women's Franchise movement was going strong," at a time when the family first returned to Ireland, "...so we marched out to the Suffragette meetings and we paraded along with the women. We marched carrying banners or giving out leaflets and calling for support for the Suffragettes."[20]

In Ireland, Francis Sheehy Skeffington became a close friend of Connolly. He and his wife were ardent feminists, as well as pacifists and Socialists. In his paper, the *Irish Citizen,* in November, 1911, he described Connolly as: "the soundest and most thorough-going feminist among all the Irish labor men."[21]

In the hectic days of the 1913 strike and lockout in Dublin, Connolly addressed a crowded suffragette meeting. Many of the working women who had been locked out of the factories attended. The common interests of labor and the women's movement was his subject. Women and labor alike had been tricked by every capitalist political party. Their own efforts, alone, would achieve freedom. He reiterated something he had said more than once -- that no militant action for or by women had failed to win his support.[22] He sent the beleaguered suffragettes of London, and elsewhere, as C. Desmond Greaves put it, "many a message of support."

One of these was: "When trimmers and compromisers disavow you, I, a poor slum-bred politician, raise my hat in thanksgiving that I have lived to see this resurgence of women."[23]

---

[19] *Harp,* March, 1909.
[20] Ina Connolly Heron, Unpublished Manuscript.
[21] Van Voris, p. 101.
[22] *Ibid.,* p. 115.
[23] Greaves, p. 292.

To a letter from John Matheson, who was still a member of the Scottish SLP, he replied: "I am unfeignedly glad to hear that you are on the right side in this woman's business. The attitude of most Socialists, including the chief Socialist press... is just beneath contempt. All glory to the women, say I! Their hearty rebellion is worth more than a thousand speeches of the doctrinaires, with which the Socialist movement of all parties, and none more than your own, is infected. I am with the militants, heart and soul."[24]

Connolly recognized the importance of training women for leadership in the causes in which he was involved. Madame Markievicz' growing identification with the workers' cause and the activities of the union, under Connolly's tutelage is elsewhere described here. She was one of the first to join the Irish Citizen Army. In 1909, she had organized the Fianna na hEireann, an organization formed for the avowed purpose of training boys to fight against England's domination of Ireland. He influenced Helen Molony, outstanding in the fight for women's rights, an actress in the Abbey Theatre, and a nationalist, to lend her talents to the organization of working-class women.[25]

The remarkable militant nationalist, Maud Gonne, called him "the bravest man I know," and was associated with him in a number of dramatic mass campaigns for Ireland's freedom. Madame Markievicz, Mrs. Sheehy Skeffington, Helen Molony, Winifred Carney, who was his secretary before and during the Rising--all these women were deeply influenced by Connolly, initially drawn to him by his devotion to the cause for women's rights.

The position of women entered into many of Connolly's polemics. *Labor, Nationality and Religion,* written in 1910, while he was still in the United States, but first published in Ireland upon his return, defended the tenets of Socialism against Father Kane, S.J.'s Lenten Discourses, in Ireland.[26]

Using Bebel as his springboard, Father Kane declared that Socialism, which believed that state was above all, would ruin the home, "rob the father... of his God-given right to be master in the citadel of his home...

---

[24]Connolly Archives, Letter, Connolly to Matheson, June 6. 1913.

[25]Ina Connolly Heron's unpublished manuscript: "He wrote me to go to see Miss Helen Molony who was an actress in the Abbey Theatre to invite her to come to Belfast to help him organize the Mill girls... She was... afraid it would cut her off too much from the Theatre... However it was not very long afterwards that she finally took up the cause of Labor and devoted her whole time to the building of the Irish Women Workers' Union... this became her life work."

[26]Connolly, *Labour, Nationality and Religion,* pp. 232-240.

would banish home's queen from what ought to be her kingdom; it would break the marriage bond, which alone can safeguard the innocence and the stability of the home; it would make the wife... practically a tenant at will... it would kidnap the child."

The critic, replied Connolly, could not comprehend the concept of a state which "should be a social instrument in the hands of its men and women, where state powers would be wielded as a means *by the workers* instead of... as a repressive force *against the workers.*"

He addressed Father Kane's use of the term: "Socialist doctrine of divorce." He stated: "The divorce evil of today arises not out of Socialist teaching but out of that capitalist system, whose morals and philosophy are based upon the idea of individualism and the cash nexus as the sole bond in society. Such teaching destroys the sanctity of the marriage bond, and makes of love and the marriage bed, things to be bought and sold."

He emphasized: "There is no Socialist government in the world today... and the least Socialist nations and classes have the most divorces: America and its capitalist class, for example."

Connolly found himself in the position of praising Bebel's work, as it referred to children under Socialism. Father Kane, quoting Bebel, drew the conclusion: "All boys and girls, as soon as they are weaned, are to be taken from their parents and brought up." Connolly refuted the Irish priest's conclusions that the child, under Socialism, would grow up "without the hallowed influence of a happy home."

Bebel had not said anything which justified that statement, he declared: "There is simply the statement that it is the duty of the State to provide for the care, education and physical and mental development of the child. All the rest is merely read into the statement by the perverted malevolence of our critic."

In his pamphlet, *The Re-Conquest of Ireland,* published in 1915, and consisting of articles that had appeared previously in the *Irish Worker,* a penetrating chapter, simply entitled "Woman", emphasized women's super-exploitation and called for labor to be her firmest ally, in order to bring about the Reconquest.

"The worker is the slave of capitalist society," he wrote. "The woman worker is slave of that slave." In Ireland, she had exhibited "an almost damnable patience. She has toiled on the farms from her earliest childhood, attaining usually to the age of ripe womanhood, without ever being vouchsafed the right to claim as her own, a single penny of the money earned by her labor... The daughters of the Irish peasantry have been the cheapest slaves in existence--slaves to their own family, who were in turn, slaves to all social parasites of a landlord and gombeen-ridden community."

Marriage was no way out. "Marriage... usually means that, to ʌthe outside labor, she has added the duty of a double domestic toil... Of what use to such sufferers can be the reestablishment of any form of Irish State if it does not embody the emancipation of womanhood?"

Continued Connolly: "In its march towards freedom, the working class of Ireland must cheer on the efforts of those women, who, feeling on their souls and bodies the fetters of the ages, have arisen to strike them off." In the end, only the working class can be women's passport to her freedom. "Whosoever carries the outworks of the citadel of oppression, the working class alone can raze it to the ground."[27]

[27]James Connolly, The Re-Conquest of Ireland, pp. 42-48.

CHAPTER XXIV

NATIONALISM AND SOCIALISM

Throughout his career, Connolly consistently advocated the theory that the struggle for Ireland's freedom from British imperialism was inseparable from the struggle for socialism. This closely paralleled the teachings of Lenin, who was to write theoretical works on the self determination of nations as a support for the working-class revolution.

A number of Socialist leaders, however, were hostile to the idea. To this day, opponents of Connolly in Ireland, attacking from the right and the left, continue assailing his position on the national question. Some charge that Connolly, suddenly, on the eve of the 1916 Rising, abandoned his support of socialism and labor, to defect to the "enemy" camp of Irish nationalism. Sean O'Casey, in his early career, was one of these attackers.

T.A. Jackson, the English Marxist, took exception: "His theoretical proposition that Nationalism and Socialism in an oppressed country, were not opposites -- as mechanical pseudo-Marxism supposed--but were complementary... was treated as a 'dangerous heresy'... by reformist 'socialists'... It was, however, accepted and applauded by a group of young men on the 'left' of English and Scottish Marxism, and was finally vindicated by the teachings of Lenin and Stalin."[1]

As early as January, 1897, in *Shan Van Vocht,* the Republican magazine edited by Alice Milligan, in Belfast, Connolly advocated unity with the nationalists to overthrow the British, but with maintenance of the independent program and organization of the workers to achieve socialism. "If you remove the English army tomorrow and hoist the green flag over Dublin Castle, " he warned, "unless you set about the organization of the Socialist Republic, your efforts would be in vain. England would still rule you... through her capitalists, through her landlords, through her financiers, through the whole array of commercial and individualist institutions she has planted in this country and watered with the tears of our mothers, and the blood of our martyrs... Nationalism

---

[1]T.A. Jackson, p. 369.

without Socialism -- without a reorganization of society on the basis of a broader and more developed form of that common property which underlay the social structure of Ancient Erin -- is only national recreancy."[2]

He warned the non-socialist nationalists against "stereotyping our historical studies into a worship of the past... Our nationalism is not merely a morbid idealizing of the past, but is also capable of formulating a distinct and definite answer to the problems of the present and a political and economic creed, capable of adjustment to the wants of the future."[3]

To the proponents of the renascence of the Gaelic language, he declared, although "the movement has great promise of life in it... you cannot teach starving men Gaelic; and the treasury of our national literature will and must remain lost forever to the poor wage-slaves who... toil from early morning to late at night for a mere starvation wage." He advised: "Your proper place is in the ranks of the Socialist Republican Party, fighting for the abolition of this accursed social system."[4]

In the United States, one of his most popular dissertations on Irish self-determination and Socialism appeared in *Socialism Made Easy*. In the section entitled "Shop Talks," which consisted of questions and answers, he attacked the "Professional Irish."

The workers' question: "Our Irish American leaders tell us that all we Irish in this country ought to stand together and use our votes to free Ireland?" The response: "Sure, let us free Ireland! Never mind such base, carnal thoughts as concern work and wages, healthy homes, or lives unclouded by poverty.

"*Let us free Ireland!* The rackrenting landlord, is he not also an Irishman, and wherefore should we hate him? ...yea, even when he raises our rent.

"*Let us free Ireland!* The profit-grinding capitalist, who robs us of three-fourths of the fruits of our labor, who sucks the very marrow of our bones... is he not an Irishman, and mayhap a patriot, and wherefore should we think harshly of him?" The victory of bourgeois nationalism would not meet the needs of the workers. The capitalist would call on all classes and creeds to join together, and "after his victory, the slums, unemployment, sweating of the workers will continue as before. But it will all take place

---

[2]Connolly, *Socialism and Nationalism*, pp. 22-27.
[3]*Ibid.*
[4]*Ibid.*, "The Language Movement," from the *Workers' Republic*, October 1, 1898, pp. 58, 59.

under the Green Flag." In evictions, "...the evicting party... will wear green uniforms and the Harp without the Crown, and the warrant turning you out on the roadside will be stamped with the arms of the Irish Republic. Now isn't that worth fighting for?"

The conclusion: The Irish Socialists were the true Nationalists. "Let us... organize for a full, free and happy life FOR ALL OR FOR NONE."[5]

When Connolly was first working out a Marxist program with other Irish socialists in 1897, he sent Maud Gonne an article for her *L'Irlande Libre,* published in Paris. Addressed to the Irish nationalists, he wrote: "The great mass of the Irish people know full well that if they had once conquered that political liberty which they struggle for with so much ardor, it would have to be used as a means of social redemption before their well-being would be assured."[6] This was the year, also, when his *Erin's Hope* was published. It consisted of four articles which had appeared in *Shan Van Vocht* and the *Labour Leader.* It explored the theme that the struggle for nationhood was, essentially, a social struggle.[7]

The tactics for achieving socialism were varied, according to Connolly. For many years, he advocated the De Leonite "Take and Hold" formula. Socialism would be achieved through the economic "force" of the industrial unions, which, at the victory of socialism, would administer government by the workers. He also saw the possibility of socialism being achieved through use of the ballot. Even during such periods, he did not exclude the possibility of other measures. In times of peace, as he later wrote, the methods must be different than in times of war. The peaceful road, if possible, he consistently advocated, but if those who opposed socialism used violence against it, that must be met.

In August, 1899, in the *Workers' Republic,* he demanded: "The whole of Ireland for the people of Ireland--their public property, to be owned and operated as a national heritage, by the labor of free men in a free country... When you ask us what are our methods, we reply, 'Those which lie nearest our hands!'"[8] Tactics must be flexible, to meet particular situations. The article written for *L'Ireland Libre* declared that modern socialism now relied on..."peaceful conquest of the forces of government in the interests of the revolutionary ideal." At its conclusion, however, he described those

[5]Connolly, *Socialism Made Easy,* "Shop Talks."
[6]*Socialism and Nationalism,* "Socialism and Irish Nationalism, " from *L'Irlande Libre,* 1897, pp. 33-38.
[7]Connolly, *Erin's Hope,* p. 11.
[8]*Socialism and Nationalism,* p. 32, from *Workers' Republic,* August 5, 1899.

who could be described as friends of the socialists as "those who would not hesitate to follow that standard of liberty, to consecrate their lives in its service, even should it lead to the terrible arbitration of the sword."[9]

In "Workshop Talks," ten years later, he advised labor: "While the forces of government are in the hands of the rich... the governing power must be wrested from the hands of the rich, peaceably if possible, forcibly if necessary."[10] In both cases, the peaceful ballot, Connolly was saying, but if that fails, then the armed struggle.

Connolly was a forceful proponent of proletarian internationalism. In his early Irish years, he made clear that his party, the Irish Socialist Republican Party, did not stand for chauvinist hatred. English workers, too, were oppressed by English exploiters. "At the worst, we can but charge them with a criminal apathy in submitting to slavery and allowing themselves to be made an instrument of coercion for the enslavement of others...". The socialists, through their socialism, impelled by reason, not tradition, "...arrive at the same conclusion as the most irreconcilable Nationalist. The governmental power of England over us must be destroyed...".[11] Nevertheless the Irish Socialists would not consent to lose their identity in the nationalist movement. They wanted only the "alliance and friendship" of the nationalists. Connolly put it: "Brothers, but not bedfellows."[12]

In May, 1909, he wrote prophetically, in the *Harp,* of the struggle of India for independence. "The universe is about tired of this British Empire and I, for one, hope that the natives of India will, ere long, drive it from their shores into the sea."[13] Connolly condemned the Irish American leaders who ignored the anti-imperialist struggles in India and their significance to Ireland.

In Connolly's time, the Irish American politicians in Tammany Hall, in New York, were in their brightest hour. Much of the corrupt political life centered in the saloons. Every St. Patrick's Day, hangers-on of Tammany Hall, Mayors, and Governors, donning high hats, marched at the front of parades, with bands booming and green flags flying. Connolly despised these men as betrayers of the Irish workers.

"Despite all their highfalutin' phrase-dropping" of an Ireland " 'free

[9]*Ibid.,* p. 37. For another point of view, see Horace B. Davis, *Nationalism and Socialism,* pp. 119-128.
[10]Connolly, *Workshop Talks, The Meaning of Socialism,*
[11]*Socialism and Nationalism,* pp. 35, 36.
[12]*Ibid.*
[13]*Harp,* May, 1909.

from the center to the sea,' the Irish American political spouters or professional patriots have in their mind's eye, an Ireland of landlords and tenants and capitalists and laborers...". This meant "an Irish underpaid working class, an Irish army of starving unemployed, an Irish poorhouse with Irish paupers, sweated and degraded Irish women and children, broken-hearted Irish laboring men, and a few, fat, insolent Irish millionaires, telling us, in Irish, about the glorious prosperity of our native land... an Ireland patterned after the industrial pattern of America."[14]

Connolly recognized that the Sinn Fein movement, which was organized toward the end of 1905 and led by Arthur Griffith, would play a key role in Irish political life. Its position, proposing breaking away from traditional participation in the English Parliament, was progressive, as opposed to the stance of the Parliamentary Party group, led by John Redmond, whose policy of working within Parliament displayed subservience to England. Redmond and his followers conceived the role of nationalism as holding the balance of power between the Tory Conservatives and the Liberal Party, in England.

Connolly, master of the united front, applauded the nationalist aspirations of Sinn Fein and its program of Irish self-reliance. At the same time he extended the hand of friendship, he criticized the movement's limitations and presented the position of the Irish socialists.

The Sinn Fein slogan: "Ourselves Alone," stated Connolly, was "a good name and a good motto." It "teaches the Irish people... that dependence upon forces outside themselves is emasculating in its tendencies and has been and will ever be disastrous in its results... That is a part of Sinn Feinism I am most heartily in agreement with, and indeed with the spirit of Sinn Fein, every thinking Irishman who knows anything about the history of his country, must concur."[15]

As the Sinn Fein movement developed, the Gaelic language movement was showing new strength, along with a number of other aspects of Irish culture and art, all reflecting the renewed nationalist aspirations. He wrote, in April, 1908: "Small nations should not consent to the extinction of their own language or culture" -- by rapacious imperialism. "It is not necessary that Irish Socialists should hostilize those who are working for the Gaelic language... In this, we can wish the Sinn Feiners good luck."[16]

Connolly's support of Sinn Fein stopped short, however, at Griffith's

---

[14]*Ibid.*, September, 1908.
[15]*Ibid.*, April, 1908.
[16]*Ibid.*

opposition to labor struggles. In 1904, Griffith had issued his *Resurrection of Hungary,* which he considered the ideological basis for Sinn Fein. He glorified the "Hungarian system," the dual monarch of Austria-Hungary. The Hungarians had won independence from Austria in 1867, but the system of exploiter and exploited remained. Griffith's economic program was designed to appeal to the petty-bourgeoisie. He opposed confrontation of the employing class by the workers.

Padraic Colum, Griffith's biographer, commented: "That Hungary was run by great landlords in the interest of great landlords was not noted by Arthur Griffith; that Hungary as a State oppressed the non-Magyar people, as the Austrians had opposed the Hungarians, was not told by him... To Griffith, the salient thing was that Hungary had achieved her independence."[17]

Connolly opposed this anti-working class position, noting: "The overwhelming majority of the producing classes in Hungary are denied the right to vote by the possessing classes, who dominate their parliament... the misery of town and country workers is so great that the country is in a chronic state of rebellion and unrest... the military and armed police are more often employed to suppress peaceable demonstrations in Hungary than in Ireland. We are inclined to wonder if Sinn Fein orators know these things, or are they only presuming upon the ignorance of the Irish workers?"[18]

Was there a possibility of unity of action between the Sinn Feiners and the Socialists? In the *Irish Nation* of January 23, 1909, his "Sinn Fein, Socialism and the Nation," supported the position of a correspondent of *The Peasant,* who had written: "A rapprochement between Sinn Fein and Socialism is highly desirable." He agreed, but only after making clear differences, as well as similarities, in the objectives of Sinn Fein and the Socialists. A simple platform was necessary, with the understanding that "as much as possible shall be left to future conditions to dictate and as little as possible settled now by rules or theories...".[19]

The Marxist concept of Nationalism was spelled out by him in an article in the *Harp* of March, 1909. In part, he wrote: "If Nationalism means that the people shall own the land of the country, as they formerly did, [under an early Irish primitive communist society] and also the factories,

---

[17]Padraic Colum, *Ourselves Alone,* p. 78.

[18]*Harp,* April, 1908.

[19]*Socialism and Nationalism,* "Sinn Fein, Socialism and the Nation," p. 87, from the *Irish Nation,* January 23, 1909.

machines, railways, shipping and all else necessary to the carrying on and maintenance of social welfare and an Irish civilization, then Socialism is not opposed to Nationalism. If Nationalism means the cultivation of national characteristics merely, such as language, literature, history... then though Socialism is not by any means opposed to these, it is opposed to such a shallow understanding of the national idea, excluding as it does, the conception of an economically free people."

Connolly's writings were often illuminated by trenchant and dramatically simple expressions of his concepts. His next sentence was a case in point, "In the world of action and thought," he wrote, "there is no good cause that has not a friendly relation to Socialism -- there is no good cause it will not assist."[20]

In this article, he remarked: "Some innocent people cannot see what the rise of a modern labor movement in Ireland has to do with the question of freedom for Ireland. Poor souls, they never paused to consider what is meant by the word, 'Ireland.' They never paused to ask themselves which of the classes in Ireland were interested in freeing the country; which is keeping it in subjection... a class that is interested in having a plentiful supply of Irish cheap labor cannot be expected to do anything to abolish the cheapness of that labor...the oppression of Ireland keeps labor plentiful and cheap. The Irish capitalist and the English government are in entire agreement upon the proposition that the Irish worker should be skinned; they only disagree as to which of them should have the biggest piece of skin."[21]

He described socialism, in July, 1909, as leading to "the highest, the purest, the holiest form of nationality." To obtain it -- political action (the ballot). But "if they fail," he admonished, again demonstrating the flexibility of his approach, "they must resort to the methods of the men of 98 and '67." [Insurrectionary force, used by Wolfe Tone and the Fenians.]

"Nationality," he said, "is reflected in our music, in our language, in our literature, in our customs, in our games and pastimes...". Under capitalism, he noted, only the rich have the opportunity to cultivate the arts; under socialism, it would be vastly different. "Our nationality is not even half developed. Only under socialism, will Irish culture be developed to its fullest extent."

The unifying of the socialist - nationalist struggle was no simple matter. In 1911, in Ireland, he observed that among those who advocated political

[20]*Harp*, March, 1909.
[21]*Ibid.*

freedom were Irish capitalists, who could be "intensely conservative in the social or economic field...". He warned that people must not be blinded that these capitalist nationalists "may be purblind bigots in their opposition to all other movements making for human progress."

On the other hand, "even among Socialists, many... seeing the socially reactionary character of much of the agitation for national freedom, become opposed... because of the anti-Socialist character of some of its advocates."

The Socialist Party was steering a correct course. "It recognizes that national political freedom is an inevitable step towards the attainment of universal economic freedom, but it insists that the non-Socialist leaders of merely national movements should be regarded... as champions of the old social order and not exalted into the position of popular heroes by any aid of Socialist praise or glorification."[22]

Several years later, Connolly's daughter, Ina, had an experience which exemplified the respect held for Connolly and the acceptance by a number of leading militant middle-class nationalists of his theories. A few came close to understanding his politics.

Ina, out of work in Belfast, received an invitation to stay with Countess Markievicz in Dublin. She was met at the station by the legendary Sir Roger Casement (later hanged by the British). He shook her hand and asked: "Is this the little Northern warrior that is going to set Ulster ablaze? What is it you want?"

Ina answered: "An Irish Republic." Casement gazed at her. "I don't think that would satisfy your father, " he said. As Ina recalled: "At once I corrected myself and said: 'An Irish *Workers'* Republic." [23]

On the eve of the Rising, in 1916, Connolly reiterated his socialist position on the national question. In an article, "The Irish Flag," written for the *Workers' Republic,* one of many such articles written by him during those decisive weeks, he called for the Rising and made a statement on the leading role of labor and labor's armed force-- the Irish Citizen Army.

The Council of the Irish Citizen Army, he began, "has resolved, after grave and earnest consideration, to hoist the green flag of Ireland over Liberty Hall, as over a fortress held for Ireland by the arms of Irishmen... Where better could that flag fly than over the unconquered citadel of the Irish working class, Liberty Hall, the fortress of the militant working class

---

[22]*Socialism and Nationalism,* "Mr. John Redmond, M.P.," pp. 75-81, from *Forward,* March 18, 1911.

[23] Ina Connolly Heron, "James Connolly," *Liberty,* July, 1966, p. 51.

of Ireland?

"We are out for Ireland for the Irish... Not the rack-renting, slum-owning landlord; not the sweating, profit-grinding capitalists; not the sleek and oily lawyers; not the prostitute pressmen-- the hired liars of the enemy... Not these, but the Irish working class, the only secure foundation upon which a free nation can be reared.

"The cause of labor is the cause of Ireland; the cause of Ireland is the cause of labor. They cannot be dissevered. Ireland seeks freedom; Labor seeks that an Ireland free should be the sole mistress of her own destiny, supreme owner of all material things within and upon her soil. Labor seeks to make the free Irish nation the guardian of the interests of the people of Ireland...".

The working class is placed in the vanguard of the nationalist movement, by virtue of its own objectives. "Is it not well and fitting," he asks, "that we of the working class should fight for the freedom of the nation from foreign rule, as the first requisite for the free development of the national powers needed for our class?... On Sunday, April 16, 1916, the green flag of Ireland will be solemnly hoisted over Liberty Hall, as the symbol of our faith in freedom, and as a token to all the world that the working class of Dublin stands for the cause of Ireland, and the cause of Ireland is the cause of a separate and distinct nationality."[24]

After Connolly's execution, Madame Markievicz, representing the thinking of nationalists who revered Connolly's leadership, though non-socialists, wrote: "To us who loved and who trusted him, the writings he left, will always be the gospels of our Nationality."[25]

---

[24]Connolly, *Labor and Easter Week,* "The Irish Flag," pp. 173-176, from *Workers' Republic,* April 18, 1916.
[25]Constance de Markievicz. Also Greaves, pp. 242, 403. R.M. Fox, p. 12.

CHAPTER XXV

SEAN O'CASEY VS. CONNOLLY

At the time the Easter Rising loomed on the political horizon, Sean O'Casey was theoretically a pacifist. A non-Socialist, he was opposed to socialist involvement in nationalist movements. In the course of his lifetime, his point of view changed, so that he became a Communist and applauded the efforts of the Soviet people to build a workers' socialist society.

It is useful to consider his early political life since his opposition to Connolly's position was revived by anti-Connolly, anti-Communist sects in Ireland, who supported O'Casey's attacks on the right of subject nations to fight for self-determination against imperialism, in a coalition of classes.[1]

Furthermore, in the United States, O'Casey's anti-revolutionary plays and writings, of his early years, are widely circulated, notably, "The Plough and the Stars," and O'Casey's later socialist position is comparatively obscure. Friends of O'Casey should find an understanding of his early defeatism a factor, not only in understanding Irish socialist history, but also for appreciation of the theoretical distance travelled by him over the years.

According to the early O'Casey, Connolly departed from his former loyalty to international working-class objectives, when he fought for Ireland's independence from Great Britain. His avowed dislike of Connolly, personally, was the visible tip of the glacier. Basic, as in the Connolly-De Leon controversies, were fundamental political differences-displayed by O'Casey only. Connolly, even in his letters, avoided any direct attack or criticism against O'Casey.

One of O'Casey's first major disagreements with Connolly was on the role of the Irish Citizen Army. He believed its activities should be confined to illegal work and guerrilla warfare.[2] On the other hand, Connolly

---

[1]The British and Irish Communist Organization, in its journal, *The Irish Communist*, expresses this view, for instance.

[2]Sean O'Casey, *Drums Under the Windows*, p. 338.

recognized the maturing of a revolutionary Republican movement in the midst of imperialist war and advocated a visible workers' army, which could rally the masses against England and fight for a Workers' Republic.

O'Casey was an ardent nationalist at the beginning of his political life. Prior to the 1913 strike, he sharply criticized the members of the Transport Workers Union, of which he was a member, who wanted to break with the nationalist Republican movement.[3] He was a staunch supporter of the union during the 1913 strike and lockout and when the right-wing nationalists fought labor and supported the employers, O'Casey changed his position and condemned the entire nationalist movement. Such men as Pearse, MacDermott, Clarke, Ceannt, members of the Irish Republican Brotherhood, within the Military Council of the Volunteers, who favored cooperation with the Irish Citizen Army and with Labor, in the struggle against the war and British domination, were not excluded from his condemnation. (All these men were executed after the defeat of the Rising.)

He wrote a steady stream of articles against the Irish Volunteers, embracing the position which he had fought a few months earlier. He took a De Leonite position against *any* united front. Labor must stand alone, "against all opposition."[4] He bitterly attacked Pearse, although Pearse supported the 1913 strike. [5] Eamonn Ceannt had resigned from Sinn Fein on the basis of Arthur Griffith's anti-labor stand. He, like Pearse, worked closely with Connolly. [6]

Connolly called on the support of middle-class nationalist sympathizers, many of whom, through him, grew to understand labor's position. He recognized, too, that most of the rank and file nationalists were not employers but workers or poor farmers. He endorsed the nationalist cultural movements of Irish intellectuals such as the campaign for teaching Irish in the public schools. Sean O'Casey expressed a contrary view.[7]

---

[3]O'Casey, *Feathers from the Green Crow*, p. 16, "Nationalism," from Irish Freedom, March 1913; pleas for labor's participation in the Republican movement were made in the *Irish Worker*, in a series of articles attacking "Euchan," who took the same position on the national question that O'Casey embraced a few months later, pp. 24, 88-95.

[4]*Feathers*, pp. 30-33; 83-86; 107-109; 116.

[5]*Irish Worker*, February 21, 1914, "Volunteers and Workers," by O'Casey. See *Feathers*, pp. 103-108. His charges against Pearse, "worse than all," that he had scabbed by riding trams during the 1913 strike were repudiated even by the *Irish Communist*, December, 1972, p. 23.

[6]Greaves, p. 274.

[7]*Feathers*, pp. 35-37, "Down With Gaedhilge," pp. 37-39, "The Gaelic Movement Today," p. 23.

Tom Clarke wrote to John Devoy in the United States: "Larkin's people, for some time past have been making war on the Irish Volunteers. I think this is largely inspired by a disgruntled fellow named O'Casey."[8]

After the onset of World War I, in view of the crucial need for unity, Connolly stopped O'Casey's attacks on the Volunteers in the *Irish Worker*. O'Casey, secretary of the Citizen Army, went on the offensive. He demanded that Madame Markievicz, a devoted follower of Connolly, sever her connectons with the nationalist movement. The alternative was for her to resign from the Citizen Army.

His resolution was defeated in the Executive Committee and in the subsequent membership meeting. Larkin demanded that O'Casey withdraw his resolution and apologize to Madame Markievicz. O'Casey refused and resigned from the Citizen Army.[9] Those who disagreed with O'Casey at that time often became victims of his subjective retaliation. This was reflected in his caricatures of Madame Markievicz. She was tireless in supporting labor's struggles in the pre-Rising period. An ardent Republican, she organized a nationalist youth movement, became a Captain in the Irish Citizen Army and played a heroic role in the 1916 Rising. O'Casey made it clear that he thought she was completely worthless. He wrote that he had "never seen the countess doing anything anyone could call a spot of work." She did not understand Ireland. "She never understood the workers and never tried to." During the 1913 strike, the union had made her an honorary member for her services in the relief kitchens and she was awarded an "Address" for "unselfish and earnest labors".[10]

The Story of the Irish Citizen Army, published in 1919, was O'Casey's first work. There is possibly no writing more poignant than O'Casey's description of his need for an advance on the book's sale, in order to pay the undertaker, who refused to bury his mother, without payment beforehand.[11] In this work, O'Casey accused Connolly of turning his back on the working class. "It is difficult to understand," he wrote, "the almost revolutionary change that was manifesting itself in Connolly's nature. The labor movement seemed to be regarded as a decrescent force, while the essence of nationalism began to assume the finest elements of his nature...

---

[8]John Devoy, p. 395.

[9]O'Casey, *The Story of the Irish Citizen Army,* Van Voris, pp. 121, 127-151, 152.

[10]Connolly Archives, "Address from the Irish Transport and General Workers' Union to Countess Constance de Markievicz in 1914." This plaque, framed and hung on her wall, was one of her most cherished possessions.

[11]O'Casey, *Inishfallen Fare Thee Well,* "Mrs. Casside Takes a Holiday."

The high creed of Irish nationalism became his daily rosary, while the higher creed of international humanity that had so long bubbled from his eloquent lips was silent forever, and Irish labor lost a leader."[12]

O'Casey denied that Connolly was an Irish *socialist* martyr. The slogan across the top of Liberty Hall, "We Serve Neither King Nor Kaiser but Ireland," he said, was "directly contrary to his life-long teachings of socialism." O'Casey's book, written about the 1914-1916 period, almost entirely omitted the important effect of World War I, in bringing the Irish movement to a new high determination to wrest freedom from Great Britain.

In his biography of Connolly, Greaves described O'Casey's position as "extraordinary." He commented: "O'Casey declared 'Labor lost a leader.' But he should have asked, 'What is required of a labor leader.'? ... Connolly had glimpsed the depth of the abyss. Here was a crisis so radical as to require, and therefore to make possible a democratic revolution. Connolly placed this objective before him and followed it like a star."[13]

Gabriel Fallon, in his biography of Sean O'Casey, shed light on O'Casey's thinking, around the time of the publication of his first work. Fallon was considered by O'Casey as his closest "Buttie" in the early 1920s. They walked the streets of Dublin together, exchanging ideas. Later, diverging ideologies divided them. Fallon, then, with some surprise, discovered that O'Casey was a pacifist. He quoted a passage from *The Story of the Irish Citizen Army,* in which O'Casey, sitting on the grass in union-owned Croydon Park, listening to union speeches, contemplated the daisy beside him. "One was forced to ask the question, "wrote O'Casey, "was all the strife with which man's life was colored, a shining light or a gloomy shade?... Here, with one's head in the bosom of nature, to what a small compass shrinks even the Constitution of the Irish Citizen Army. How horrible is a glistening oily rifle to one of the tiny daisies that cowers in a rosy sleep at my very feet.".

Fallon concluded: "This man was a pacifist. And yet, according to the book, he continued to associate with men who were preparing themselves for battle. This I could not understand." To Fallon, *The Story of the Irish Citizen Army* was an "anomaly... written after that army had gone into action in the Rebellion of 1916, after its leader, James Connolly, wounded in the defense of the General Post Office had been taken, strapped to a

---

[12]*Story of the Irish Citizen Army.*
[13]Greaves, *Liam Mellows and the Irish Revolution,* p. 104. *The Life and Times of James Connolly,* p. 371.

stretcher, to the prison yard of Kilmainham Gaol and there summarily shot with his volunteer comrades".[14]

O'Casey deemed Francis Sheehy-Skeffington, the pacifist, the real hero of the Easter Rising -- not Connolly, nor Pearse. Skeffington's principles against violence prohibited him from bearing arms. However he demonstrated his support to the rebellion by tending the wounded and attempting to prevent looting behind the lines. However, he was pictured by O'Casey as a contrast to the Rising: "He was the living antithesis of the Easter Insurrection; a spirit of peace enveloped in the flame and rage and hatred of the contending elements, absolutely free from all its terrifying madness."[15]

Sean O'Casey's play about the Easter Rising, "The Plough and the Stars," was offered by the Abbey Theatre for the first time on Monday, February 8, 1926. Its characters -- participants in the Easter Rising -- are comic, shabby, shoddy people, cowards and self-seekers all. The leadership of the Irish Citizen Army is exemplified by Clitheroe, a weak, ambitious, fearful man. He leaves the army when he believes he has been denied a commission as an officer. He discovers that his wife, Nora, hid the commission and, an officer after all, he goes out to fight and die. Nora, a snivelling, whining woman, goes insane, mourning for her dead husband. Nor does any woman in the play comprehend the meaning of the struggle for Irish freedom. Fluther Good (played by Barry Fitzgerald, later of the Hollywood movies) is a drunken clown. The "socialist" of the play, The Covey, is an ignorant lout, constantly spouting flamboyant, meaningless phrases. He joins the others in a looting spree during the fighting. They return with their trophies and sit down to play cards.

There is no honest reflection in the play about Easter Week, its causes, its leaders and the men and women who fought bravely to win freedom. There is no portrayal of the period, the War and the crisis of British imperialism, in which the Rising occurred.[16] The principles of Connolly and his courage are missing. Connolly himself -- the leading socialist of Ireland, the outstanding labor leader, the Commander of the Rising in Dublin -- is absent. Instead, an obscure early statement of Pearse, glorifying the spilling of blood as Ireland's necessity, was the "Voice" of the Rising. O'Casey later conceded that when Pearse made this statement, Connolly strongly criticized him.[17]

[14]Gabriel Fallon, pp. 55, 56, 57.

[15]*Story of the Irish Citizen Army*. Also *Feathers*, p. 177.

[16]O'Casey, "The Plough and the Stars," pp. 160 ff. *The Sean O'Casey Reader*.

[17]George Gilmore, *Labor and the Republican Movement*. He wrote that Connolly's comment on Pearse's statement on blood-letting was: "Blithering idiot."

There can scarcely be divided opinion on O'Casey's superb writing talent. He created pictures of the Dublin slums that caught the attention of the world. Yet, it is a fact that his fancy, his biting irony, his brilliant comedy were, in "The Plough and the Stars," directed against the Irish working class, depicting the workers as caricatures and their revolt as laughable.

How far the O'Casey cult is being used against Connolly's Marxism is evidenced by Saros Cowasjee in his *Sean O'Casey, The Man Behind the Plays.* In "The Plough and the Stars," states Cowasjee, "O'Casey was holding up to ridicule the heroics of second rate men. And the second rate men were among those who most objected to the play." [18] To Cowasjee, the essence of "The Plough and the Stars" was that O'Casey pictured the Irish Republicans as personifying "ingrained cowardice". Their "unheroic actions", according to Cowasjee, had "brought death, destruction, suffering on innocent women and children". [19]

In, *Drums Under the Windows,* O'Casey continued his attacks against the leaders of the Rising. As in the *Story of the Citizen Army,* in his autobiographical novel, published twenty-seven years later, personal animosity against Connolly is apparent. Connolly never merely walked; he "waddled." He had "a rather commonplace face," a "thick-lipped sensuous mouth." Granting his "luminous" eyes, O'Casey did not like Connolly's nose. It was "a little too thick." Also "a firm and fleshy neck bulged out" over his collar... He was "a little surly."[20]

According to O'Casey, "commonplace outcries" filled the pages of the *Workers' Republic.* It was a "childish thought" for Connolly to feel that recruiting impoverished Irishmen into the British Army could be stemmed. In the 1940s, while he praised Connolly as a labor leader, in programs of Connolly Commemoration meetings, issued by the Transport Workers Union of New York, in his *Drums Under the Windows,* O'Casey still called the uprising "Naked foolishness. A child's pattern of war." The Rising defeated, O'Casey lamented: "All our dreams gone -- the Sinn Fein madmen have tossed them into insignificance. Their blow at England has fallen on the head of Ireland, and all is lost as well as honor."[21]

The reception in Ireland of O'Casey's "Plough and the Stars" should not

[18]Saros Cowasjee, pp. 18, 84 ff.
[19]*Ibid.*
[20]*Drums,* pp. 12-17. With devastating contempt, O'Casey describes a socialist open-air meeting where Connolly was the principal speaker.
[21]*Ibid.,* pp. 399 to end.

have surprised him. The martyrs of the Rising were Ireland's heroes; the Rising, though defeated, had been a cause close to the hearts of those who cherished Irish freedom. The play was introduced in the midst of strife between the Irish Free State and the Republicans, who felt the Free State was the creature of Great Britain. On the fourth night of the production, a large gathering of protesters demonstrated against the play. Yeats, head of the Theatre, by then a Senator of the Irish Free State, had invited the Free State President, the Finance Minister and the Lord Chief Justice to the performance.[22] At the interruption to the play, Yeats called the police. For days afterward, the actors declaimed under the eye of the of the polce.

A small group had objected to the play on moral grounds -- presentation of a prostitute as one of the characters. The main body of demonstrators, however, protested the debasing of the Rising. Hannah Sheehy Skeffington and Maud Gonne led the group. This was not the first time Maud Gonne had clashed with Yeats.Many years before, after a short immersion in the nationalist effort, Yeats tried to induce her to leave the struggle, marry him, and "live a peaceful life."[23] She refused.

He soon turned to an "anti-political" policy in the Theatre. "In the... struggle... Art for Art's sake or Art for Propaganda -- we were on different sides," Maud Gonne wrote. At one time Yeats issued a circular to all prospective playwrights setting forth his policy: "We do not desire propaganda plays; nor plays written to serve some obvious moral purpose; for art seldom concerns itself with those interests or opinions that can be defended by argument, but with realities of emotion and characters that become self evident when made vivid to the imagination."[24]

Fallon, an actor in "The Plough and the Stars," described the play's difficulties on the first night. The "inveterate theatre-goer," Joseph Holloway, on the arrival of the Free State leaders in the audience, gave voice to his Republican sympathies. "There they go, the bloody murderers," he loudly told those around him. Fallon continued: "The author of the *Plough* was in the vestibule of the theatre, surrounded by a crowd of patriotic women..." who "were begging him to write plays that would honor Ireland's hereos and not defame them."[25]

---

[22]Fallon, pp. 90-98. It is not within the scope of this book to go into the Civil War and the Black and Tan occupation of Ireland. Greaves' *Liam Mellows* gives a detailed history of the period.

[23]Maud Gonne, p. 324.

[24]Zack Bowen, pp. 65-67. Colum, *My Irish Years*. Also see Mary Colum, *Life and the Dream*.

[25]Fallon, 90-98.

The Literary and Historical Society of University College, Dublin, proposed a debate on the merits of the play. O'Casey agreed to be present. The debate was held in a hall in Merrion Row. Professor Clery, of the college, presided. Hannah Sheehy-Skeffington and Maud Gonne protested again that the play was an insult to the participants in the 1916 Rising.

In writing about it, O'Casey labelled the women who demonstrated against his play as "squealers." Members of Cumann na mBan, the Society of Women (a branch of the Volunteers), "they said O'Casey was a renegade, a friend of England." He added: "There wasn't a comely damsel among them."[26]

O'Casey continued the debate in a controversy with Mrs. Skeffington in the Dublin newspapers. His defense of the character, Nora, Clitheroe's wife, was a remarkable exposition of his conception of women. Women, he wrote, are only concerned with the security of their families. Nora spoke for all womanhood. "The safety of her brood is the true morality of every woman."[27] As to Mrs. Skeffington: "The heavy-hearted expression by Mrs. Sheehy-Skeffington about 'the Ireland that remembers with tear-dimmed eyes all that Easter Week stands for' makes me sick... When Mrs. Skeffington roars herself into the position of dramatic critic, we cannot take her seriously. She is singing here on a high note, wildly beyond the range of her political voice, and can be given only the charity of our silence."[28]

He also paid his respects to Maud Gonne. She was no longer beautiful. "But the poor old woman, whose voice was querulous, from whom came many words that were bitter and but few kind... she was changed utterly, for no wrinkle of glory now surrounded that crinkled, querulous face... Shadows now were all its marking, shadows where the flesh swelled or where the flesh had sagged."[29]

Maud Gonne, Mrs. Sheehy-Skeffington, Countess Markievicz, three Irish Republican women, champions of labor and of freedom for Ireland-- all were loathed and ridiculed by O'Casey. The authors of this book have a letter, written by Maud Gonne in her eightieth year, twenty one years after O'Casey depicted her as a worn-out scarecrow of a woman. It is a lively letter, written to an American trade-union leader, in support of Irish

---

[26] *The Sean O'Casey Reader,* p. 780.
[27] O'Casey, *Blasts and Benedictions,* "The Plough and the Stars. A Reply to the Critics."
[28] *Ibid.,* pp. 93-95.
[29] *The Sean O'Casey Reader,* p. 782.

Republican political prisoners. She indicated considerable activity on their behalf in Ireland and applauded Gerald O'Reilly's pamphlet, "They Are Innocent," written about them.[30] Hannah Sheehy Skeffington, after the Rising, spent years fighting for a Republic in Ireland and for workers' democracy on a world scale. She was treasurer of the Irish Women's Relief Committee to aid the anti-fascist fighters in Spain in the 1930s.[31]

There is no clearer exposition of the relationship of art and politics than the evaluation of Irish culture in relation to the struggle for Irish freedom which is in the Minutes of the Royal Commission to Investigate the Rising, published in 1916. Sir Augustine Birrell, Secretary for Ireland, chief representative of Great Britain, revealed how closely the British government followed events in the Abbey Theatre. The objective was to keep revolutionary Republicanism out of Irish art. Satisfaction was expressed that the Theatre was not anti-English.

Birrell, who was forced to resign because of the Rising, said that in the period immediately preceding the Rising, the Abbey Theatre "was a curious situation to watch, but there was nothing suggestive of revolt or rebellion, except in the realm of thought. Indeed, it was quite the other way. The Abbey Theatre made merciless fun of mad political enterprise, and lashed with savage satire some historical aspects of the Irish revolutionary... This new critical tone and temper... was the deadly foe of the wildly sentimental passion which has once more led so many brave young fellows to a certain doom, in the belief that in Ireland any revolution is better than none. A little more time and but for the outbreak of the war, this new critical temper would, in my belief, have finally prevailed, not indeed to destroy national sentiment (for that is immortal) but to kill by ridicule, insensate revolt. But this was not to be."[32]

Sean O'Casey's autobiographical *The Temple Entered* recounts his reaction to the reception of his "Plough and the Stars." "In his heart, he despised, more bitterly than ever, the ones who made it necessary for a writer to defend a work so many hated and so few admired." He decided on voluntary exile. "Write to please the Mary MacSwineys, [one of the leaders of the Republican movement] the Countess Markieviczs, the Madame Gonne-McBrides [her name by marriage] -- Jesus Christ, the very thought was laughable."[33]

---

[30]Letter, Maud Gonne to Gerald O'Reilly, December 9, 1949.

[31]Hannah Sheehy Skeffington, *British Militarism As I Have Known It*. George Gilmore, *The 1934 Republican Congress*. See *The Worker*, March 20, 1938, column by Elizabeth Gurley Flynn.

[32]*Sinn Fein Rebellion Handbook*, also see Richard Elman, *Yeats, The Man and the Masks*.
[33]*Sean O'Casey Reader*, p. 783.

He mourned: "The Easter Rising had pulled down a dark curtain of eternal separation between him and his best friends." The critics at home in Ireland "were no good. He would have to go a long way from the cliques of Dublin."[34] Two critics now began to enter his thoughts "one Irish, curiously enough, and the other American...". He meant George Bernard Shaw and the cyncial, defeatist George Jean Nathan. O'Casey heaped praises on Nathan and concluded: "The Irish drama critics, even those who were poets, could now go to hell, for Sean!" O'Casey left Ireland for England.

Mike Gold, working class author and Marxist critic, was moved to comment on "The Plough and the Stars," movie version. He concluded that the fault for "the saddest of flops" rested on the original material. O'Casey, he commented, was no revolutionary, but "a muddled liberal," who "did not understand the great place of Easter Week in history, and hence he could not portray it dramatically." The play, according to Gold, was "A jellyfish fantasy."

He observed: "In these days... a school of liberalistic writers stands by wringing its hands. These writers call themselves pacifists and preach the futility of all revolt... Their message has a great appeal for the comfortable middle class...". Written for his column, "Change the World," in the *Daily Worker* of February 15, 1937, Gold commented: "What a program of futility, cowardice and impatience. But it is the same program O'Casey had for Ireland. His play was really an artistic statement of this shabby, un-Irish creed." Whatever gains, won in the Irish Free State, unsubstantial though they might be, were gained not by "weeping", said Gold, but "...bought with the blood of James Connolly and Padraic Pearse and their comrades." The revolt failed, but it was "the prelude to a chain of people's revolutions that overthrew the Kaiser and Czar and finished the war."[35]

O'Casey responded to this criticism in the Foreword of a selection of his plays published in 1954. He approved, he said, of those "accredited critics of the Drama whose integrity as regards the Drama must be equal to that of the playwright...". He referred to critics Brooks Atkinson and George Jean Nathan, who had praised his play. But "...those resentful of any harm to their petted humbug, closeted cliche, or pietistic stutter, frightened of losing their fear, who shout out under the name of God to shut tight the

---

[34]*Ibid.,* p. 789.

[35]*Daily Worker,* February 15, 1937, "Change the World," by Mike Gold. Padraic Colum, although supporting the Irish Free State fully, also felt that the Easter uprising had forced the British government to grant concessions to the Irish people. He said there would have been no Free State, without the Rising.

mouth that tries to utter some whisper of the truth. All sorts and conditions of men, all ranks, from a Lord Chamberlain of his late Majesty of England, who didn't like the theme of one play, to the (leftist) Mister Mike Gold up in New York, who didn't like the theme of another, or the playwright either... Well, the only retort to a boo is a bah!"[36]

Though he never comprehended James Connolly's combination of the struggles for national independence of Ireland with the achievement of socialism, correspondence with Gerald O'Reilly of the Transport Union of New York, revealed that O'Casey had to some extent re-evaluated Connolly's working-class contribution. In a letter dated April 26, 1945, he enthusiastically praised Larkin and added: "Of course, Connolly was a great fellow too, dogged, true, and incorruptible but he hadn't the amazing magnetism and lovable personality of Larkin."[37] For the 34th Commemoration celebration, held in the Hotel Capitol, New York, May 12, 1950, O'Casey sent a message: "In the war for a right life for all, and not a privileged few, I greet you on this occasion, commemorating the work and example of Jim Larkin and Jim Connolly, who led the Irish workers in the fight for the life that was their due." He told of his work with Larkin. "I was with him and Jim Connolly when the workers fought the good fight of 1913... And we shall fight here, and you fight there, to bring into being the time when all things created, all things made, shall be created... not for profit, but for use by all the people... We have to thank these two great men for a lot of the strength that is in us today."

, O'Casey's later articles, plays and letters disclose his development toward a Communist philosophy. Of O'Casey's *The Star Turns Red,* a play sympathetic to Communism, George Jean Nathan, his long-time advocate, said: "Communism, one fears, has now adversely affected Sean O'Casey as a dramatic artist." Defeatism and workers' disasters were acceptable themes, but a play where Jim Larkin was the main character, was unacceptable.[38]

O'Casey's wife, Eileen, in her biography of her husband, described some of his later associates and activities. In 1960, he was finishing *The Star Turns Red.* He was writing articles for the *Daily Worker* of London, as well as for the Soviet *International Literature.* Jim Larkin visited and they talked about old times. Veterans of the Spanish Civil War as well as Russian editors and publishers met with him.[39]

---

[36]Sean O'Casey, *Selected Plays,* pp. xxvi-xxvii.
[37]Letter, Sean O'Casey to Gerald O'Reilly, April 26, 1945.
[38]Saros Cowasjee, p. 170.
[39]Eileen O'Casey, p. 166.

The family had varied reactions to the 1956 events in Hungary. Niall, the beloved young son of the O'Casey's, soon to die of leukemia, was against the suppression of this anti-Soviet action. He objected to violence under any circumstances. Eileen found a long memorandum, in answer to a "very forthright" letter from his son, in O'Casey's effects. O'Casey wrote: "Niall had little experience of the cruelties of strife, for he was but six when the Second World War was alive, whilst I over a long life had known the Boer War, the First World War, the Easter Rising in Ireland, the Black and Tan Terror, the Irish Civil War, and then the terrible strife let loose by Hitler, not forgetting the Western refusal to open its eyes to what Hitler did in Spain, leading to the first growth of his gigantic egomania that finally slew five million Jews, and sent to the grave many millions of old and young in almost every country in Europe, in a vast and deep attempt to make himself the Lord of Creation, and stamp out the power of Socialism, fully grown in the USSR and bud-ripening in many other countries."

Niall did not understand, O'Casey wrote, the implication of Mindszenty's possible ascension to be "head of Hungary, Prince Primate; and Niall had never read what the Prince Primate had been in Hungary or what he would be as dictator of the country."

Eileen disagreed with Sean and could not understand his position that "anybody who has blacklegged or informed... should be shot." She said: "I was still surprised that hating cruelty and oppression as he did, he seemed completely to accept the need for those harsh measures in Hungary."[40]

Ronald Ayling, editor of an O'Casey anthology, remarked, on O'Casey's support of Communism: "O'Casey joined the editorial board of the *Daily Worker* [in England] in 1940 when the Nazi advance in Europe was proceeding without check, and his most obviously Communist play, *The Star Turns Red,* was published and produced at the same time. "His whole-hearted support of international Communism and his admiration for the achievements of the Soviet Union never wavered before, during or after the Second World War... Several American critics who were friendly with him were obviously embarrassed by his avowed political standpoint."[41]

In an interview with O'Casey, in April, 1959, Saros Cowasjee noted that at that time, he showed a more comprehensive grasp of social change. "I am not a pacifist," he told the author. "I believe in fighting for my rights." Of *The Star Turns Red,* Cowasjee commented: "It is clear that O'Casey had now discarded his pacifism for a militant attitude which justifies the

---

[40]*Ibid.,* pp. 250, 251.
[41]*Blasts and Benedictions,* p. xv.

sacrifice of human life for the achievement of political ends." In the *Plough and the Stars,* said Cowasjee, he offered no solution to the problem which was stated. In *Red Roses for Me,* "He had discarded his earlier pacifism for the belief that one must fight for one's rights... This departure is due to a positive development in O'Casey's outlook. The cynicism of his early plays has been replaced in his later ones by a vision of hope for the future...".[42]

This evaluation seems valid. Why was O'Casey's approach to Easter Week, in the *Plough and the Stars* completely negative? Because in it, he saw no "vision of hope." Connolly followed the star that Sean O'Casey could not then see.[43]

[42]Saros Cowasjee, p. 176.

[43]In his later years, O'Casey was highly interested in American affairs. In Eileen O'Casey's book about her husband, there is a lengthy letter from O'Casey to Barrows Dunham which reviews Dunham's book, *Man Against Myth.* Dunham, an advocate of civil rights, was forced to leave the teaching staff of Temple University as the result of the "witch hunts" of the Dies Committee on UnAmericanism, in the '30s. O'Casey also maintained correspondence with Gerald O'Reilly, trade union organizer and mainspring in the organizing of commemoration meetings honoring James Connolly. At our request, he reviewed this correspondence and we quote an excerpt from his letter of July 18, 1974 to us: "It looks as if Sean O'Casey passed on, never regretting his differences with James Connolly. The pity of it is, or was, that as far as I know, no one ever seriously questioned him on this sort of a grudge he expressed in some articles...".

CHAPTER XXVI

CONCLUSION

"YOUR BEAUTIFUL LIFE, JAMES!"
THE RISING BECOMES HISTORY

The Republicans faced the overwhelming military forces of the British Empire and stubbornly fought in the center of Dublin. The Republic of Ireland, declared in the Proclamation, existed for six days. Thousands of British troops were brought in as reinforcements and heavy artillery shelled Dublin. Battleships pushed up the Liffey, to bombard Liberty Hall and other key buildings at close range. The center of Dublin, finally, was reduced to rubble.

Under Prime Minister Asquith's orders, by May 12, 1916, all seven leaders of the revolt and signers of the Proclamation had been executed. The *New York Daily (Socialist) Call* kept labor and socialists of the United States informed of events in Ireland. On April 26th, an eight-column headline, flashed the news: "Riots Rage in Capital. Rebels Capture Dublin After Fierce Street Fighting."[1] On the following day, the news appeared under the heading "Martial Law Has Been Proclaimed in Dublin County." Asquith proclaimed the "Sinn Fein Society... an illegal organization," the members to be "dealt with accordingly."[2] Every nationalist, socialist and labor anti-war organization was "dealt with accordingly." Rigid censorship was imposed. Nevertheless stories about the Rising continued to flow into the United States.

Asquith announced that the Irish revolt was spreading. Major General Sir John Maxwell, former Commander-in-Chief in Egypt, with a history of bloody suppression of the people, was appointed dictator of Ireland. Redmond and Carson demanded, in Parliament, that the "Dublin rioters," be put down "now and forever more."[3]

---

[1]*New York Evening Call,* April 26, 1916.
[2]*Ibid.,* April 27, 1916.
[3]*Ibid.,* April 28, 1916.

On Saturday, April 29th, the *Call* reported the rebellion was still "raging full blast." Under the headline: "Main Dublin Street Afire, Revolt Spreads," the story asserted that both press and public admitted that England was confronted by "the gravest crisis since the war began."

On that same day, in Dublin, the Republican forces, under Pearse and Connolly, surrendered to prevent further bloodshed. Connolly was severely wounded in the leg, the bone shattered and the wound becoming gangrenous. A prisoner, he was taken by stretcher to the Castle.[4] Pearse, in his last communique, issued the day before from "Headquarters, Army of the Republic, General Post Office Building," paid "homage to the gallantry of the soldiers of Irish Freedom... who wrote with fire and steel the most glorious chapter in the later history of Ireland... They have redeemed Dublin from many shames, and made her name splendid among the names of cities."

Pearse said he would name only "Commandant General James Connolly, Commanding the Dublin Division. He lies wounded but is still the guiding brain of our resistance...". He blamed MacNeill and his followers for the defeat. "I am satisfied that... we should have accomplished the task of enthroning, as well as proclaiming the Irish Republic as a Sovereign State, had our arrangements for a simultaneous rising of the whole country, with a combined plan as sound as the Dublin plan has proved to be, been allowed to go through on Easter Sunday." He called MacNeill's disruption, a "fatal countermanding order."[5]

The May first , *Call* carried the news: "The Rebel Leaders Have Surrendered Unconditionally." The issue also reported that Connolly, "the Chief Leader," had been shot. The dispatch could have referred to his being wounded, but the paper interpreted it that he had met his death.

The *Call* expressed contradictory positions on the Rising. One editorial, taking McNeill's position, described the Rising as a mistake: "The day of the insurrectionary barricade is gone." The Dublin workers should have waited until the end of the war. In any case, the use of force to secure socialism, in the opinion of the writer, was questionable.[6] The May 4th edition, two days later, paid unreserved tribute to Connolly and to the Rising.

This editorial, "Ireland's Victims," in part, commented: "For twenty years, Connolly was an active, a faithful and an able fighter for the

---

[4]*Sinn Fein Rebellion Handbook*, p. 43.
[5]*Ibid.*, pp. 43, 44.
[6]*Call*, May 2, 1916.

proletariat... He labored with tongue and pen, faced danger, endured privation and imprisonment and in the end, he laid down his life, not for Irish national independence alone, but for the emancipation of the Irish people, along with all other peoples, from every form of class rule... Many an Irish laborer will shed a few bitter tears and then... continue the fight. The seeds of Socialist thought and of revolutionary socialist feeling that Connolly sowed in the old sod will sprout. Soldiers' boots canot trample them to death. The Irish blood that has been shed will water them to stronger life. And James Connolly's name will be spoken with love, when the Redmonds as well as the Carsons, have been mercifully cast out of mind... James Connolly, known above the others, greater than the others, will live in the History of Ireland."[7]

Connolly, however, was still alive. For another week, he would remain a prisoner in the Castle. The British military, after the surrender, shot down many Irish civilians. Court martials began and execution of the leaders of the Rising followed, in rapid succession.

Agna (Ina) was sent to visit Connolly, since she was the least likely member of the family to be arrested. She reported back that no one was permitted to see him, but a nurse had told her that her father was very weak. Lillie was subsequently informed that she could see her husband. She visited him with Fiona. She told Nora: "He is very ill. He couldn't move in the bed." His shattered leg had been placed in a "cage." Lillie was again permitted to visit her husband, with Nora, on Tuesday, May 9. Connolly had been court-martialled, but sentence had not yet been imposed. Nora reported her father's words to them: "The cause is safe now. Our fight will put an end to recruiting. Irishmen will now realize the absurdity of fighting for another country when their own is enslaved."[8]

Nora firmly believed that the protest of English and American labor and the Irish-American movement had halted her father's execution. But Connolly's fate was undoubtedly sealed when William Martin Murphy published in his newspaper, the *Independent*, several bitterly venomous attacks, demanding Connolly's immediate execution.

One of the last conversations Connolly had with his wife and daughter concerned the youth of Ireland. Nora, on May 9th, told her father that among a number of boys under sixteen, who had been released from prison, was his son. Roddy, who had kept his identity a secret from his jailers. Connolly reflected: "Roddy was in the fight and has been

---

[7]*Ibid.*, May 4, 1916.
[8]Nora Connolly O'Brien, pp. 314-319.

imprisoned for his country and he is not yet sixteen. He has made a great start in life, hasn't he, Nora?"[9] He told them of the boy he later found to be only fourteen, who had helped carry his stretcher, under the shelling. "...He would move his body in such a way that he might receive the bullet instead of me... We cannot fail now. These young lads will never forget."[10]

An affidavit among the O'Brien papers in the National Library in Dublin tells of the last visit of Lillie and Nora to Connolly. It is signed by both of them. At midnight, on May 11th, a military motor drove up to the O'Brien home, where they were staying. The family was informed, according to the affidavit: "The prisoner, James Connolly, was very weak and wished to see his wife and eldest daughter." They were driven to Dublin Castle and directed up a flight of stairs. At the landing, and at the top of the stairs stood soldiers, with fixed bayonets. Soldiers, with fixed bayonets, too, guarded the door through which they entered to see James Connolly.

"My father was lying in the bed with his head turned to the door." As soon as he saw them, he said: "Well, I suppose you know what this means." Lillie said: "Not that, James, not that."

Nora continued her narrative: "My father said, 'Yes, for the first time, I dropped off to sleep and they wakened me to tell me that I was to be shot at dawn.'

"My mother cried out: 'Your life, James. Your beautiful life.'

" 'Well, Lillie,' he answered, 'Hasn't it been a full life, and isn't this a good end?'

"I told him of the execution of Padraic Pearse, Thomas MacDonagh and all the others. He was silent for a while. I think he thought he was the first to be executed. Then he said: 'Well, I am glad that I am going with them'." Before they left him, he took Nora's hand and secretly slipped a paper into it.[11]

Asquith, in the dead of night, travelled to Dublin, to be there at the kill. He arrived in Dublin in the morning, Friday, May 12th.[12] At dawn on that day, Connolly was taken on a stretcher to Kilmainham Prison. There, propped up in a chair, he was shot. The requests for his body for burial, by the Connolly family, were refused.

---

[9]*Ibid.,* p. 319.

[10]Nora Connolly, *The Unbroken Tradition,* pp. 182, 183.

[11]Connolly Archives, Document No. 19, "Affadavit of Discovery, Statement by Nora Connolly." Signed by Nora and Lillie Connolly.

[12]*Sinn Fein Rebellion Handbook,* p. 204.

After their last visit to him, Nora, with her mother, brother and sisters weeping around her, held out the paper which her father had given her. With difficulty, amid the stifled sobs around her, she painfully read the statement, which as addressed: "To the Field General Court Martial, held at Dublin Castle, on May 9th, 1916."

In part, Connolly wrote: "We went out to break the connection between this country and the British Empire, and to establish an Irish Republic. We believed that the call we then issued to the people of Ireland, was a nobler call, in a holier cause, than any call issued to them during this war, having any connection with the war. We succeeded in proving that Irishmen are ready to die,. endeavouring to win for Ireland those national rights which the British Government has been asking them to die to win for Belgium. As long as that remains the case, the cause of Irish Freedom is safe.

"Believing that the British Government has no right in Ireland, never had any right in Ireland, and never can have any right in Ireland, the presence, in any one generation of Irishmen, of even a respectable minority, ready to die, to affirm that truth, makes that Government forever a usurpation and a crime against human progress.

"I personally thank God that I have lived to see the day when thousands of Irish men and boys and hundreds of Irish women and girls, were ready to affirm that truth, and to attest it with their lives, if need be." It was signed, "James Connolly, Commandant-General, Dublin Division, Army of the Irish Republic."[13]

In the United States, a meeting was held in Carnegie Hall, New York on May 14th, to protest the executions. Many prominent Irish-Americans spoke. James Oneal, labor historian, writer and lecturer, in the May 21st Sunday *Call,* honored Connolly and expressed outrage against the British. He wrote: "The revolt of the Irish people has been suppressed with a butchery that has shocked the world by its frightfulness... The brutal murders... came as a shock to the great mass of the people." High financial circles in the United States had economic ties with Britain, and sympathy had been developed for the people of Belgium, but it became apparent there was little choice between English and German imperialists, he charged. "At the first assertion of Irish wrongs during the war," he continued, "the thin veneer of civilization that covers the Westminster government cracked and all the brutal ferocity of the ruling class found vent in the most shocking murders of modern times." The murdered men

---

[13]Nora Connolly O'Brien, *Portrait of a Rebel Father,* pp. 325, 326.

represented "the flower of Irish life...". Connolly was "the most thoroughgoing Socialist of the murdered men...".[14]

V.I. Lenin defended the importance of the Easter Rising to the world revolutionary movement, in a lengthy discussion, in the autumn of 1916.[15] Karl Radek had condemned the Irish Rising as a "putsch" -- a narrow conspiracy, without a mass base. Representing the leftists among the Polish Social Democrats, he opposed slogans of self determination of nations and of the right of subject nations to secession from "Big Power" nations. In the debate, the attitude towards the Irish revolt became a test of what was a Marxist attitude on self determination. Radek and his group held that the vitality of small nations, sapped by the imperialist powers which dominated them, could not play any effective role. Support of their purely national strivings was useless.[16]

Lenin refuted such conclusions. The Irish Rising, he contended, was part of the general severe crisis of world capitalism, one of a series of revolts which took place in the colonies. He described the rebellion in Ireland as one "which the 'freedom-loving' English, who did not dare to extend conscription to Ireland, suppressed by executions." He argued against an article, "A Played Out Song," in the May 9, 1916 *Berner Tagwacht,* which was signed with the initials K.R. It described the Irish question as an agrarian question and the nationalist movement remained only as a *"purely urban petty bourgeois movement,* [Lenin's emphasis] which, notwithstanding the sensation it caused, had not much social backing..." the peasants having been appeased by reforms. Thus the Irish Rebellion was a "putsch."

"Monstrously doctrinaire and pedantic," Lenin called this appraisal of the rebellion. He pointed out this coincided with the viewpoint of the Russian bourgeois Cadets, "who also dubbed the rebellion, 'The Dublin Putsch,' "[17]

Lenin included the Irish-American movement, which supported the Republican cause in Ireland, as part of the evidence of mass backing. He wrote: "The century-old Irish national movement, having passed through various stages and combinations of class interests, expressed itself, *inter alia,* in a mass Irish National Congress in America (*Vorwarts,* March 20,

---

[14]*Call,* May 21, 1916.
[15]V.I. Lenin, *Collected Works, 1916-1917,* Vol. XIX. "The Discussion on Self Determination Summed Up," p. 299.
[16]*Ibid.*
[17]*Ibid.,* pp. 300, 301.

1916) which passed a resolution calling for Irish independence." The movement "expressed itself in street fighting, conducted by a section of the urban petty bourgeoisie and a *section of the workers,* after a long period of mass agitation, demonstrations, suppressions of papers, etc. Whoever calls *such* an uprising a 'putsch' is either a hardened reactionary or a doctrinaire, hopelessly incapable of picturing to himself a social revolution as a living phenomenon."[18]

The Irish National Congress or "Race Convention," which Lenin considered significant, took place March 4th and 5th, 1916 and included 2300 delegates from all walks of life. John Devoy called it, "The largest assemblage of Irish delegates that ever met in America up to that time." The lengthy Declaration of Principles and Policy followed the line of the Proclamation of the Irish Republic. Undoubtedly reflecting Connolly's class struggle orientation, it declared that England "has brutalized humanity and stifled conscience, in order that her ruling classes may thrive and live in luxury and wealth, even though her unskilled working classes be the most degraded and poverty-stricken people of all Europe." Representing the combined thought of Irish Americans of varied economic and political backgrounds, it was an anti-imperialist document. Nevertheless, it expressed blatant racism in one sentence, alluding to "the supremacy of the white race." As noted earlier, this was a period in which some "Socialists" and "labor leaders" were guilty in this area.[19] The Declaration demanded, in conclusion, that Ireland be, "cut off from England and restored to her rightful place among the nations of the earth."[20]

Lenin denounced the sectarians who opposed supporting national movements based on an alliance with the middle class. "To imagine that social revolution is *conceivable* [Lenin's emphasis throughout] without revolts by small nations in the colonies and in Europe, without the revolutionary outbursts of a section of the petty bourgeoisie *with all its prejudices,* without the movement of non-class conscious proletarian and semi-proletarian masses against the oppression of landlords, the church, the monarchy, the foreign nations, etc., to imagine this, means *repudiating social revolution.* Only those who imagine that in one place an army will line up and say 'We are for Socialism,' and in another place, another army will say 'We are for imperialism,' and that this will be the social revolution,

---

[18]*Ibid.*
[19]See chapter here on the *Harp,* which discusses the attitude of the Socialists to Blacks.
[20]John Devoy, pp. 449-457.

only those who hold such a ridiculously pedantic opinion could vilify the Irish Rebellion by calling it a 'putsch.' Whoever expects a 'pure' revolution will *never* live to see it. Such a person pays lip service to revolution, without understanding what revolution is."[21]

Lenin analyzed the causes of the failure of the revolt: "They rose prematurely, when the European revolt of the proletariat had *not yet* matured. Capitalism is not so harmoniously built that the various springs of rebellion can immediately merge of their own accord, without reverses and defeats... Only in premature, partial, sporadic, and therefore unsuccessful revolutionary movements will the masses gain experience...".

The relation of the Irish struggle for independence to the English working class concerned Karl Marx. In a letter to Frederick Engels, in December, 1869, he wrote: "Quite apart from all phrases about international and 'humane' justice for Ireland...*it is in the direct and absolute interest of the English working class to get rid of their present connection with Ireland.* [Marx's emphasis]... The English working class will *never accomplish anything* before it has got rid of Ireland. The lever must be applied in Ireland. That is why the Irish question is so important for the social movement in general!"[22]

Marx, among other actions to foster Irish independence, brought a resolution to that effect into the International Workingmen's Association.[23] It included the statement: "A people which enslaves another people, forges its own chains."

During the days of crisis in 1916 and after the execution of Connolly, important sections of American labor made it clear that they understood the meaning of Connolly's work and the Easter Rising in Ireland. Federations of Labor, in the main industrial areas of the nation, protested the actions of the British government. The Detroit Federation of Labor demanded that: "James Connolly, the Irish toiler who is in prison, wounded, awaiting possible death for his part in the Irish rebellion, shall be given fair play." The Chicago Federation of Labor cabled its protest to Asquith.

The May 12th issue of the *Detroit Labor News,* which carried news of labor's actions, also contained an eloquent tribute to Connolly by Jim

---

[21]Lenin, pp. 301, 302, 303. Also p. 286.

[22]Marx, Engels, *Ireland and the Irish Question,* p. 284.

[23]Dirk Struik, in his *Birth of the Communist Manifesto,* noted the attention paid by Marx and Engels to the Irish struggle and the position of the Irish who had fled to English slums from famine and oppression. There, as cheap labor, they disunited the English and Irish working class. (pp. 74-79.)

Larkin, which called for unions and individuals to immediately cable protests to the British Government. "Ireland and the Irish workers have given hope and inspiration to all the workers of the countries engaged in this holocaust in Europe," he declared.[24]

The May 26th issue of the same paper reported the "Murder of Connolly." The Illinois State Federation of Labor responded by cabling Asquith. "New York's Central body, in common with Detroit and other central labor organizations throughout the country," the paper reported, "has condemned the slaughter of these unionists."

The resolution of the New York unions, introduced by Thomas Rock, of the Pavers and Rammermen's Union, declared: "The very principles of humanity and good government have been outraged by the execution of the men who surrendered as prisoners of war." It claimed that Connolly and Clarke were American citizens, "who during their residence in the United States were actively interested in organized labor." Expressing "abhorrence and condemnation of the military executions in Dublin," it called on President Wilson and the State Department to demand reparations "for the murder by court martial of American citizens."[25]

The depth of support in the United States for the Irish Republicans is evidenced also in a secret letter, written to Sir Edward Grey, in London, by British Ambassador Spring-Rice, which pleaded for the Home Rule Bill to be adopted for Ireland, as a means of stemming the mounting protests. He wrote, June 16th: "Our cause, for the present, among the Irish here, is a lost one." He wrote further, on July 31st: "The only occasions on which Congress has intervened or attempted to intervene in the present war, were to prevent a blockade of cotton and to prevent the execution of Irish rebels... irritation among the Irish here has reached a degree of intensity as great as in the '80s."[26]

Madame Markievicz, who had been given a life sentence, but was later released from prison, wrote about Connolly, as she had known him: "He was a man of genius and of great nobility of character. He was 'class conscious' and class consciousness in him developed a great and self-sacrificing love for the men and women of his class, which was coexistent with and coordinate with a great love of his country."[27]

In 1924, eight years after Connolly's death, Arthur MacManus

---

[24]*Detroit Labor News,* May 12, 1916.
[25]*Ibid.,* May 26, 1916.
[26]Van Voris, p. 207.
[27]Constance de Markievicz, p. 4.

considered Connolly's meaning to the working class of Ireland, in the (English) *Communist Review*: "The self-sacrificing character of the man's whole life and work, his optimism in moments of darkness... his valor, fortitude and courage in action, these have impressed themselves deep down on the affection of the masses of the people of Ireland. His whole life was unquestionably devoted to the revolutionary working class movement." He concluded: "Connolly was the first Irishman to give the Irish struggle its real and true historic significance. He was the first who saw it all the time as a revolutionary struggle."[28]

The bodies of the martyrs of the Rising were buried in quicklime, at Arbor Hill, now a sacred spot for the Irish people. It was hoped by the British Government that Connolly and the others would be forgotten. But like the American, Joe Hill, Connolly "never died." The defeated Easter Rebellion, it was conceded by Padraic Colum and others, was the basic cause for Ireland's securing the concession of the Free State. It is of record that the Irish people, in 1918, by a general strike, did prevent conscription. The Rebellion in Ireland played its part in delaying the entry of the United States into the war. Its influence went far beyond Ireland's shores, as Lenin explained.

James Connolly, had he lived, it is likely, would not have been completely satisfied with these achievements. Based on his life, it is clear that he would have continued his work -- writing, organizing, fighting -- settling finally only for a Workers' Republic, in a free, united socialist Ireland, a goal he moved toward all his life.[29]

---

[28]The late John Williamson, Librarian of the Marx Memorial Library, London, provided this article.

[29]The Souvenir Issue of *Liberty,* publication of the Irish Transport and General Workers Union, May, 1965, contains the following pertinent articles: "Headquarters for Workers' Freedom," (Unsigned); "The Workers' Army That Inspired A Nation," by Frank Robbins; "More Than Fifty Years Progress." Also see *Jim Connolly and Irish Freedom,* by G. Schuller, *The Glorious Seven* by Seamus G. O'Kelly, *Poems of the Irish Revolutionary Brotherhood,* Edited by Padraic Colum and Edward J. O'Brien, *My Irish Year,* and *Cross Roads in Ireland,* both by Padraic Colum, the latter two books discussing the peasants and Ulster.

BIBLIOGRAPHY

American History, A Survey, Richard N. Current, T. Harry Williams, Frank Freidel, New York, Alfred A. Knopf, 1965.

American Socialism, 1900-1960, Edited by H. Wayne Morgan, Englewood Cliffs, New Jersey, Prentice Hall, Inc., 1964.

Aptheker, Herbert, *Urgency of Marxist-Christian Dialogue,* New York, Harper and Row, 1970; *A Documentary History of the Negro People in the United States,* Vol. 1, New York, Citadel Press, 1951.

Beard, Charles and Mary, *Basic History of the United States,* New York, Doubleday Doran & Co., 1944.

Bebel, August, *Woman Under Socialism,* Translated by Daniel De Leon, New York, Schocken Books, 1971. (Reprinted from N.Y. Labor News Press, edition of 1904.)

Bell, Thomas, *Pioneering Days,* London, Lawrence & Wishart, 1941.

Bernstein, Samuel, *First International in America,* New York, Augustus M. Kelley, 1962.

Bloor, Ella Reeve ("Mother"), *We Are Many,* New York, International Publishers, 1940.

Bowen, Zack, *Padraic Colum, A Biographical-Critical Introduction,* London and Amsterdam, Feffer & Simons, Inc., Carbondale and Edwardsville, Southern Illinois University Press, 1970.

Brewer, Kara P., *American Career of James Connolly,* Thesis presented to Department of History, University of the Pacific, 1972.

Brissenden, Paul F., *The Industrial Workers of the World. A Study of American Syndicalism,* New York, Russell and Russell, Columbia University Press, 1919. (Reissued 1920 and 1957.)

Burke, T.N., Very Rev., *Ireland's Case Stated. In Reply to Mr. Froude,* New York, P.M. Haverty, 1873.

Burns, Elinor, *British Imperialism in Ireland,* Dublin, City and County Workers Books, 1931.

Chaplin, Ralph, *Wobbly, The Rough and Tumble Story of an American Radical,* Chicago, University of Chicago Press, 1948.

Colum, Mary, Life and the Dream, Dublin, Dolmer Press, 1966.

Colum, Padraic, *Cross-Roads in Ireland,* New York, The MacMillan Company, 1941

    My Irish Year, New York, James Pott & Co., 1912.

    Ourselves Alone, New York, Crown Publishers, 1959.

Commemoration Committee Brochure for Wolfe Tone Week, June 22,

1913, Dublin, Brian O'Higgins.

Connolly, Nora, *The Unbroken Tradition,* New York, Boni and Liveright, 1918. (Also see Nora Connolly O'Brien.)

Connolly, James, Fragmentary Notes, London, *Communist Review,* July, 1925.

    Introduction by Arthur MacManus.

    Connolly Archives, William O'Brien Papers, National Library, Dublin.

    Erin's Hope, Dublin, New Books Publications, 1968. (First published in 1897.)

    "Industrialism and the Trade Unions," *International Socialist Review,* February, 1910.

    Labor and Easter Week, 1916. A selection from the writings of James Connolly. Edited by Desmond Ryan, Dublin, At the Sign of the Three Candles, reprinted 1966.

    Labor in Irish History, Dublin, New Books Publication, 1967. (First published in 1910.)

    Labor, Nationality and Religion, reprinted in *The Workers' Republic. A Selection from the Writings of James Connolly.* Edited by Desmond Ryan, Dublin, At the Sign of the Three Candles, 1961.

    The New Evangel, (part of *Erin's Hope and the New Evangel*) Dublin, New Books Publications, 1968. (First issued 1901.)

    Old Wine in New Bottles, New Age, 1914. Issued by the Irish Transport and General Workers Union in Dublin in 1921 and 1934.

    Re-Conquest of Ireland, Dublin and Belfast, New Books Publications, 1968. (First Published in 1915.)

    Revolutionary Warfare, Dublin, New Books Publications, 1968. This originally consisted of lectures printed in the *Workers' Republic.*

    Socialism Made Easy, Chicago, Charles H. Kerr & Co., 1909.

    Socialism and Nationalism. A Selection from the Writings of James Connolly. Dublin, At the Sign of the Three Candles, 1948.

    The Workers' Republic. A Selection from the Writings of James Connolly. Edited by Desmond Ryan, Dublin, At the Sign of the Three Candles, 1951.

Cowasjee, Saros, *Sean O'Casey, The Man Behind the Plays,* New York, St. Martin's Press, 1964.

Creel, George, *Ireland's Fight for Freedom,* New York and London, Harper & Bros.

Cronin, Sean, *The Revolutionaries,* Dublin, Republican Publications, 1971.

Davis, Horace B., *Nationalism and Socialism,* New York and London, Monthly Review Press, 1967.

Deasy, Joseph, *The Teachings of James Connolly,* New Books, Dublin.

De Leon, Daniel, *As To Politics,* New York Labor News Co., 1907.
> "Burning Question of Trade Unionism," included in *Socialist Landmarks,* First printing by New York Labor News Co., 1904.
> *Flashlights of the Amsterdam Congress,* New York Labor News Co., 1906.
> *Socialist Economics in Dialogue,* New York Labor News Co., 1935.
> *Socialism vs. Anarchism,* an address delivered October 31, 1901. Reprinted by New York Labor News Co. many times from 1901.
> *Watson on the Gridiron,* New York Labor News Co., 1926. (A compilation of articles written in 1909.)
> *Warning of the Gracchi,* New York Labor News Co., 1903. Reprinted many times.
> "What Means This Strike", included in *Socialist Landmarks.* New York Labor News Co., 1952. An address delivered February 11, 1898.

Devoy, John, *Recollections of an Irish Rebel. The Fenian Movement,* Estate of John Devoy, 1929, Irish American Collection, Villanova College.

Ellman, Richard, *Yeats, The Man and the Masks,* New York, The Macmillan Co., 1948.

Ellis, P. Berresford, *A History of the Irish Working Class,* New York, George Braziller, 1973.

Engels, Frederick, *Origin of the Family, Private Property and the State,* New York, International Publishers, 1964.

Fallon, Gabriel, *Sean O'Casey, The Man I Knew,* Little Brown Co., Boston and Toronto, 1965.

Flynn, Elizabeth Gurley, *I Speak My Own Piece,* New York, Masses and Mainstream, 1955.

Papers, American Institute for Marxist Studies.
Foner, Philip S., *History of the Labor Movement in the United States,* Vol. 3, New York, International Publishers, 1964.
    Ibid., Vol. 4, International Publishers, 1965.
Foster, William Z., *American Trade Unionism,* New York, International Publishers, 1947.
    From Bryan to Stalin, New York, International Publishers, 1937.
    History of the Three Internationals, International Publishers, 1955.
Fox, R.M., *James Connolly, The Forerunner,* The Kerryman, Ltd., 1946.
The Founding Convention of the IWW, June 27 - July 8, 1905. Reprint of stenographic report, New York Labor News Co., 1905. Reprinted by Merit Publishers, New York, 1968.

Gallacher, William, *Revolt on the Clyde,* New York, International Publishers.
Gilmore, George, Labor and the Republican Movement, a pamphlet.
    The 1934 Republican Congress, Dochas Coop Society, Ltd., Dublin.
Greaves, C. Desmond, *The Life and Times of James Connolly,* International Publishers, New York, 1971. (London, Lawrence and Wishart, 1961)
    Liam Mellows and the Irish Revolution, London, Lawrence & Wishart, 1971.

Hass, Eric, *Capitalism, Breeder of Race Prejudice,* New York Labor News Co., 1964.
    The SLP and the Internationals, New York Labor News Co., 1949.
Haywood, William D., *The Autobiography of Big Bill Haywood,* New York, International Publishers, 1929.
Heron, Ina Connolly, "James Connolly," a series of articles published in their organ, *Liberty,* by the International Transport and General Workers Union, Dublin, from March 1966 through October, 1966.
Herreshoff, David, *American Disciples of Marx,* Detroit, Wayne State University Press, 1967.

Jackson, T.A., *Ireland Her Own,* London, Cobbett Press, 1946.
Johnson, Oakley C., *Marxism in U.S. History, 1876-1917,* New York, A.I.M.S. and Humanities Press, 1974.
Johnson, Olive, "Daniel De Leon, Our Comrade," from *Symposium,* New

York Labor News Co., 1918.

    Socialist Labor Party, 1890-1930, Part II, New York Labor News Co., 1931.

Kendall, Walter, *The Revolutionary Movement in Britain - 1900-1921.,* London, Weidenfeld & Molloy, 1969.

Kipnis, Alexander, *The American Socialist Movement, 1897-1912,* New York, Columbia University Press, 1952.

Larkin, Emmet, *Life of James Larkin,* University of Chicago.

1913. Jim Larkin and the Dublin Lock-out, Dublin, Workers Union of Ireland, 1964.

Larkin, James, "The Irish Rebellion," New York, *New Masses,* July, 1916.

Lassalle, Ferdinand, *Gessammelte Reden u. Lehrifteh,* 11-S. 58, Quoted in Mark and Engles, *Correspondence, 1846-1895,* New York, International Publishers, 1934.

Leaders and Men of the Easter Rising, Edited by F.X. Martin, O.S.A., Ithaca, N.Y., Cornell University Press, 1967.

Le Caron, Henri, Major, *Twenty-five Years in the Secret Service. The Recollections of a Spy,* London, William Heinemann, 1893.

Lenin, *Collected Works,* Vol. XVIII, *The Imperialist War. The Struggle Against Social Chauvinism and Social Pacifisim, 1914-1915,* New York, International Publishers, 1930.

    Collected Works, 1916-1917. Vol. XIX. International Publishers, 1942.

    The State and Revolution, International Publishers, 1940.

    Selected Works, Vol. IX, *Party Unity and the Anarcho-Syndicalist Deviation,* International Publishers, 1937.

    Selected Works, Vol. X, International Publishers, 1943.

Levenson, Samuel, *James Connolly,* Martin Brian and O'Keeffe, Ltd., London, 1973.

de Markievicz, Constance, *James Connolly's Policy and Catholic Doctrine,* a pamphlet, publisher and date unstated.

Marx and Engels, *Correspondence, 1846-1895,* New York, International Publishers, 1934.

    Ireland and the Irish Question, International Publishers, 1972.

Marx, Karl, *Capital,* Vol. I, New York, International Publishers, 1939.

    "Value, Price and Profit," *Selected Works,* Vol. I., International Publishers, 1933.

Minute Book, IWW Archives, Detroit, Walter P. Reuther Library, Wayne

State University.

Minutes, General Executive Board, IWW, Meeting September 25, 1908. These Minutes were pasted in Minute Book "October 4, 1906 - September 15, 1911", p. 196, IWW Archives, Wayne State University.

MacBride, Maud Gonne, *Servant of the Queen, Reminiscences by Maud Gonne MacBride,* London, Victor Gollancz, Ltd., 1938.

O'Brien, Nora Connolly, *Portrait of a Rebel Father,* Dublin, The Talbot Press; London, Rich and Cowan, Ltd., 1935.

O'Brion, Leon, "Birrell, Nathan and the Men of Dublin Castle, "*Leaders and Men of the Easter Rising,* Edited by F.X. Martin, O.S.A., Ithaca, Cornell University Press, 1967.

O'Casey, Eileen, *Sean,* London, Coward, McCann & Geoghegan, Inc., 1971.

O'Casey, Sean, *Blasts and Benedictions.* Articles and Stories by Sean O'Casey. Selected and Introduced by Ronald Ayling, London, Toronto, Macmillan; New York, St. Martin's Press, 1967.

   Drums Under the Windows, New York, The Macmillan Company, 1950. (Also 1946.)

   Feathers from the Green Crow, Edited by Robert Hogan, Columbia, University of Missouri Press, 1962.

   Inishfallen Fare Thee Well, New York, The Macmillan Co., 1956.

   The Story of the Irish Citizen Army (by P.O. Cathasaigh), Dublin and London, Maunsel & Co., Ltd., 1919.

   Sean O'Casey Reader, edited by Brooks Atkinson, Macmillan, 1968.

   Selected Plays of Sean O'Casey. Selected and with Foreword by the author. Introduction by John Gassner, New York, George Braziller, 1954.

O'Kelly, Seamus G., *The Glorious Seven,* Dublin, Irish News Service, 1965.

O'Neill, Brian, *The War for the Land in Ireland,* Introduction by Peadar O'Donnell, New York, International Publishers, 1933.

O'Reilly, Gerald, *They Are Innocent!* (pamphlet) New York, Connolly Commemoration Committee, 1947.

O'Riordan, Manus, *James Connolly in America,* Thesis submitted to the University of New Hampshire, Durham, N.H., January, 1971.

Pearse, Padraic, Speech made at the grave of Wolfe Tone, Commemoration Committee Brochure for Wolfe Tone Week, June 22, 1913, Dublin, Brian O'Higgins. From the Collection of Gerald O'Reilly.

Quill, Michael Jr., *Justice for Ireland*, (pamphlet) Address at Irish Conference, N.Y.C., December 30, 1943.

Reeve, Carl, *The Life and Times of Daniel De Leon*, New York, A.I.M.S. and Humanities Press, 1972.
Ryan, Desmond, *James Connolly, His LIfe and Work*, London, The Labour Publishing Co., Ltd., Dublin, The Talbot Press, Ltd., 1924.
Ryan, W.P., "The Struggle of 1913," *1913. Jim Larkin and the Dublin Lockout*, Dublin, Workers Union of Ireland, 1964.

Schuller, G., *Jim Connolly and Irish Freedom*, a pamphlet, Chicago, Daily Worker Publishing Co., 1926.
Shannon, Cathal, "James Connolly. The Man and His Work." *Liberty Magazine*, publication of the Irish Transport and General Workers Union, Dublin, May, 1965.
Shannon, David, *The Socialist Party of America, A History*, New York, Macmillan, 1955.
Skeffington, Hannah Sheehy, *British Militarism As I Have Known It*, a pamphlet, printed by The Kerryman, Ltd., Tralee.
Sinn Fein Rebellion Handbook, Easter, 1916, Dublin, *Weekly Irish Times*, August, 1916. Minutes of the Royal Commission of Inquiry.
St. John, Vincent, *The IWW. Its History, Structure and Methods*, Chicago, IWW, Revised 1919.
Struik, Dirk J., *Birth of the Communist Manifesto*. Includes the Manifesto, all Prefaces by Marx and Engels, drafts and supplementary material; edited and with an introduction by Struik, New York, International Publishers, 1970.
A. Symposium, *Daniel De Leon: The Man and His Work*. National Executive Committee of the SLP. Published in 1919 as a commemoration of Daniel De Leon, who died in 1914.
Thompson, Fred, *The IWW. Its First Fifty Years (1905-1955)*, Chicago, IWW, 1955.

Van Voris, Jacqueline, *Constance de Markievicz. In the Cause of Ireland*, Amherst University of Massachusetts Press, 1967.

White, J.R. Captain, *Misfit,* An Autobiography, New York, Jonathan Cape and Harrison Smith, *1930.*

Williams, Ben, *The Saga of the One Big Union,* Unpublished Manuscript, IWW Archives, Walter P. Reuther Library, Wayne University, Detroit.

The Woman Question, Selections from the Writings of Karl Marx, Frederick Engels, V.I. Lenin and Joseph Stalin, New York, International Publishers, 1951.

INDEX